HISSING

vol. 4

Kang EunYoung

Yen Press

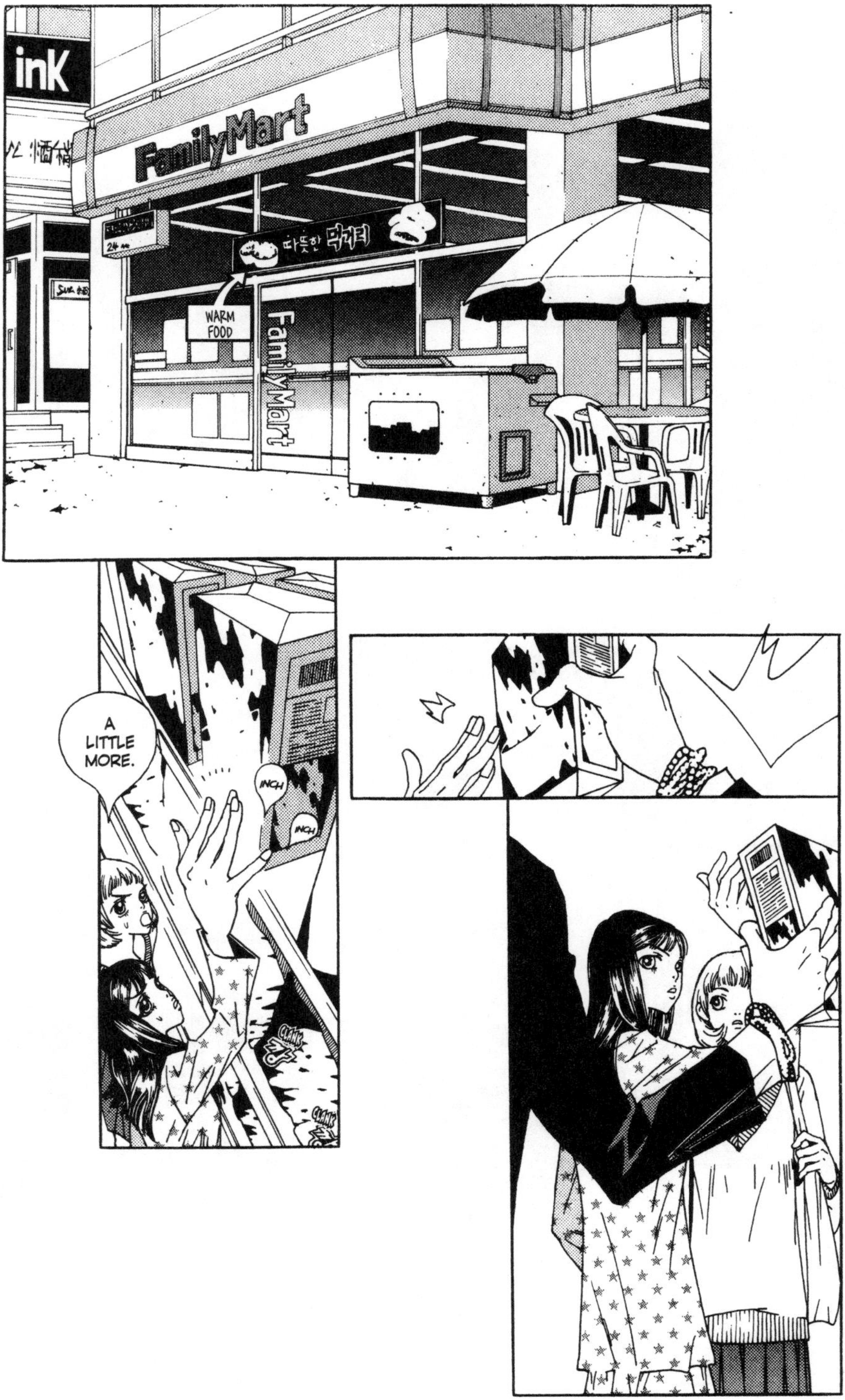
inK
FamilyMart
따뜻한 먹거리
WARM FOOD
FamilyMart
A LITTLE MORE.
INCH
INCH
CLANK
CLANK

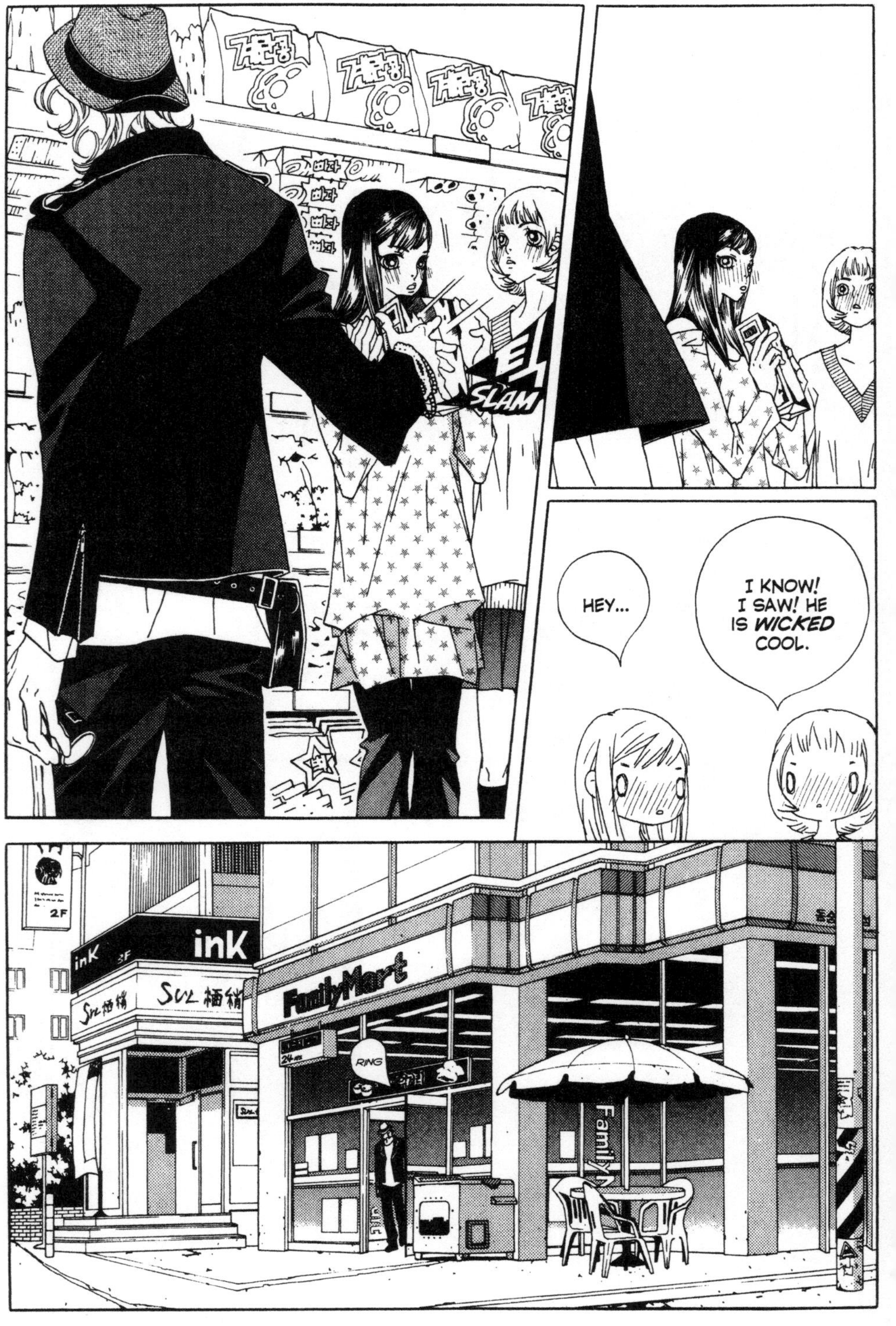
SLAM
HEY...
I KNOW! I SAW! HE IS WICKED COOL.
2F
inK
inK 3F
FamilyMart
RING

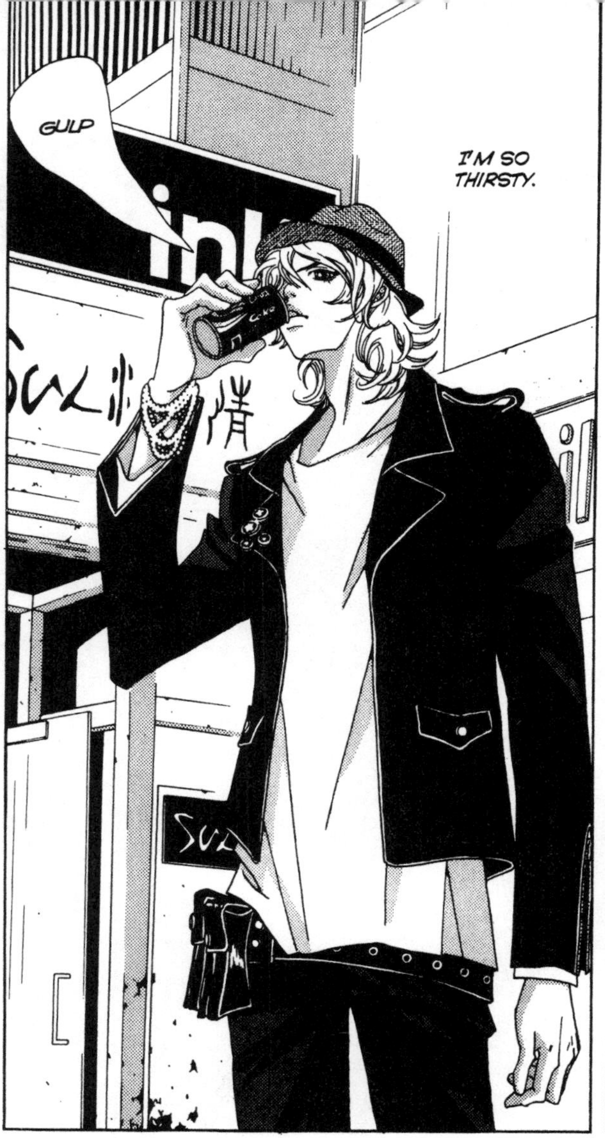
GULP
I'M SO THIRSTY.

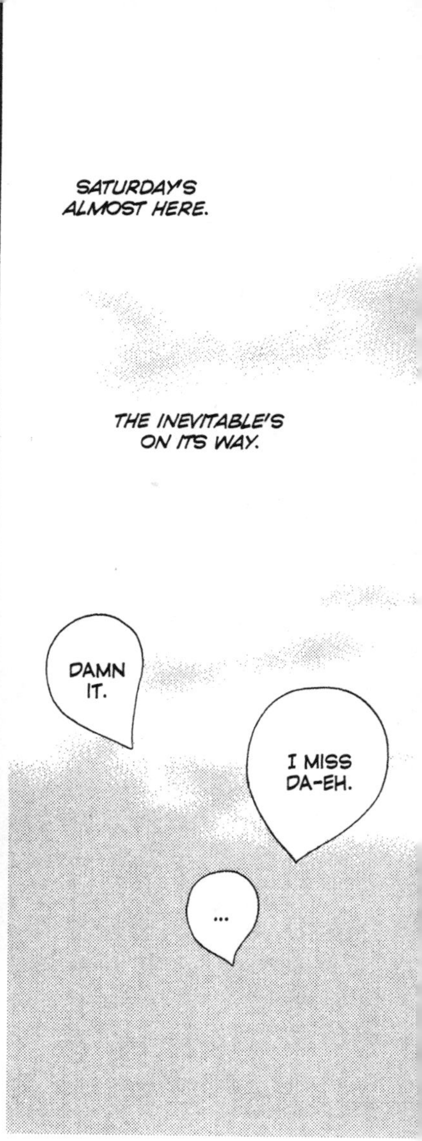
SATURDAY'S ALMOST HERE.
THE INEVITABLE'S ON ITS WAY.
DAMN IT.
I MISS DA-EH.
...

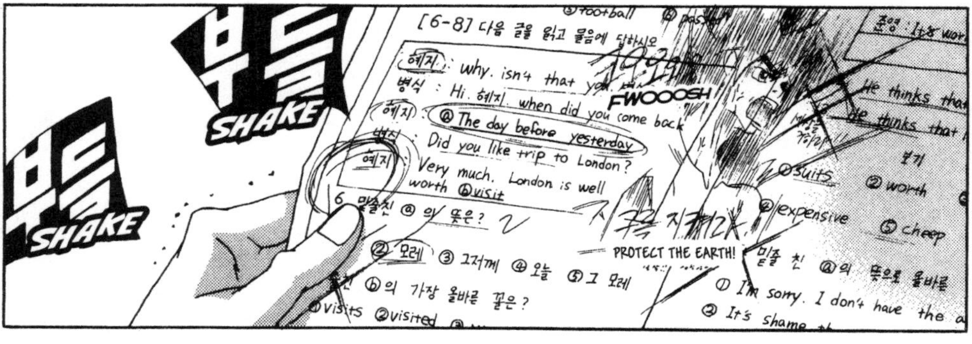
부들
SHAKE
부들
SHAKE
[6-8] 다음 글을 읽고 물음에 답하시오
혜지 : why. isn't that you.
병식 : Hi. 혜지. when did you come back
혜지 : ⓐ The day before yesterday
병식 : Did you like trip to London?
혜지 : Very much. London is well worth ⓑvisit
FWOOOSH
PROTECT THE EARTH!
He thinks that
He thinks that
①suits
②worth
④expensive
⑤cheep
① I'm sorry. I don't have the
② It's shame

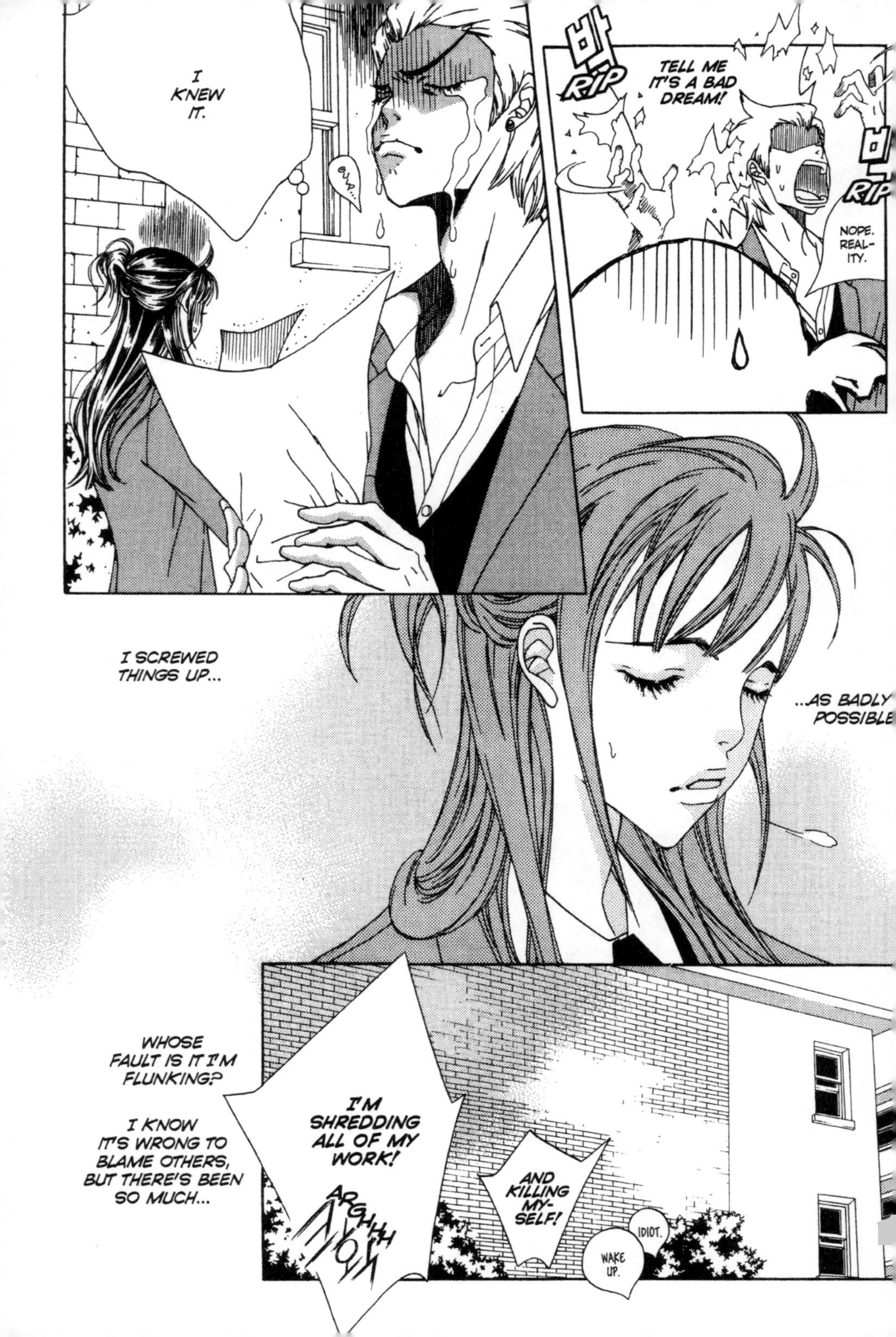
I KNEW IT.
RIP
TELL ME IT'S A BAD DREAM!
RIP
NOPE. REALITY.
I SCREWED THINGS UP...
...AS BADLY POSSIBLE
WHOSE FAULT IS IT I'M FLUNKING?
I KNOW IT'S WRONG TO BLAME OTHERS, BUT THERE'S BEEN SO MUCH...
I'M SHREDDING ALL OF MY WORK!
ARGHHH
AND KILLING MY-SELF!
IDIOT.
WAKE UP.

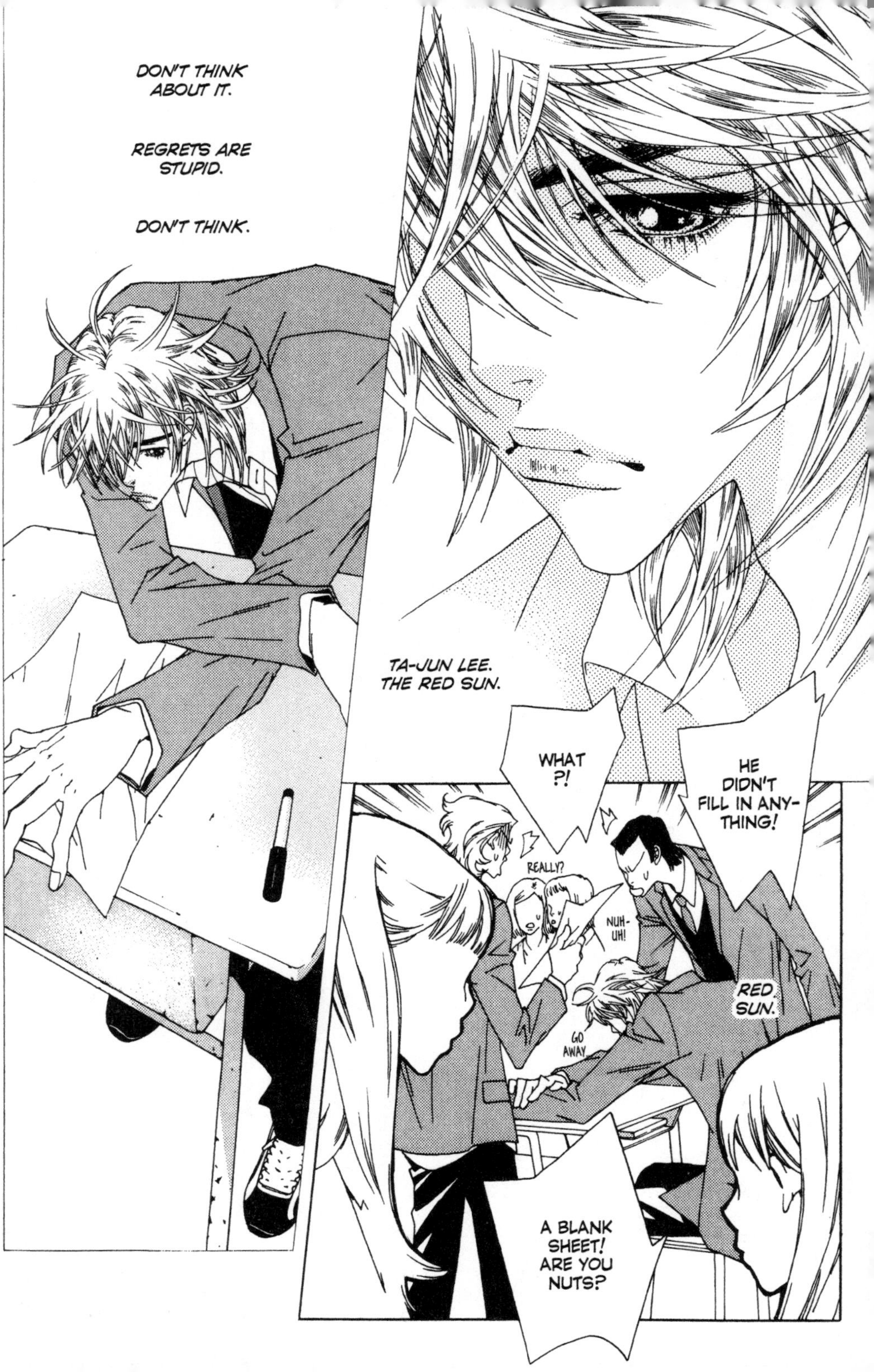
DON'T THINK ABOUT IT.
REGRETS ARE STUPID.
DON'T THINK.
TA-JUN LEE. THE RED SUN.
WHAT ?!
REALLY?
NUH-UH!
HE DIDN'T FILL IN ANY-THING!
RED SUN.
GO AWAY
A BLANK SHEET! ARE YOU NUTS?

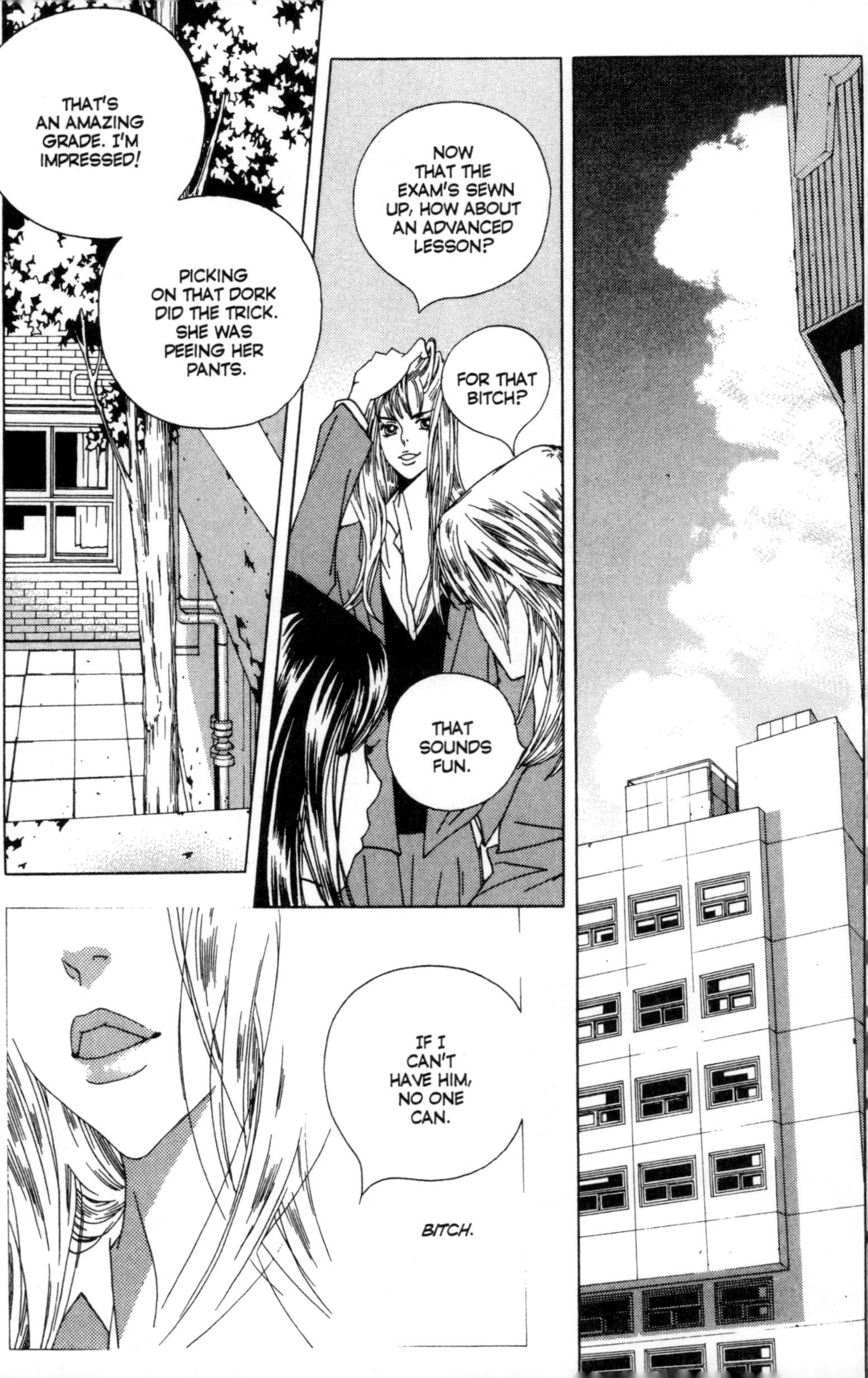
THAT'S AN AMAZING GRADE. I'M IMPRESSED!
PICKING ON THAT DORK DID THE TRICK. SHE WAS PEEING HER PANTS.
NOW THAT THE EXAM'S SEWN UP, HOW ABOUT AN ADVANCED LESSON?
FOR THAT BITCH?
THAT SOUNDS FUN.
IF I CAN'T HAVE HIM, NO ONE CAN.
BITCH.

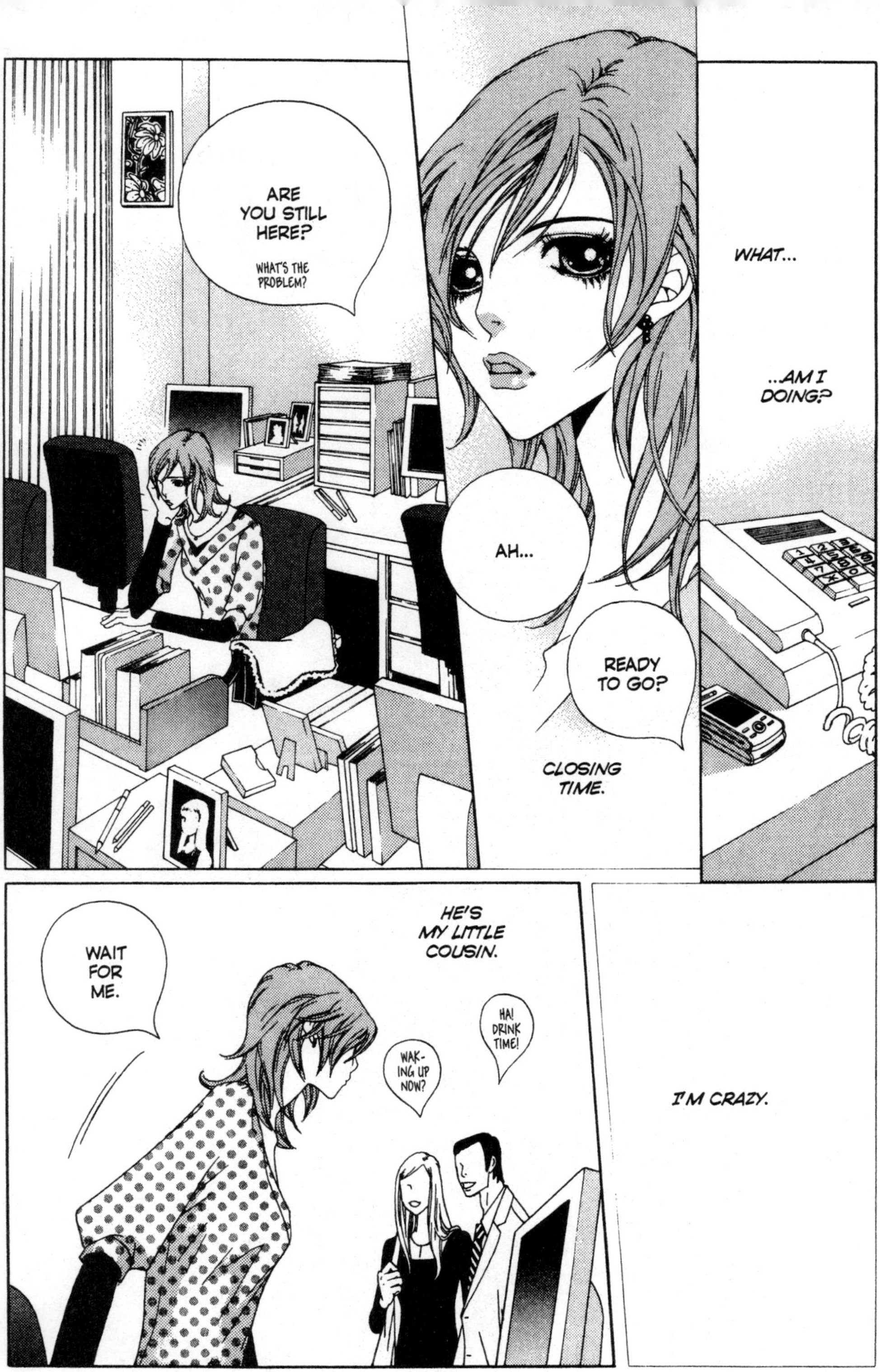
ARE YOU STILL HERE?
WHAT'S THE PROBLEM?
AH...
READY TO GO?
CLOSING TIME.
WHAT...
...AM I DOING?
WAIT FOR ME.
HE'S MY LITTLE COUSIN.
WAK-ING UP NOW?
HA! DRINK TIME!
I'M CRAZY.

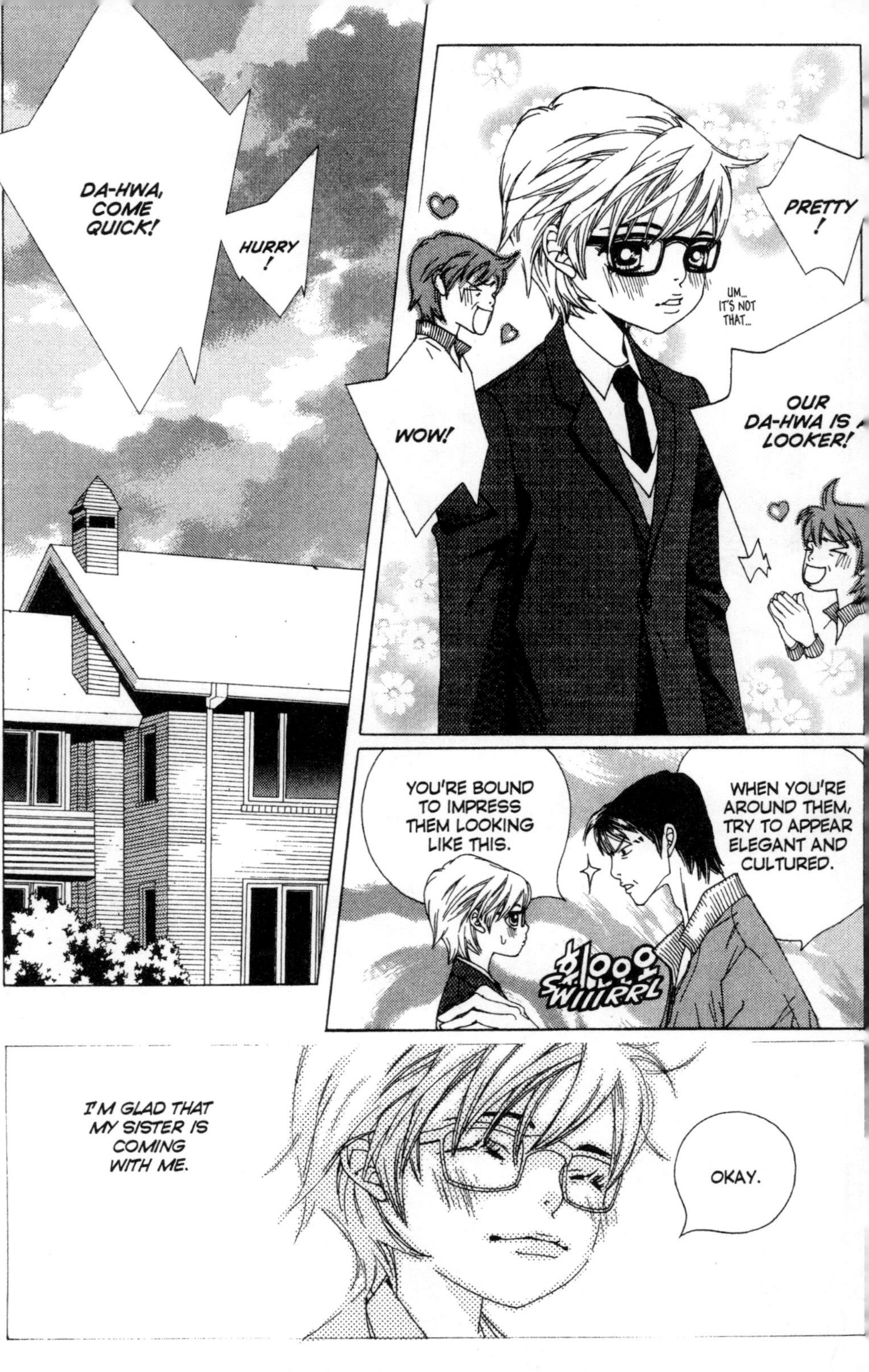
DA-HWA, COME QUICK!
HURRY!
PRETTY!
WOW!
UM... IT'S NOT THAT...
OUR DA-HWA IS LOOKER!
YOU'RE BOUND TO IMPRESS THEM LOOKING LIKE THIS.
WHEN YOU'RE AROUND THEM, TRY TO APPEAR ELEGANT AND CULTURED.
SWIIIRRL
I'M GLAD THAT MY SISTER IS COMING WITH ME.
OKAY.

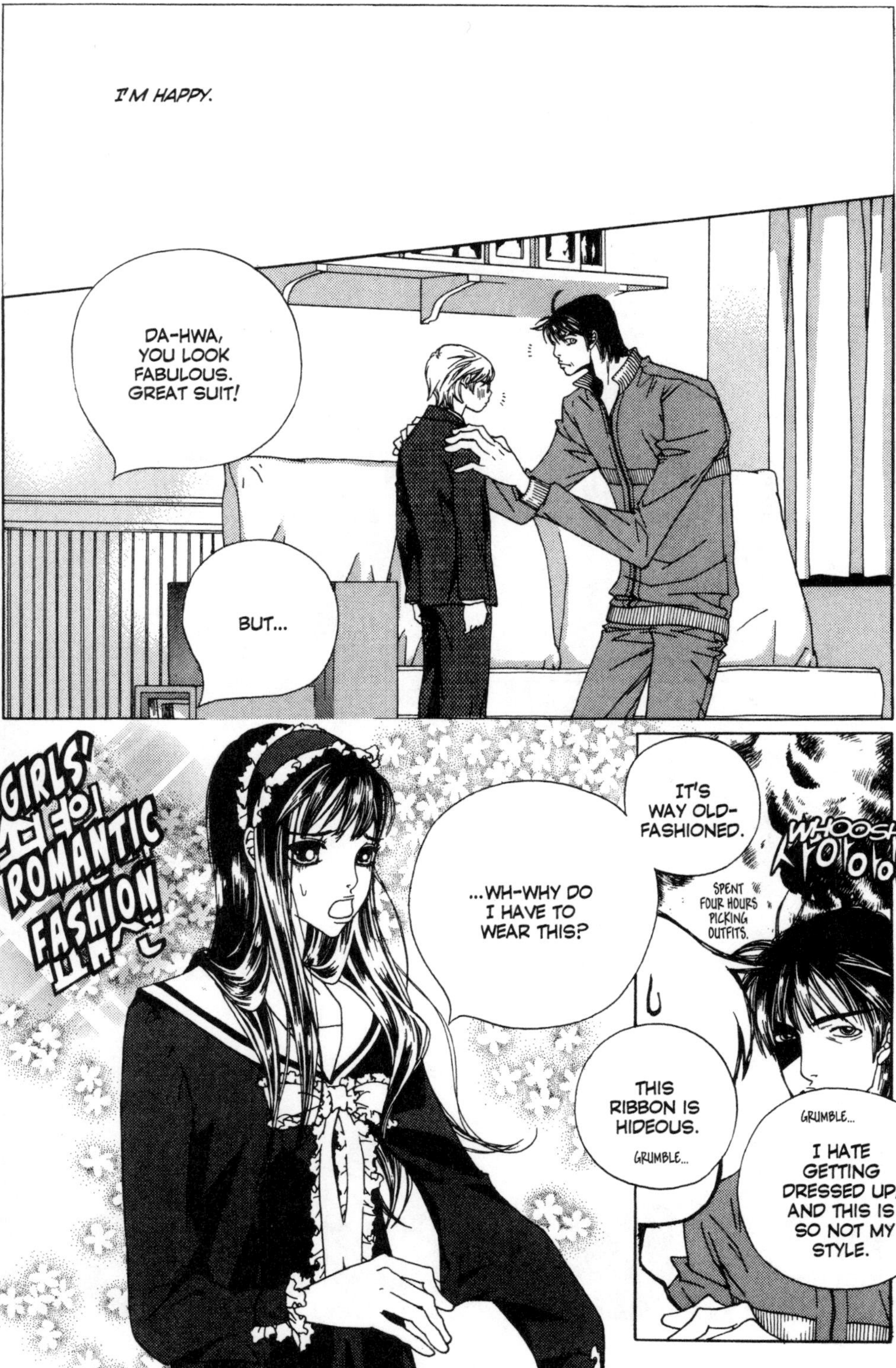
I'M HAPPY.
DA-HWA, YOU LOOK FABULOUS. GREAT SUIT!
BUT...
GIRLS' ROMANTIC FASHION!!
...WH-WHY DO I HAVE TO WEAR THIS?
IT'S WAY OLD-FASHIONED.
WHOOSH
SPENT FOUR HOURS PICKING OUTFITS.
THIS RIBBON IS HIDEOUS.
GRUMBLE...
GRUMBLE...
I HATE GETTING DRESSED UP, AND THIS IS SO NOT MY STYLE.

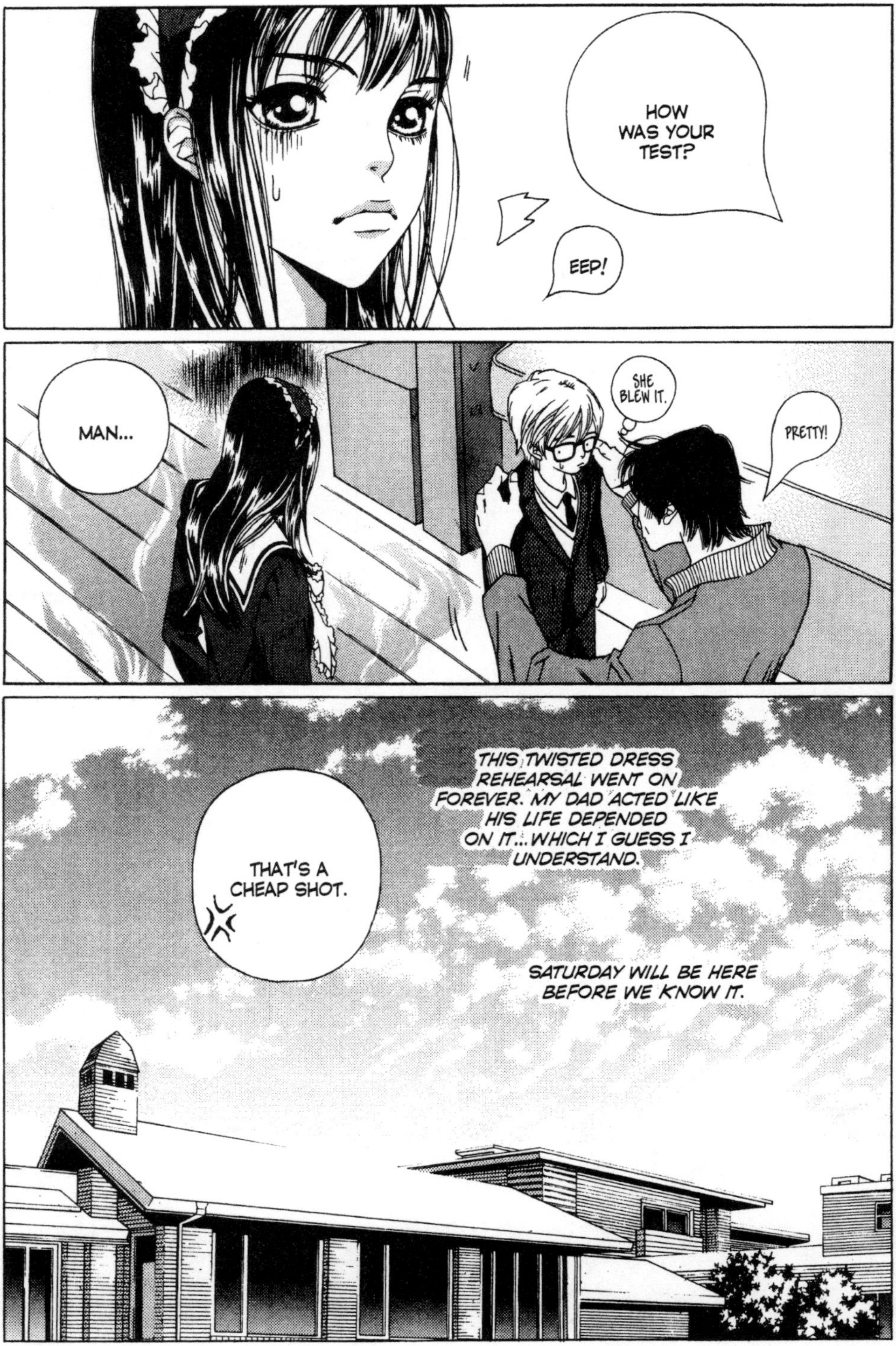
HOW WAS YOUR TEST?
EEP!
MAN...
SHE BLEW IT.
PRETTY!
THAT'S A CHEAP SHOT.
THIS TWISTED DRESS REHEARSAL WENT ON FOREVER. MY DAD ACTED LIKE HIS LIFE DEPENDED ON IT...WHICH I GUESS I UNDERSTAND.
SATURDAY WILL BE HERE BEFORE WE KNOW IT.

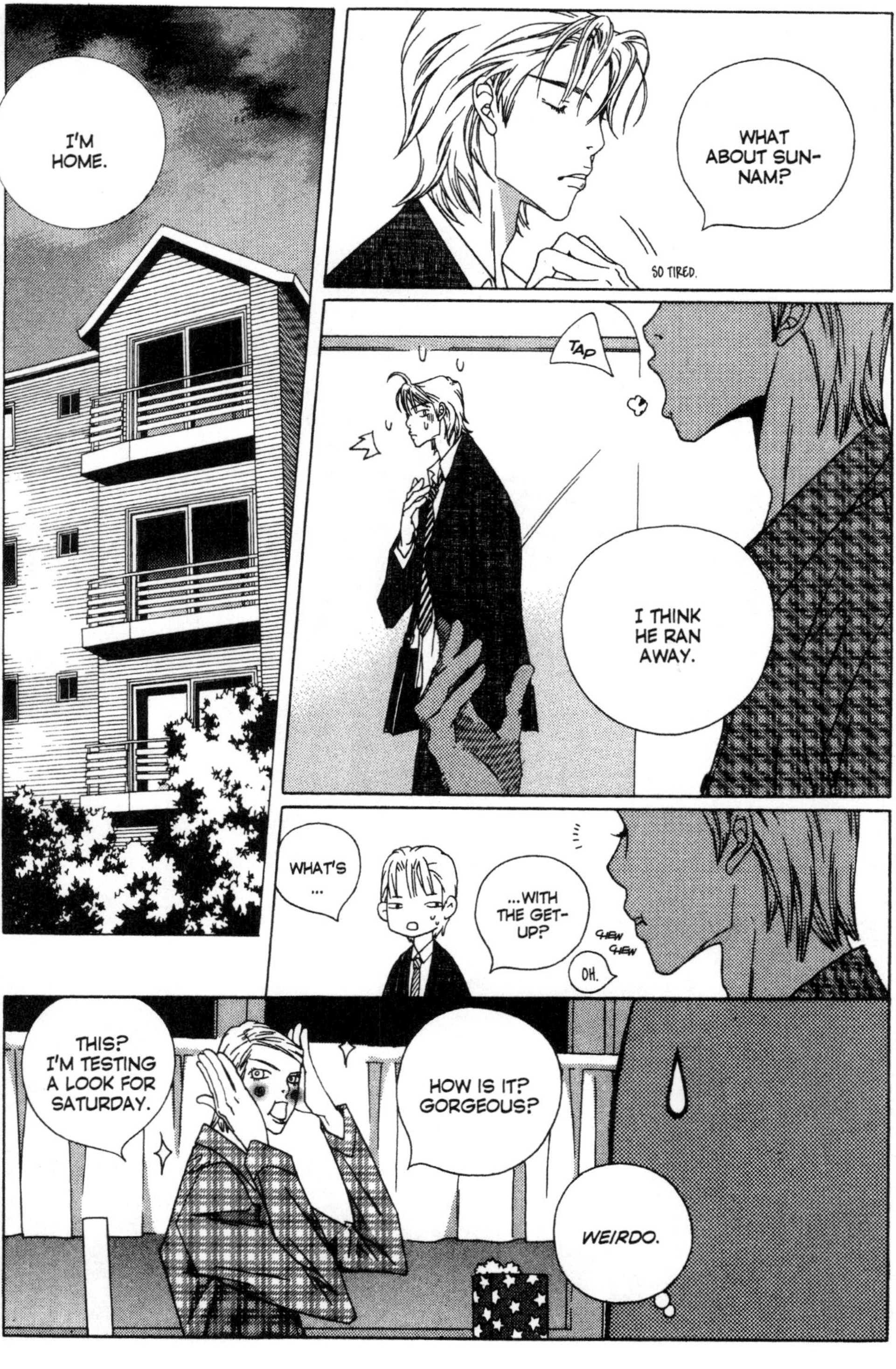
I'M HOME.
WHAT ABOUT SUN-NAM?
SO TIRED.
TAP
I THINK HE RAN AWAY.
WHAT'S ...
...WITH THE GET-UP?
CHEW CHEW
OH.
THIS? I'M TESTING A LOOK FOR SATURDAY.
HOW IS IT? GORGEOUS?
WEIRDO.

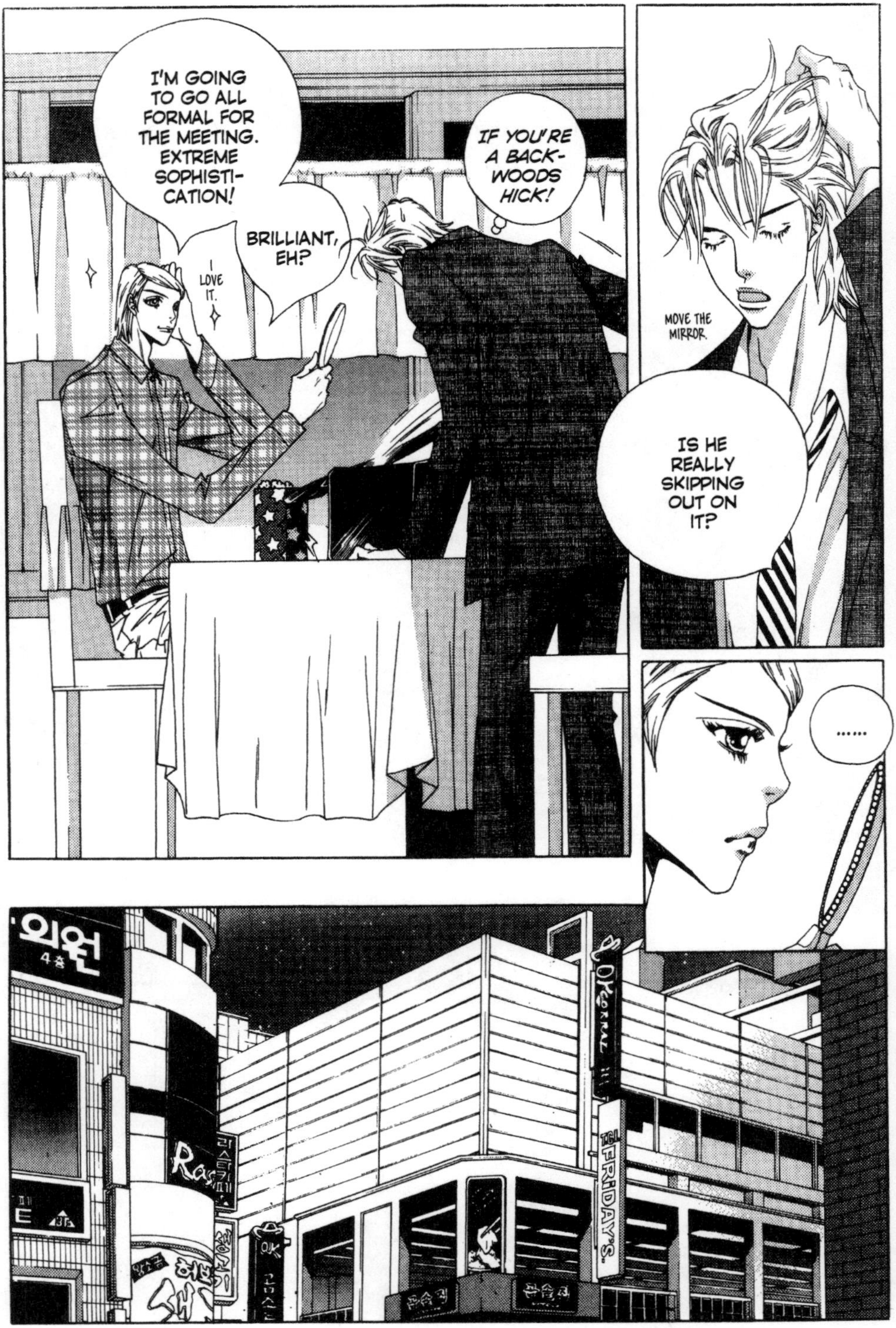
I'M GOING TO GO ALL FORMAL FOR THE MEETING. EXTREME SOPHISTI-CATION!
BRILLIANT, EH?
IF YOU'RE A BACK-WOODS HICK!
I LOVE IT.
MOVE THE MIRROR.
IS HE REALLY SKIPPING OUT ON IT?
......
외원
T.G.I. FRiDAY'S

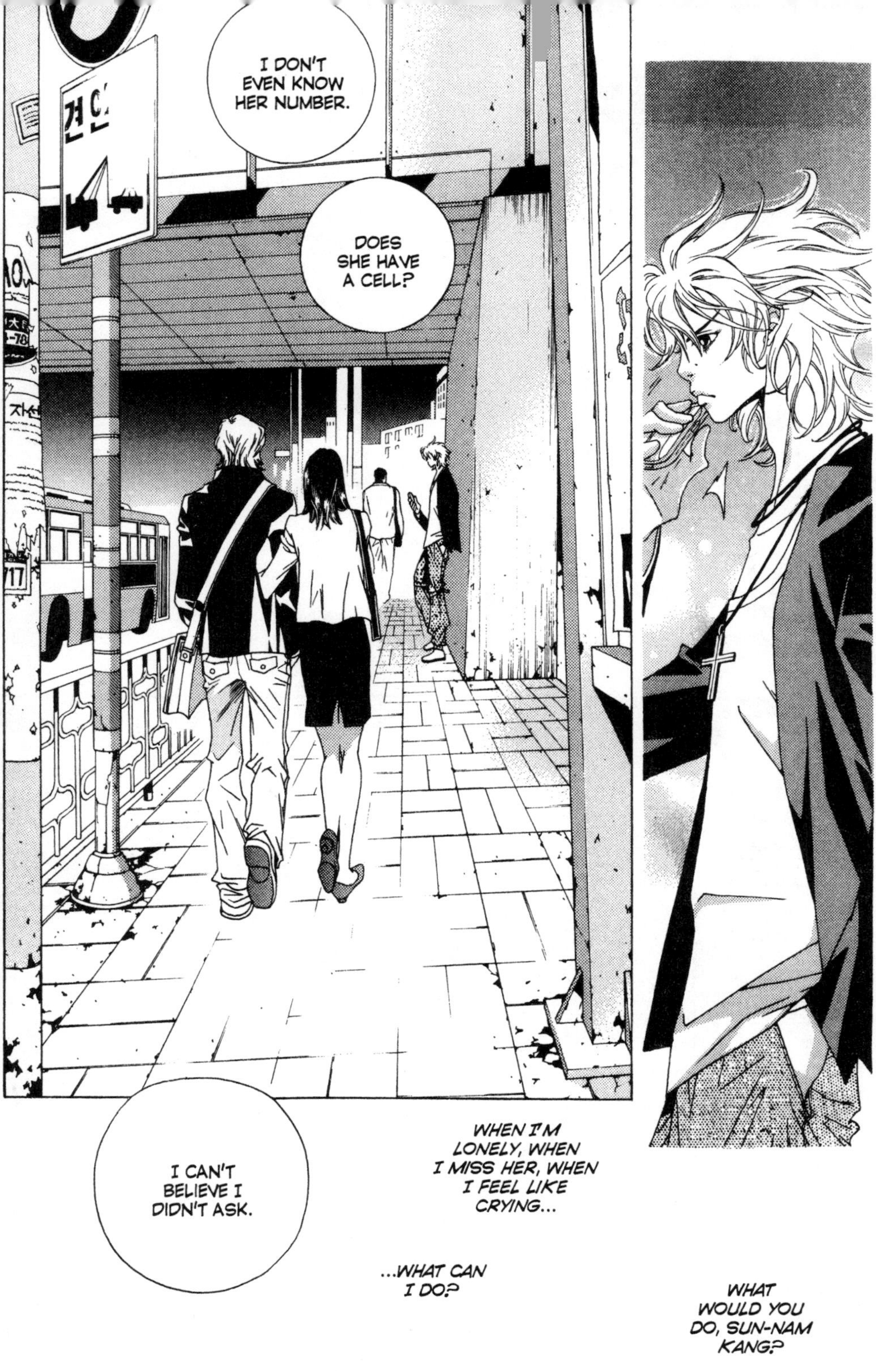
I DON'T EVEN KNOW HER NUMBER.
DOES SHE HAVE A CELL?
I CAN'T BELIEVE I DIDN'T ASK.
WHEN I'M LONELY, WHEN I MISS HER, WHEN I FEEL LIKE CRYING...
...WHAT CAN I DO?
WHAT WOULD YOU DO, SUN-NAM KANG?

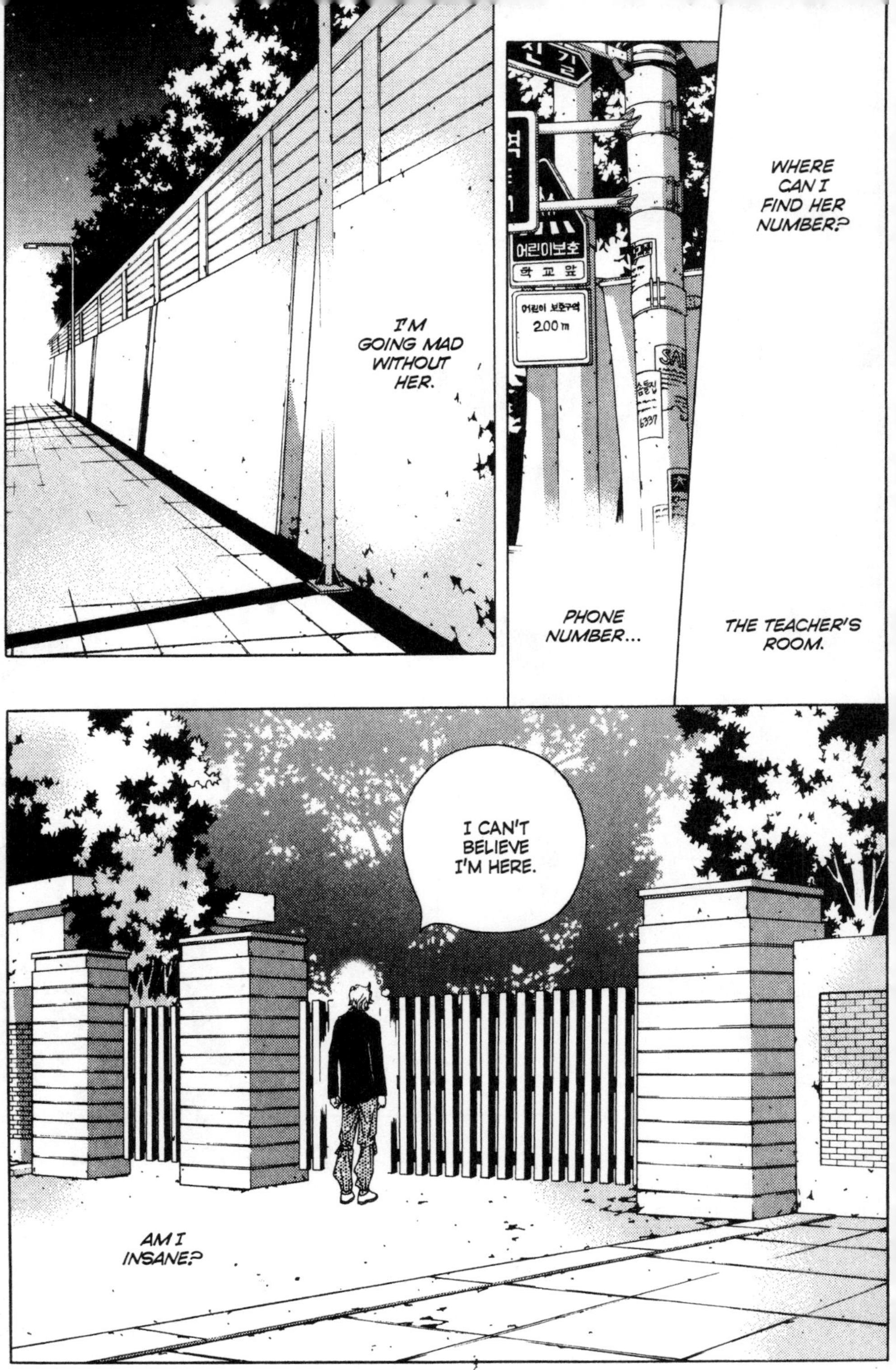
I'M GOING MAD WITHOUT HER.
어린이보호
학교앞
어린이 보호구역
200m
PHONE NUMBER...
WHERE CAN I FIND HER NUMBER?
THE TEACHER'S ROOM.
I CAN'T BELIEVE I'M HERE.
AM I INSANE?

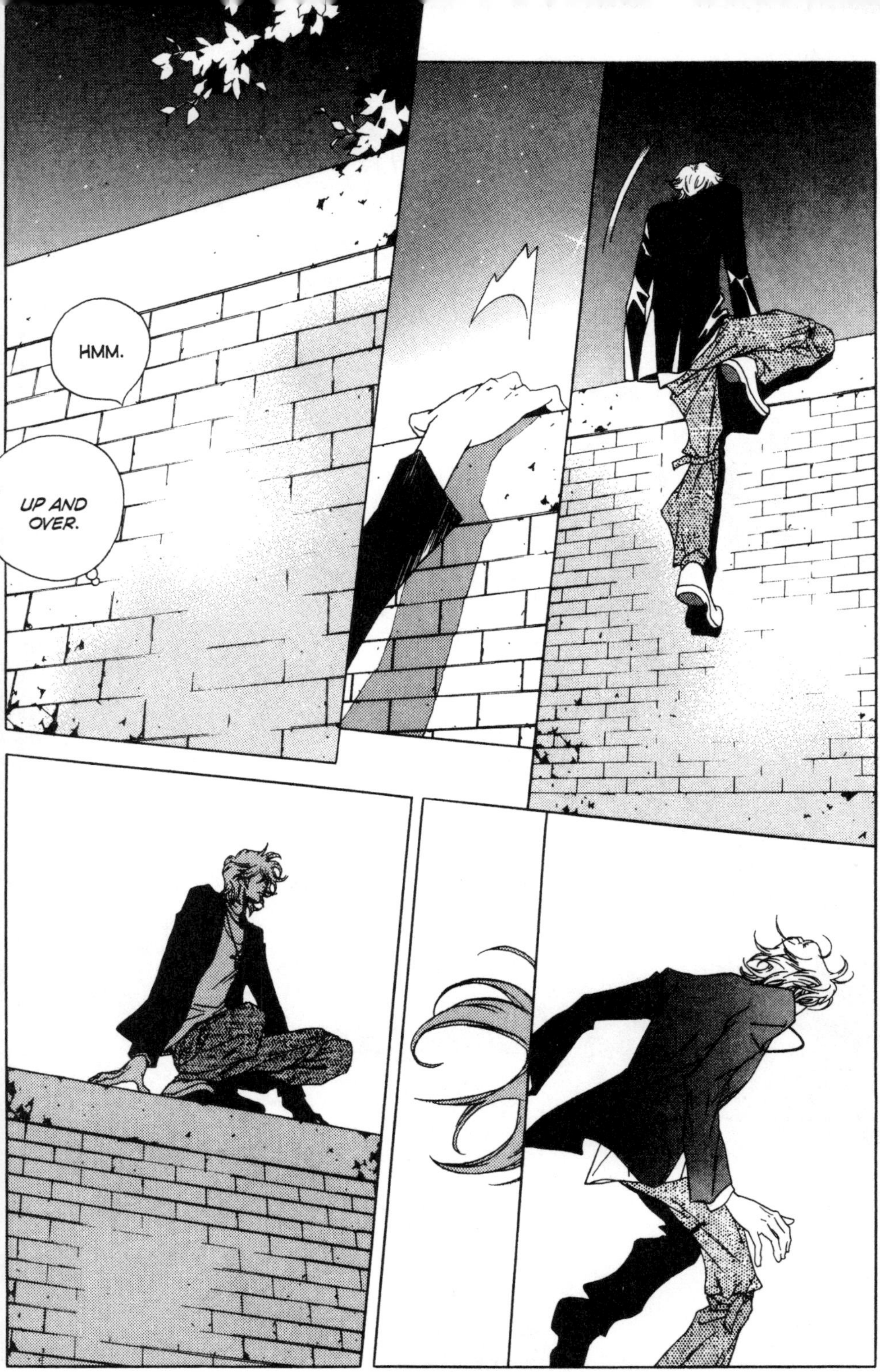
HMM.
UP AND OVER.

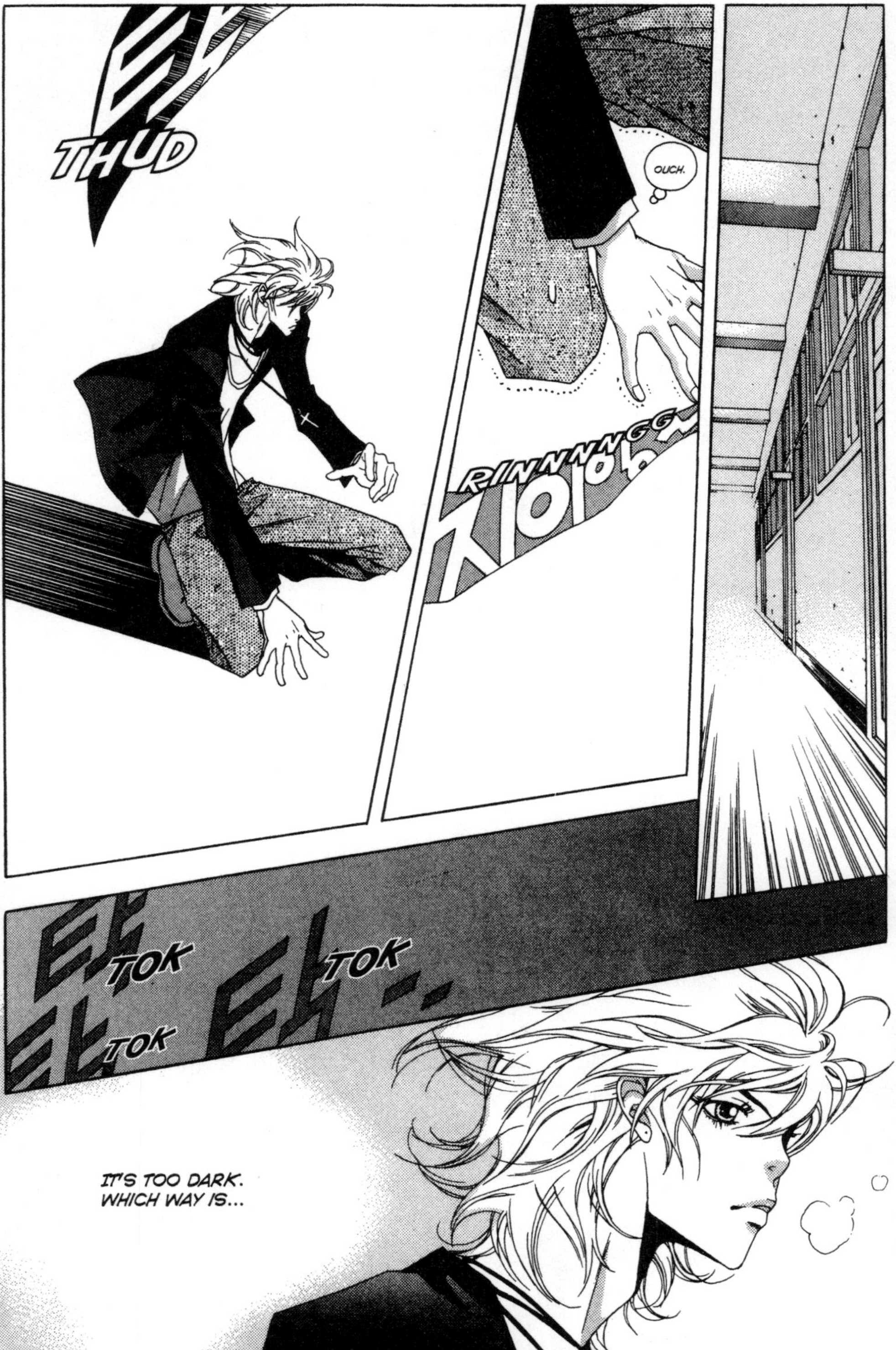
THUD
OUCH.
RINNNNNGG
TOK
TOK
TOK
IT'S TOO DARK.
WHICH WAY IS...

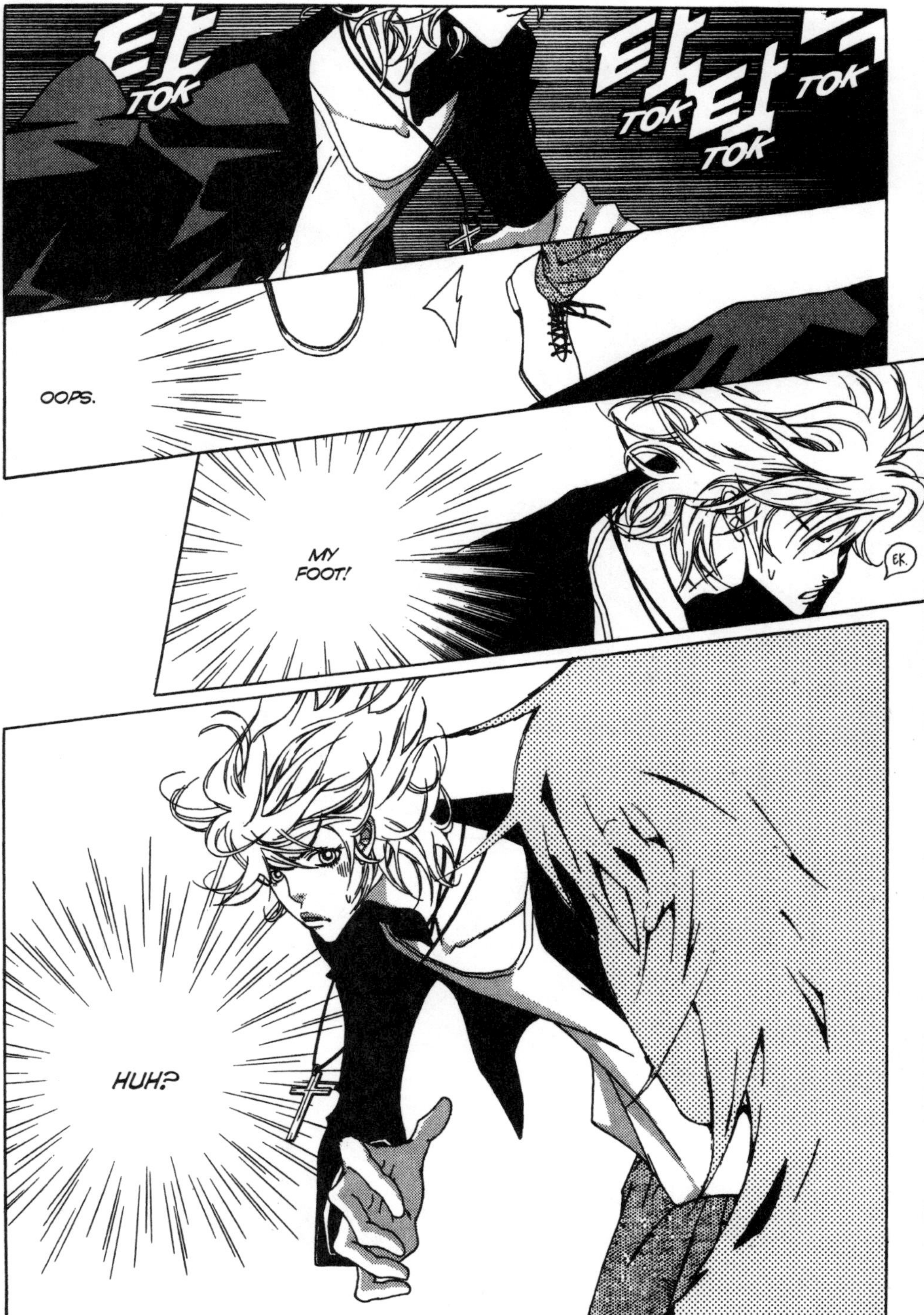
탁
TOK
탁
TOK
탁
TOK
TOK
OOPS.
MY FOOT!
EK.
HUH?

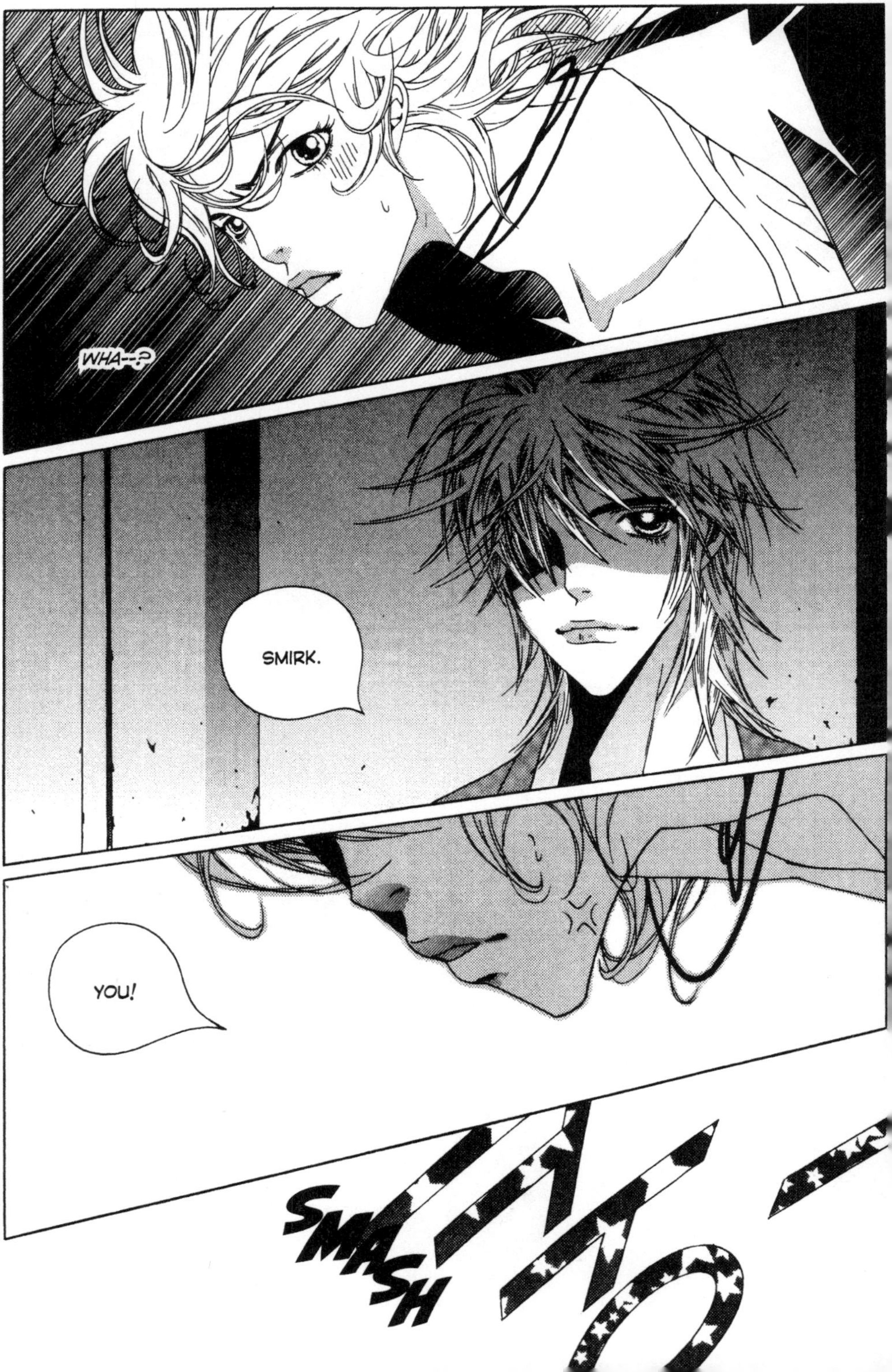
WHA--?
SMIRK.
YOU!
SMASH

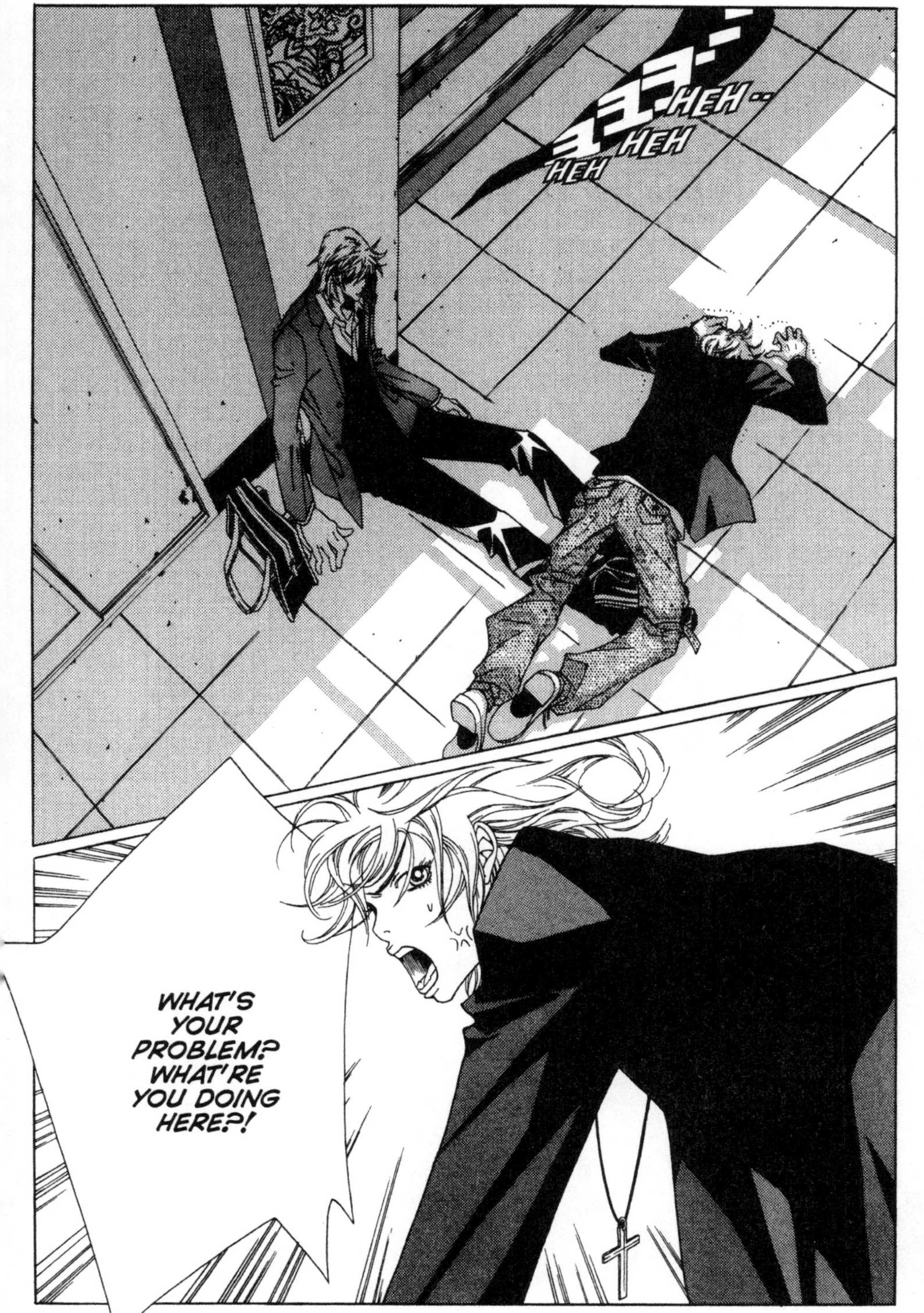
HEH.. HEH HEH
WHAT'S YOUR PROBLEM? WHAT'RE YOU DOING HERE?!

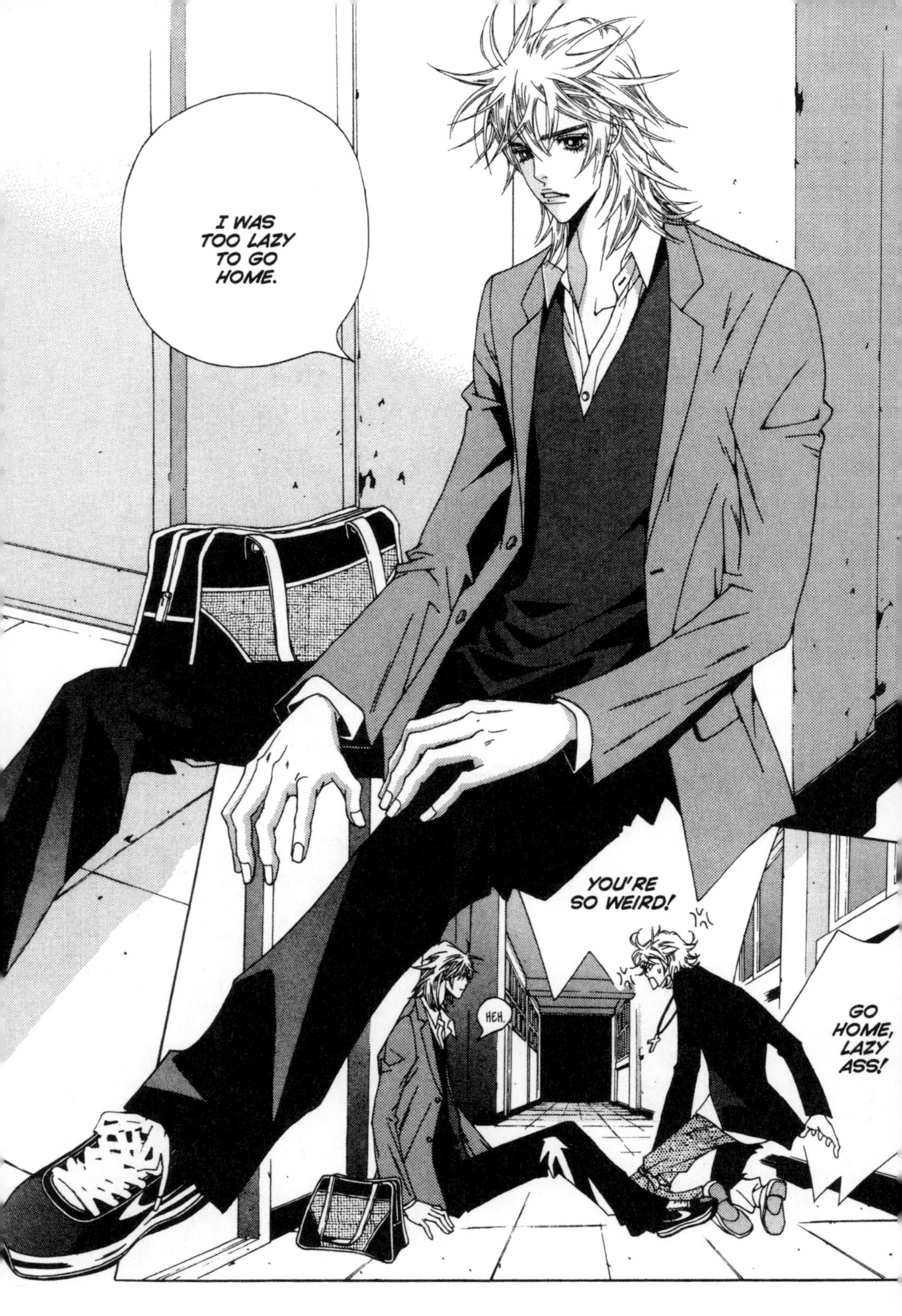
I WAS TOO LAZY TO GO HOME.
YOU'RE SO WEIRD!
HEH.
GO HOME, LAZY ASS!

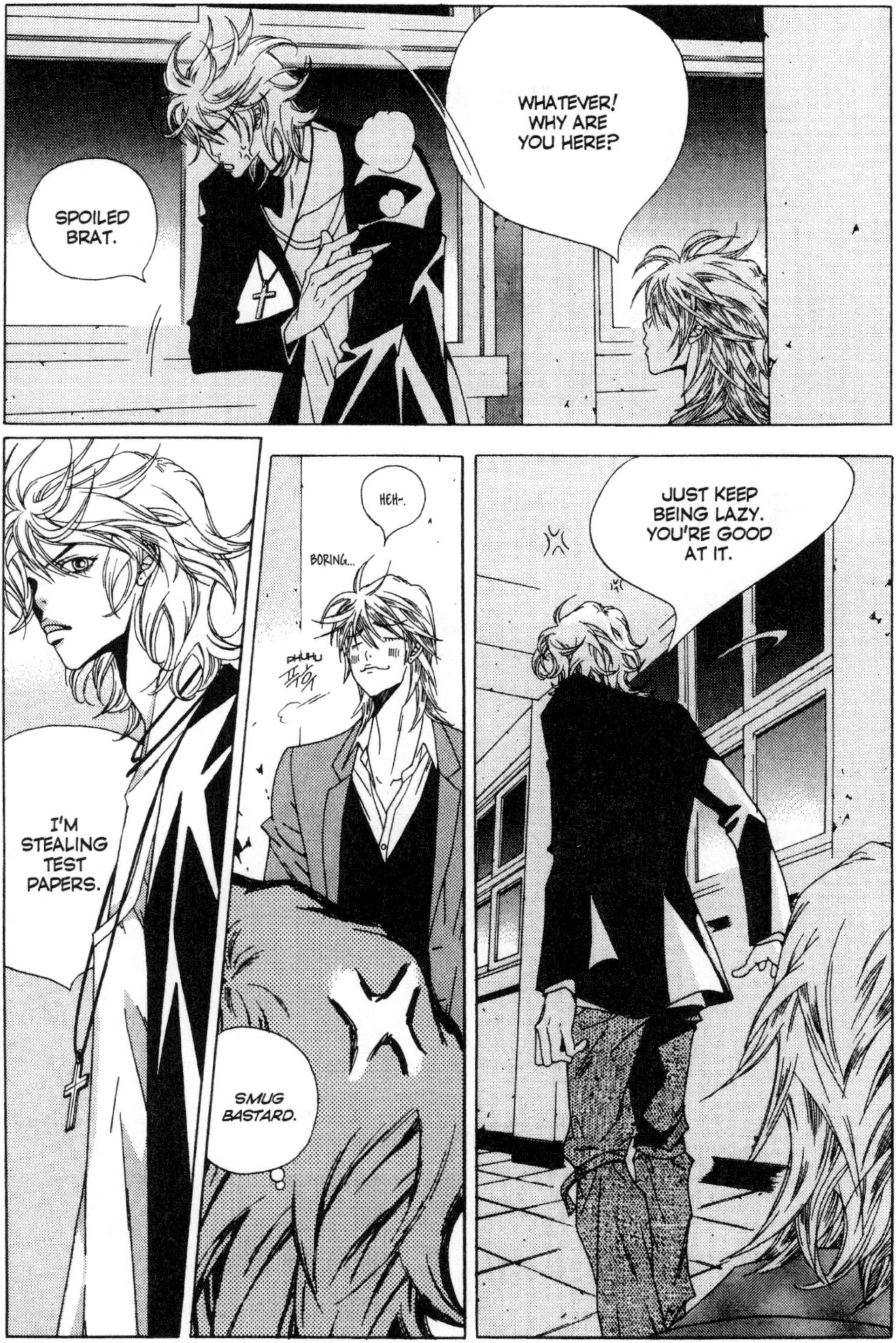
SPOILED BRAT.
WHATEVER! WHY ARE YOU HERE?
I'M STEALING TEST PAPERS.
HEH~.
BORING...
PHUHU
SMUG BASTARD.
JUST KEEP BEING LAZY. YOU'RE GOOD AT IT.

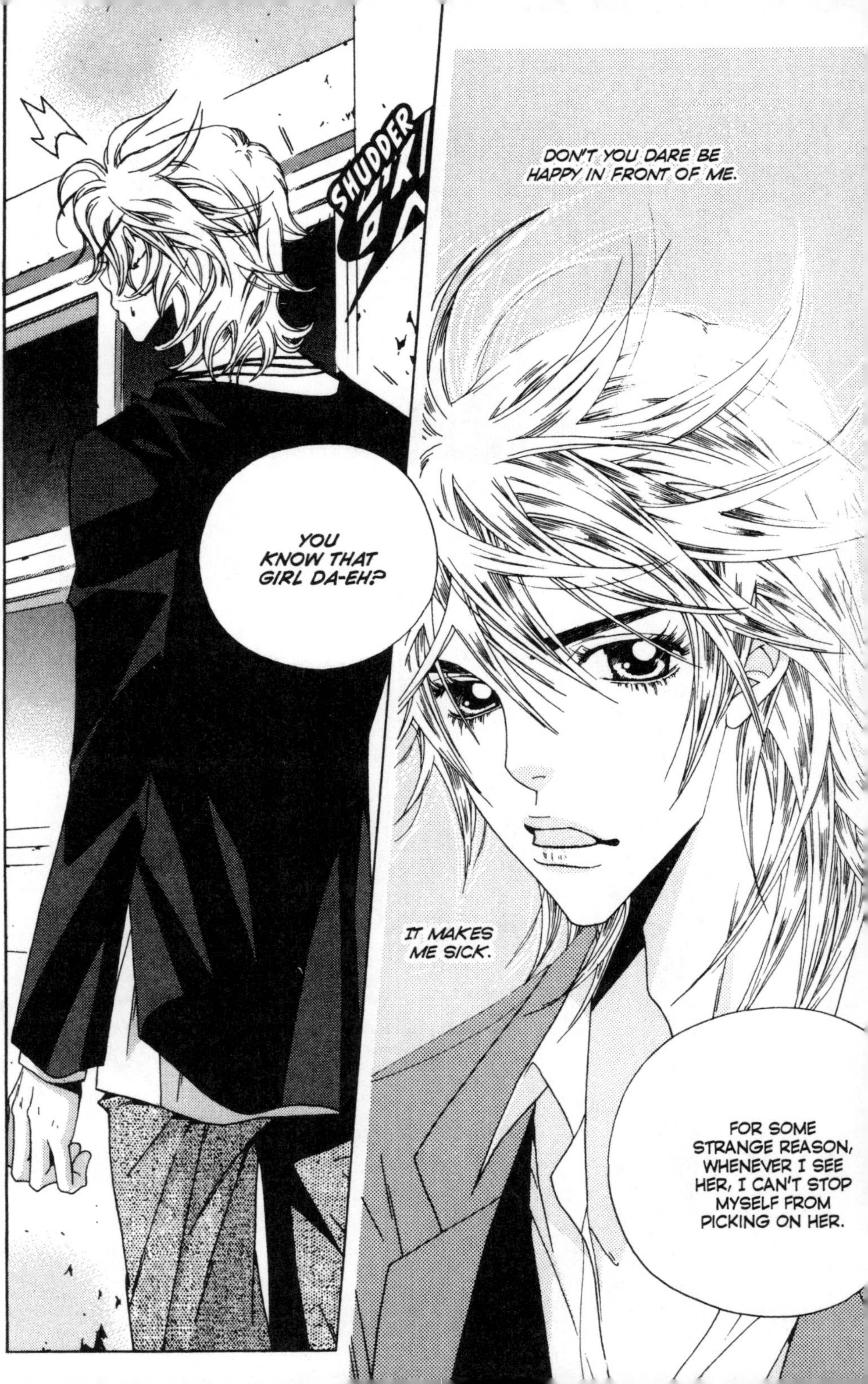
SHUDDER
YOU KNOW THAT GIRL DA-EH?
DON'T YOU DARE BE HAPPY IN FRONT OF ME.
IT MAKES ME SICK.
FOR SOME STRANGE REASON, WHENEVER I SEE HER, I CAN'T STOP MYSELF FROM PICKING ON HER.

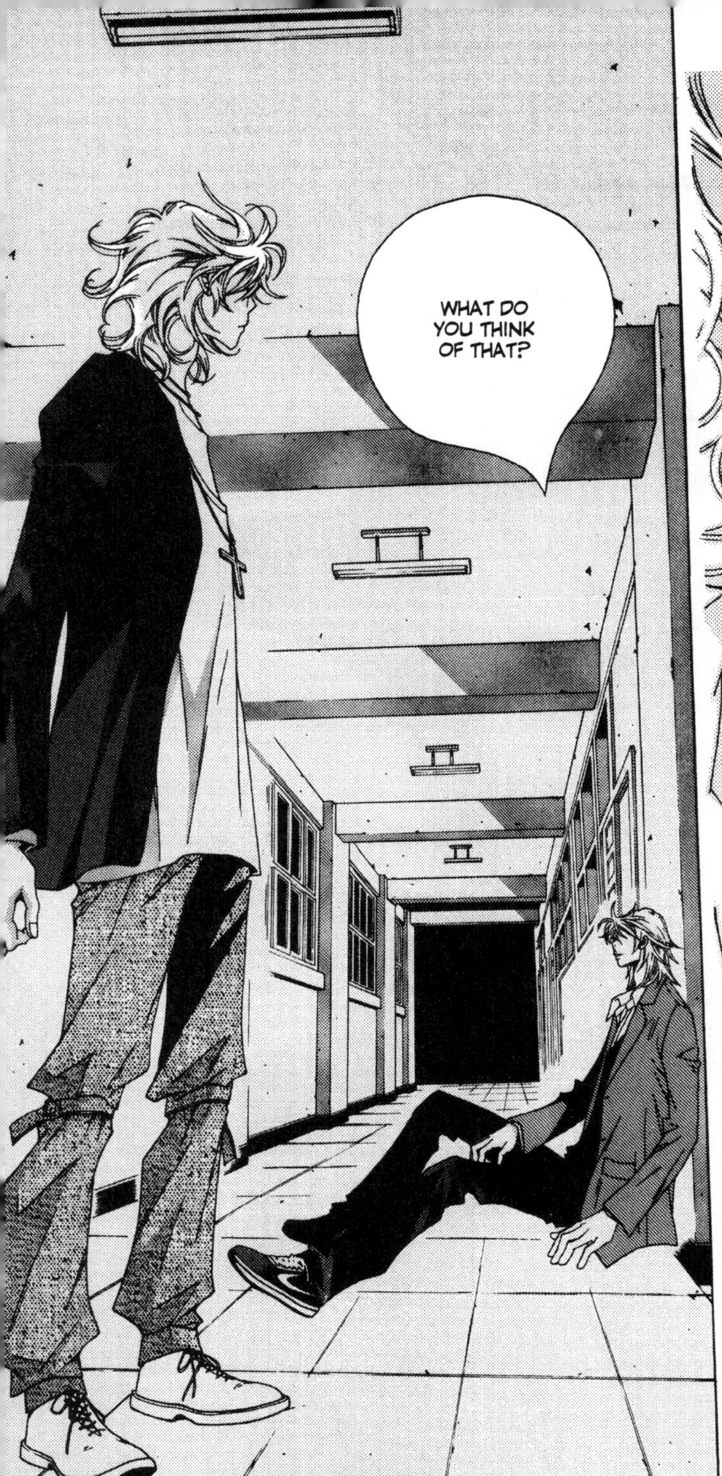
WHAT DO YOU THINK OF THAT?
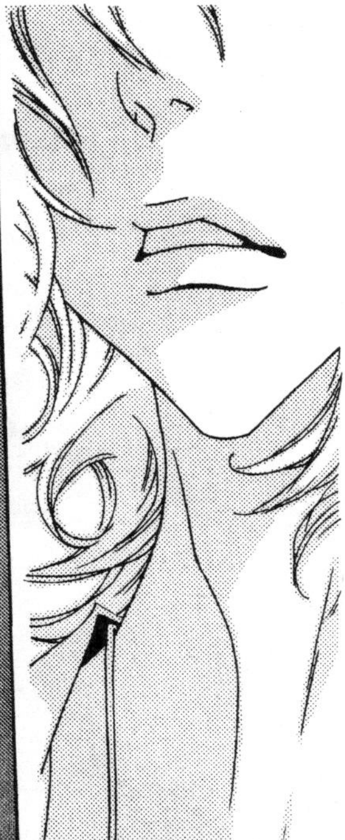
......

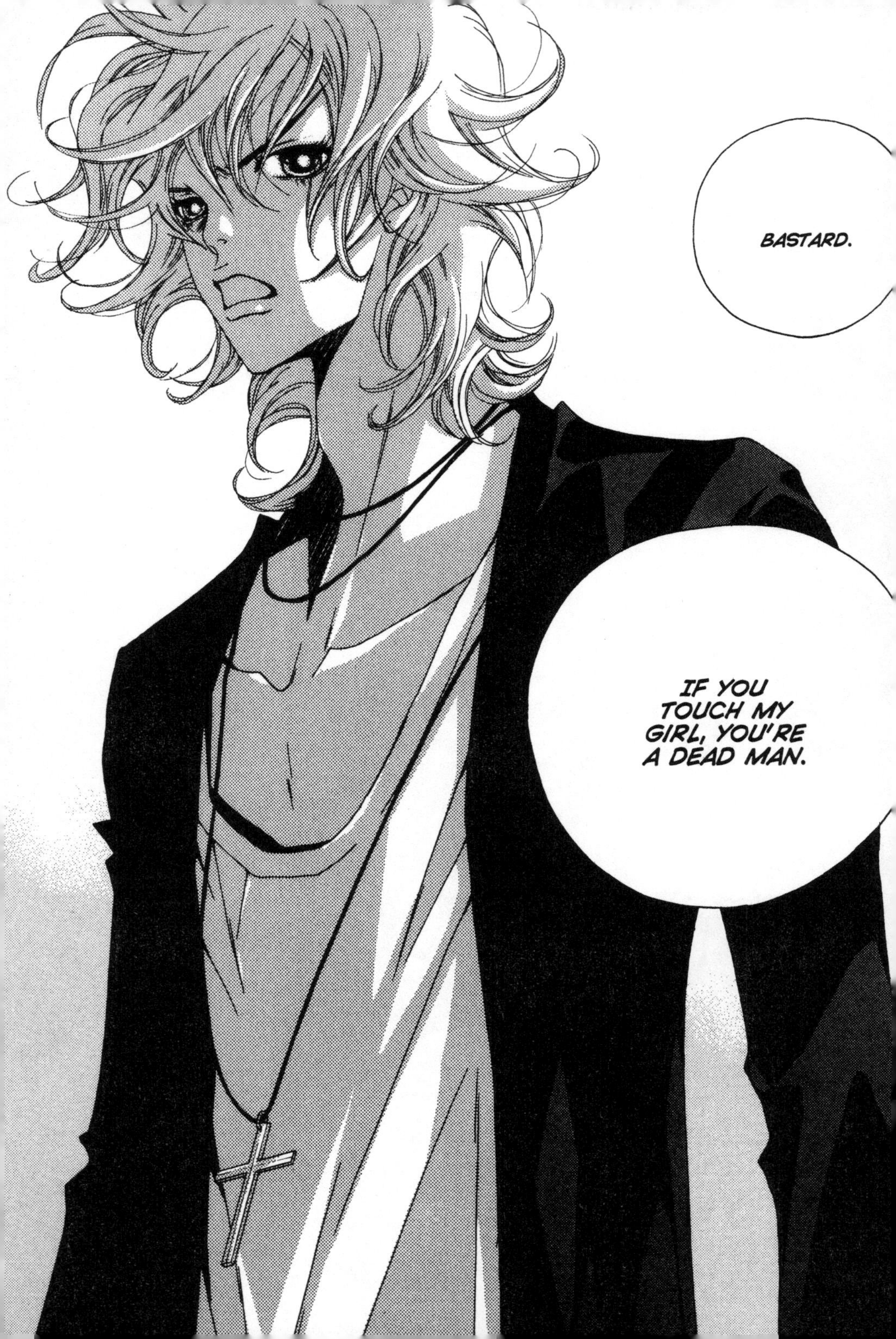
BASTARD.
IF YOU TOUCH MY GIRL, YOU'RE A DEAD MAN.

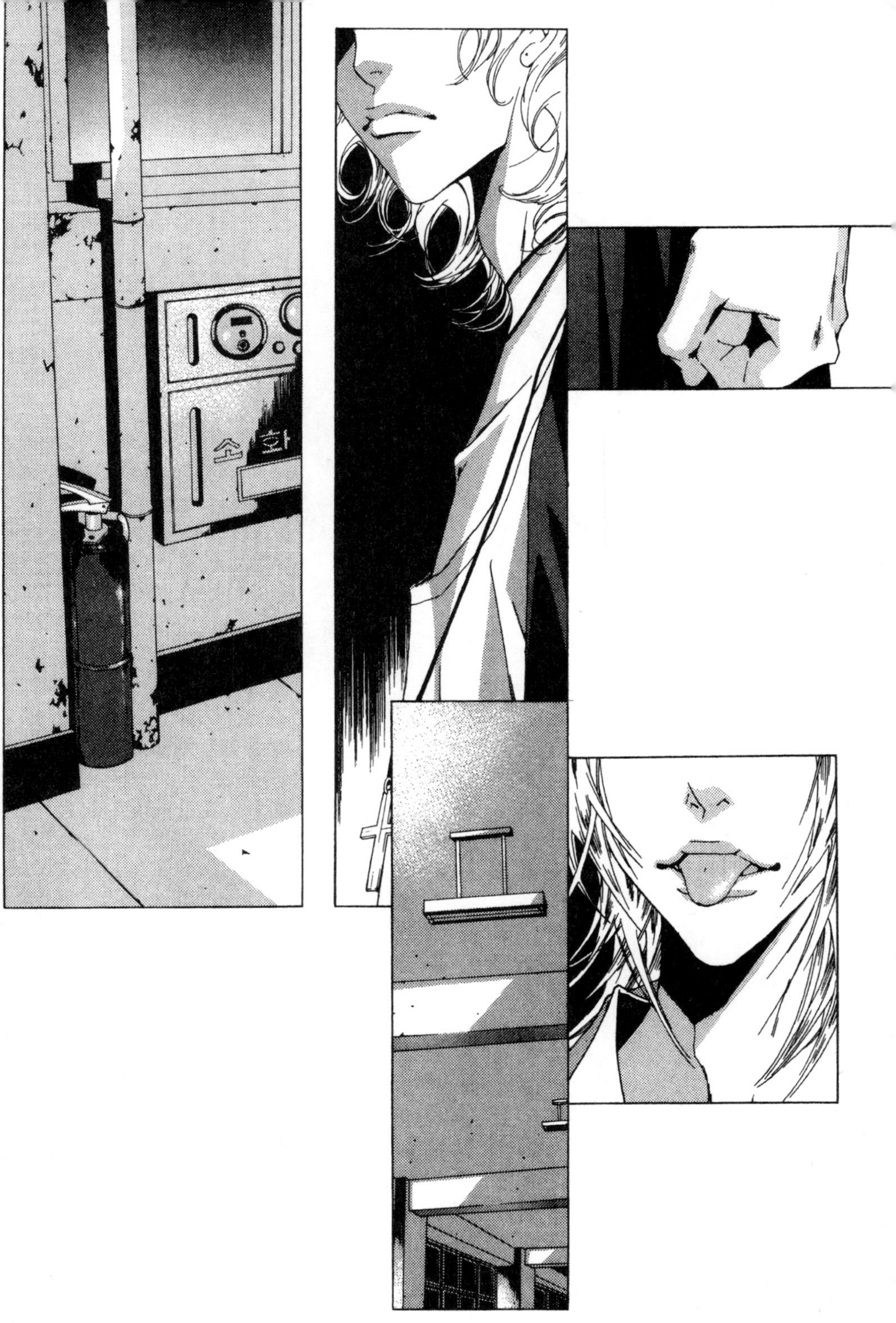

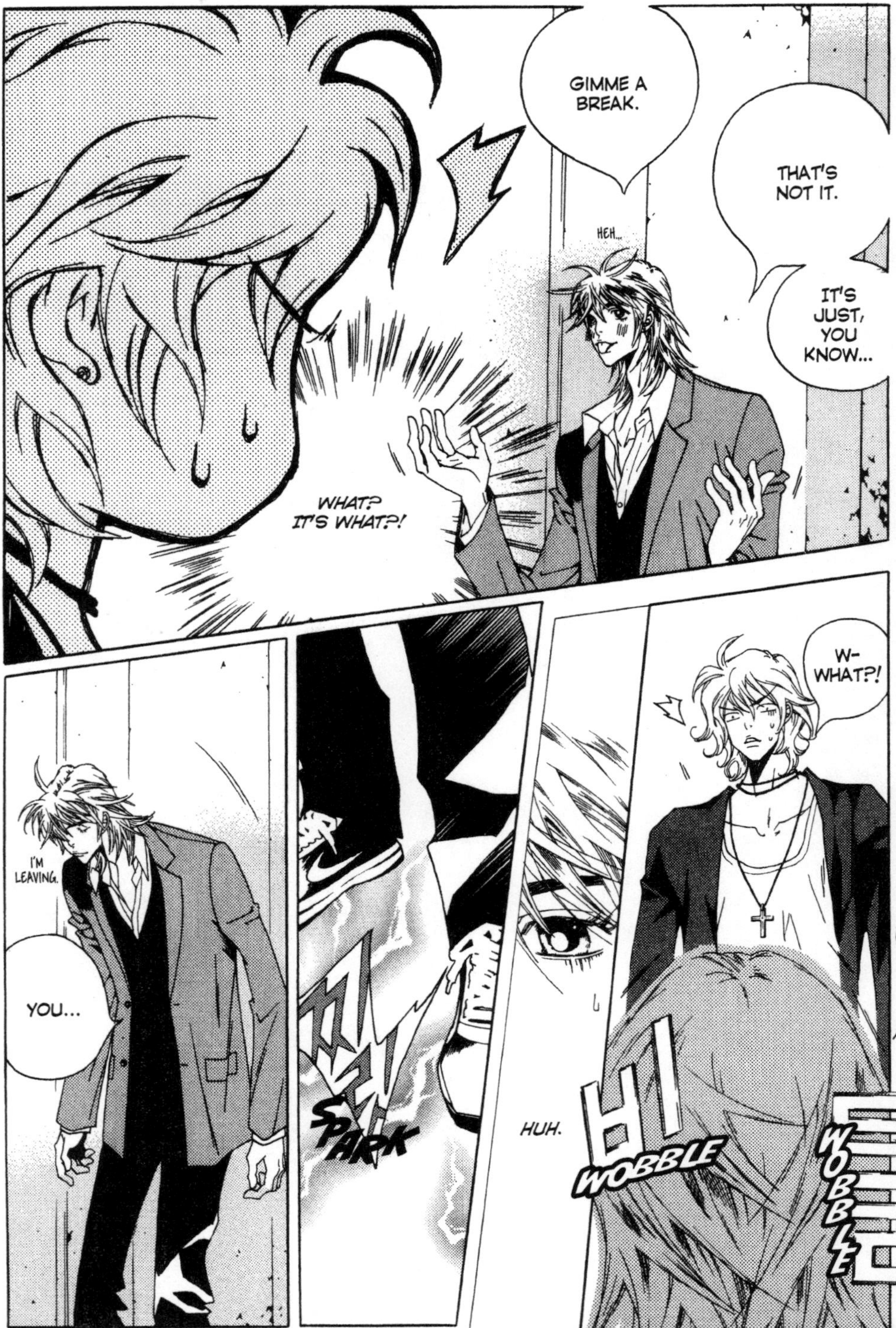
GIMME A BREAK.
HEH...
THAT'S NOT IT.
IT'S JUST, YOU KNOW...
WHAT? IT'S WHAT?!
I'M LEAVING.
YOU...
SPARK
W-WHAT?!
HUH.
WOBBLE
WOBBLE

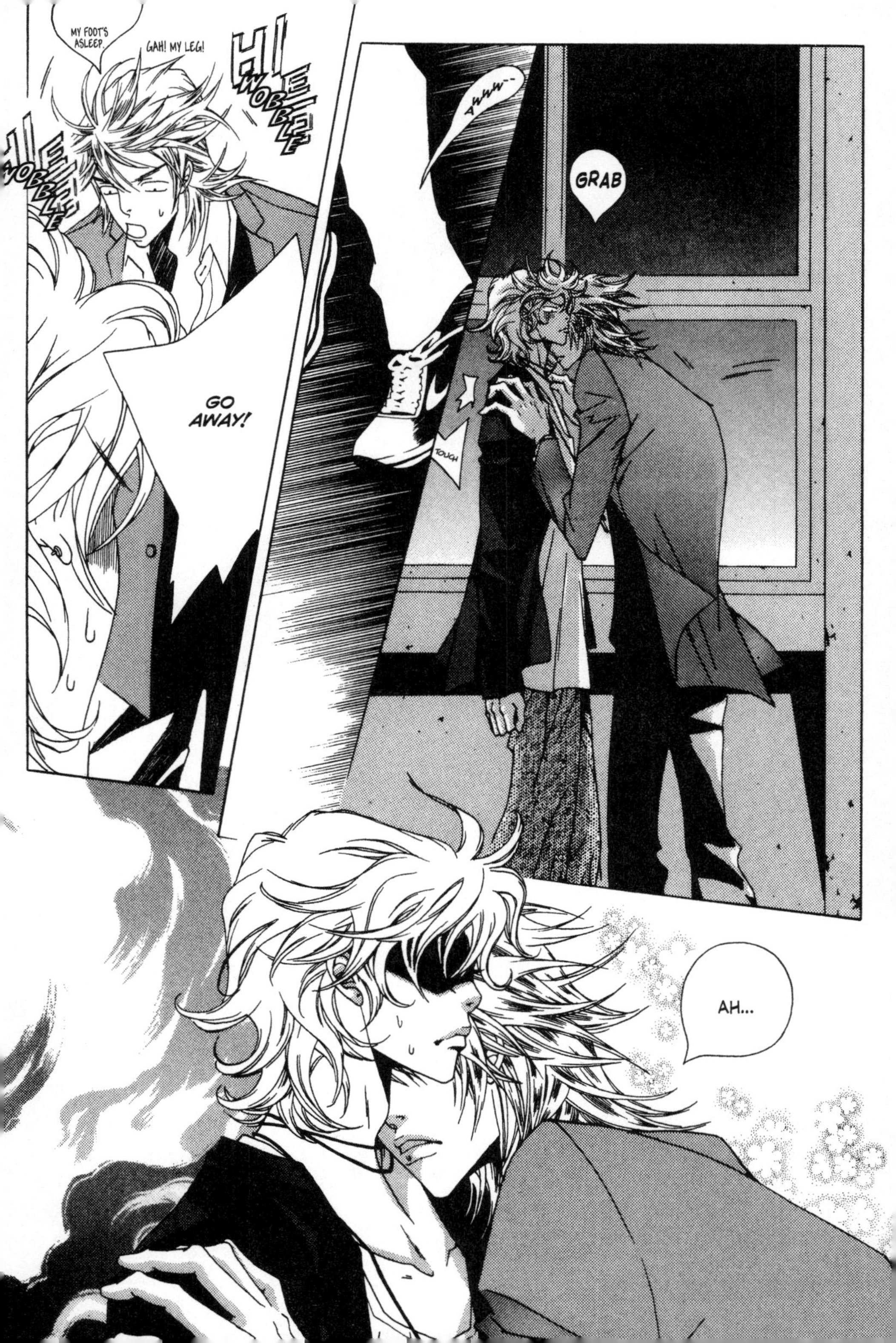
MY FOOT'S ASLEEP.
GAH! MY LEG!
HIE WOBBLE
HIE WOBBLE
GO AWAY!
AWW--
GRAB
TOUCH
AH...

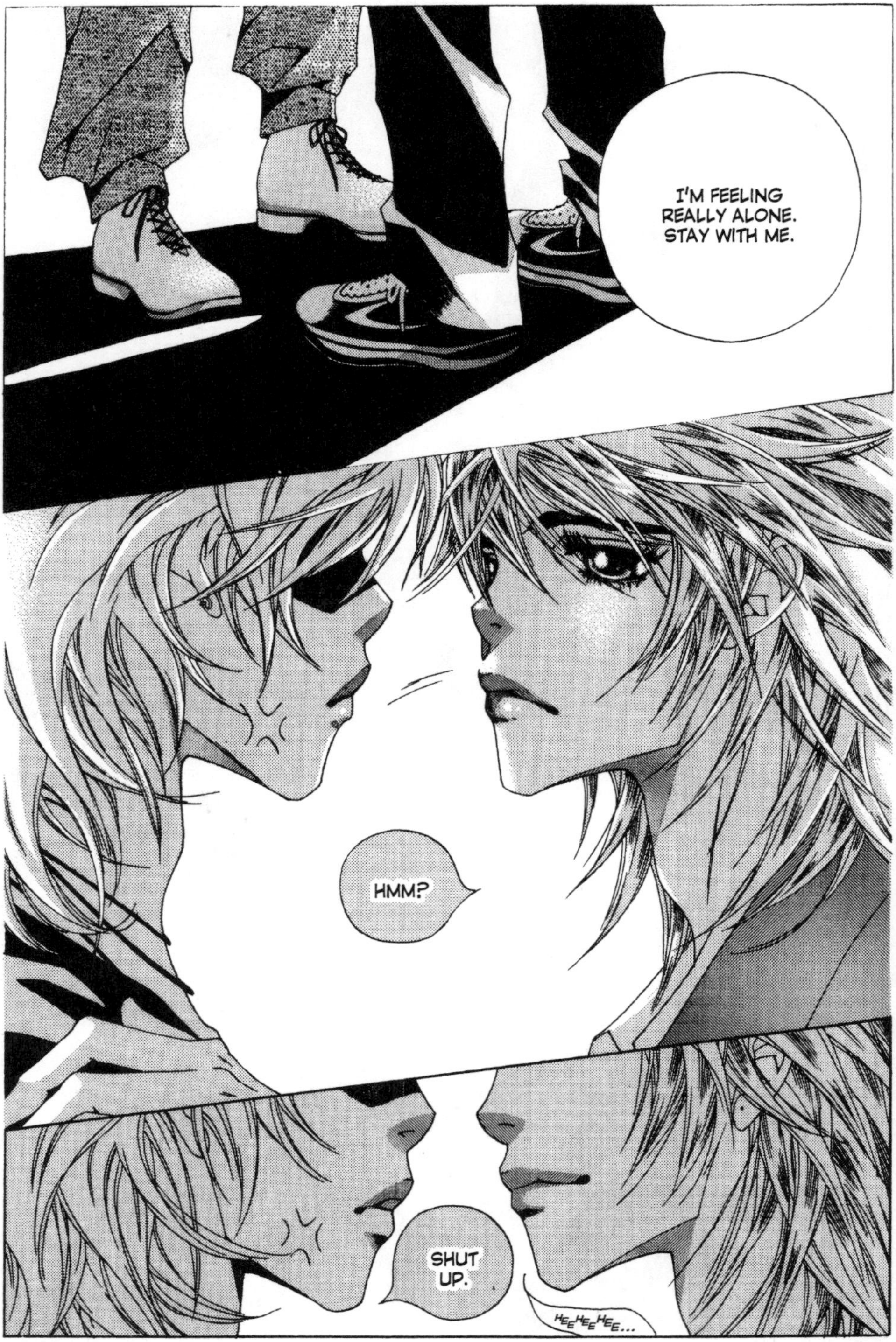
I'M FEELING REALLY ALONE. STAY WITH ME.
HMM?
SHUT UP.
HEEHEEHEE...

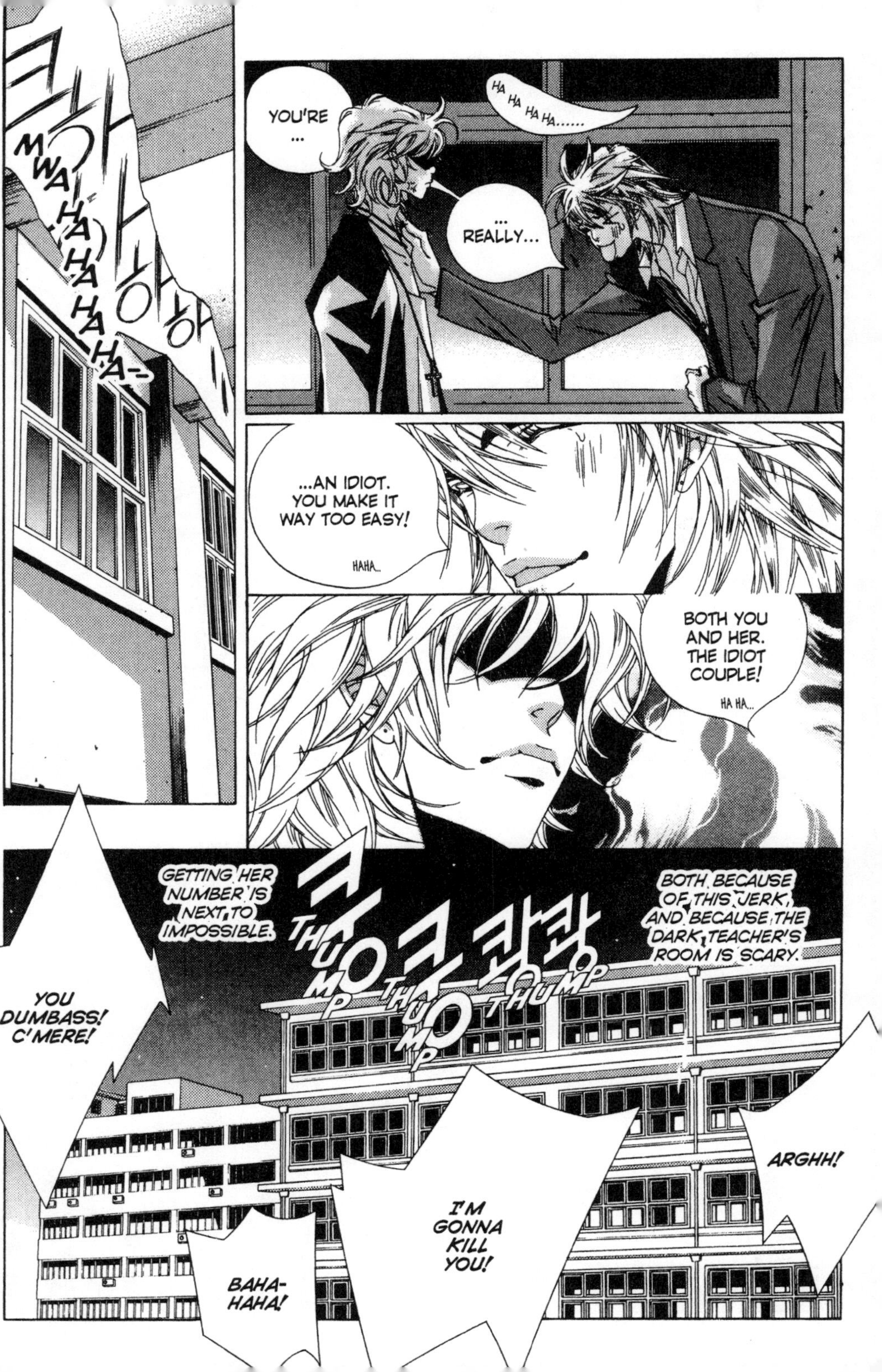
MWAHAHAHAHAHA-
YOU'RE ...
HA HA HA HA......
... REALLY...
...AN IDIOT. YOU MAKE IT WAY TOO EASY!
HAHA...
BOTH YOU AND HER. THE IDIOT COUPLE!
HA HA...
GETTING HER NUMBER IS NEXT TO IMPOSSIBLE.
THUMP THUMP THUMP
쾅쾅
BOTH BECAUSE OF THIS JERK, AND BECAUSE THE DARK TEACHER'S ROOM IS SCARY.
YOU DUMBASS! C'MERE!
BAHA-HAHA!
I'M GONNA KILL YOU!
ARGHH!

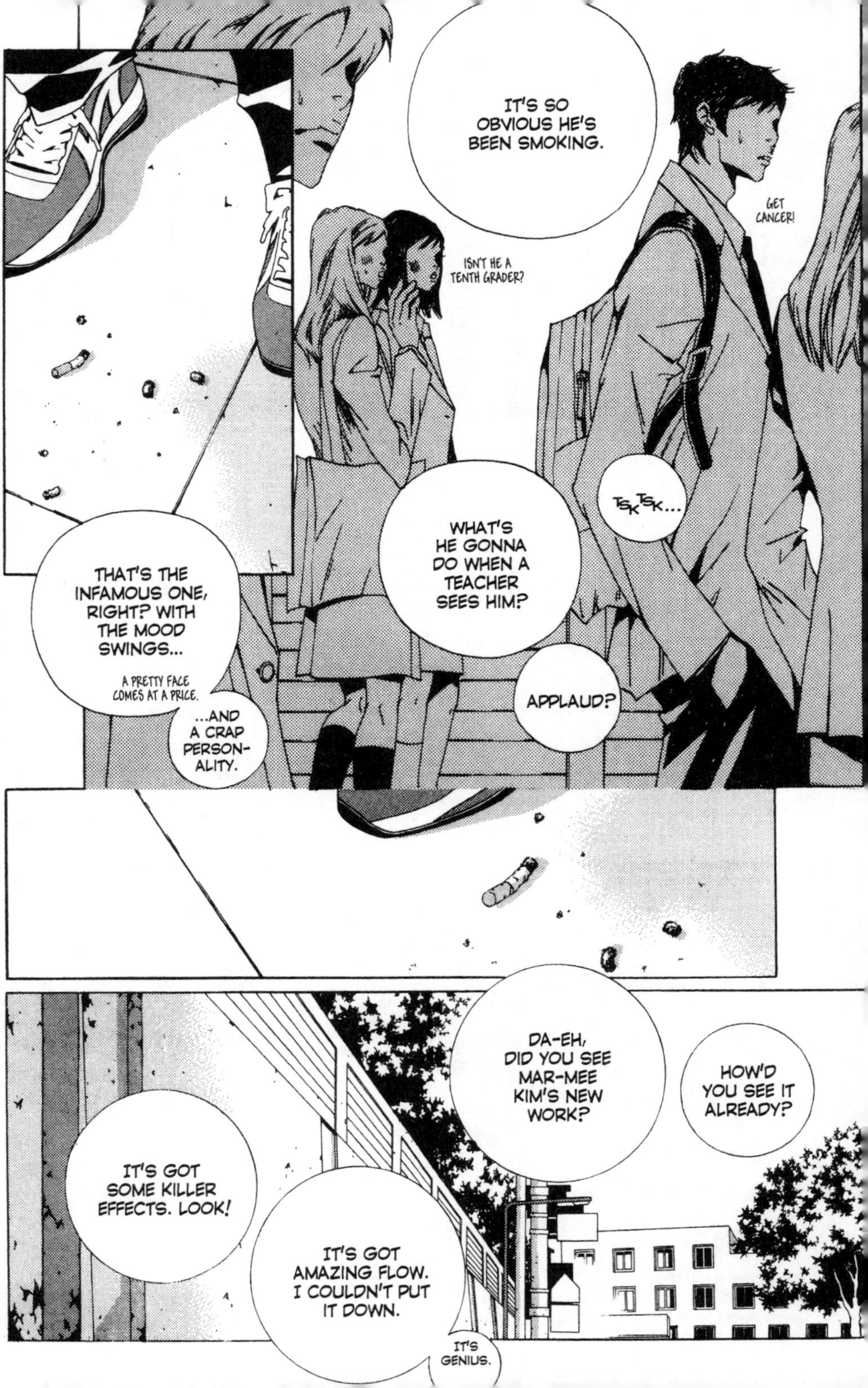
IT'S SO OBVIOUS HE'S BEEN SMOKING.
ISN'T HE A TENTH GRADER?
GET CANCER!
THAT'S THE INFAMOUS ONE, RIGHT? WITH THE MOOD SWINGS...
A PRETTY FACE COMES AT A PRICE.
...AND A CRAP PERSON-ALITY.
WHAT'S HE GONNA DO WHEN A TEACHER SEES HIM?
TSK TSK...
APPLAUD?
DA-EH, DID YOU SEE MAR-MEE KIM'S NEW WORK?
HOW'D YOU SEE IT ALREADY?
IT'S GOT SOME KILLER EFFECTS. LOOK!
IT'S GOT AMAZING FLOW. I COULDN'T PUT IT DOWN.
IT'S GENIUS.

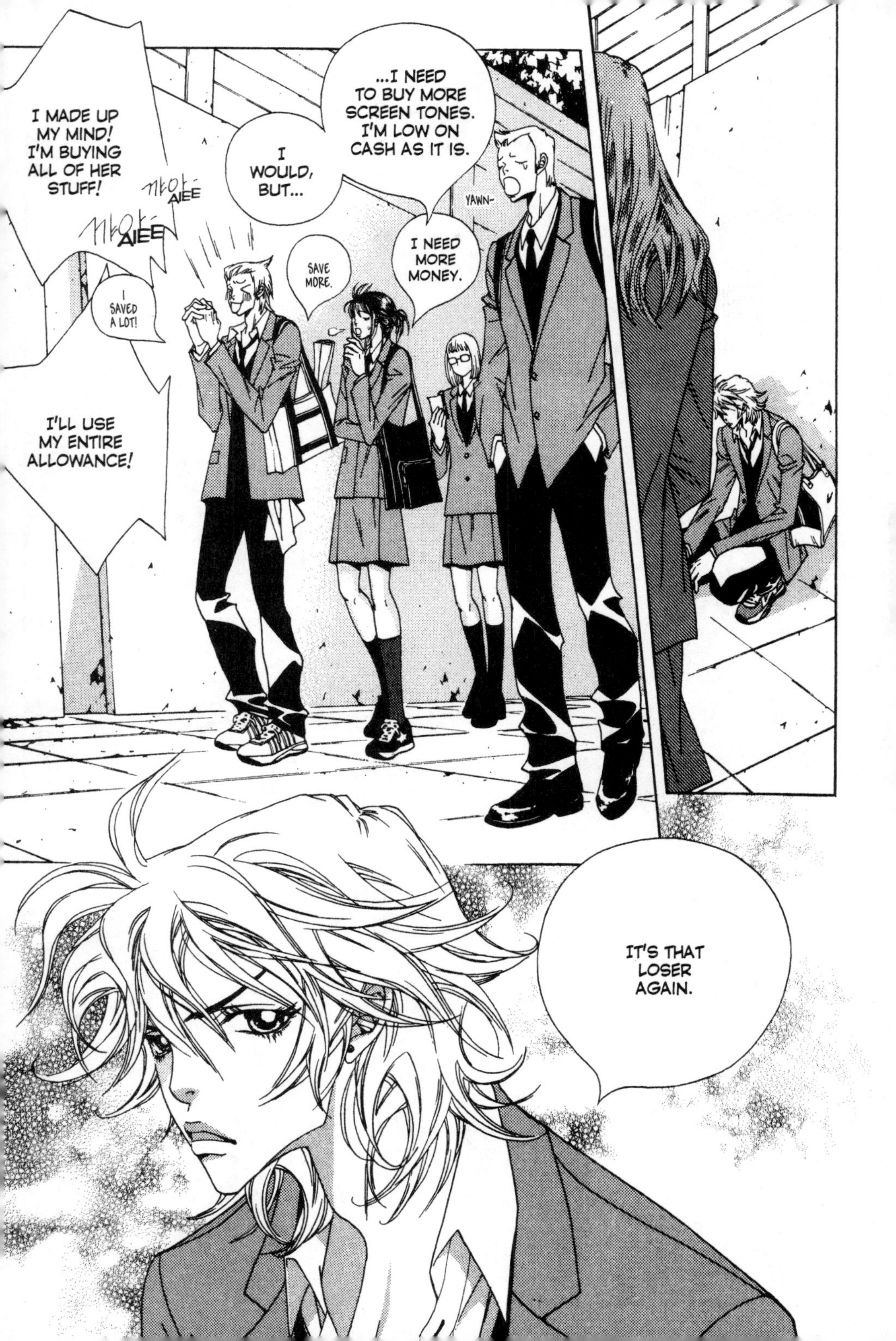
I MADE UP MY MIND! I'M BUYING ALL OF HER STUFF!
AIEE
AIEE
I SAVED A LOT!
I'LL USE MY ENTIRE ALLOWANCE!
I WOULD, BUT...
SAVE MORE.
...I NEED TO BUY MORE SCREEN TONES. I'M LOW ON CASH AS IT IS.
I NEED MORE MONEY.
YAWN~
IT'S THAT LOSER AGAIN.

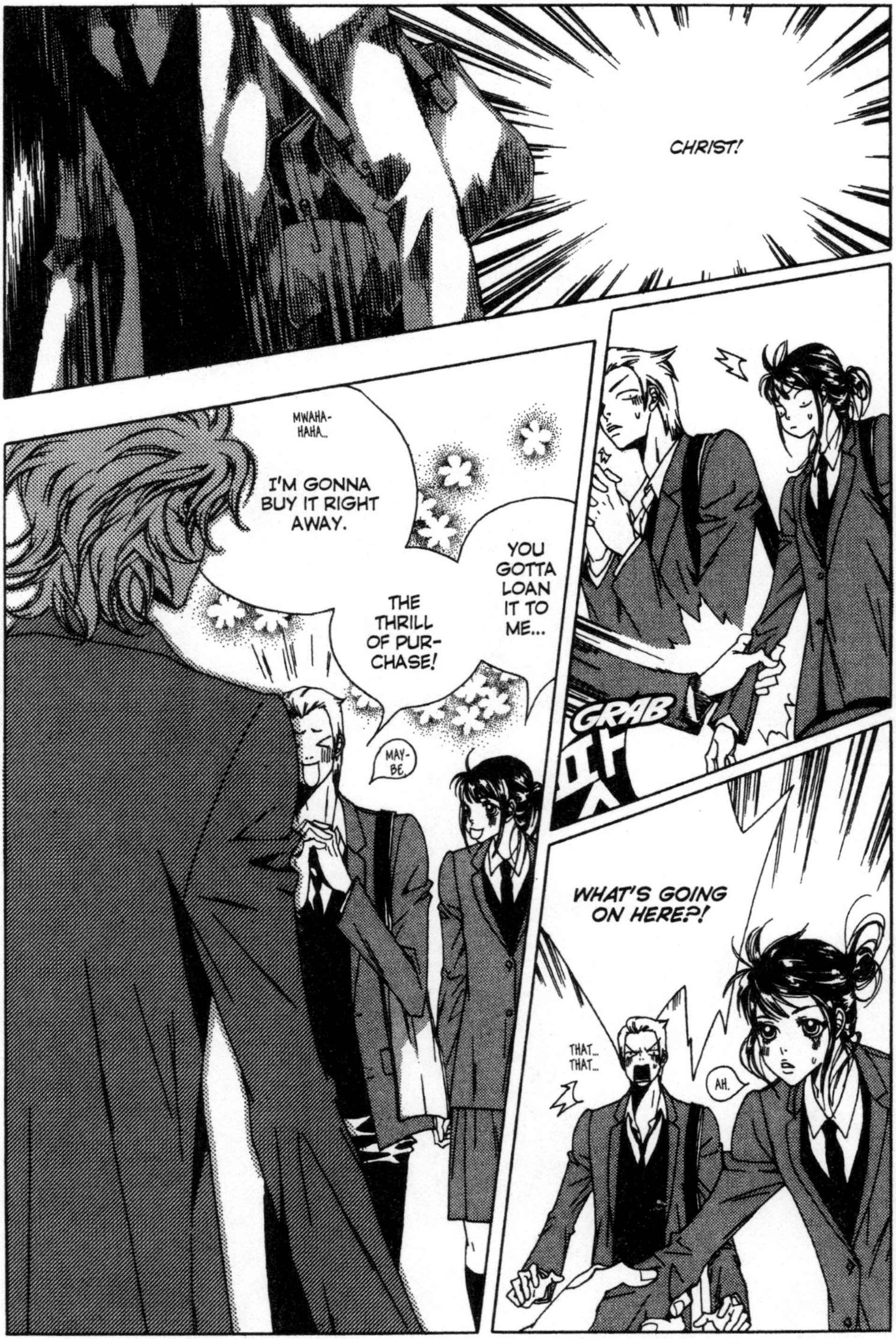
CHRIST!
MWAHA-HAHA...
I'M GONNA BUY IT RIGHT AWAY.
THE THRILL OF PUR-CHASE!
YOU GOTTA LOAN IT TO ME...
MAY-BE.
GRAB
WHAT'S GOING ON HERE?!
THAT... THAT...
AH.

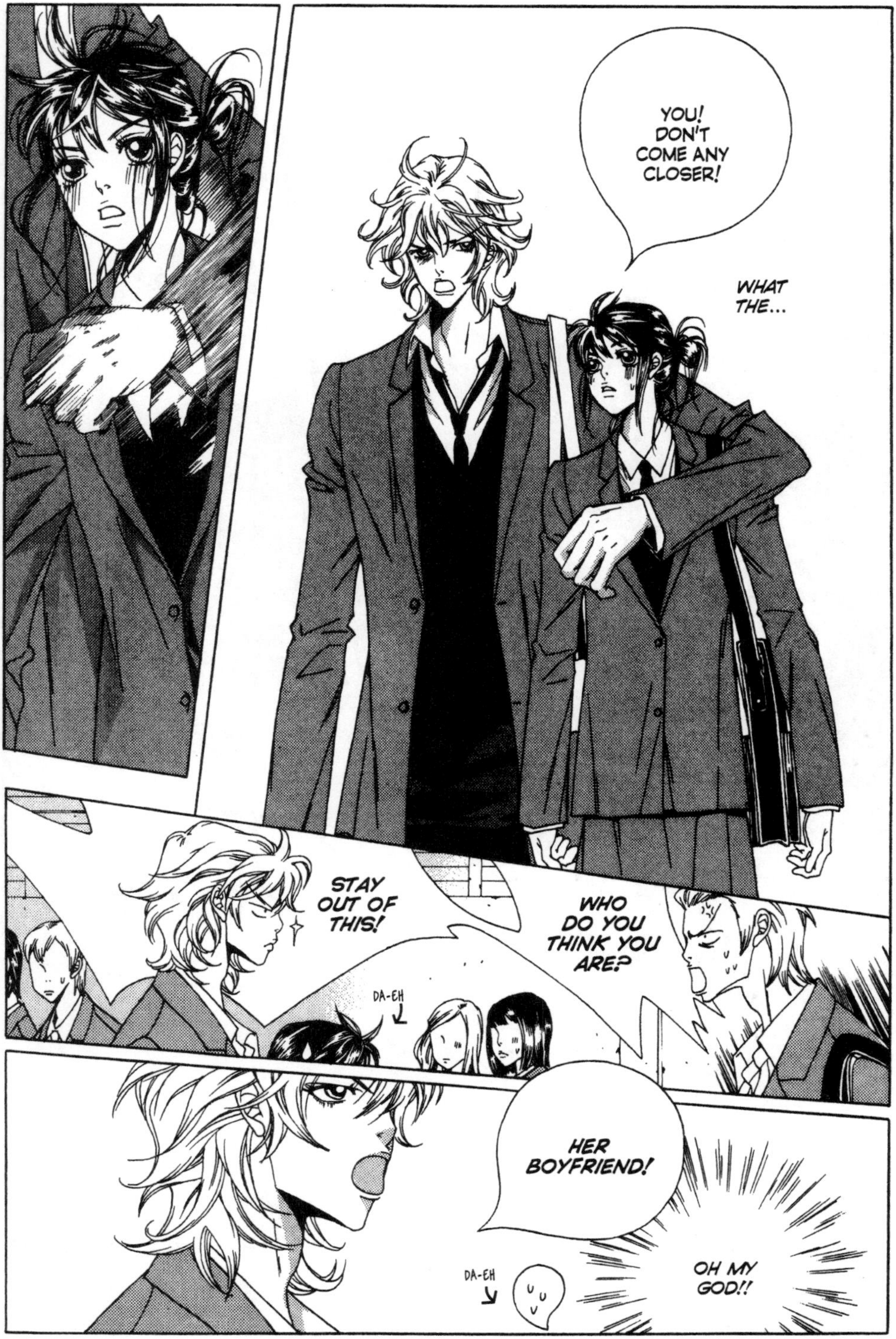
YOU! DON'T COME ANY CLOSER!
WHAT THE...
STAY OUT OF THIS!
WHO DO YOU THINK YOU ARE?
DA-EH
HER BOYFRIEND!
DA-EH
OH MY GOD!!

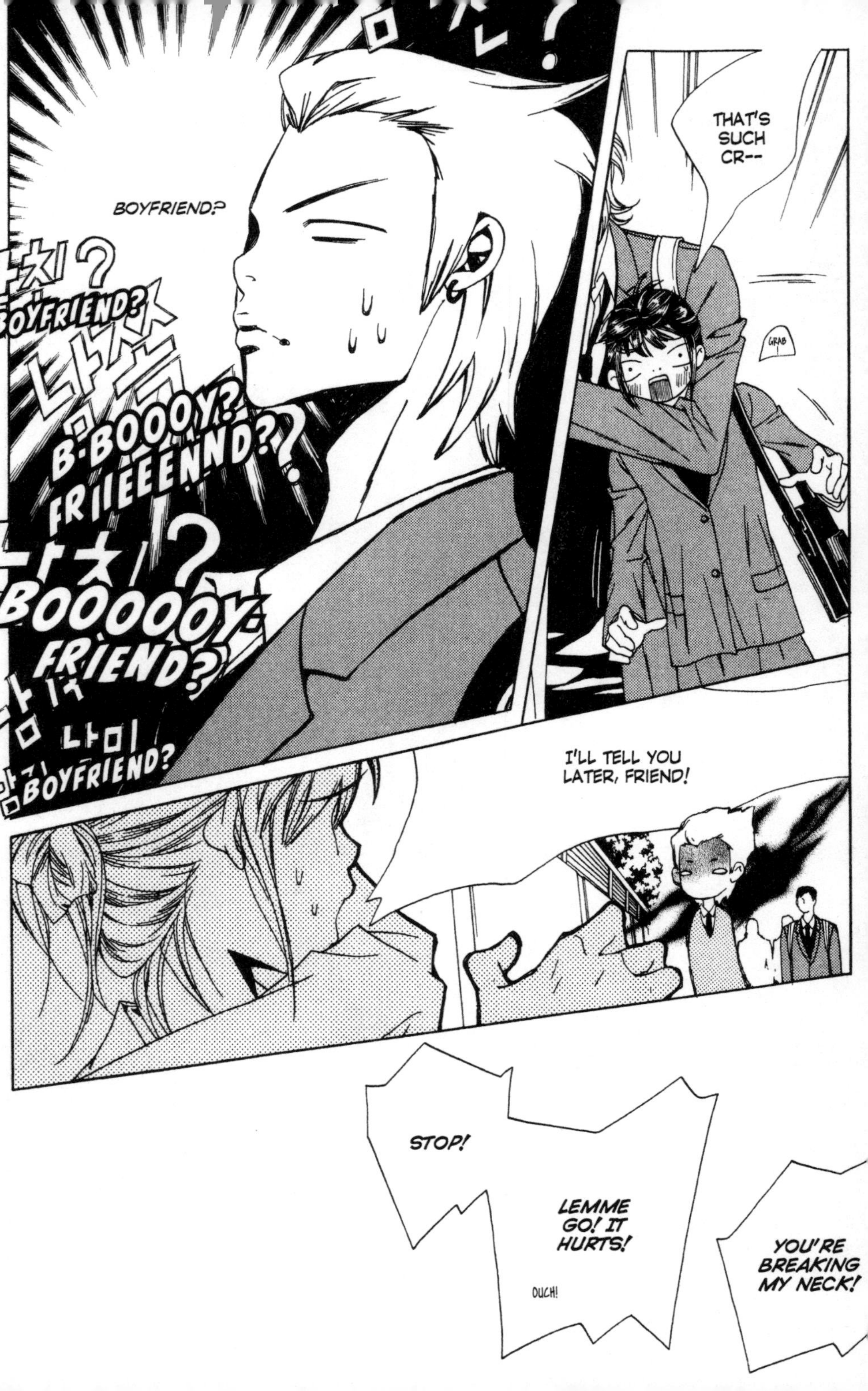
BOYFRIEND?
BOYFRIEND?
B-BOOOY? FRIIEEEENND??
BOOOOOY-FRIEND?
BOYFRIEND?
THAT'S SUCH CR--
GRAB!
I'LL TELL YOU LATER, FRIEND!
STOP!
LEMME GO! IT HURTS!
OUCH!
YOU'RE BREAKING MY NECK!

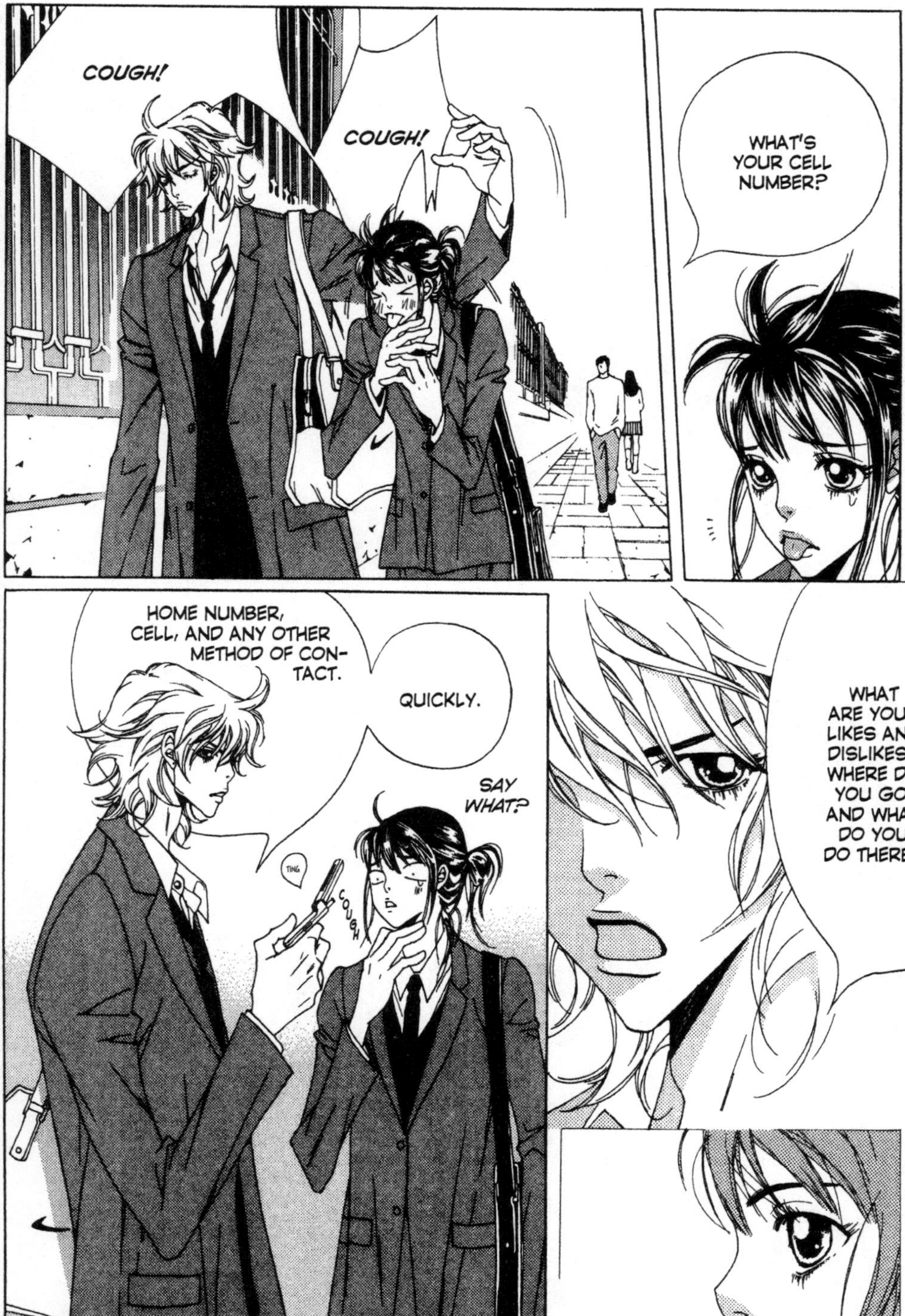
COUGH!
COUGH!
WHAT'S YOUR CELL NUMBER?
HOME NUMBER, CELL, AND ANY OTHER METHOD OF CONTACT.
QUICKLY.
SAY WHAT?
TING
COUGH
WHAT ARE YOUR LIKES AND DISLIKES? WHERE DO YOU GO, AND WHAT DO YOU DO THERE?

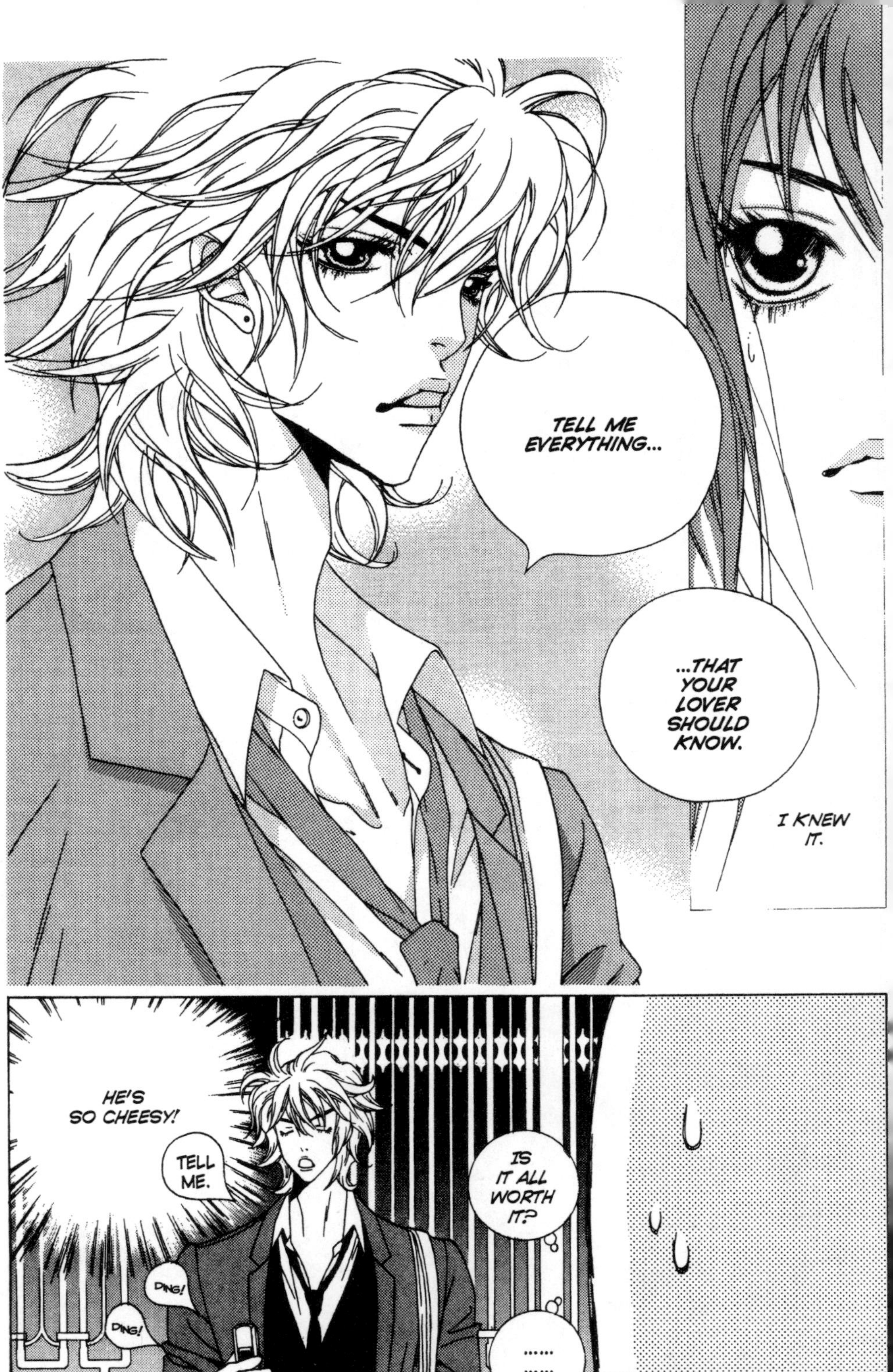
TELL ME EVERYTHING...
...THAT YOUR LOVER SHOULD KNOW.
I KNEW IT.
HE'S SO CHEESY!
TELL ME.
DING!
DING!
IS IT ALL WORTH IT?
......
......

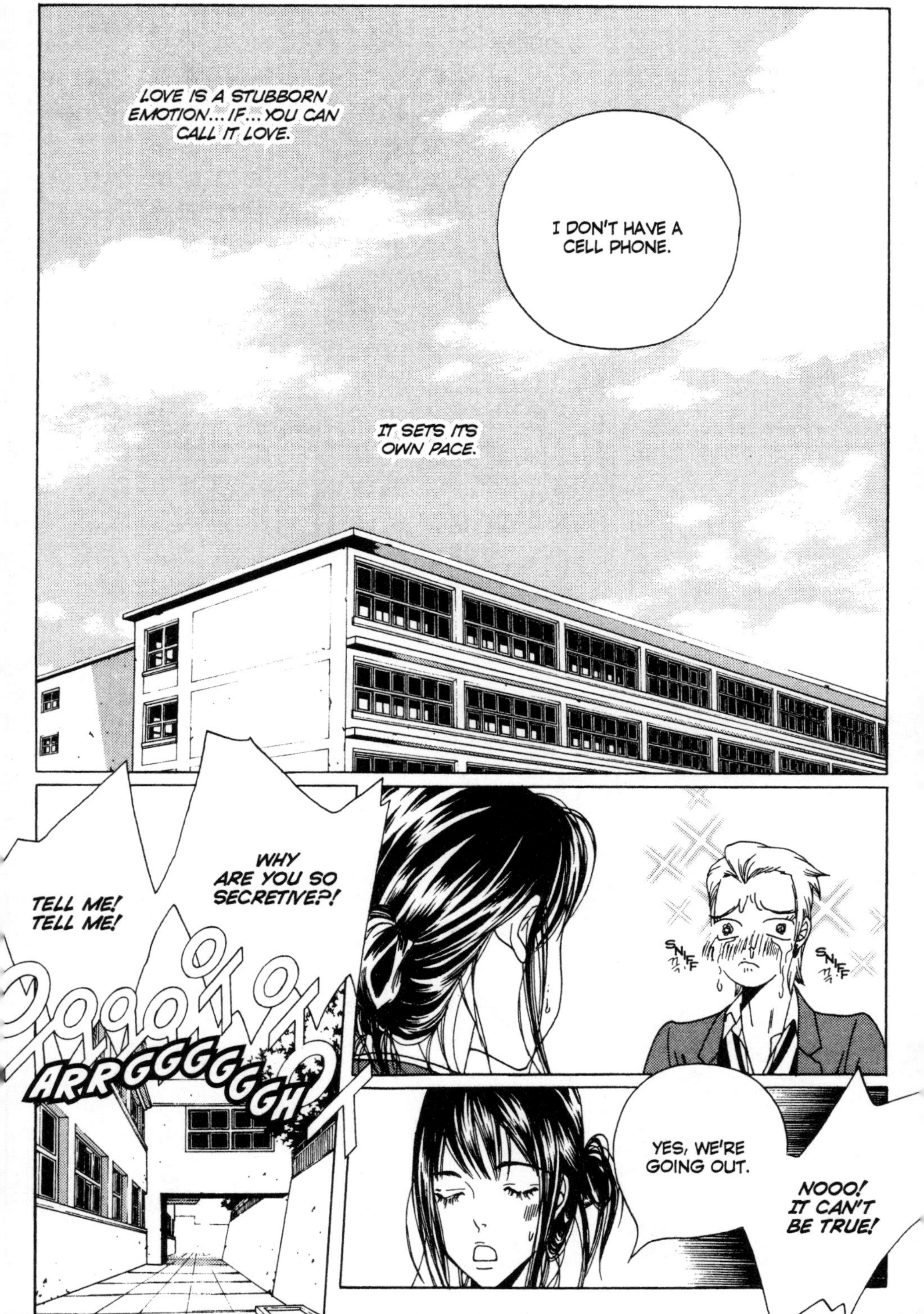
LOVE IS A STUBBORN EMOTION... IF... YOU CAN CALL IT LOVE.
I DON'T HAVE A CELL PHONE.
IT SETS ITS OWN PACE.
TELL ME! TELL ME!
WHY ARE YOU SO SECRETIVE?!
ARRGGGGGGGH
SNIFF
SNIFF
YES, WE'RE GOING OUT.
NOOO! IT CAN'T BE TRUE!

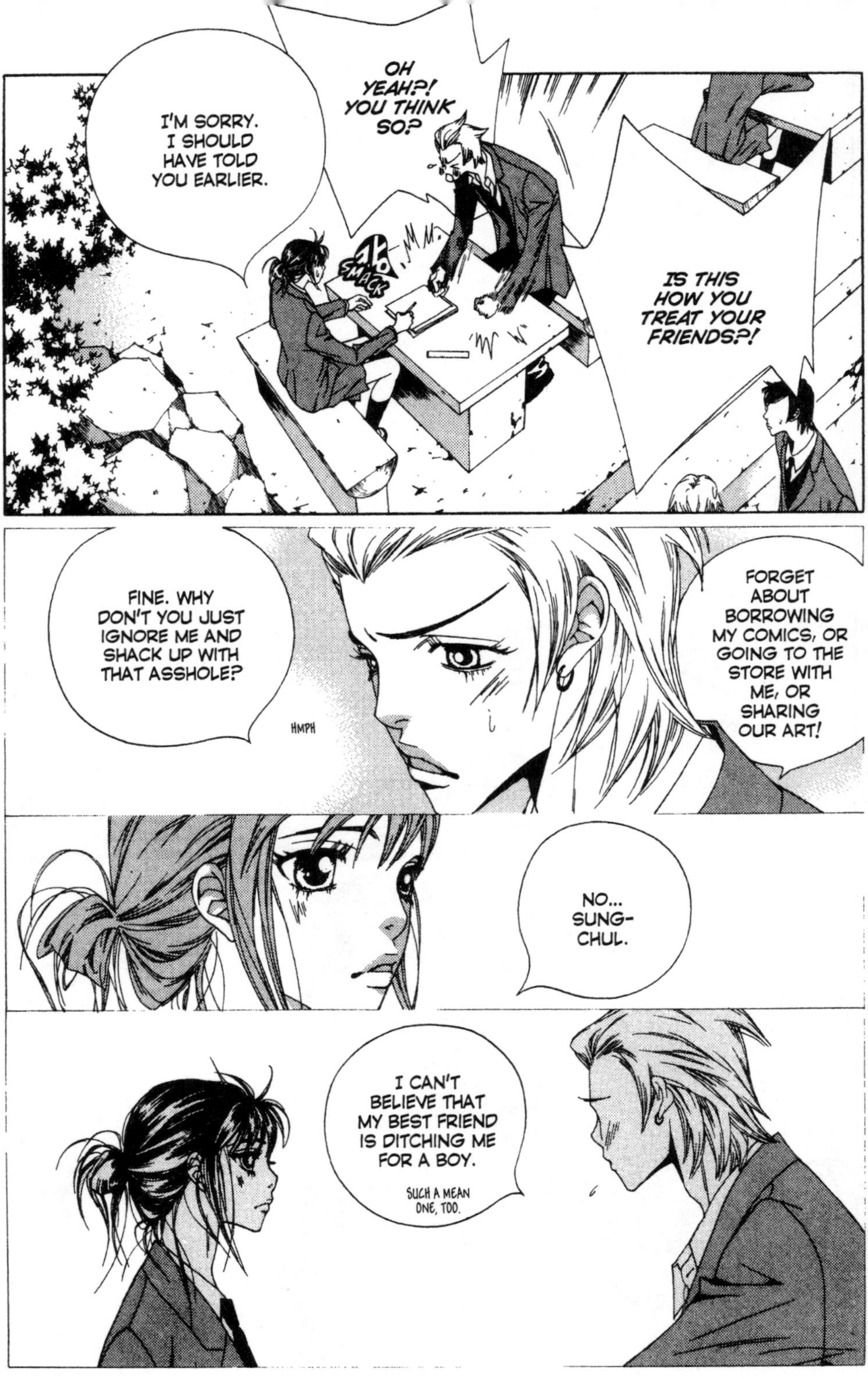
I'M SORRY. I SHOULD HAVE TOLD YOU EARLIER.
OH YEAH?! YOU THINK SO?
SMACK
IS THIS HOW YOU TREAT YOUR FRIENDS?!
FINE. WHY DON'T YOU JUST IGNORE ME AND SHACK UP WITH THAT ASSHOLE?
HMPH
FORGET ABOUT BORROWING MY COMICS, OR GOING TO THE STORE WITH ME, OR SHARING OUR ART!
NO... SUNG-CHUL.
I CAN'T BELIEVE THAT MY BEST FRIEND IS DITCHING ME FOR A BOY.
SUCH A MEAN ONE, TOO.

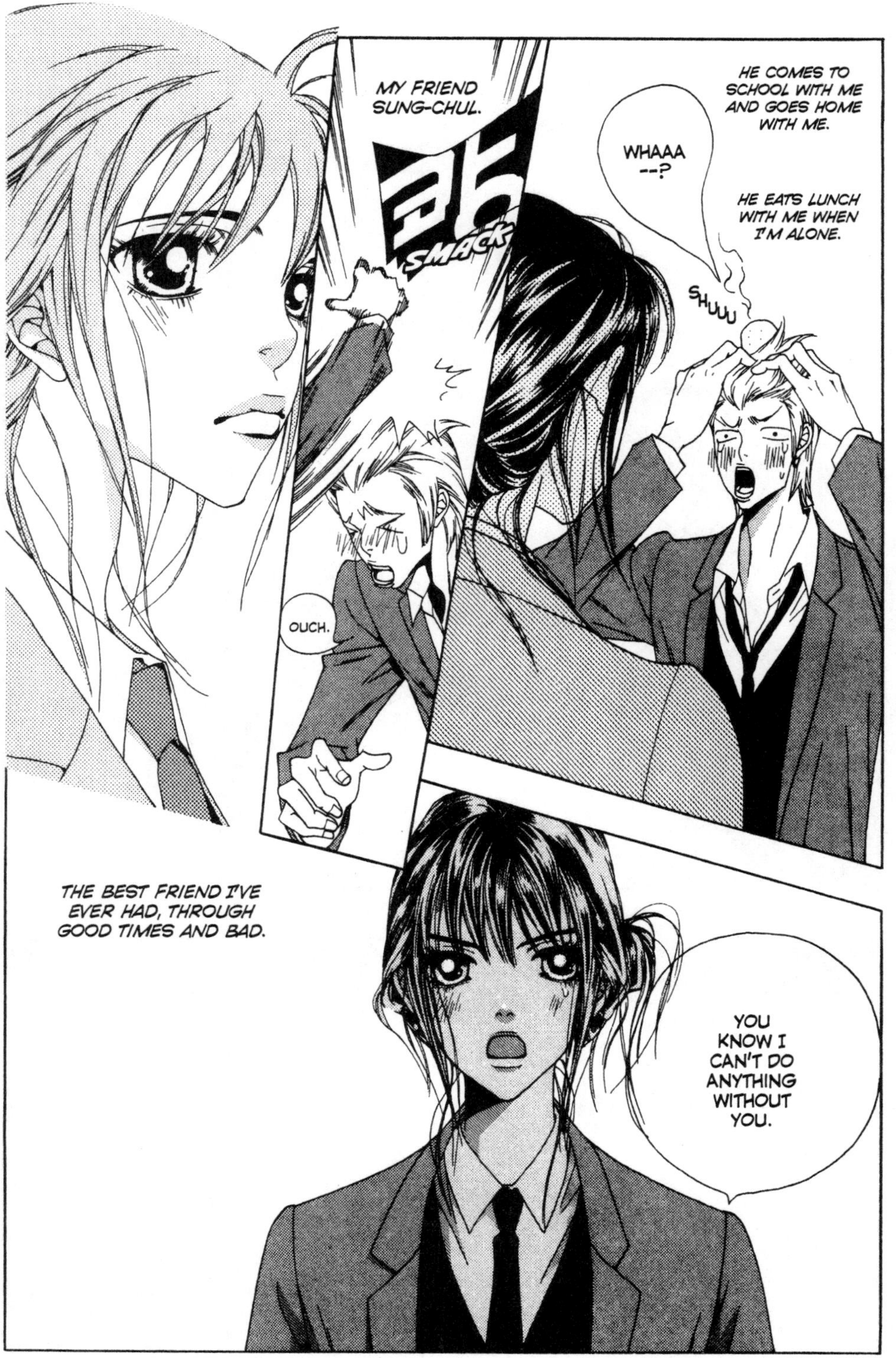
MY FRIEND SUNG-CHUL.
SMACK
OUCH.
HE COMES TO SCHOOL WITH ME AND GOES HOME WITH ME.
WHAAA --?
HE EATS LUNCH WITH ME WHEN I'M ALONE.
SHUUU
THE BEST FRIEND I'VE EVER HAD, THROUGH GOOD TIMES AND BAD.
YOU KNOW I CAN'T DO ANYTHING WITHOUT YOU.

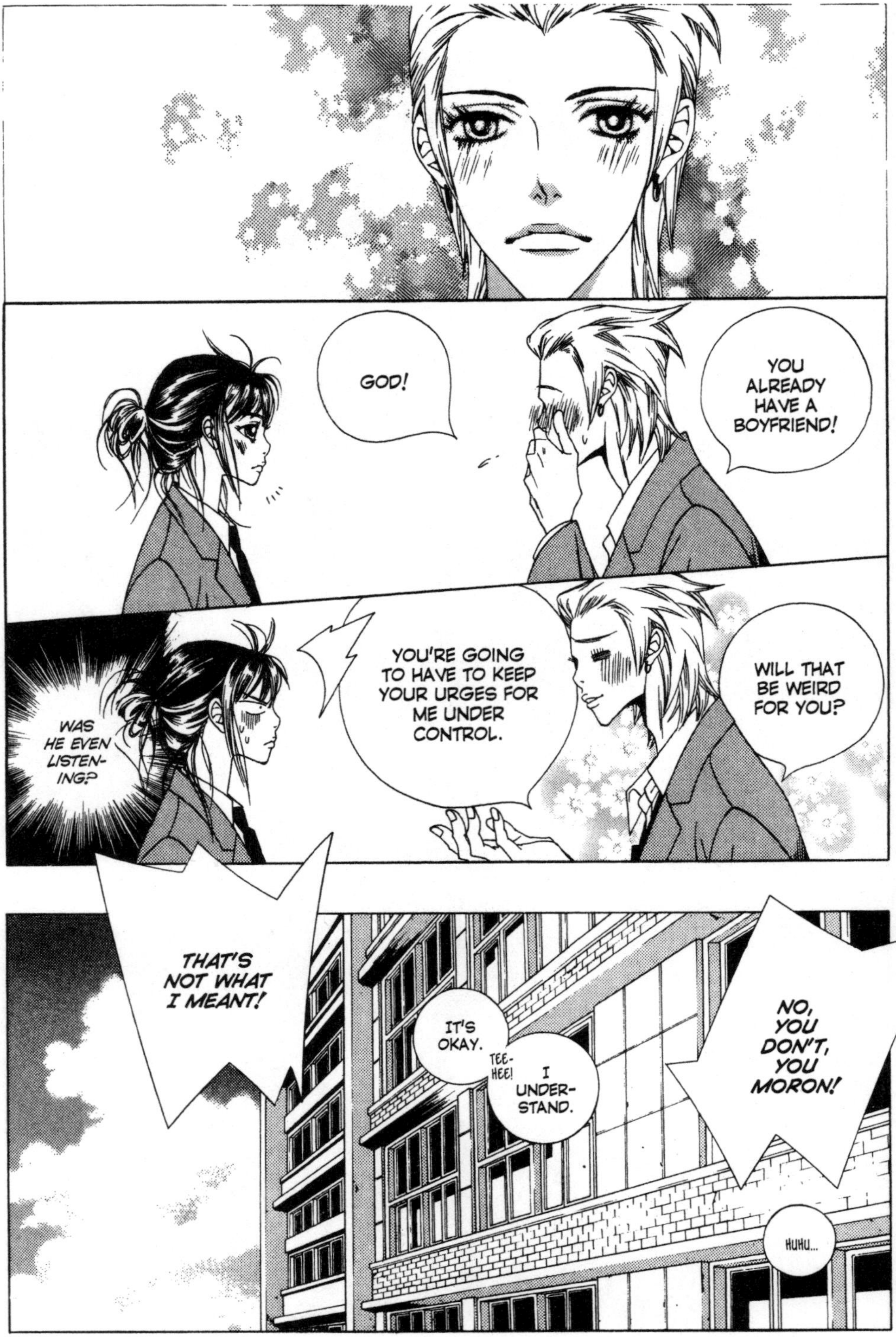
GOD!
YOU ALREADY HAVE A BOYFRIEND!
WAS HE EVEN LISTENING?
YOU'RE GOING TO HAVE TO KEEP YOUR URGES FOR ME UNDER CONTROL.
WILL THAT BE WEIRD FOR YOU?
THAT'S NOT WHAT I MEANT!
IT'S OKAY.
TEE-HEE!
I UNDERSTAND.
NO, YOU DON'T, YOU MORON!
HUHU...

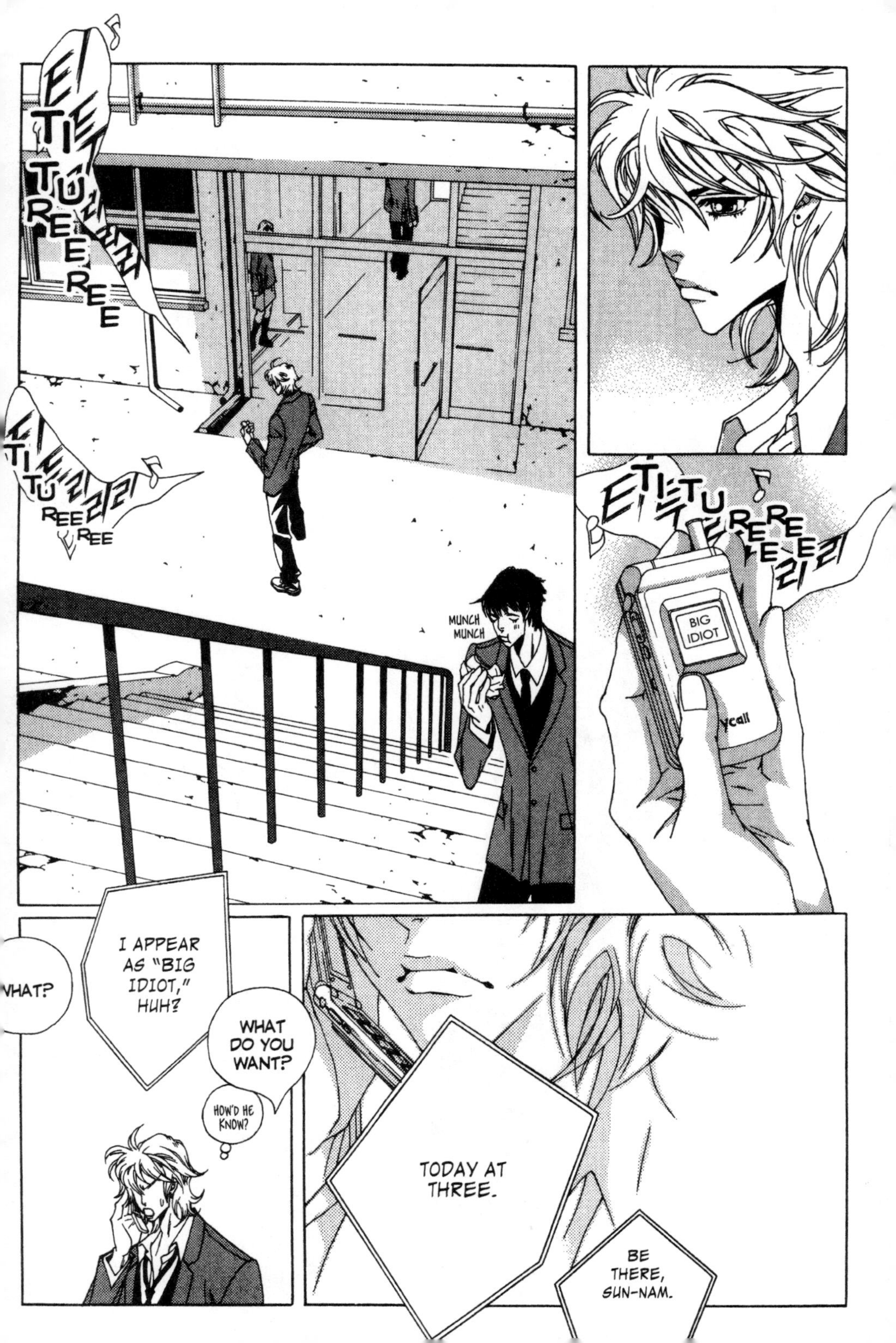

ETITIETTU TÚ REE REE REE
리리리
TITI TÚ REE REE
리리리
MUNCH MUNCH
ETI TI TU RE RE REE
리리
BIG IDIOT
ycall
WHAT?
I APPEAR AS "BIG IDIOT," HUH?
WHAT DO YOU WANT?
HOW'D HE KNOW?
TODAY AT THREE.
BE THERE, SUN-NAM.

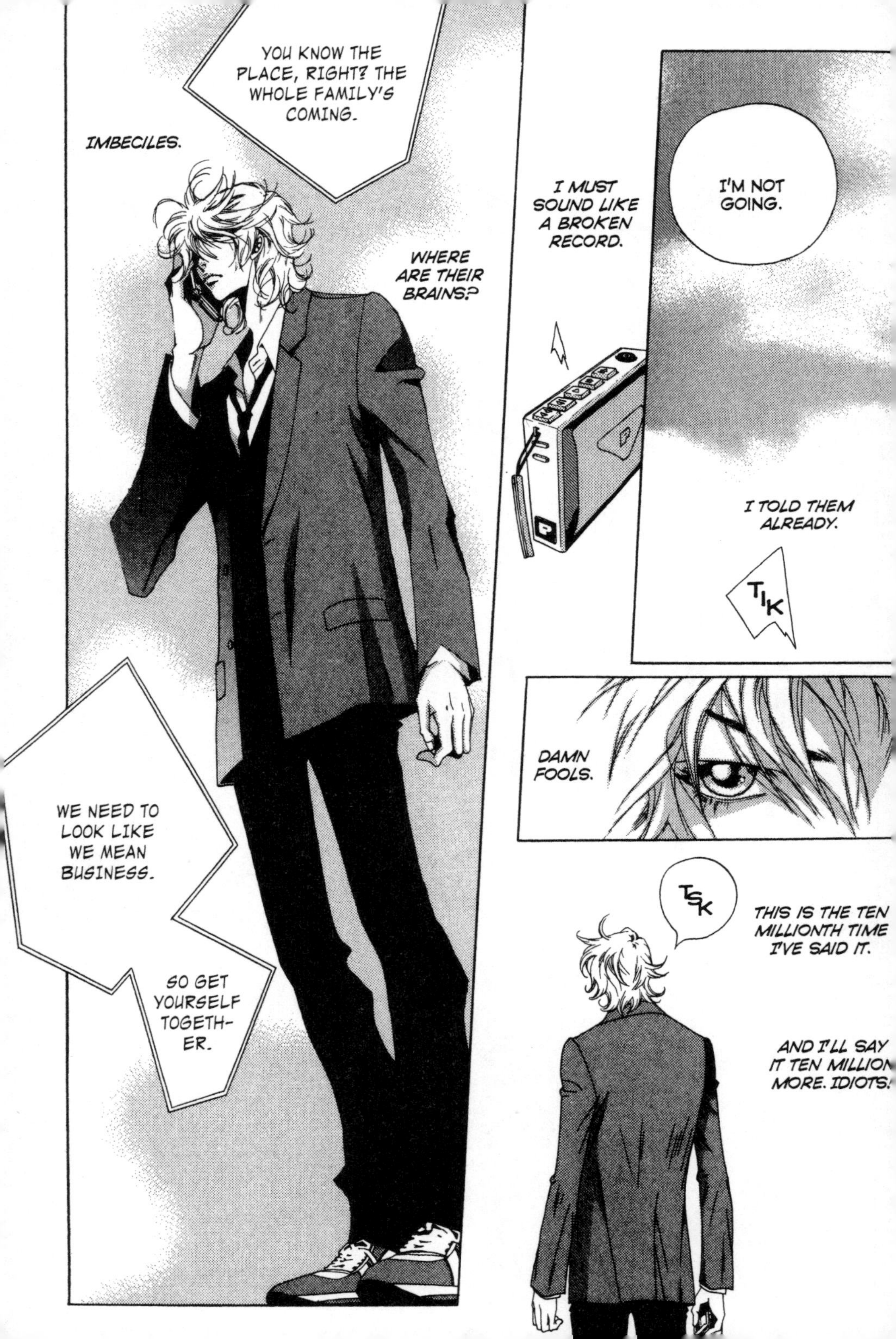
YOU KNOW THE PLACE, RIGHT? THE WHOLE FAMILY'S COMING.
IMBECILES.
WHERE ARE THEIR BRAINS?
WE NEED TO LOOK LIKE WE MEAN BUSINESS.
SO GET YOURSELF TOGETH-ER.
I MUST SOUND LIKE A BROKEN RECORD.
I'M NOT GOING.
I TOLD THEM ALREADY.
TIK
DAMN FOOLS.
TSK
THIS IS THE TEN MILLIONTH TIME I'VE SAID IT.
AND I'LL SAY IT TEN MILLION MORE. IDIOTS.

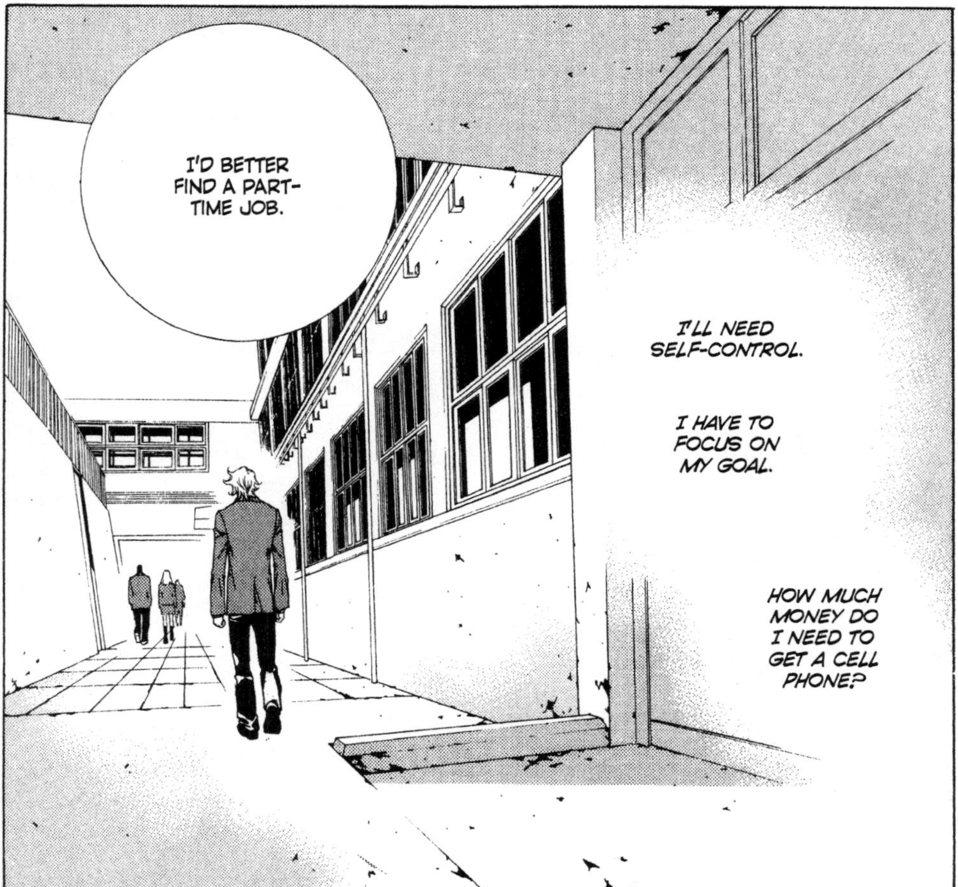
I'D BETTER FIND A PART-TIME JOB.
I'LL NEED SELF-CONTROL.
I HAVE TO FOCUS ON MY GOAL.
HOW MUCH MONEY DO I NEED TO GET A CELL PHONE?

TIME FLIES.

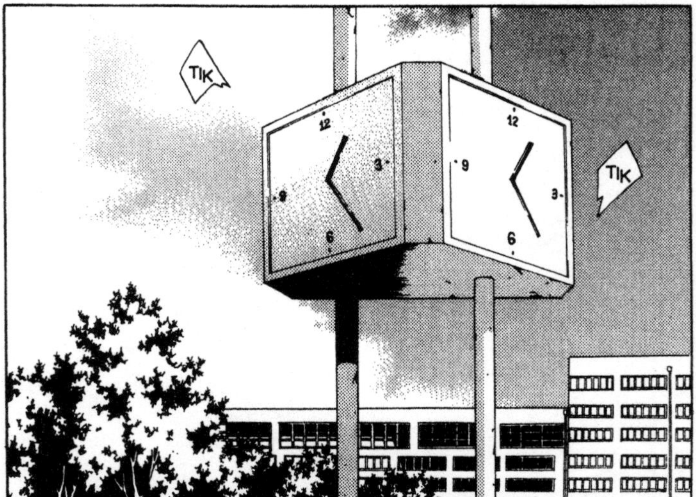
TIK
TIK

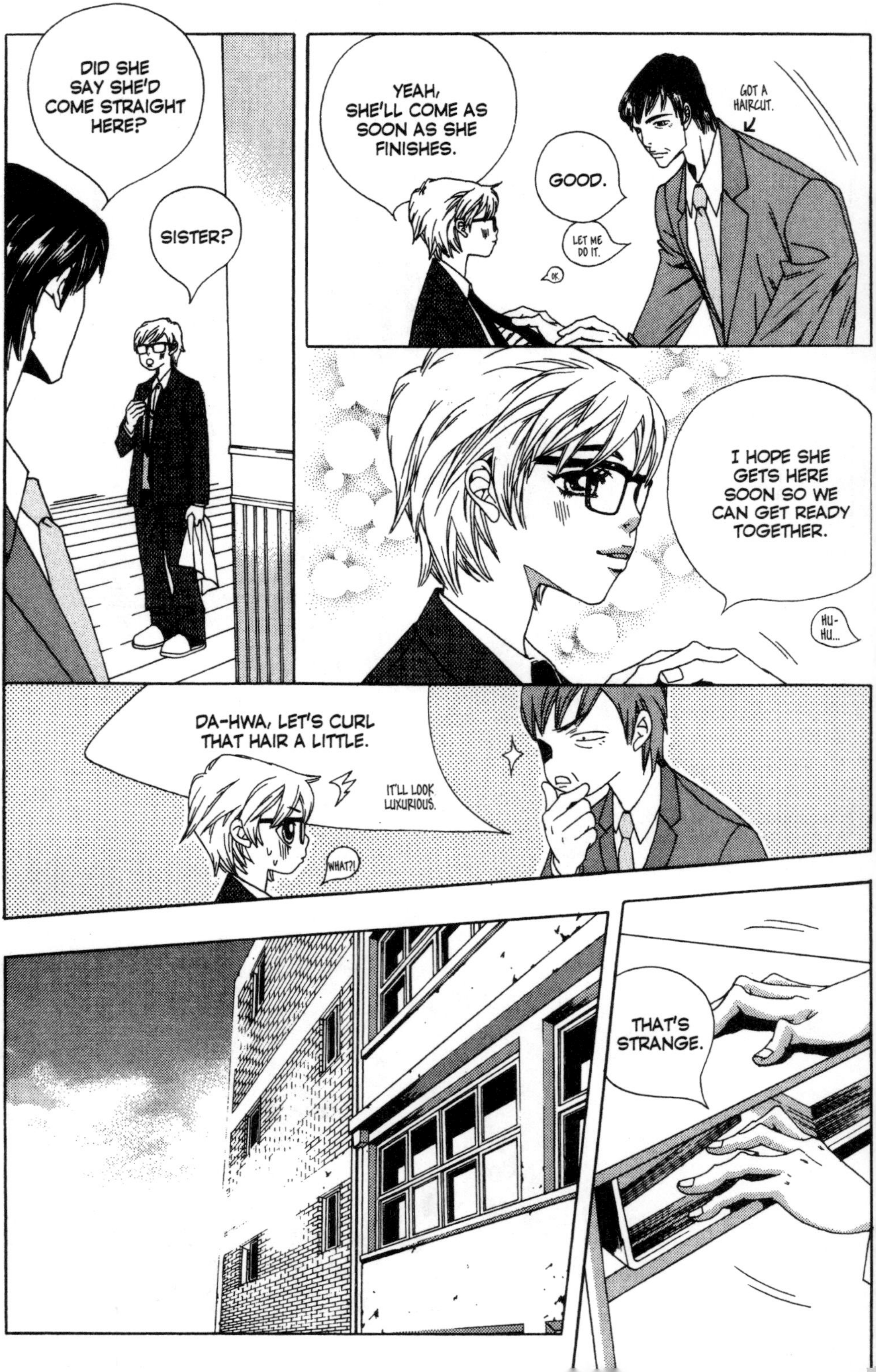
DID SHE SAY SHE'D COME STRAIGHT HERE?
SISTER?
YEAH, SHE'LL COME AS SOON AS SHE FINISHES.
GOOD.
GOT A HAIRCUT.
LET ME DO IT.
OK.
I HOPE SHE GETS HERE SOON SO WE CAN GET READY TOGETHER.
HU-HU...
DA-HWA, LET'S CURL THAT HAIR A LITTLE.
IT'LL LOOK LUXURIOUS.
WHAT?!
THAT'S STRANGE.

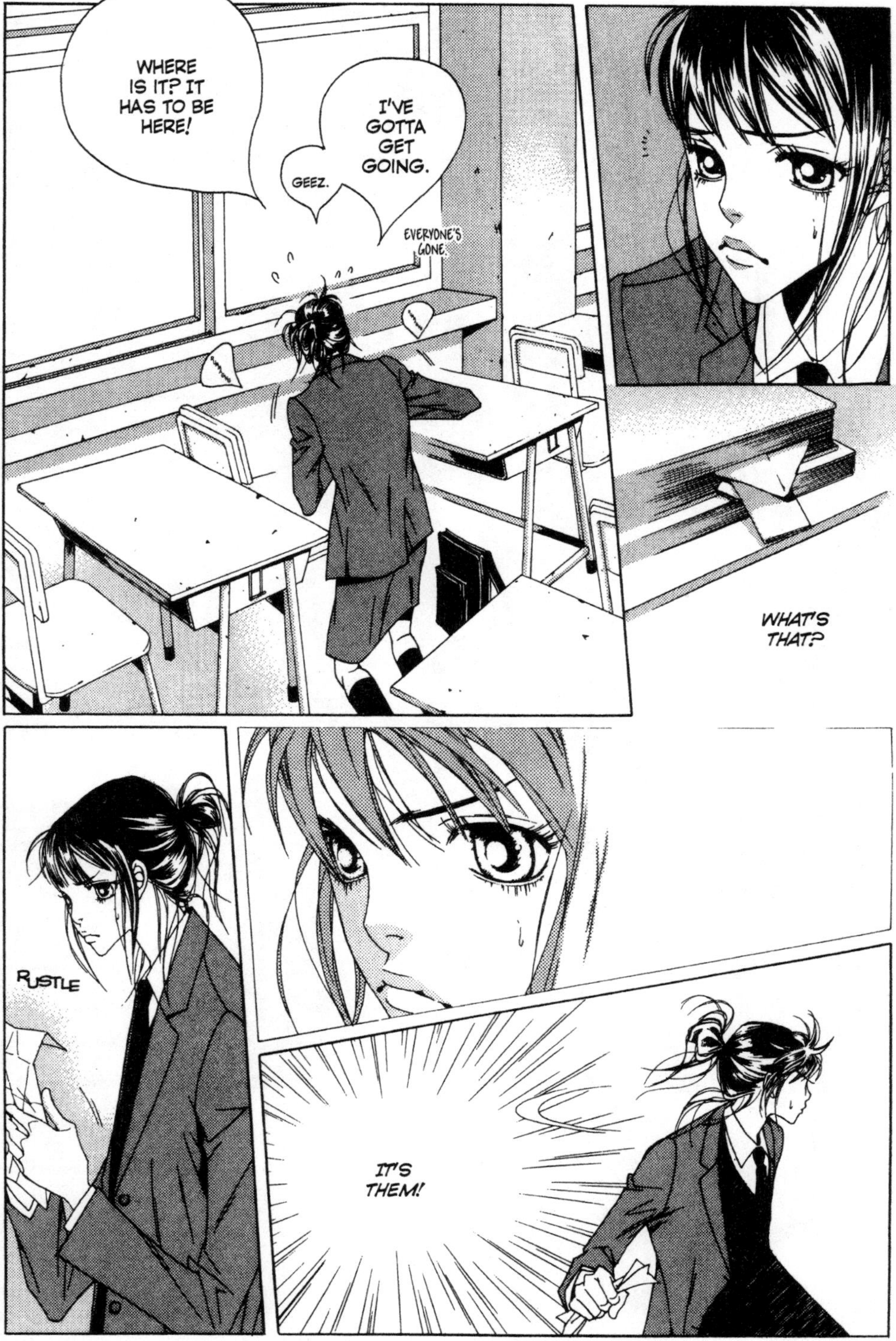
WHERE IS IT? IT HAS TO BE HERE!
I'VE GOTTA GET GOING.
GEEZ.
EVERYONE'S GONE.
WHAT'S THAT?
RUSTLE
IT'S THEM!

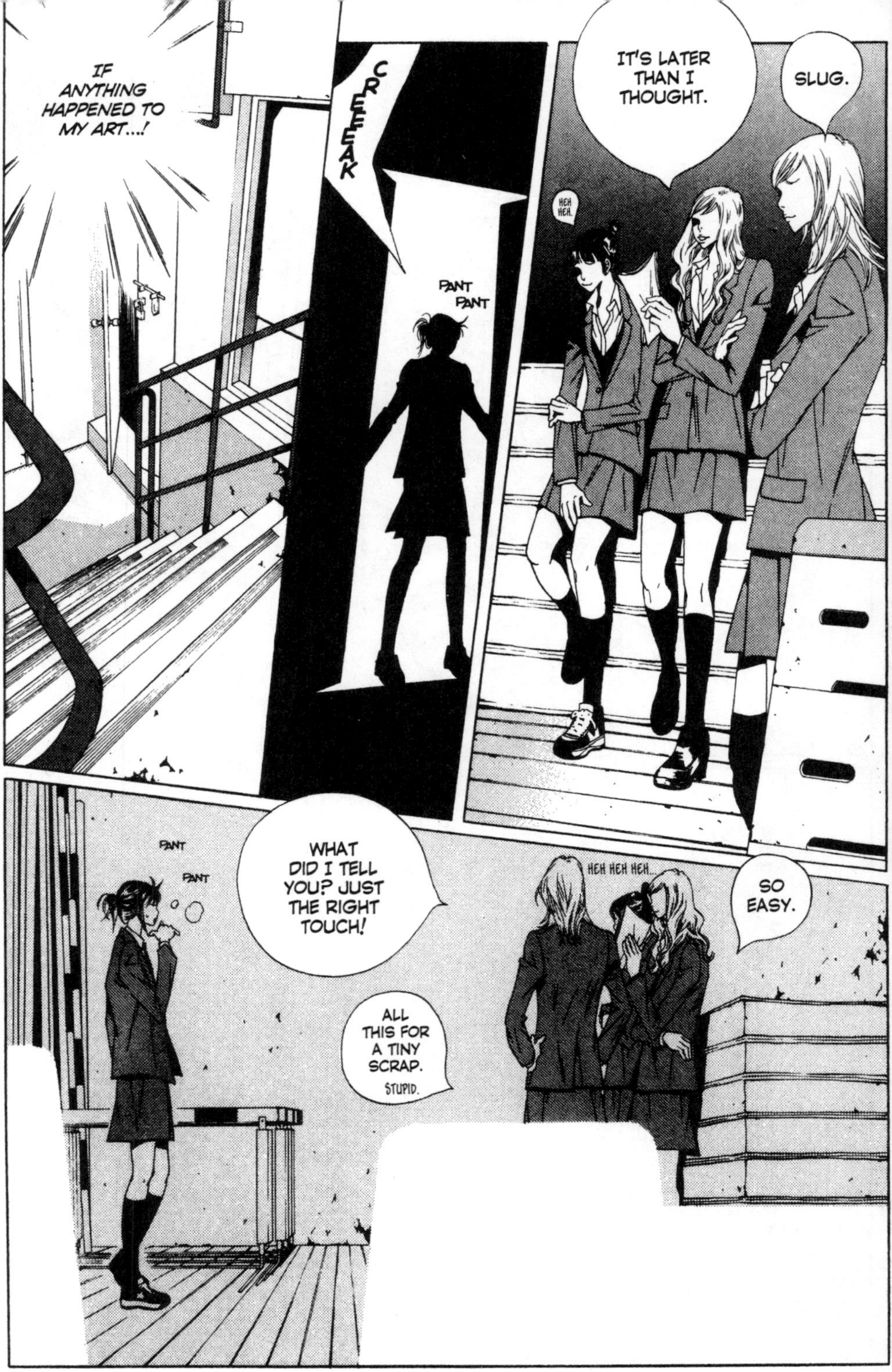
IF ANYTHING HAPPENED TO MY ART...!
CREEEAK
PANT PANT
IT'S LATER THAN I THOUGHT.
SLUG.
HEH HEH.
PANT PANT
WHAT DID I TELL YOU? JUST THE RIGHT TOUCH!
ALL THIS FOR A TINY SCRAP.
STUPID.
HEH HEH HEH...
SO EASY.

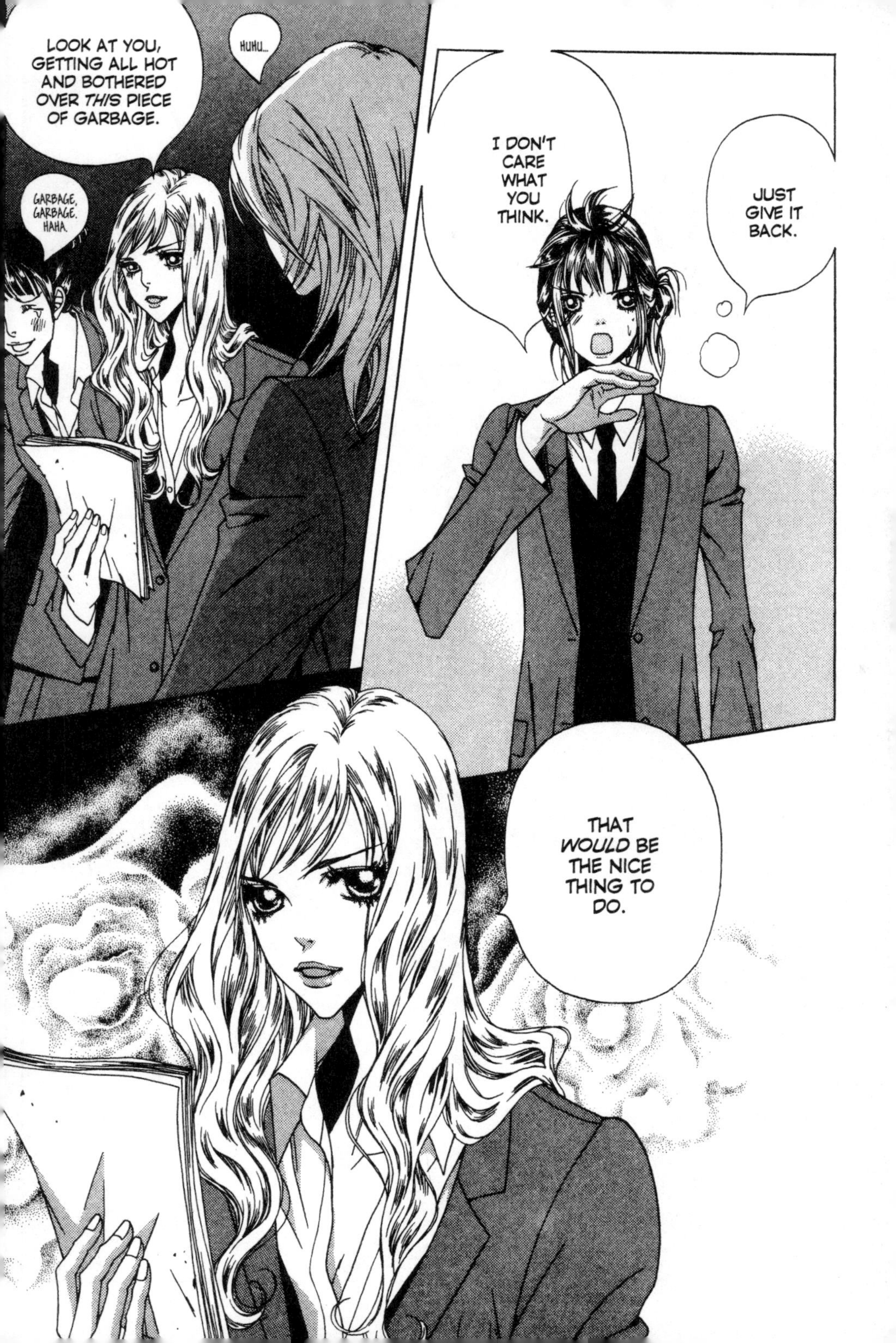
LOOK AT YOU, GETTING ALL HOT AND BOTHERED OVER *THIS* PIECE OF GARBAGE.
HUHU...
GARBAGE, GARBAGE. HAHA.
I DON'T CARE WHAT YOU THINK.
JUST GIVE IT BACK.
THAT *WOULD* BE THE NICE THING TO DO.

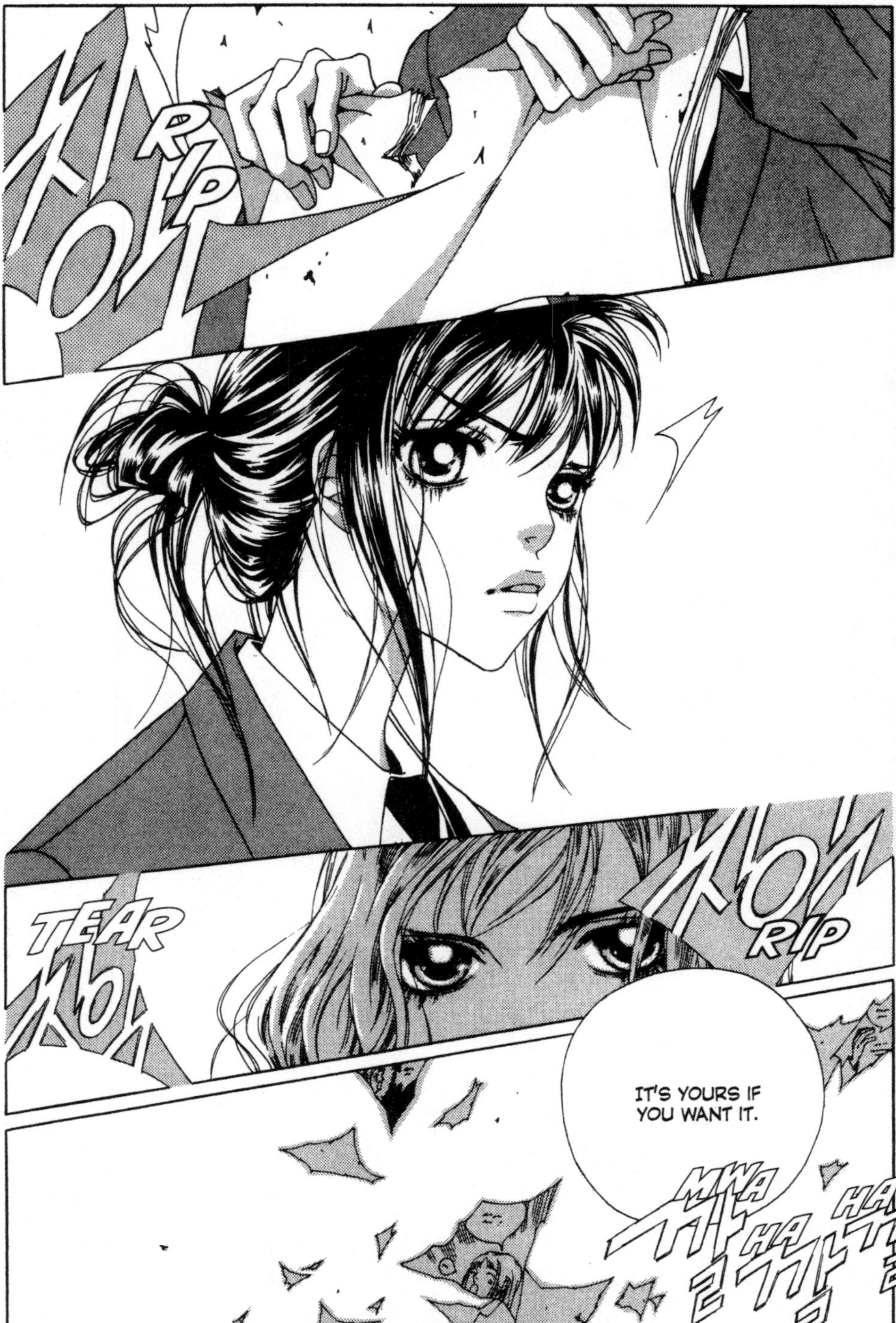
RIP
TEAR
RIP
IT'S YOURS IF YOU WANT IT.
MWA HA HA

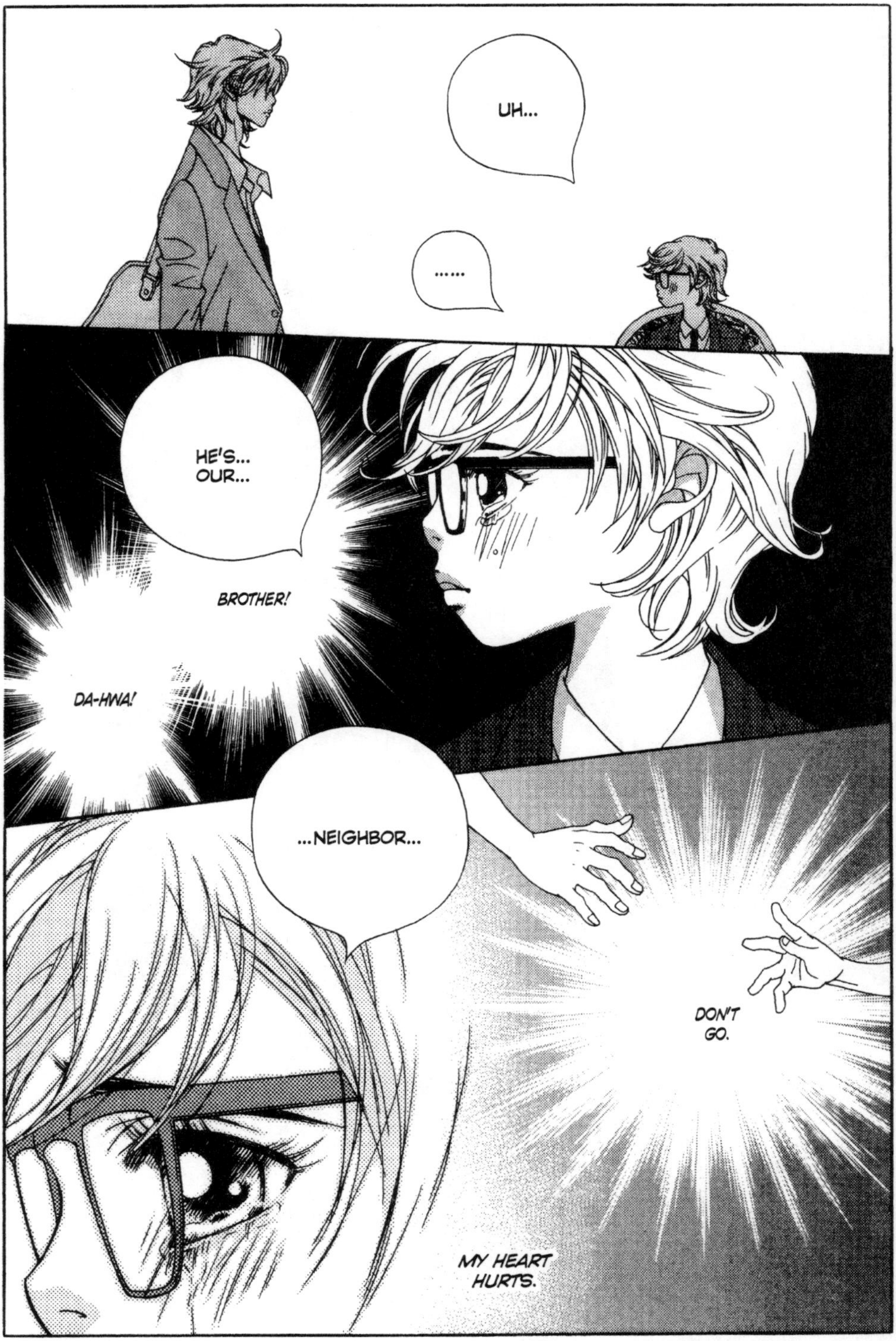
UH...
......
HE'S...
OUR...
BROTHER!
DA-HWA!
...NEIGHBOR...
DON'T
GO.
MY HEART
HURTS.

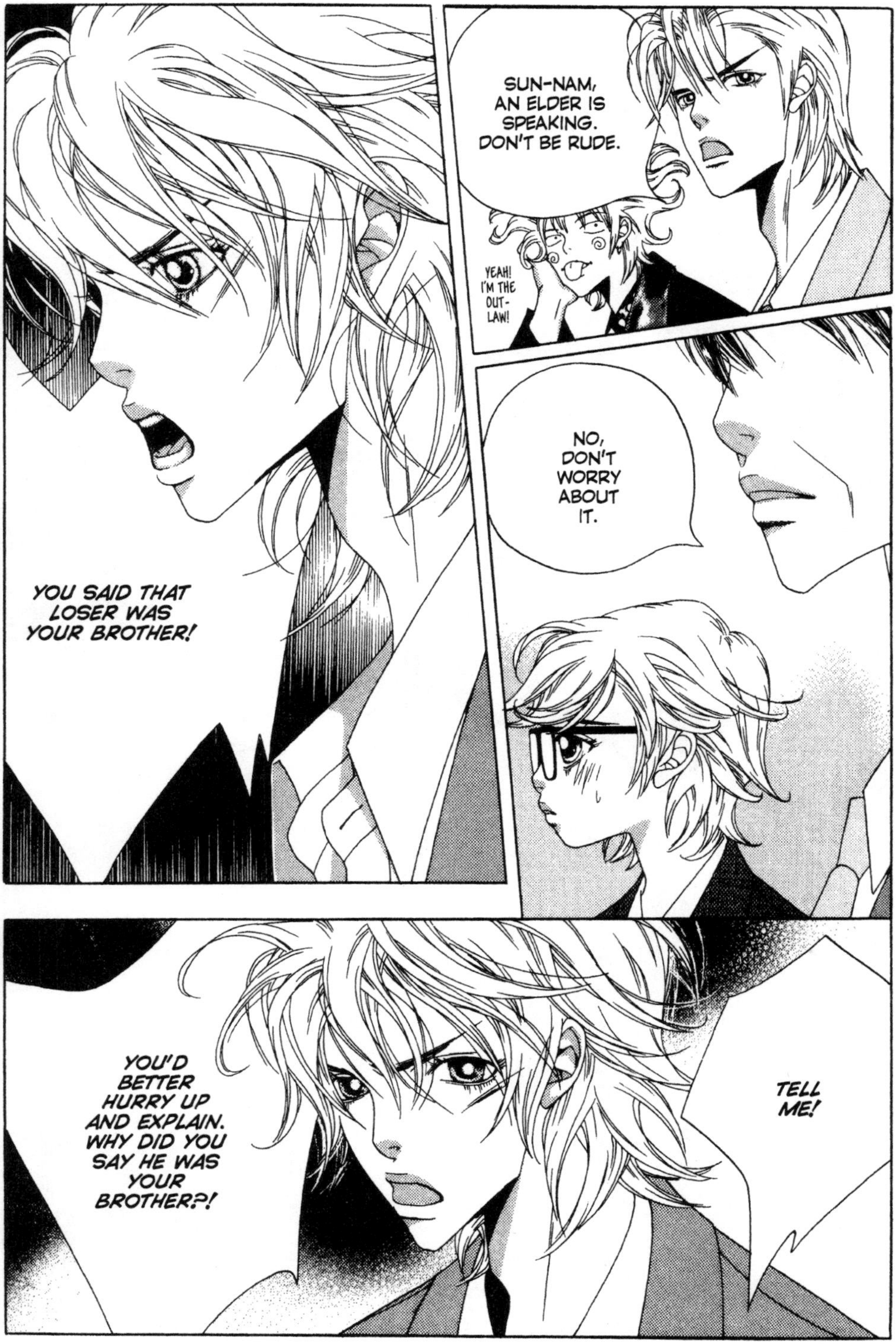
YOU SAID THAT LOSER WAS YOUR BROTHER!
SUN-NAM, AN ELDER IS SPEAKING. DON'T BE RUDE.
YEAH! I'M THE OUT-LAW!
NO, DON'T WORRY ABOUT IT.
YOU'D BETTER HURRY UP AND EXPLAIN. WHY DID YOU SAY HE WAS YOUR BROTHER?!
TELL ME!

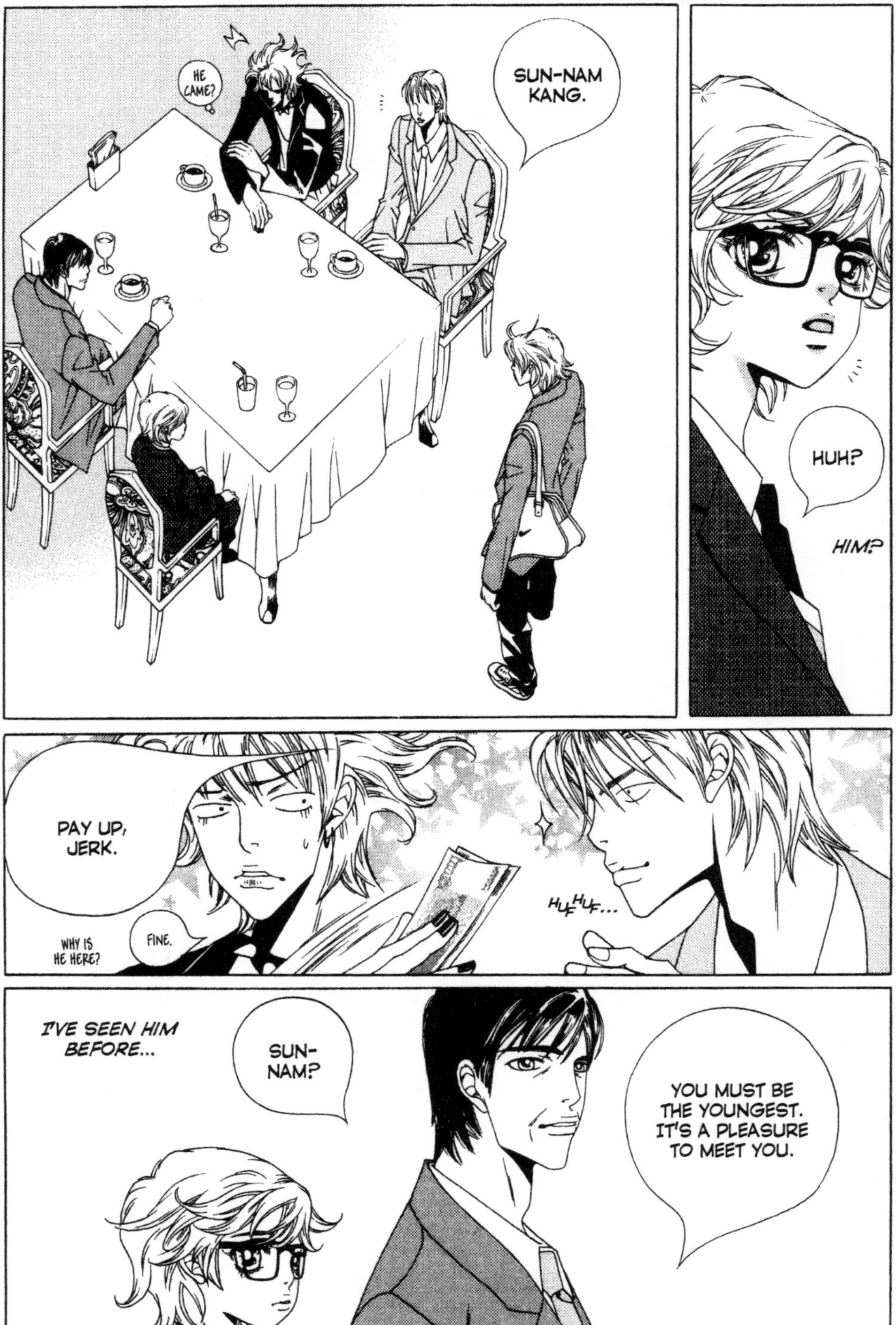
HE CAME?
SUN-NAM KANG.
HUH?
HIM?
PAY UP, JERK.
WHY IS HE HERE?
FINE.
HUFHUF...
I'VE SEEN HIM BEFORE...
SUN-NAM?
YOU MUST BE THE YOUNGEST. IT'S A PLEASURE TO MEET YOU.

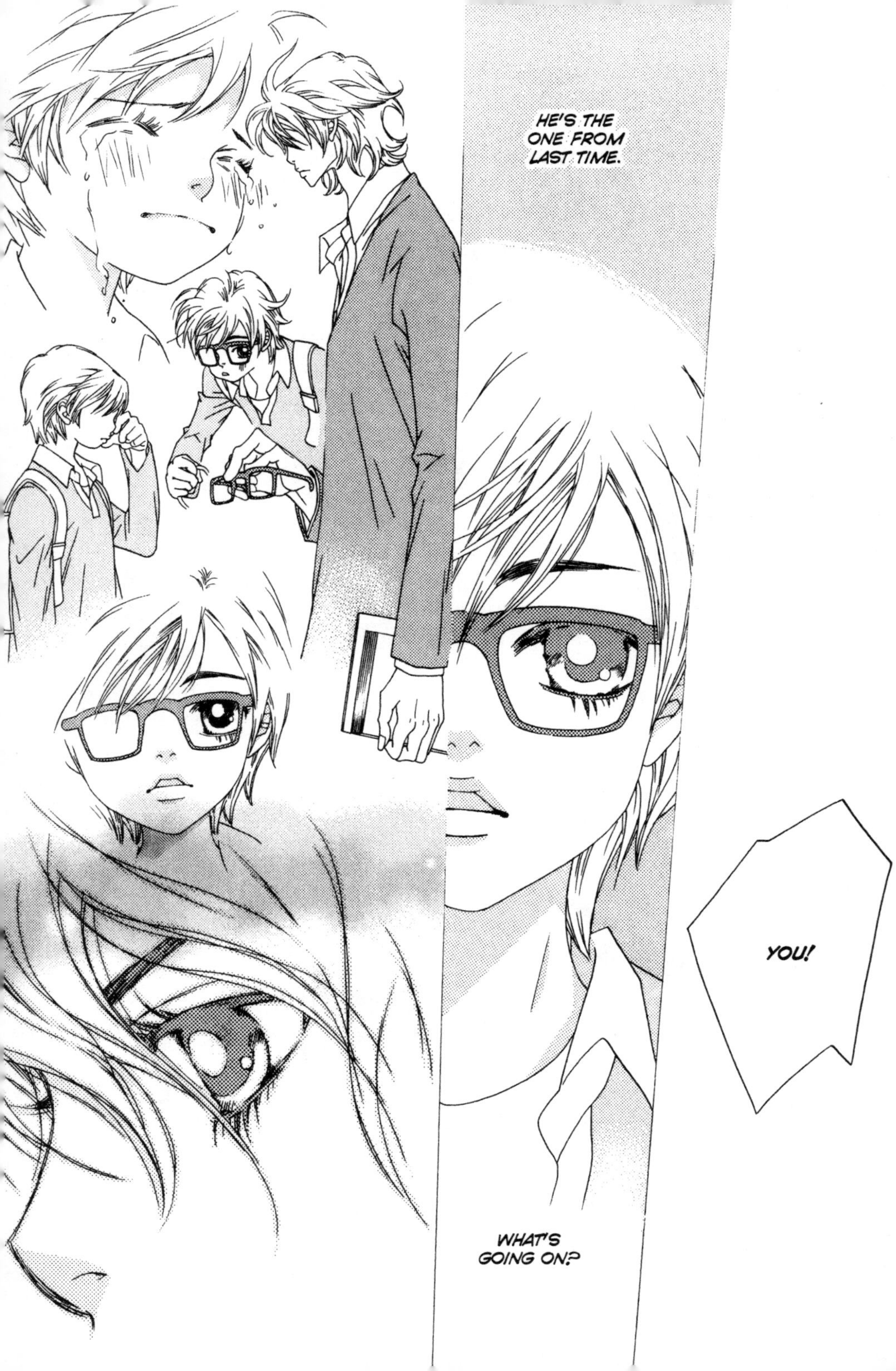
HE'S THE ONE FROM LAST TIME.
WHAT'S GOING ON?
YOU!

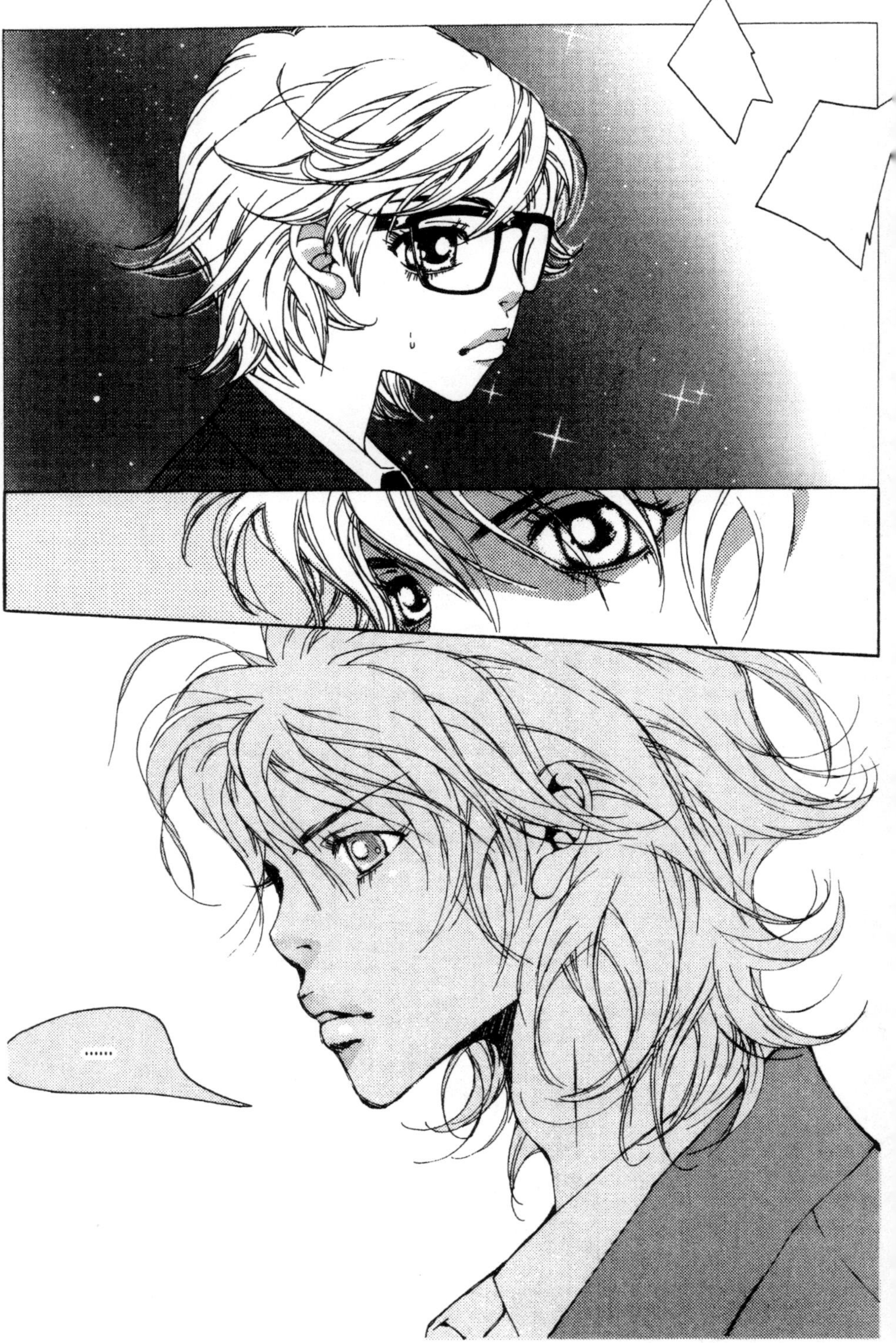
……

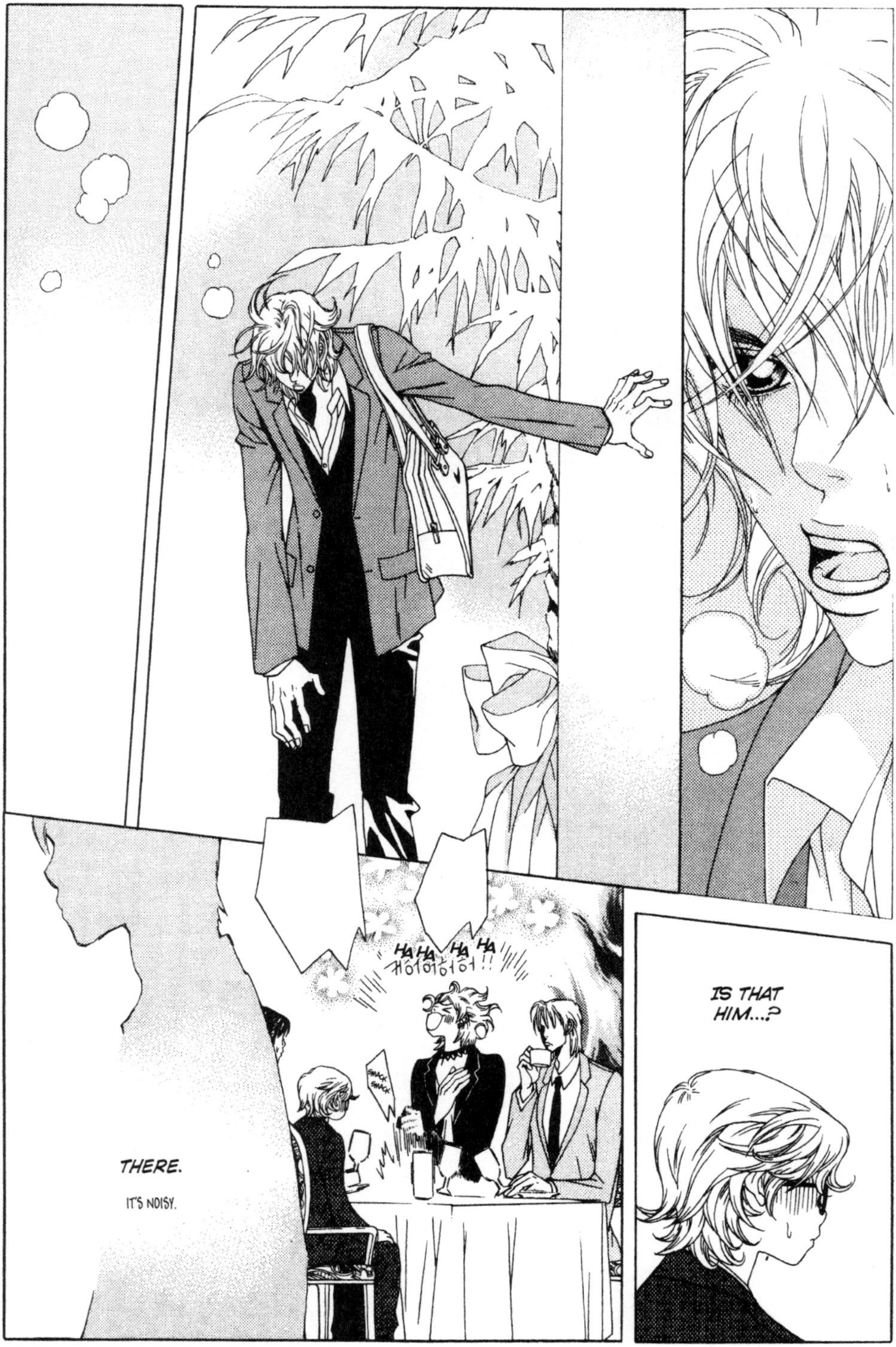
THERE.
IT'S NOISY.
HA HA HA HA
하하하하!!
SMACK SMACK
IS THAT HIM...?

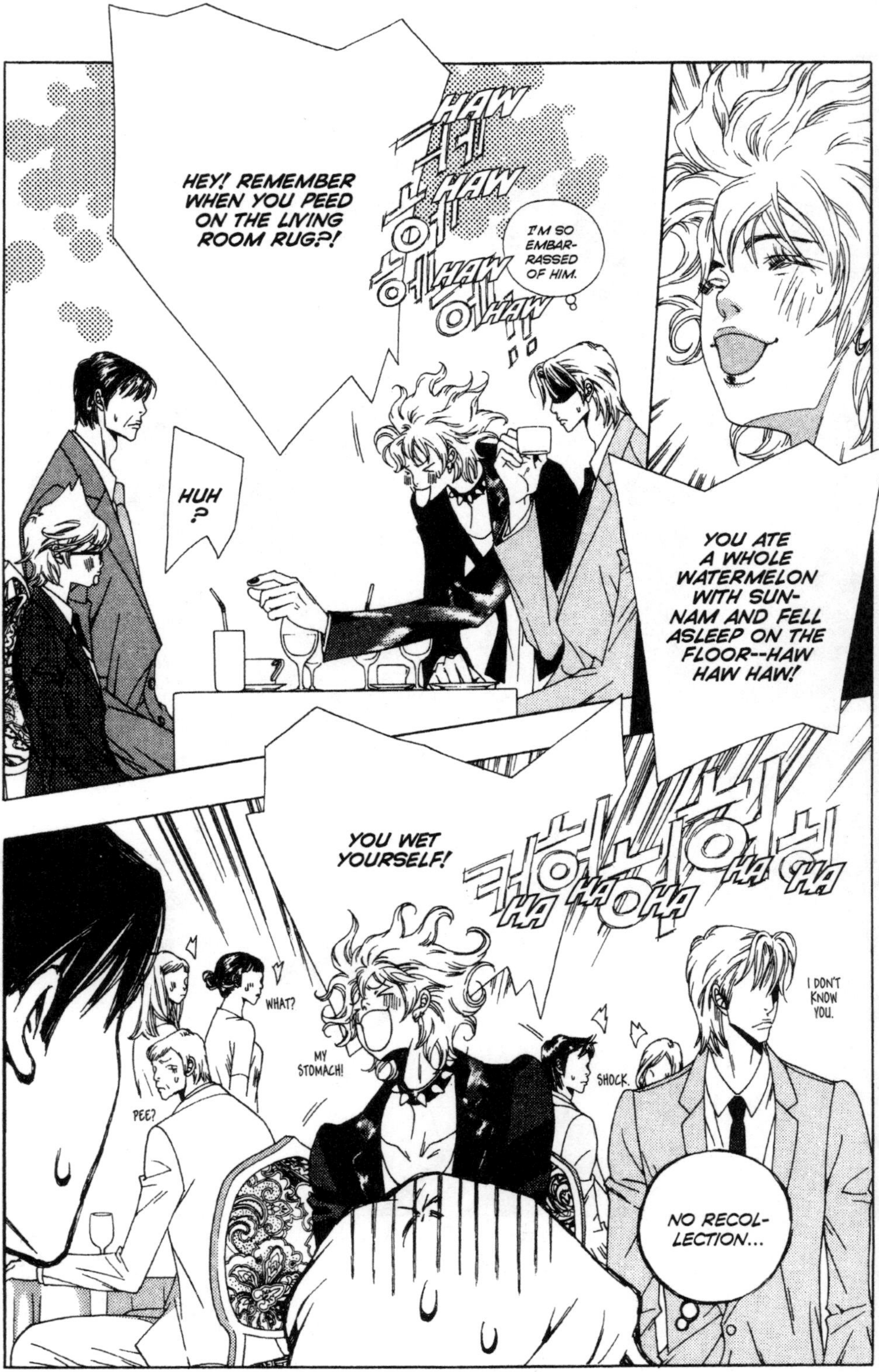
HEY! REMEMBER WHEN YOU PEED ON THE LIVING ROOM RUG?!
HAW HAW HAW HAW
I'M SO EMBARRASSED OF HIM.
HUH?
YOU ATE A WHOLE WATERMELON WITH SUN-NAM AND FELL ASLEEP ON THE FLOOR--HAW HAW HAW!
YOU WET YOURSELF!
HA HA HA HA HA
WHAT?
MY STOMACH!
PEE?
SHOCK.
I DON'T KNOW YOU.
NO RECOLLECTION...

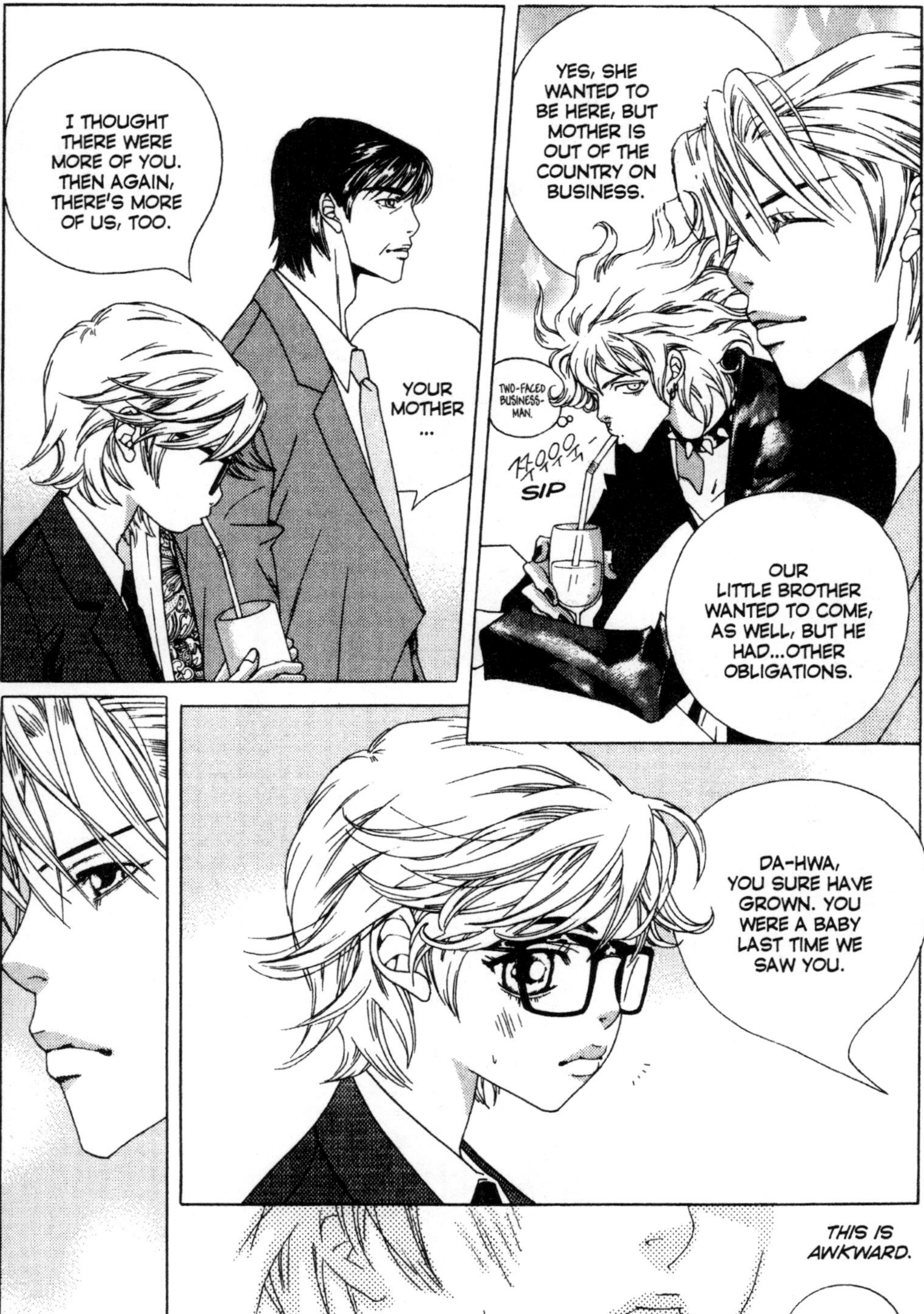
I THOUGHT THERE WERE MORE OF YOU. THEN AGAIN, THERE'S MORE OF US, TOO.
YOUR MOTHER ...
YES, SHE WANTED TO BE HERE, BUT MOTHER IS OUT OF THE COUNTRY ON BUSINESS.
TWO-FACED BUSINESS-MAN.
SIP
OUR LITTLE BROTHER WANTED TO COME, AS WELL, BUT HE HAD...OTHER OBLIGATIONS.
DA-HWA, YOU SURE HAVE GROWN. YOU WERE A BABY LAST TIME WE SAW YOU.
THIS IS AWKWARD.
YES...

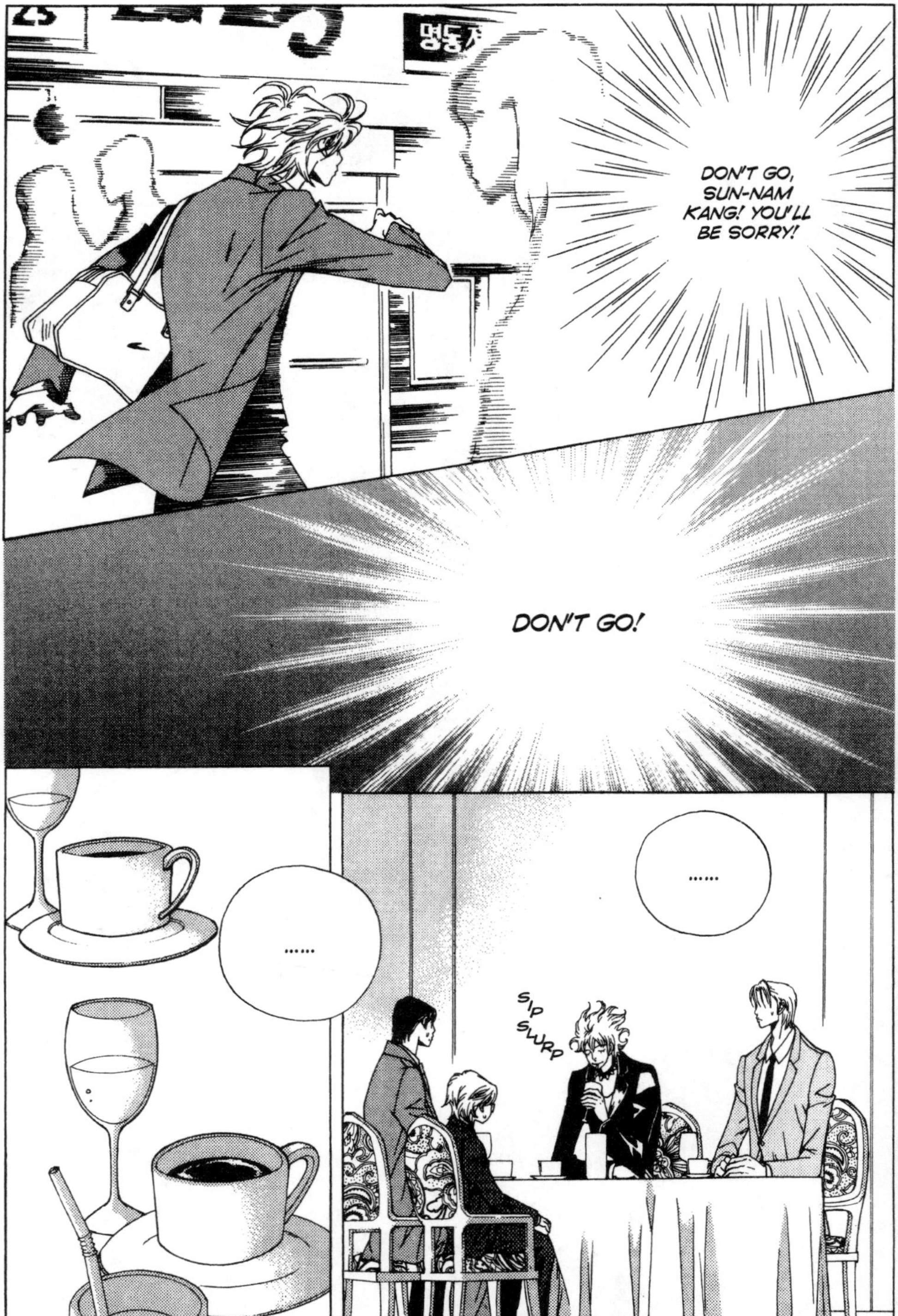
DON'T GO, SUN-NAM KANG! YOU'LL BE SORRY!
DON'T GO!
……
……
SIP SLURP

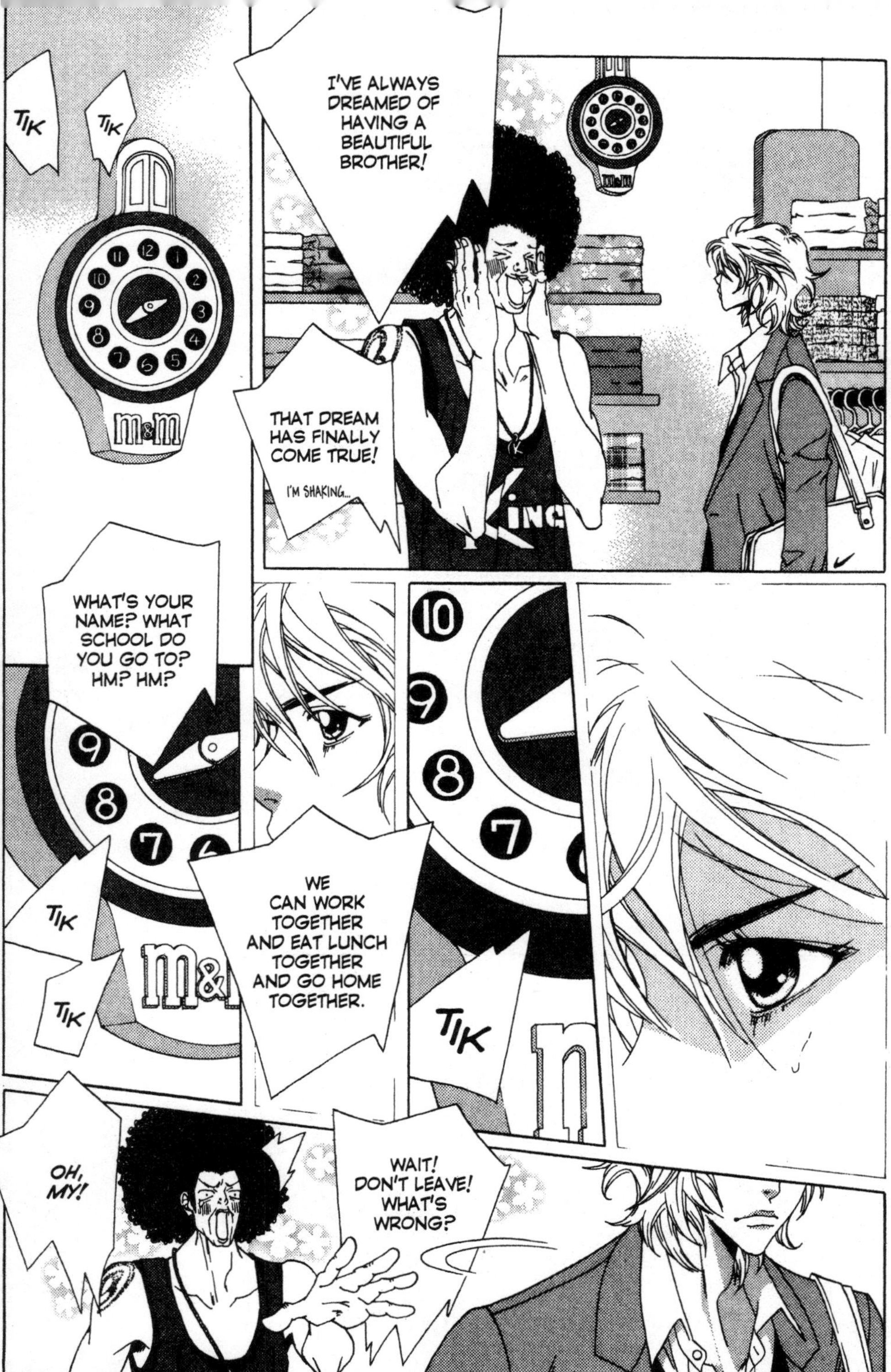
TIK
TIK
I'VE ALWAYS DREAMED OF HAVING A BEAUTIFUL BROTHER!
THAT DREAM HAS FINALLY COME TRUE!
I'M SHAKING...
WHAT'S YOUR NAME? WHAT SCHOOL DO YOU GO TO? HM? HM?
TIK
TIK
WE CAN WORK TOGETHER AND EAT LUNCH TOGETHER AND GO HOME TOGETHER.
TIK
OH, MY!
WAIT! DON'T LEAVE! WHAT'S WRONG?

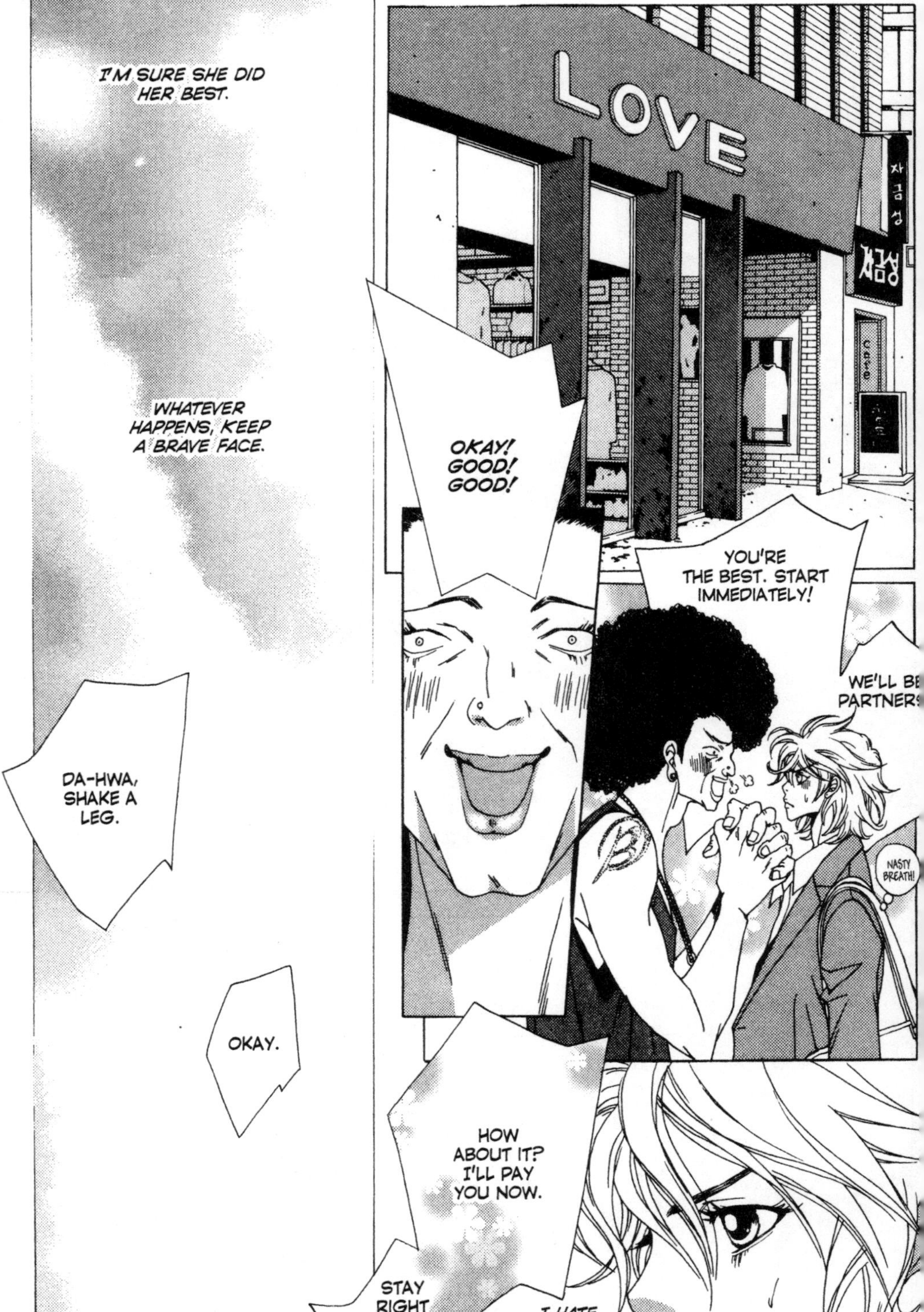
I'M SURE SHE DID HER BEST.
WHATEVER HAPPENS, KEEP A BRAVE FACE.
DA-HWA, SHAKE A LEG.
OKAY.
LOVE
자금성
자금성
cafe
OKAY! GOOD! GOOD!
YOU'RE THE BEST. START IMMEDIATELY!
WE'LL BE PARTNERS
NASTY BREATH!
HOW ABOUT IT? I'LL PAY YOU NOW.
STAY RIGHT HERE.
I HATE THIS!

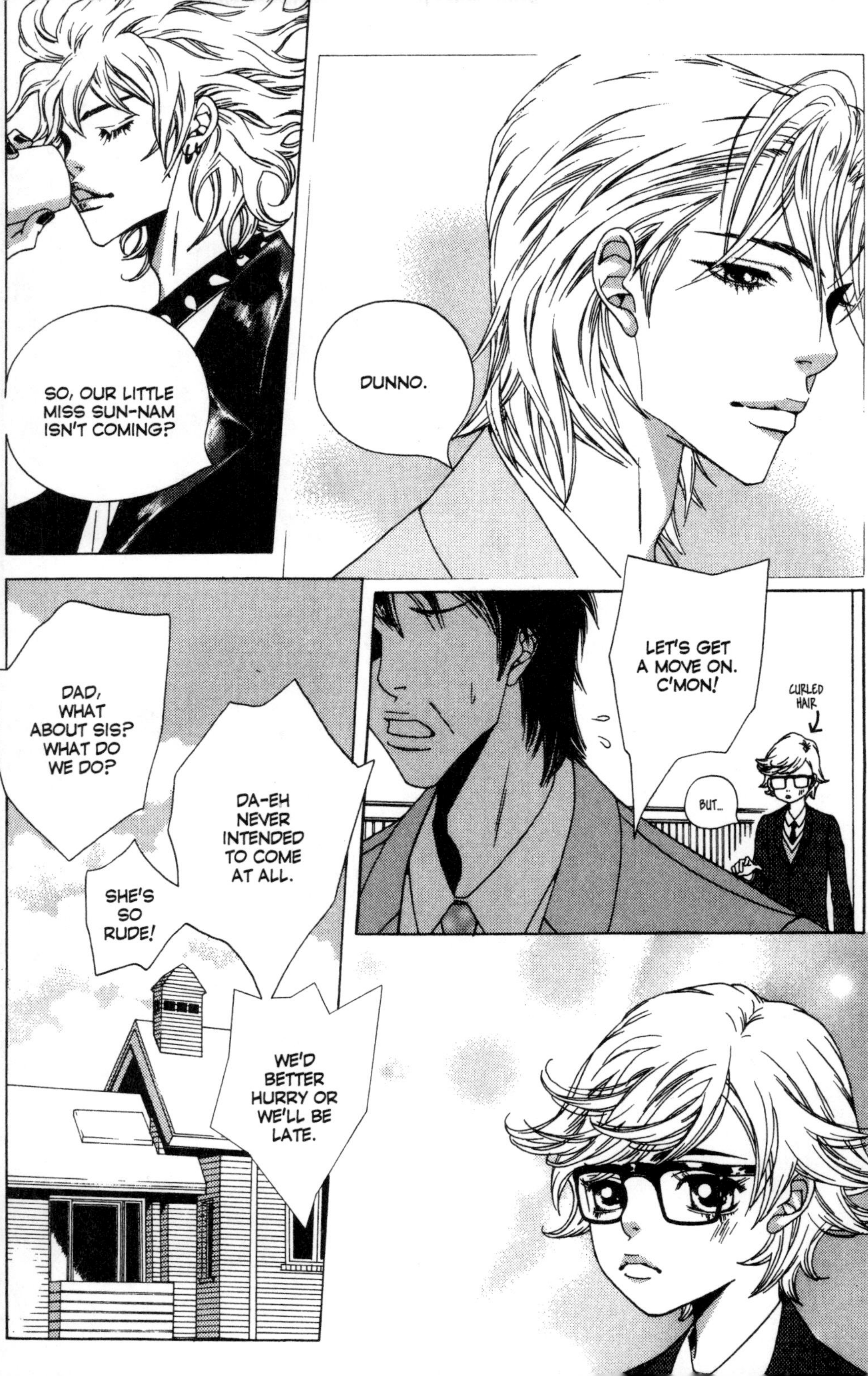
SO, OUR LITTLE MISS SUN-NAM ISN'T COMING?
DUNNO.
DAD, WHAT ABOUT SIS? WHAT DO WE DO?
DA-EH NEVER INTENDED TO COME AT ALL.
SHE'S SO RUDE!
LET'S GET A MOVE ON. C'MON!
BUT...
CURLED HAIR
WE'D BETTER HURRY OR WE'LL BE LATE.

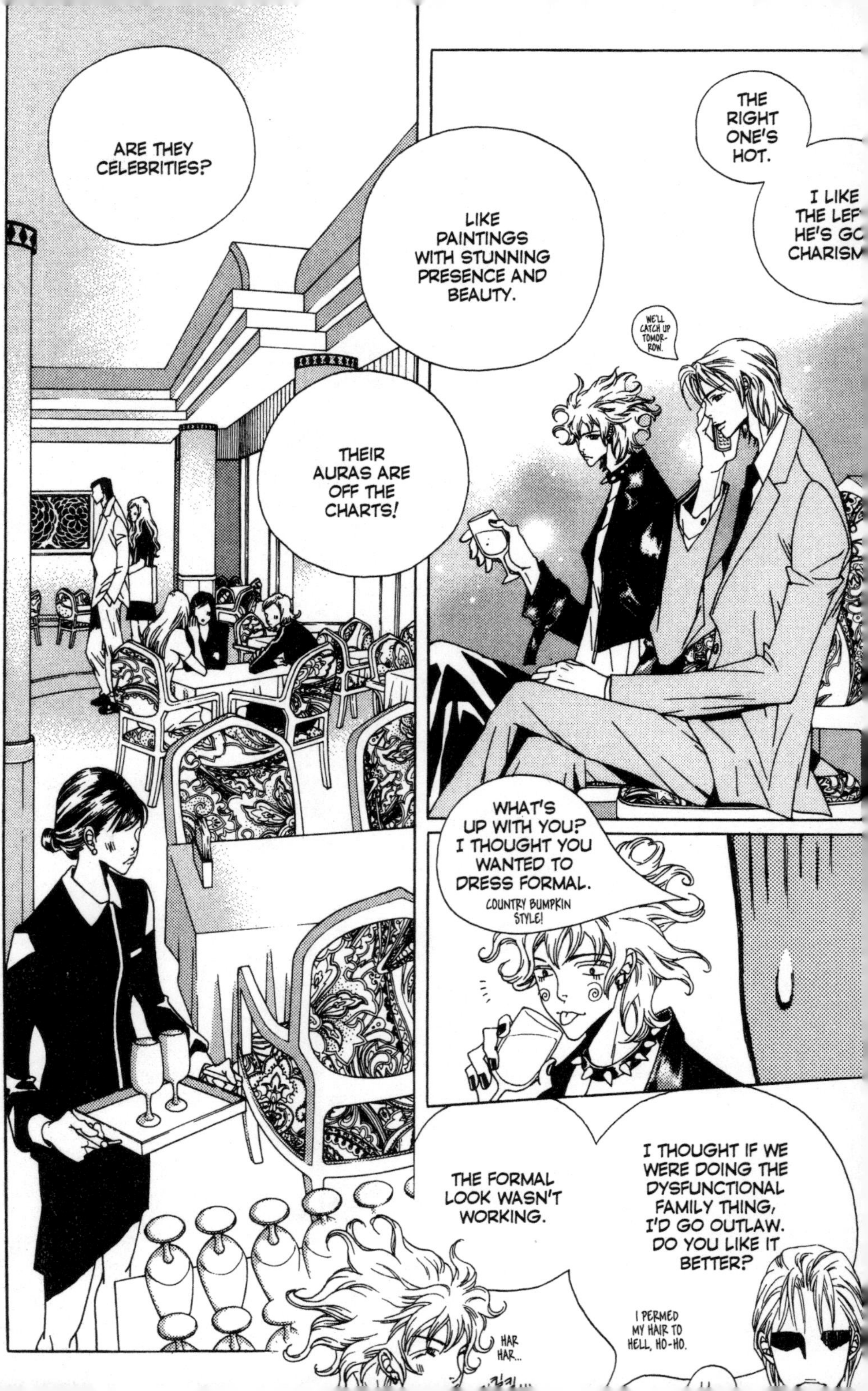
ARE THEY CELEBRITIES?
LIKE PAINTINGS WITH STUNNING PRESENCE AND BEAUTY.
THEIR AURAS ARE OFF THE CHARTS!
THE RIGHT ONE'S HOT.
I LIKE THE LEF HE'S GO CHARISM
WE'LL CATCH UP TOMOR-ROW.
WHAT'S UP WITH YOU? I THOUGHT YOU WANTED TO DRESS FORMAL.
COUNTRY BUMPKIN STYLE!
THE FORMAL LOOK WASN'T WORKING.
I THOUGHT IF WE WERE DOING THE DYSFUNCTIONAL FAMILY THING, I'D GO OUTLAW. DO YOU LIKE IT BETTER?
HAR HAR...
I PERMED MY HAIR TO HELL, HO-HO.

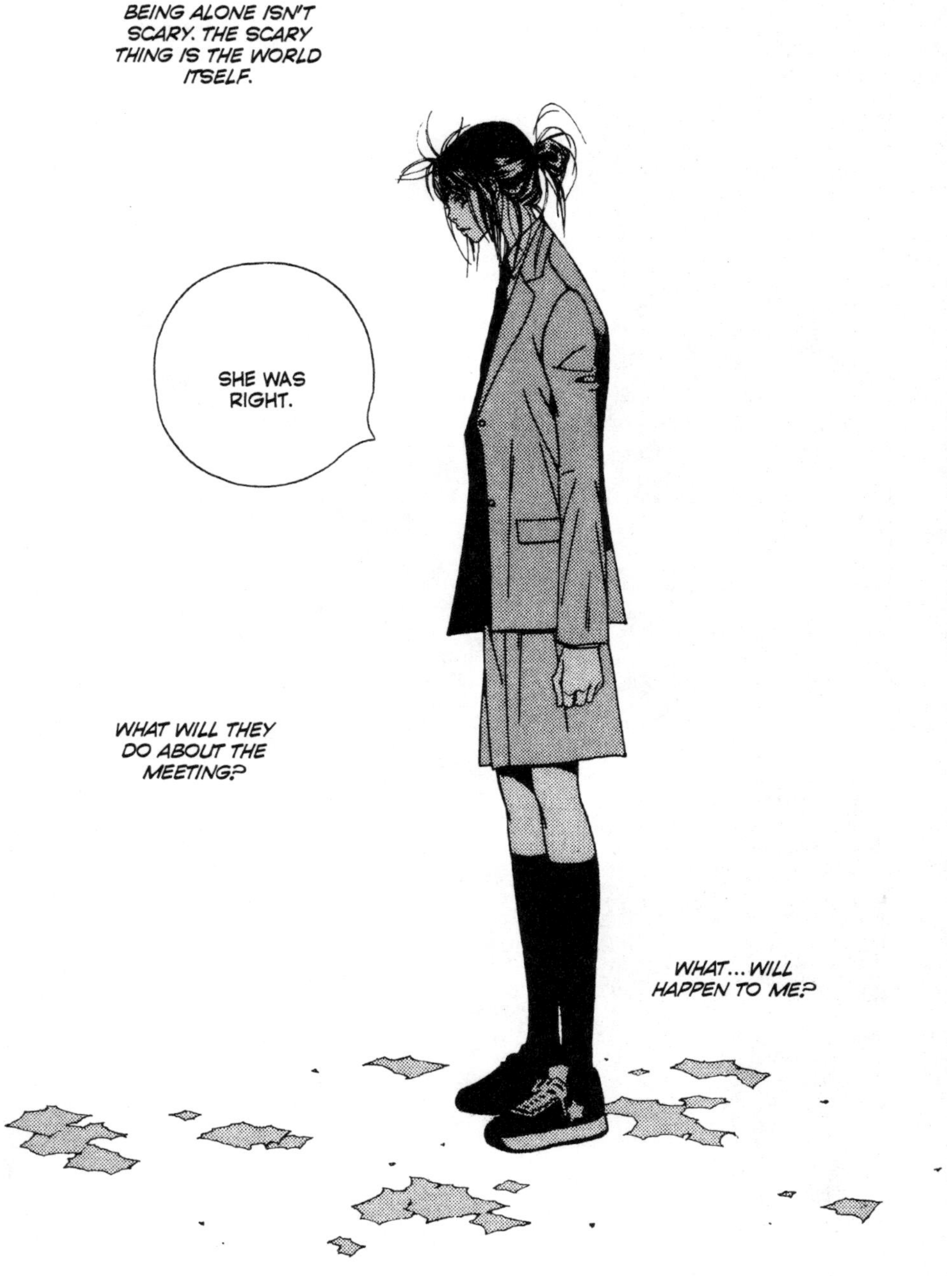
BEING ALONE ISN'T SCARY. THE SCARY THING IS THE WORLD ITSELF.
SHE WAS RIGHT.
WHAT WILL THEY DO ABOUT THE MEETING?
WHAT... WILL HAPPEN TO ME?

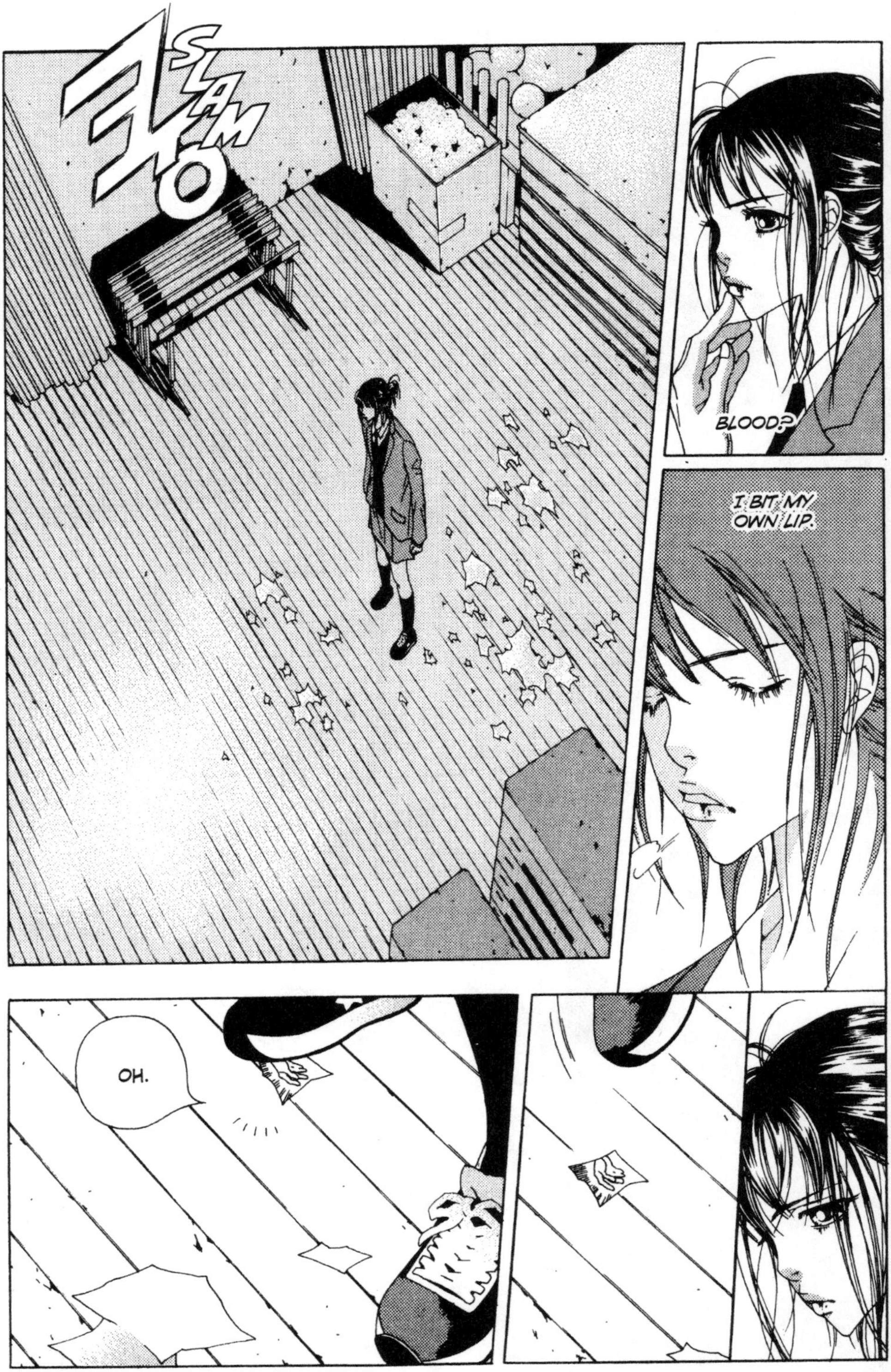
SLAM
BLOOD?
I BIT MY OWN LIP.
OH.

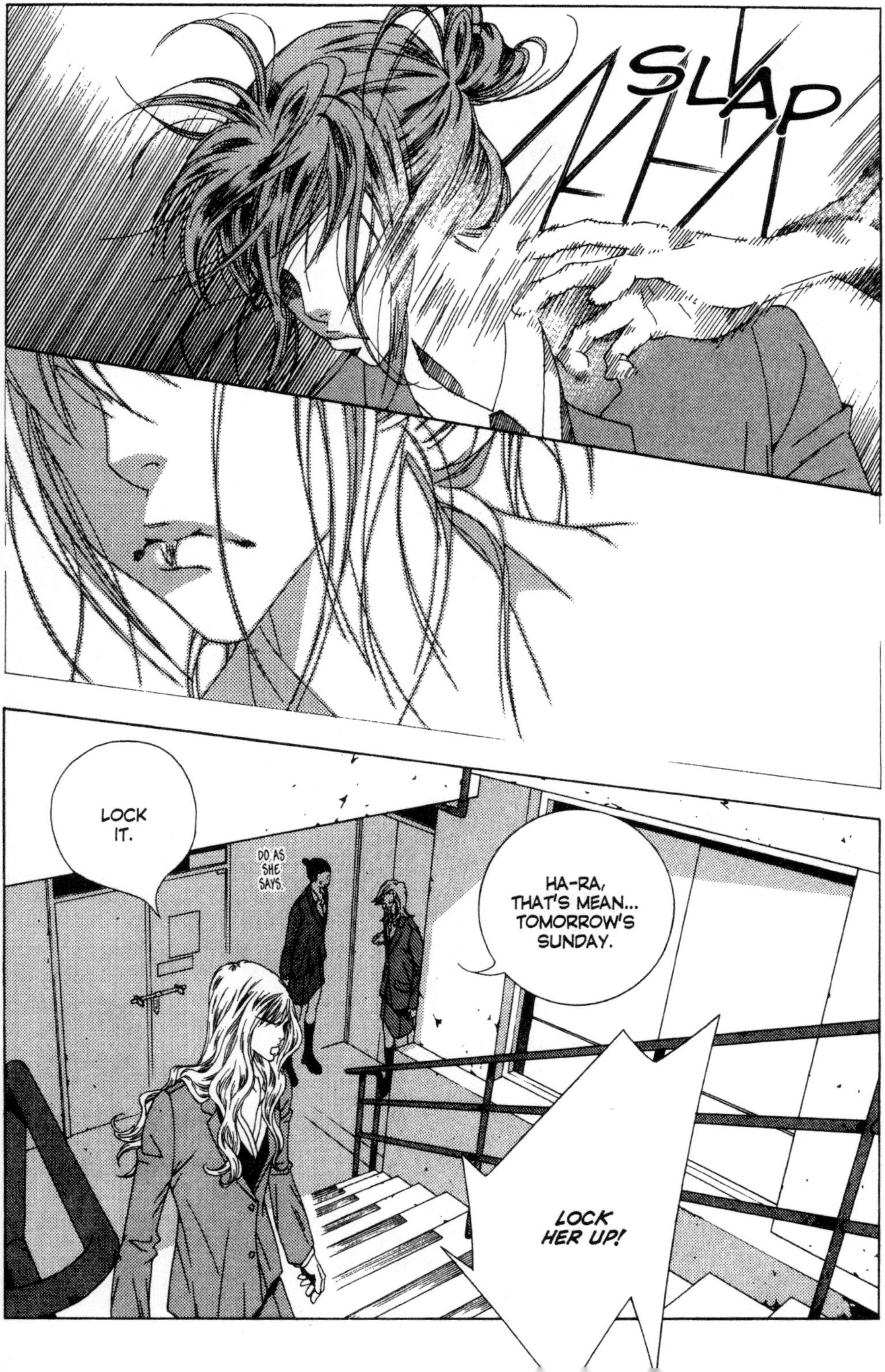
SLAP
LOCK IT.
DO AS SHE SAYS.
HA-RA, THAT'S MEAN... TOMORROW'S SUNDAY.
LOCK HER UP!

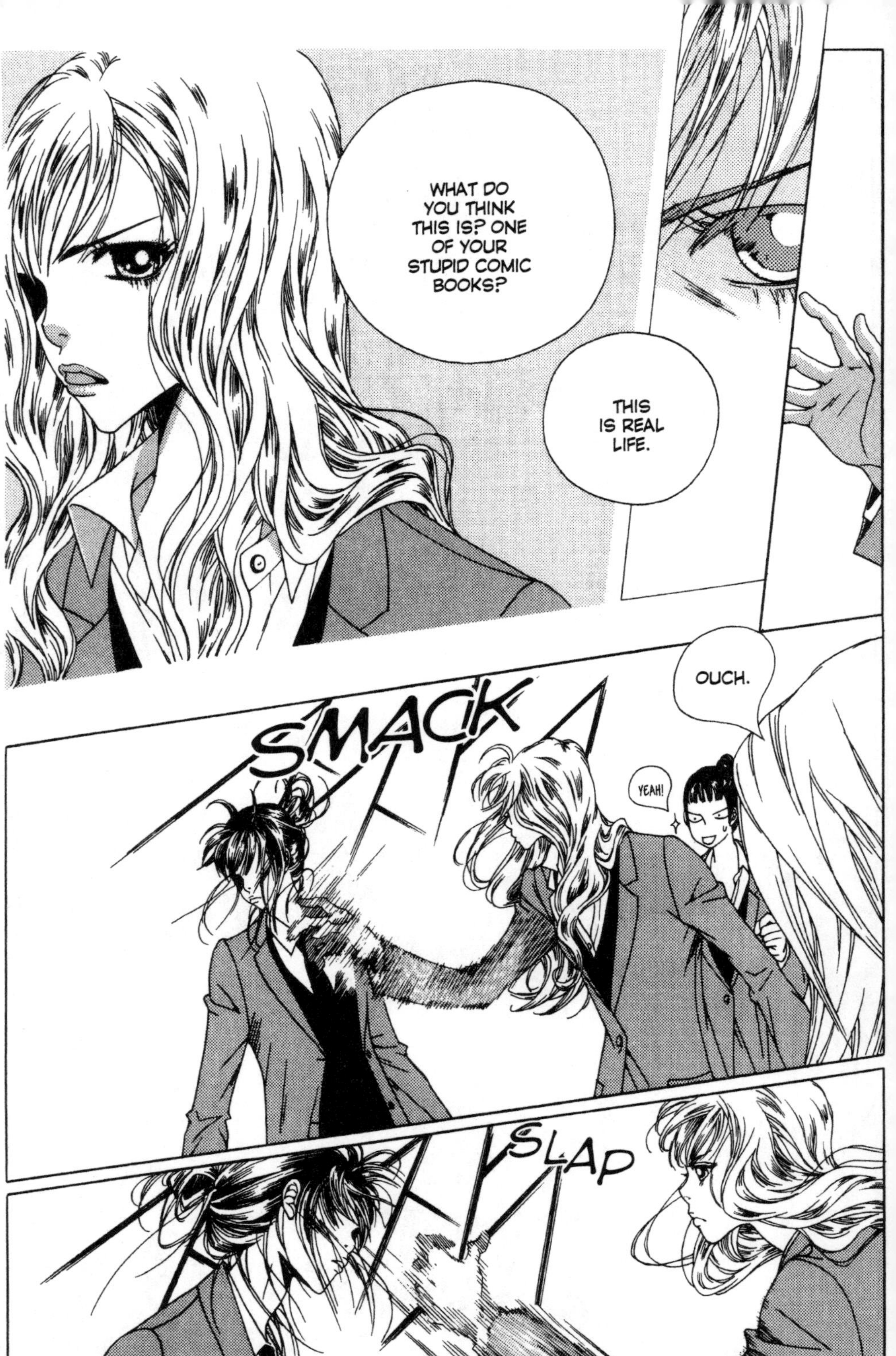
WHAT DO YOU THINK THIS IS? ONE OF YOUR STUPID COMIC BOOKS?
THIS IS REAL LIFE.
SMACK
YEAH!
OUCH.
SLAP

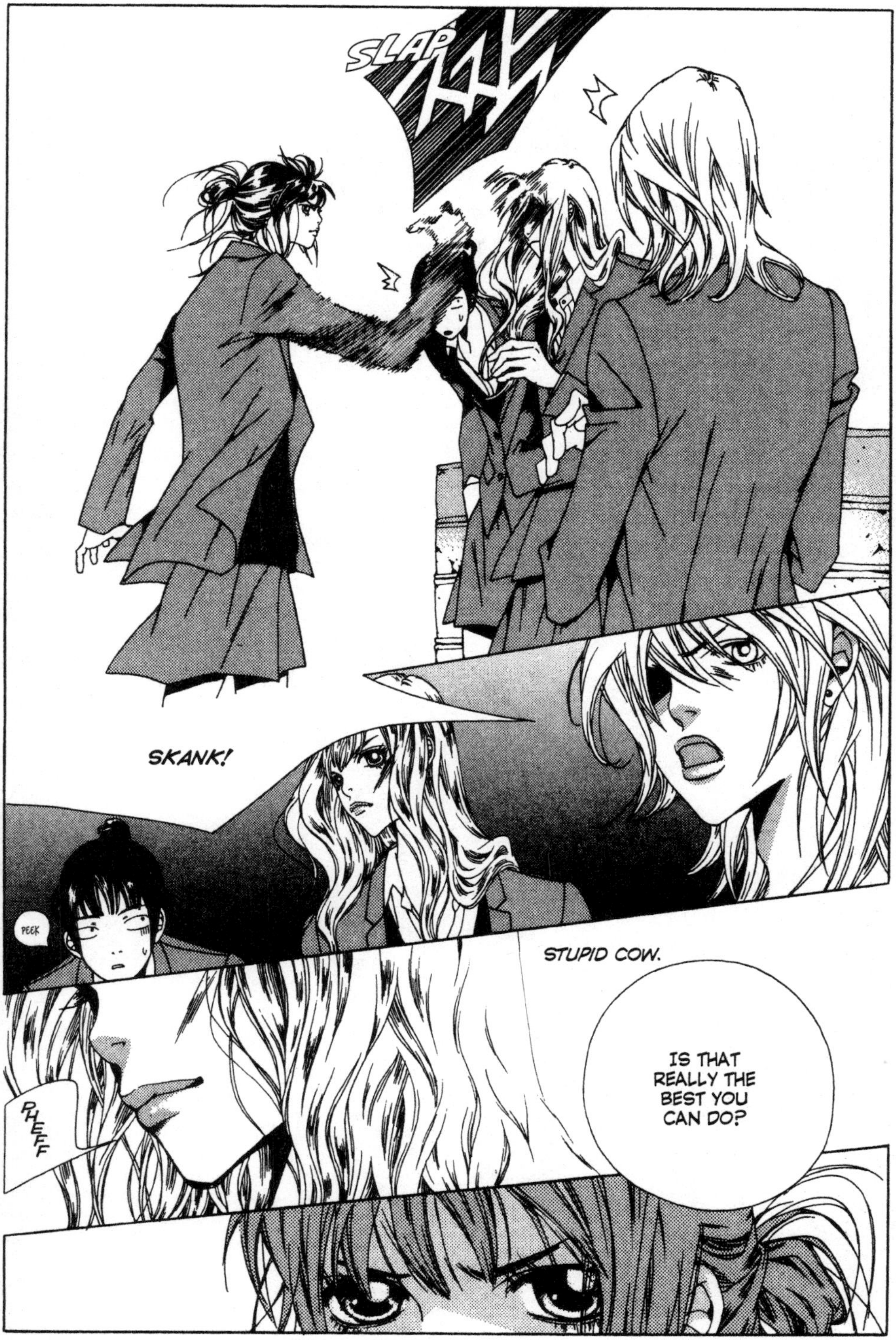
SLAP
SKANK!
PEEK
STUPID COW.
PHEFF
IS THAT REALLY THE BEST YOU CAN DO?

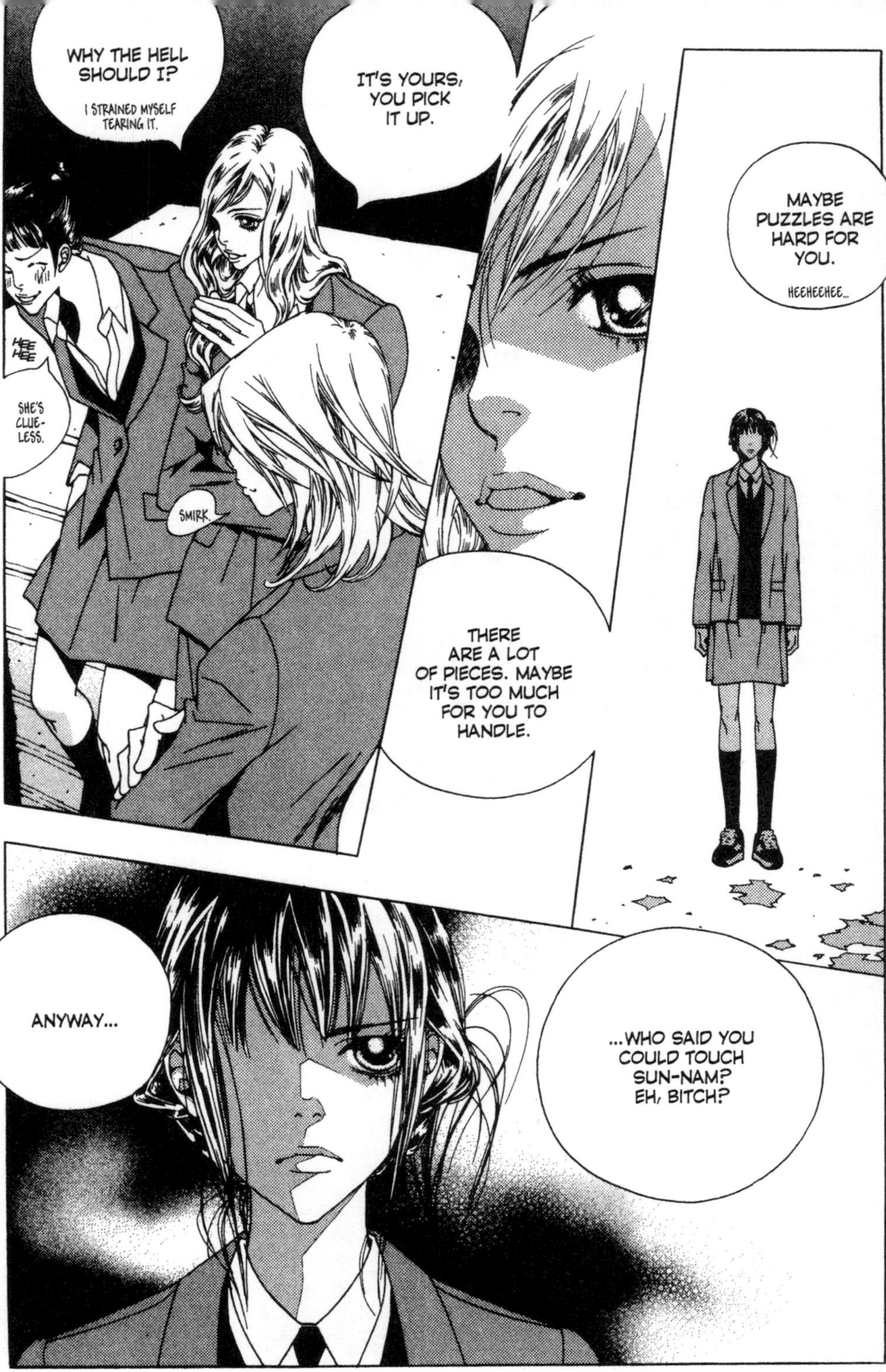
WHY THE HELL SHOULD I?
I STRAINED MYSELF TEARING IT.
IT'S YOURS, YOU PICK IT UP.
HEE HEE
SHE'S CLUELESS.
SMIRK.
THERE ARE A LOT OF PIECES. MAYBE IT'S TOO MUCH FOR YOU TO HANDLE.
MAYBE PUZZLES ARE HARD FOR YOU.
HEEHEEHEE...
ANYWAY...
...WHO SAID YOU COULD TOUCH SUN-NAM? EH, BITCH?

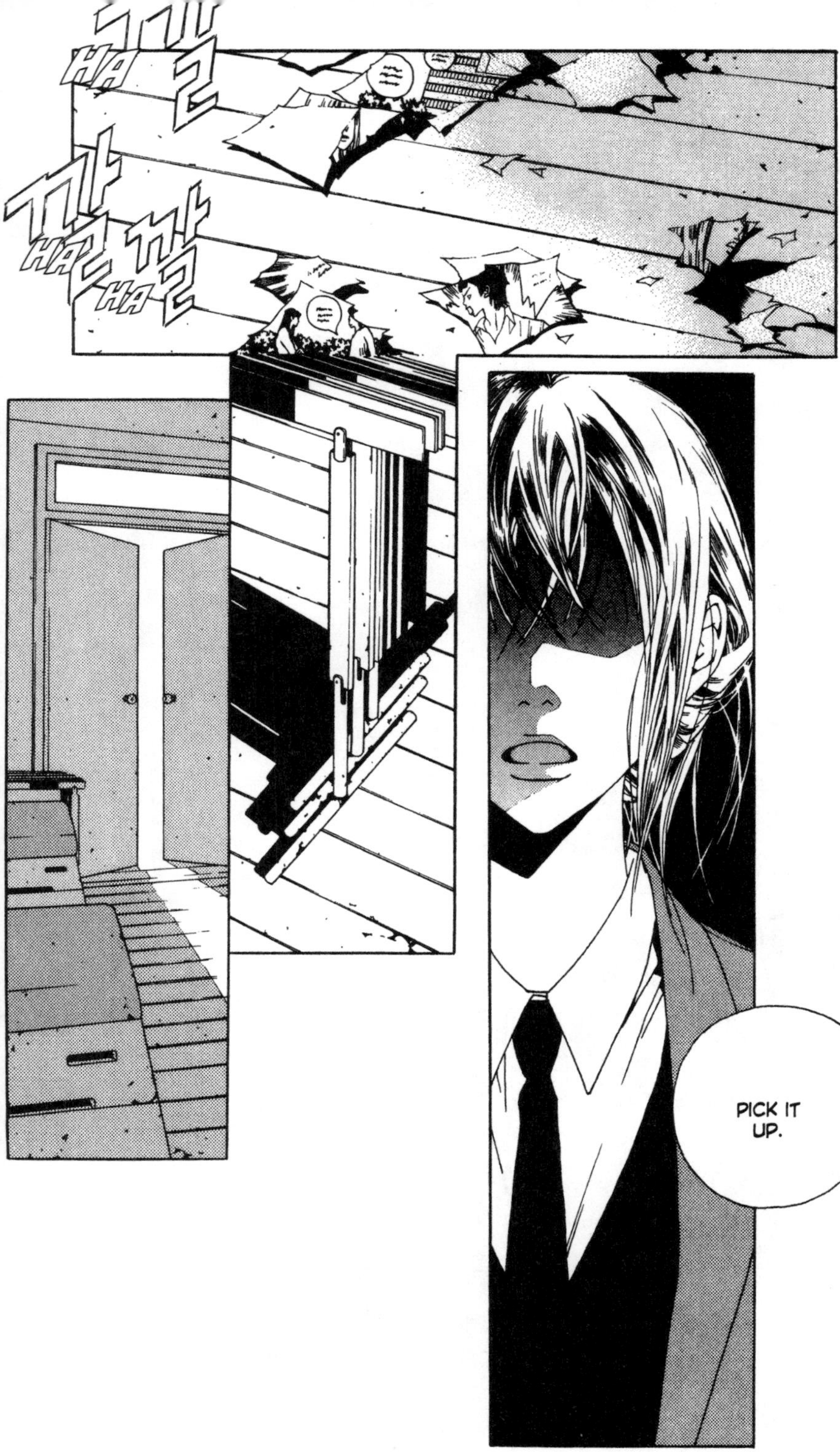
HA
HA
HA
PICK IT UP.

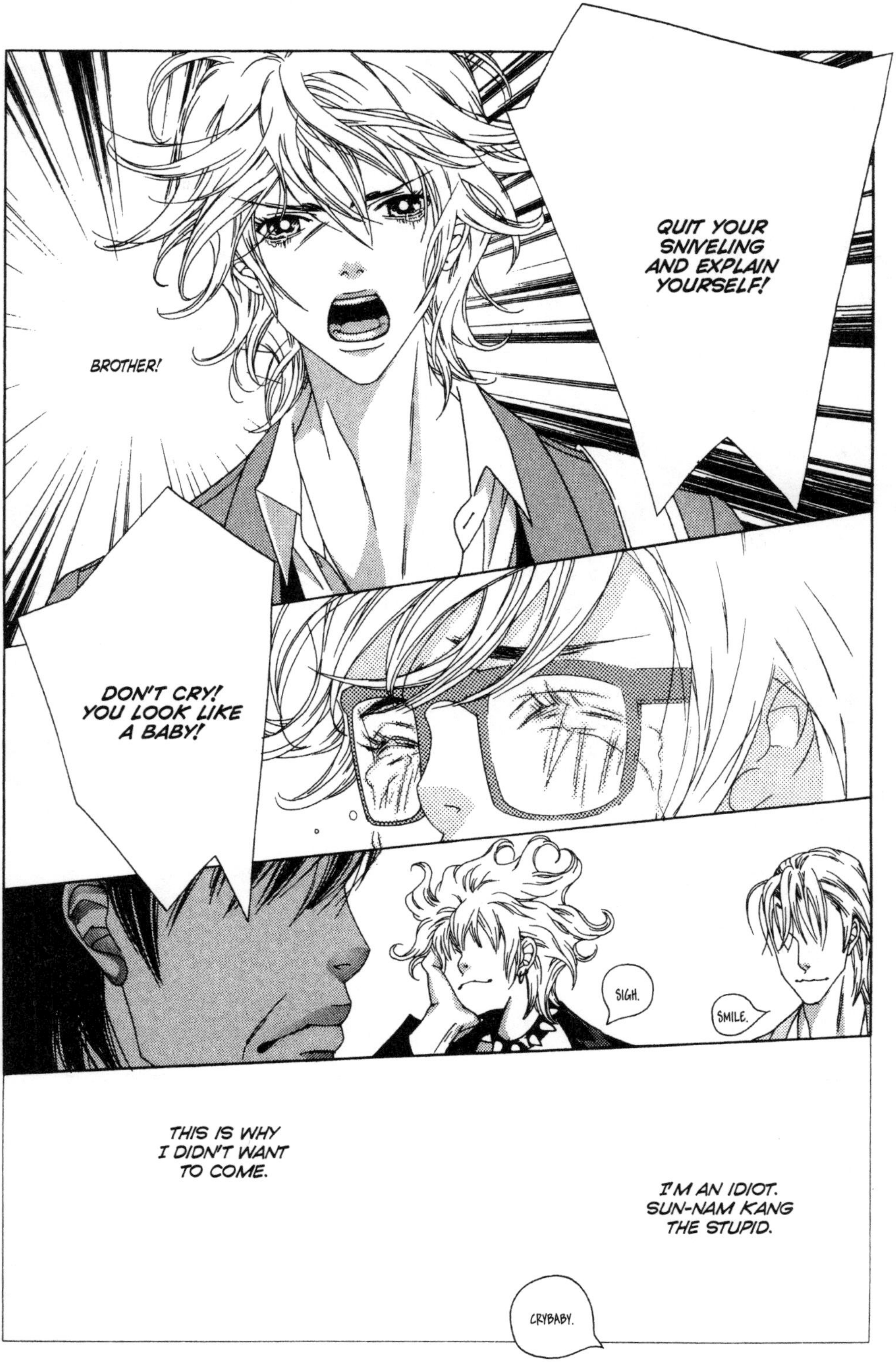
BROTHER!
QUIT YOUR SNIVELING AND EXPLAIN YOURSELF!
DON'T CRY! YOU LOOK LIKE A BABY!
SIGH.
SMILE.
THIS IS WHY I DIDN'T WANT TO COME.
I'M AN IDIOT. SUN-NAM KANG THE STUPID.
CRYBABY.

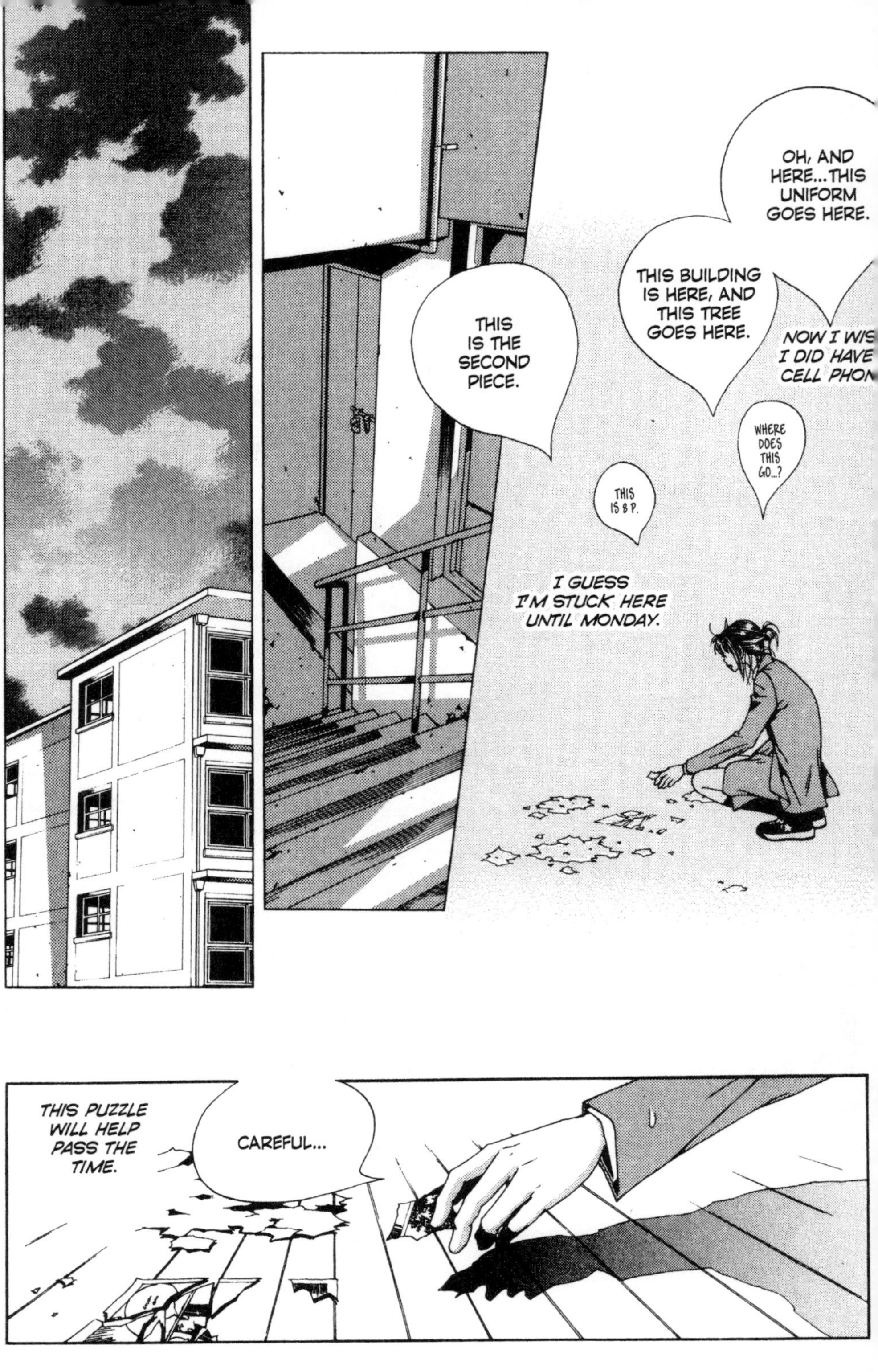
THIS IS THE SECOND PIECE.
THIS BUILDING IS HERE, AND THIS TREE GOES HERE.
OH, AND HERE...THIS UNIFORM GOES HERE.
NOW I WIS I DID HAVE CELL PHON
THIS IS 8 P.
WHERE DOES THIS GO...?
I GUESS I'M STUCK HERE UNTIL MONDAY.
THIS PUZZLE WILL HELP PASS THE TIME.
CAREFUL...

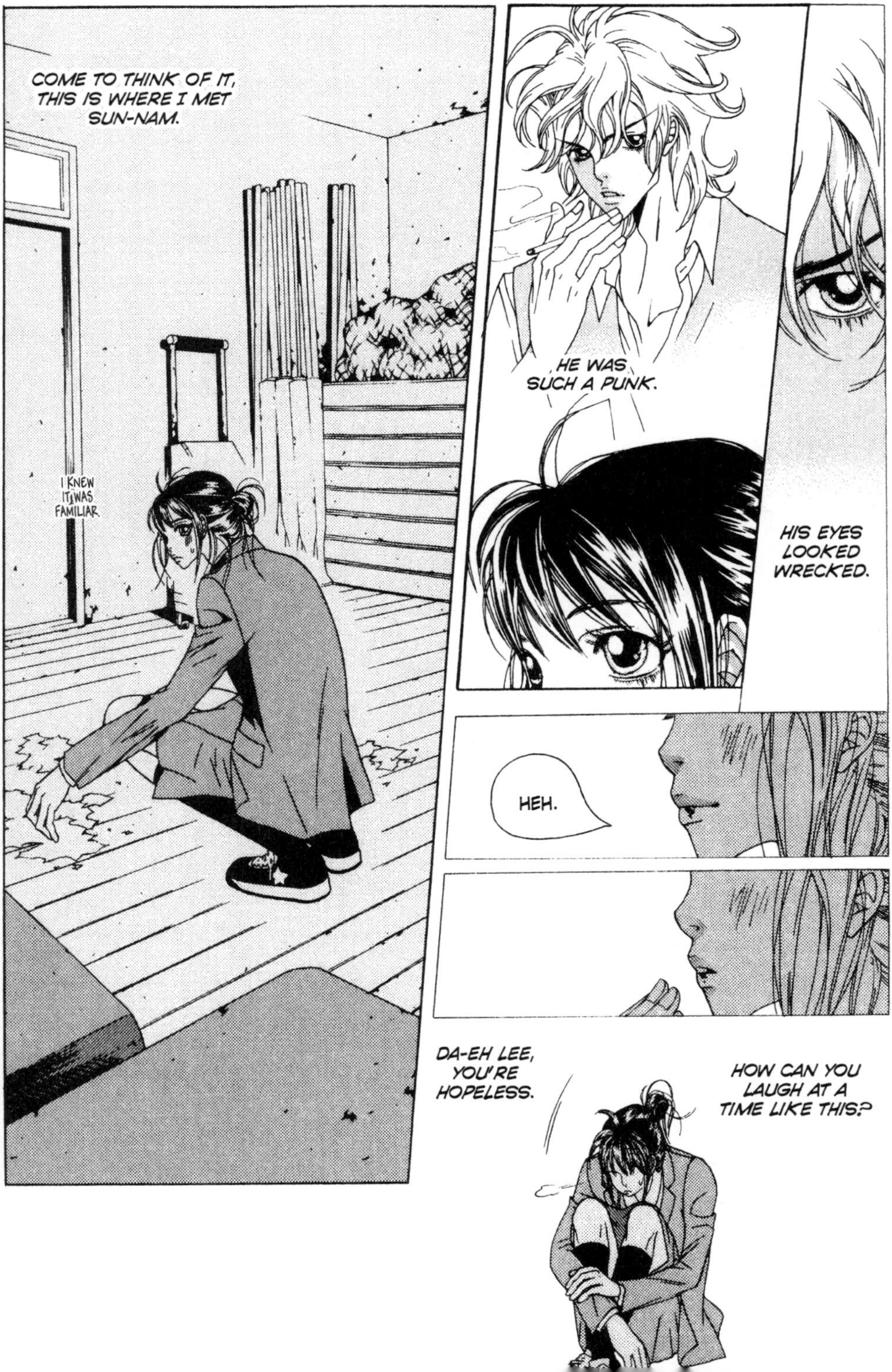
COME TO THINK OF IT, THIS IS WHERE I MET SUN-NAM.
I KNEW IT WAS FAMILIAR.
HE WAS SUCH A PUNK.
HIS EYES LOOKED WRECKED.
HEH.
DA-EH LEE, YOU'RE HOPELESS.
HOW CAN YOU LAUGH AT A TIME LIKE THIS?

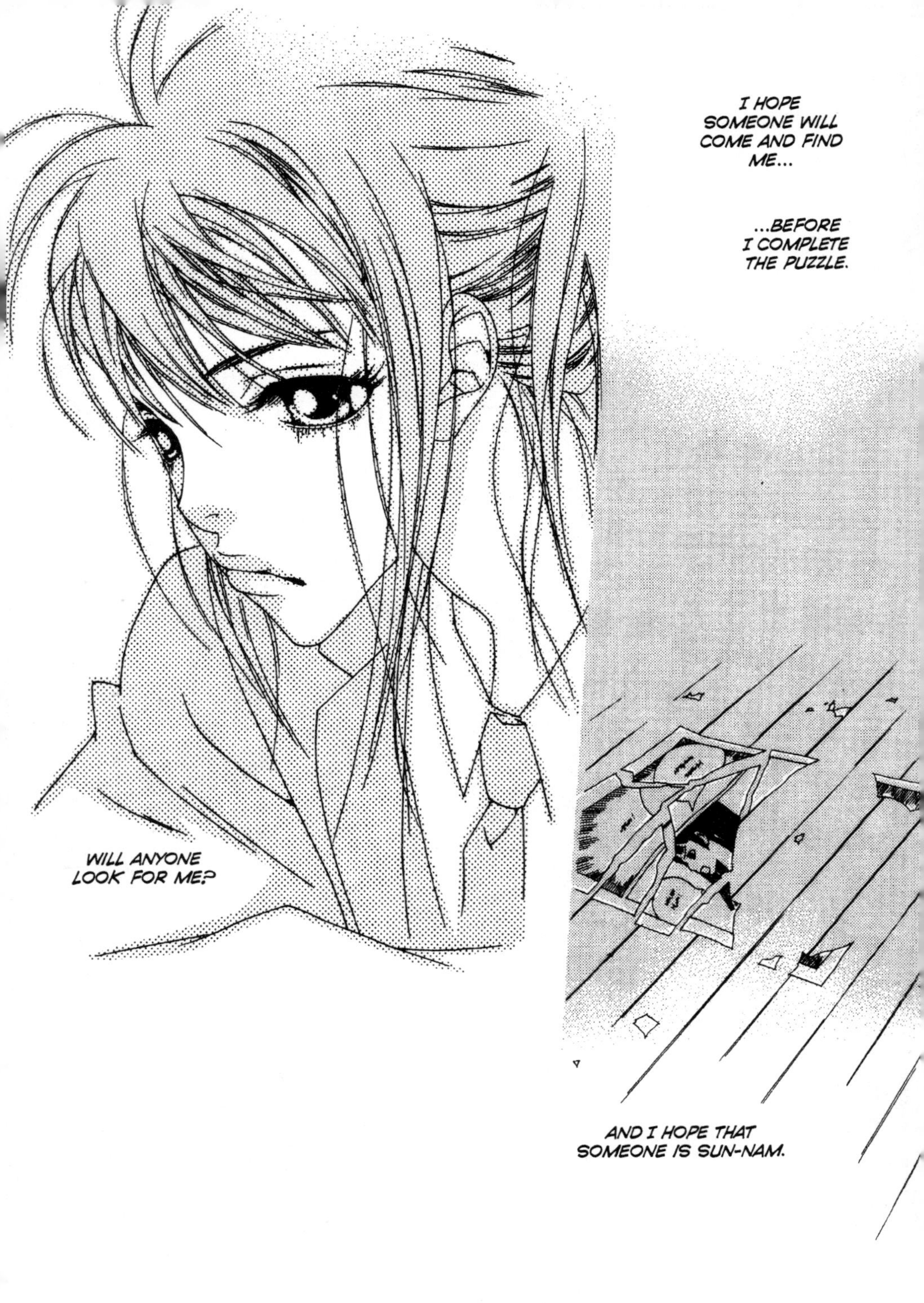
WILL ANYONE LOOK FOR ME?
I HOPE SOMEONE WILL COME AND FIND ME...
...BEFORE I COMPLETE THE PUZZLE.
AND I HOPE THAT SOMEONE IS SUN-NAM.

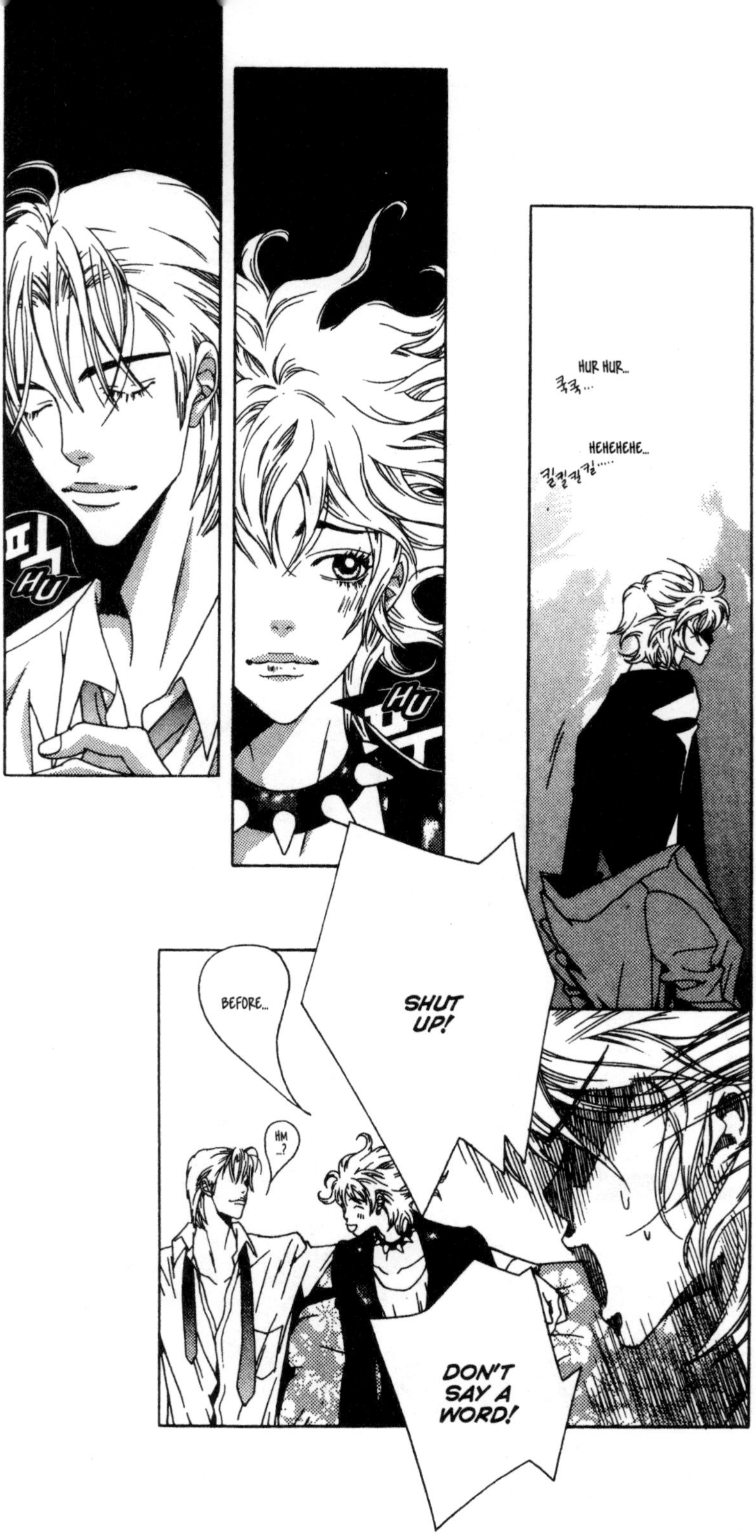
픽
HU
HU
HUR HUR...
쿡쿡...
HEHEHEHE...
킬킬킬킬.....
BEFORE...
HM ...?
SHUT UP!
DON'T SAY A WORD!

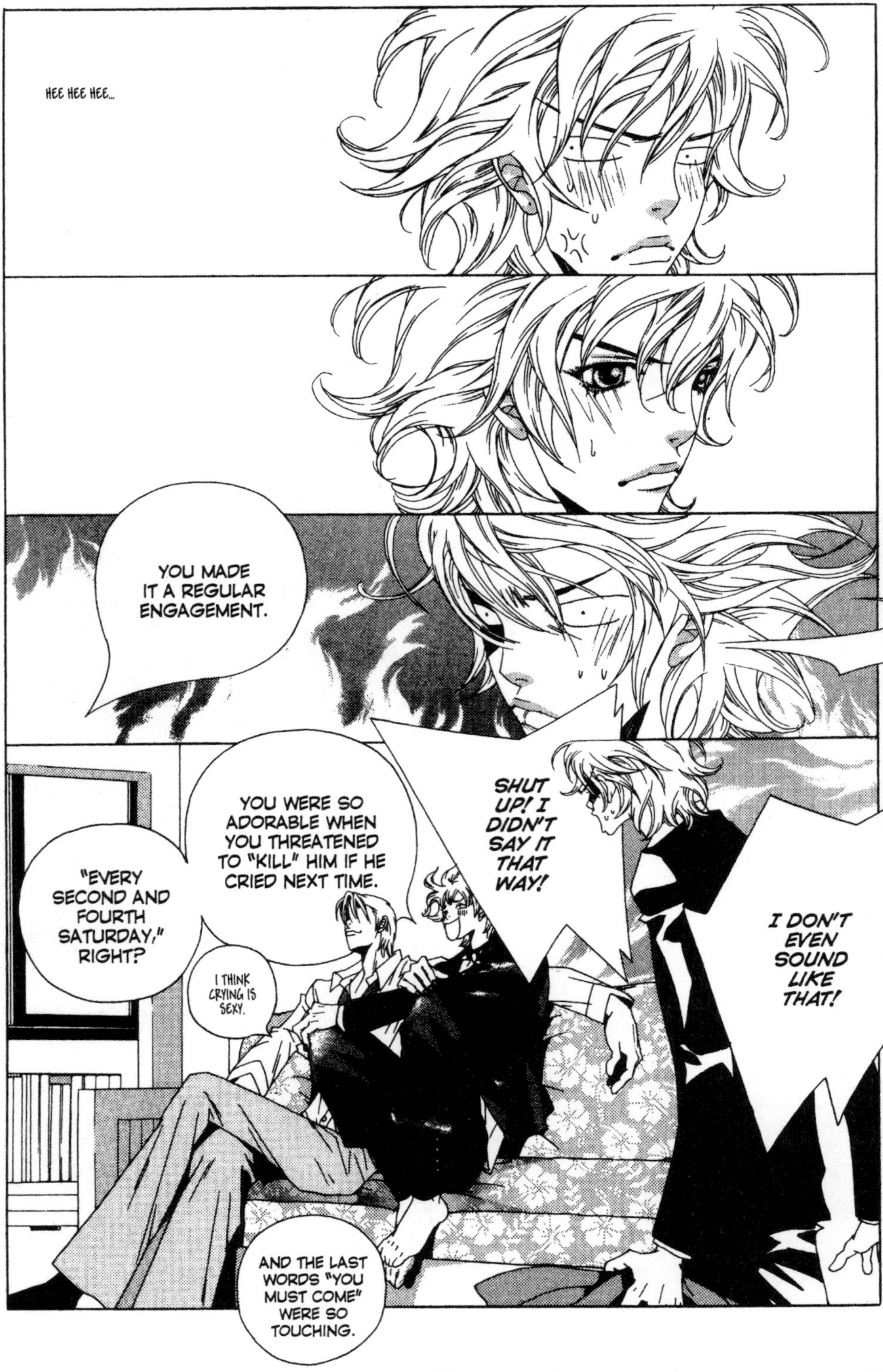
HEE HEE HEE...
YOU MADE IT A REGULAR ENGAGEMENT.
"EVERY SECOND AND FOURTH SATURDAY," RIGHT?
YOU WERE SO ADORABLE WHEN YOU THREATENED TO "KILL" HIM IF HE CRIED NEXT TIME.
I THINK CRYING IS SEXY.
AND THE LAST WORDS "YOU MUST COME" WERE SO TOUCHING.
SHUT UP! I DIDN'T SAY IT THAT WAY!
I DON'T EVEN SOUND LIKE THAT!

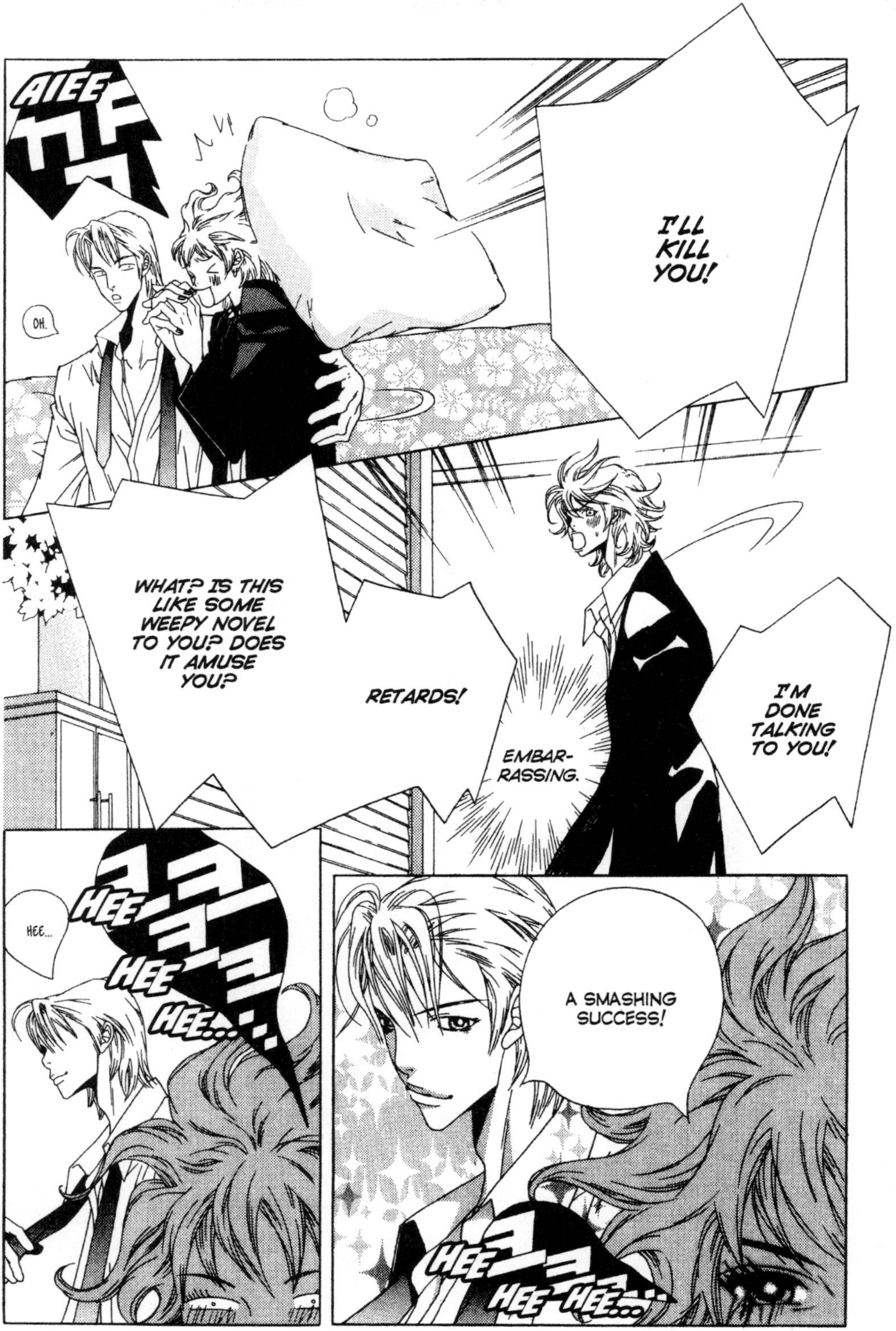
AIEE
OH.
I'LL KILL YOU!
WHAT? IS THIS LIKE SOME WEEPY NOVEL TO YOU? DOES IT AMUSE YOU?
RETARDS!
EMBAR-RASSING.
I'M DONE TALKING TO YOU!
HEE...
HEE HEE HEE...
A SMASHING SUCCESS!
HEE HEE HEE...

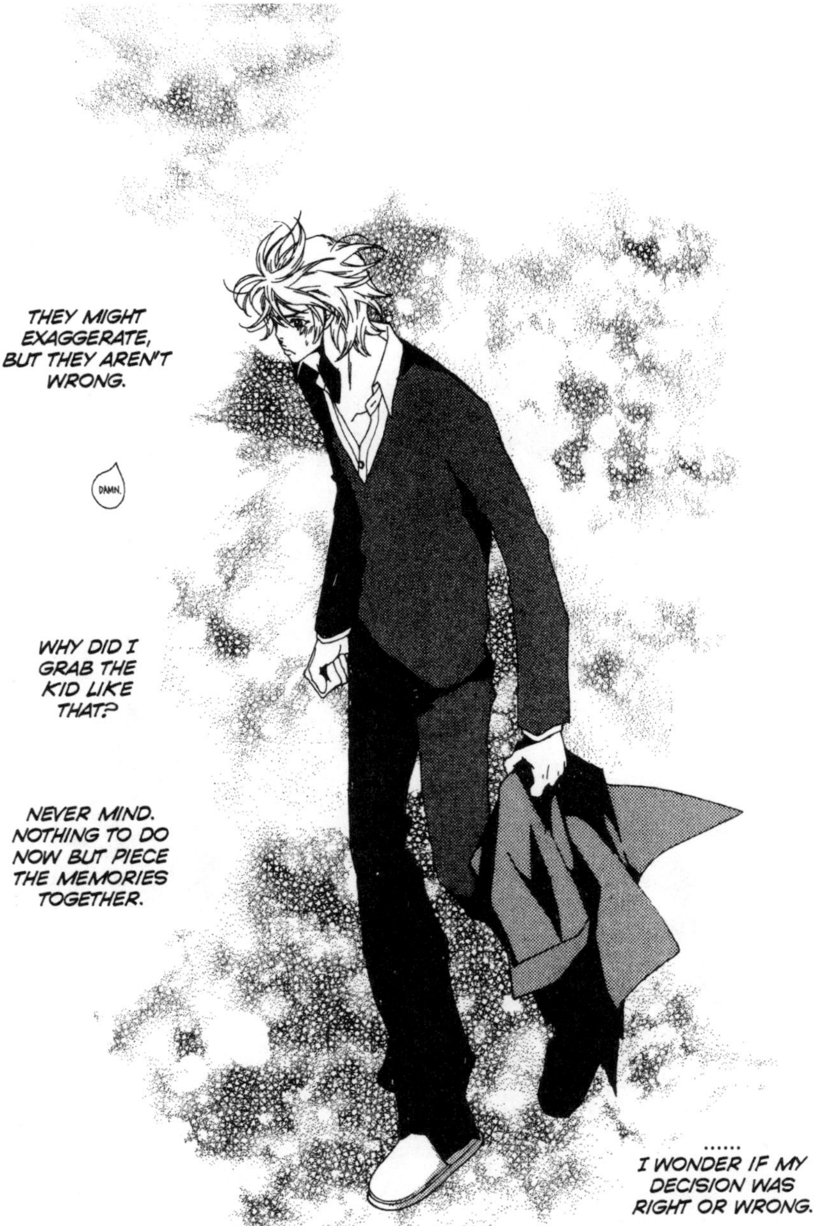
THEY MIGHT EXAGGERATE, BUT THEY AREN'T WRONG.
DAMN.
WHY DID I GRAB THE KID LIKE THAT?
NEVER MIND. NOTHING TO DO NOW BUT PIECE THE MEMORIES TOGETHER.
...... I WONDER IF MY DECISION WAS RIGHT OR WRONG.
I WANTED TO BE A BAD GUY, BUT...

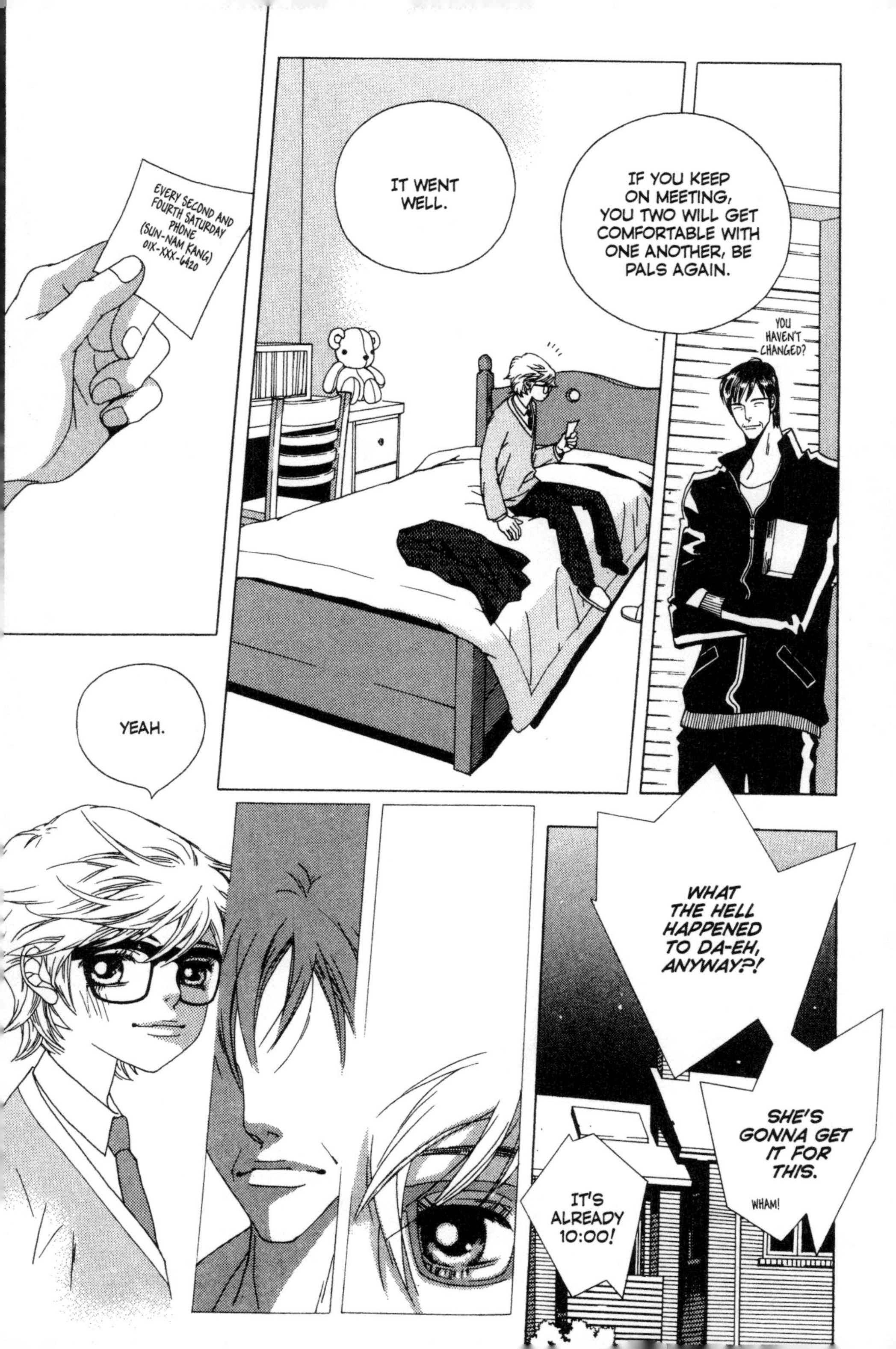
EVERY SECOND AND FOURTH SATURDAY
PHONE
(SUN-NAM KANG)
01X-XXX-6420
IT WENT WELL.
IF YOU KEEP ON MEETING, YOU TWO WILL GET COMFORTABLE WITH ONE ANOTHER, BE PALS AGAIN.
YOU HAVEN'T CHANGED?
YEAH.
WHAT THE HELL HAPPENED TO DA-EH, ANYWAY?!
SHE'S GONNA GET IT FOR THIS.
IT'S ALREADY 10:00!
WHAM!

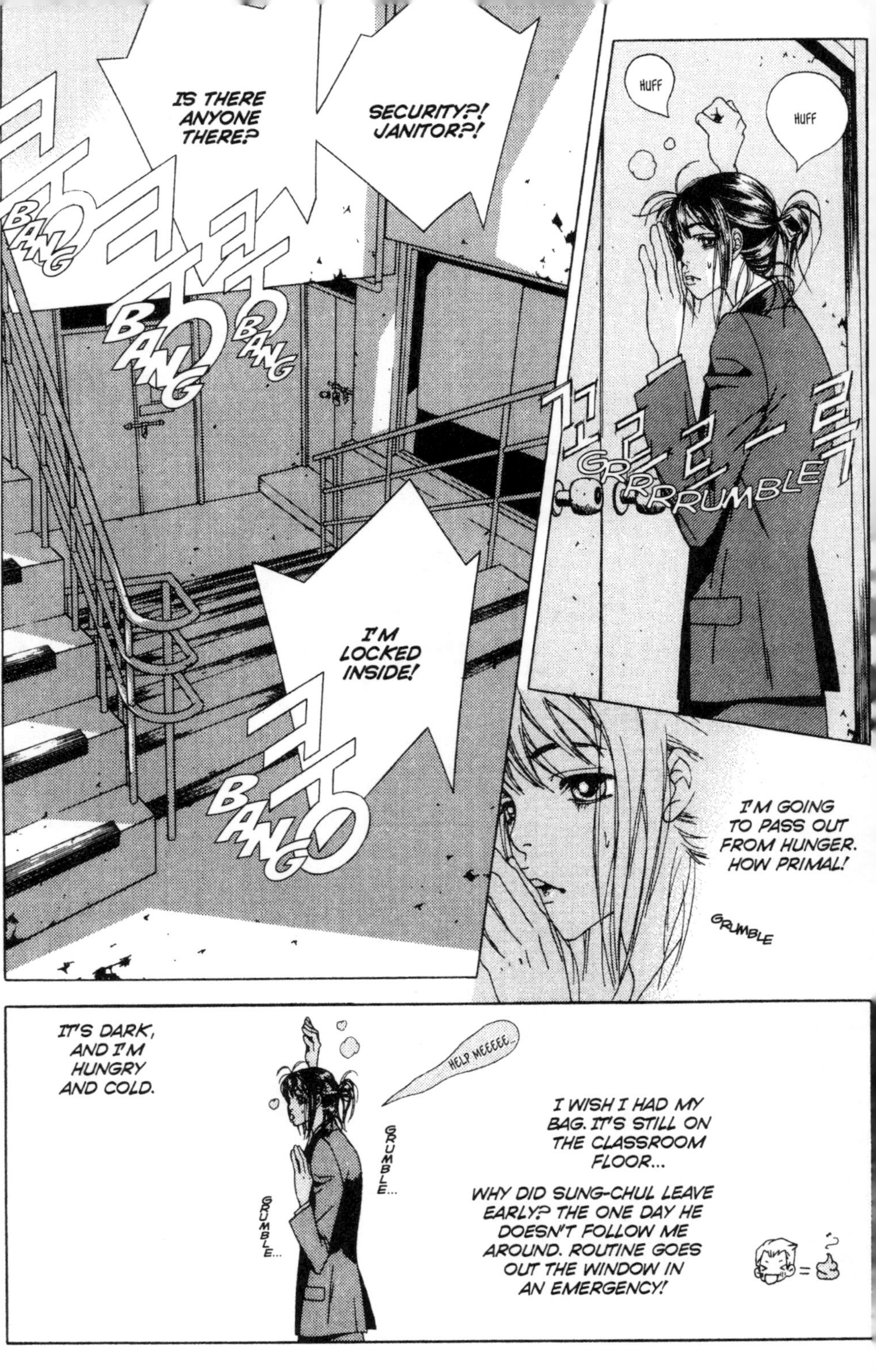
IS THERE ANYONE THERE?
SECURITY?! JANITOR?!
BANG
BANG
BANG
I'M LOCKED INSIDE!
BANG
HUFF
HUFF
GRRRRRUMBLE
I'M GOING TO PASS OUT FROM HUNGER. HOW PRIMAL!
GRUMBLE
IT'S DARK, AND I'M HUNGRY AND COLD.
HELP MEEEEE...
GRUMBLE...
GRUMBLE...
I WISH I HAD MY BAG. IT'S STILL ON THE CLASSROOM FLOOR...
WHY DID SUNG-CHUL LEAVE EARLY? THE ONE DAY HE DOESN'T FOLLOW ME AROUND. ROUTINE GOES OUT THE WINDOW IN AN EMERGENCY!

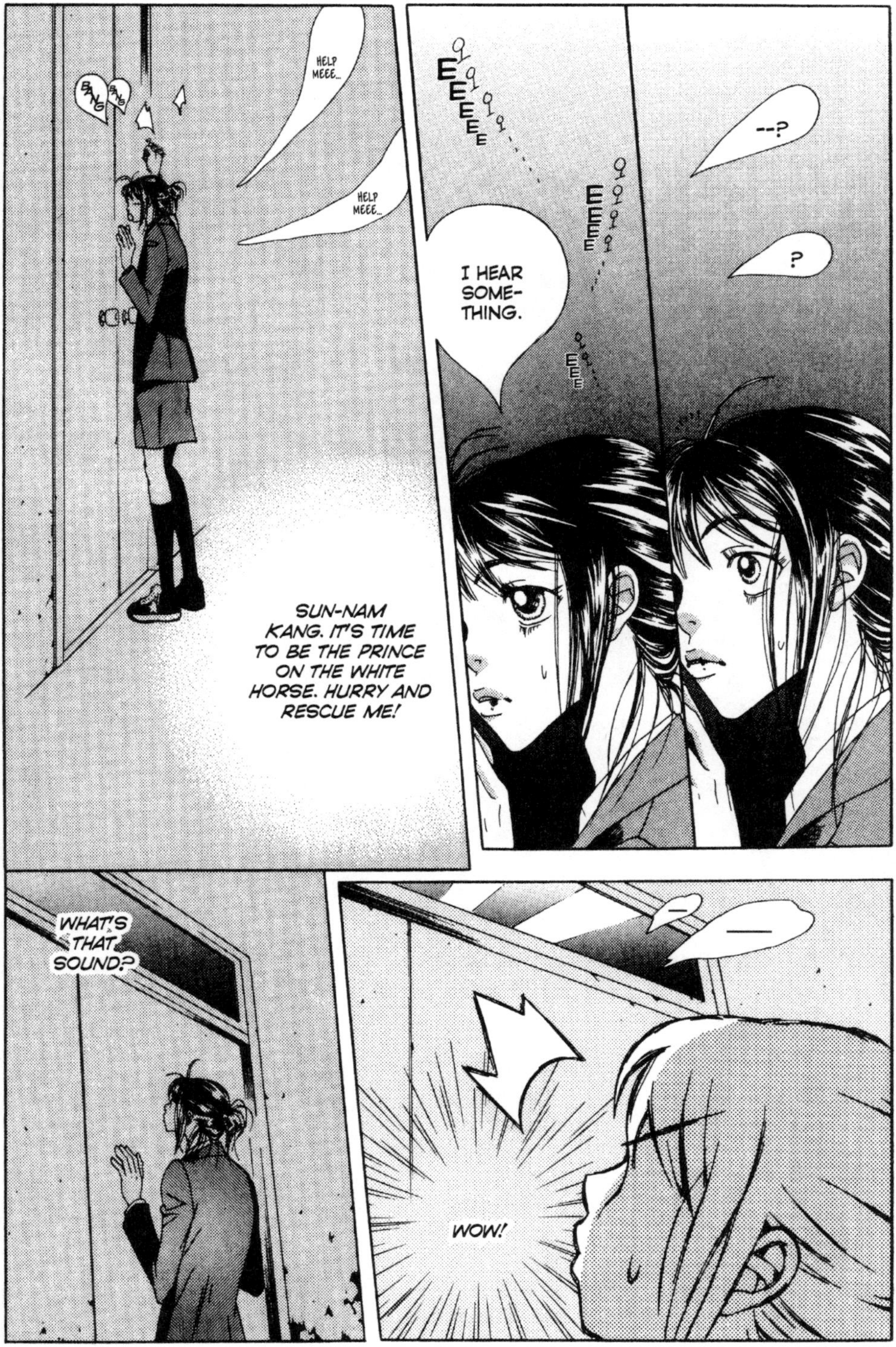
BANG
BANG
HELP MEEE...
HELP MEEE...
SUN-NAM KANG. IT'S TIME TO BE THE PRINCE ON THE WHITE HORSE. HURRY AND RESCUE ME!
EEEEE...
I HEAR SOME-THING.
EEEE...
EEE...
--?
?
WHAT'S THAT SOUND?
—
——
WOW!

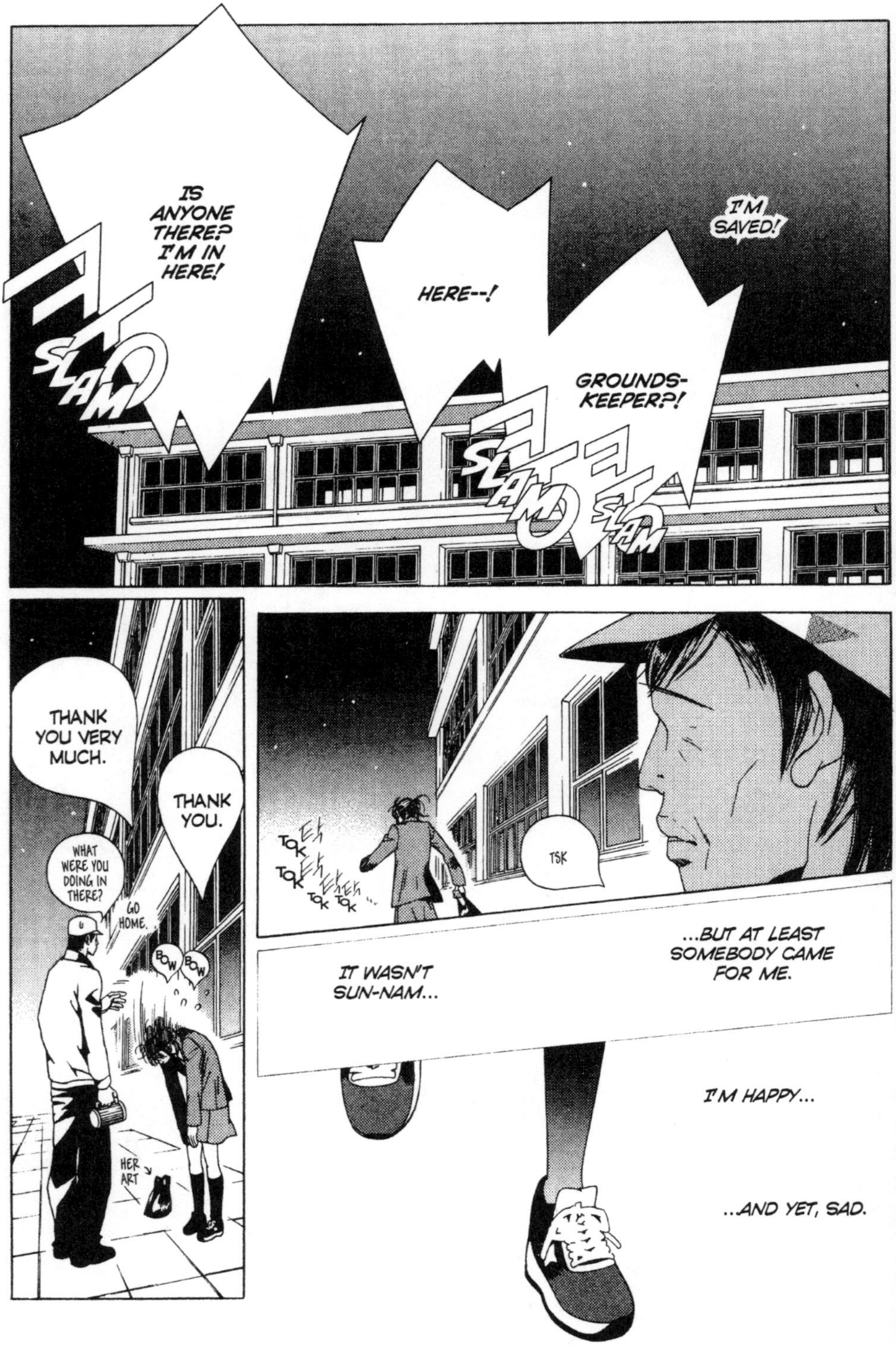

IS ANYONE THERE? I'M IN HERE!
SLAM
HERE--!
GROUNDS-KEEPER?!
SLAM
SLAM
I'M SAVED!
THANK YOU VERY MUCH.
THANK YOU.
WHAT WERE YOU DOING IN THERE?
GO HOME.
BOW
BOW
HER ART
TOK TOK TOK TOK...
TSK
IT WASN'T SUN-NAM...
...BUT AT LEAST SOMEBODY CAME FOR ME.
I'M HAPPY...
...AND YET, SAD.

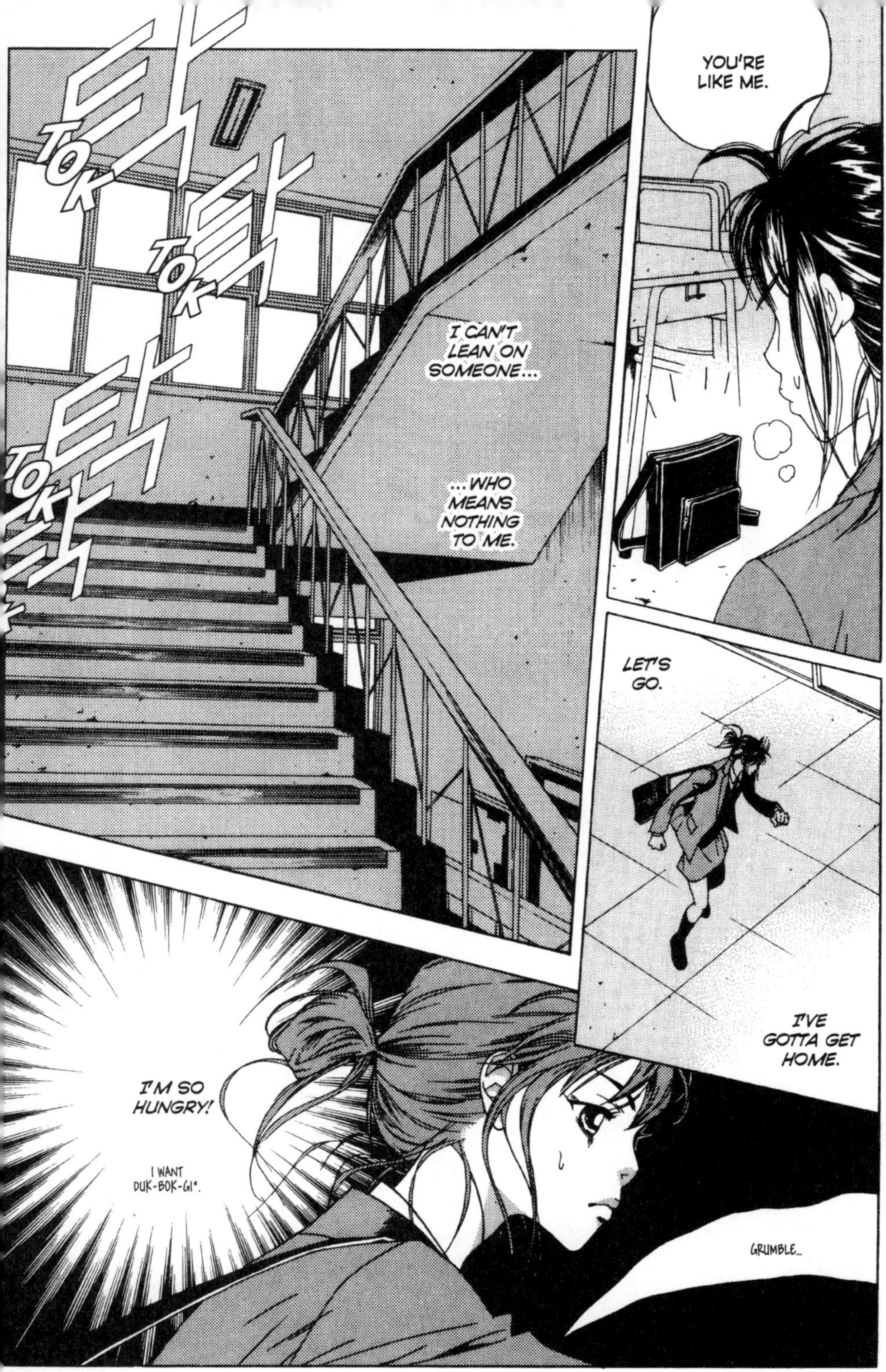
TOK
TOK
TOK
I CAN'T LEAN ON SOMEONE...
...WHO MEANS NOTHING TO ME.
YOU'RE LIKE ME.
LET'S GO.
I'VE GOTTA GET HOME.
I'M SO HUNGRY!
I WANT DUK-BOK-GI*.
GRUMBLE...

*SPICY RICE CAKES.

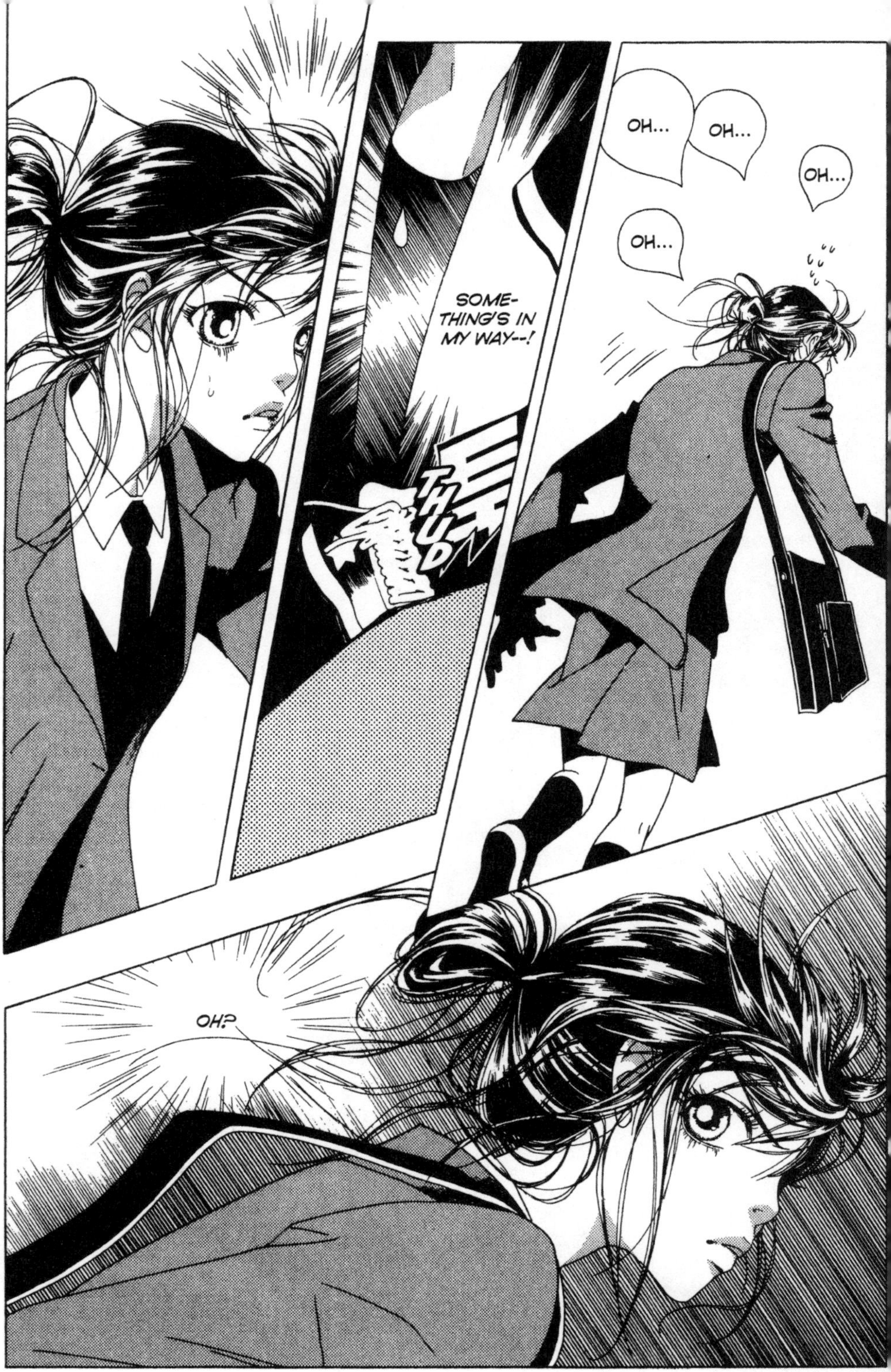
SOME-
THING'S IN
MY WAY--!
THUD
OH...
OH...
OH...
OH...
OH?

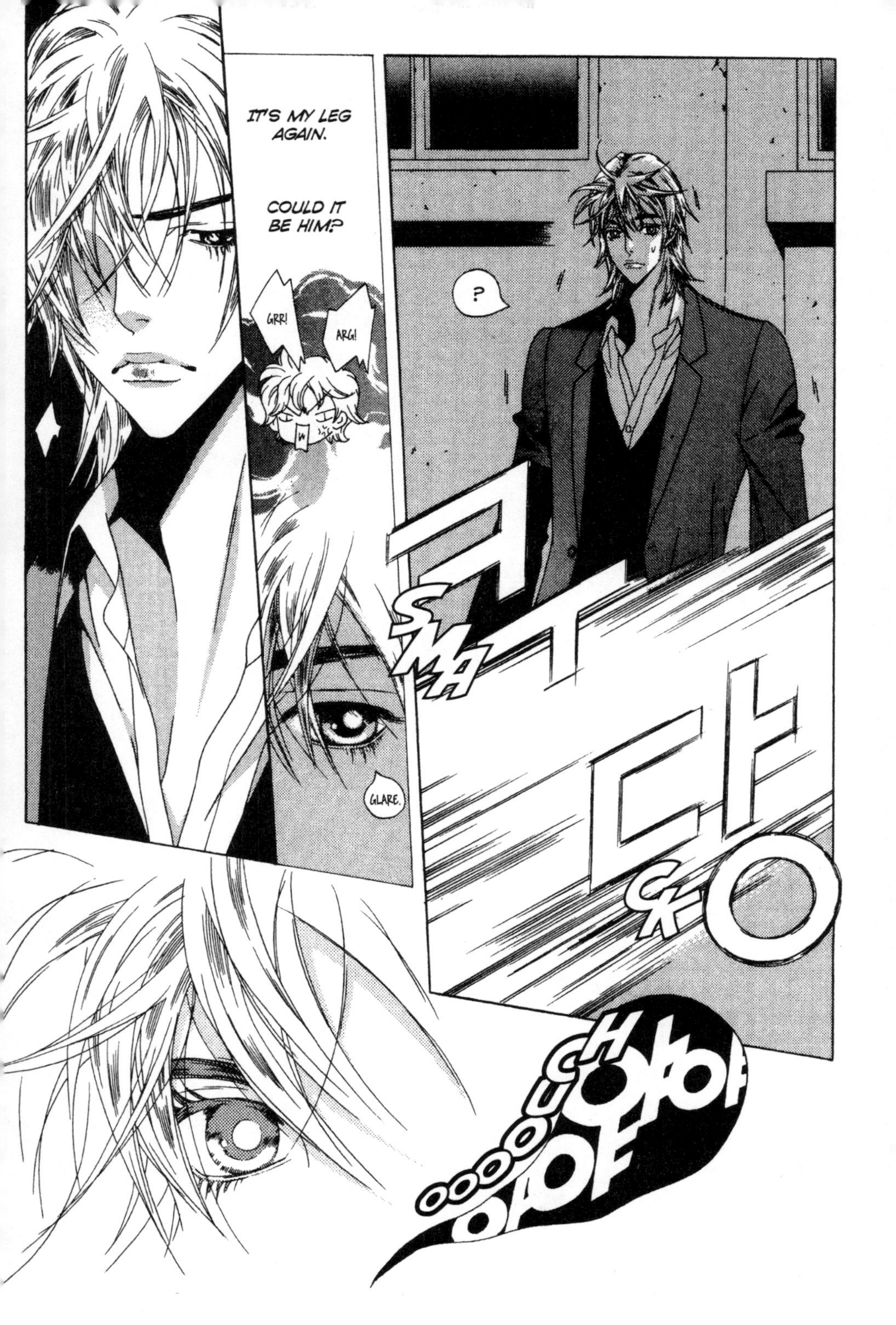
IT'S MY LEG AGAIN.
COULD IT BE HIM?
GRR!
ARG!
GLARE.
?
SMACK
OOOOOUCH

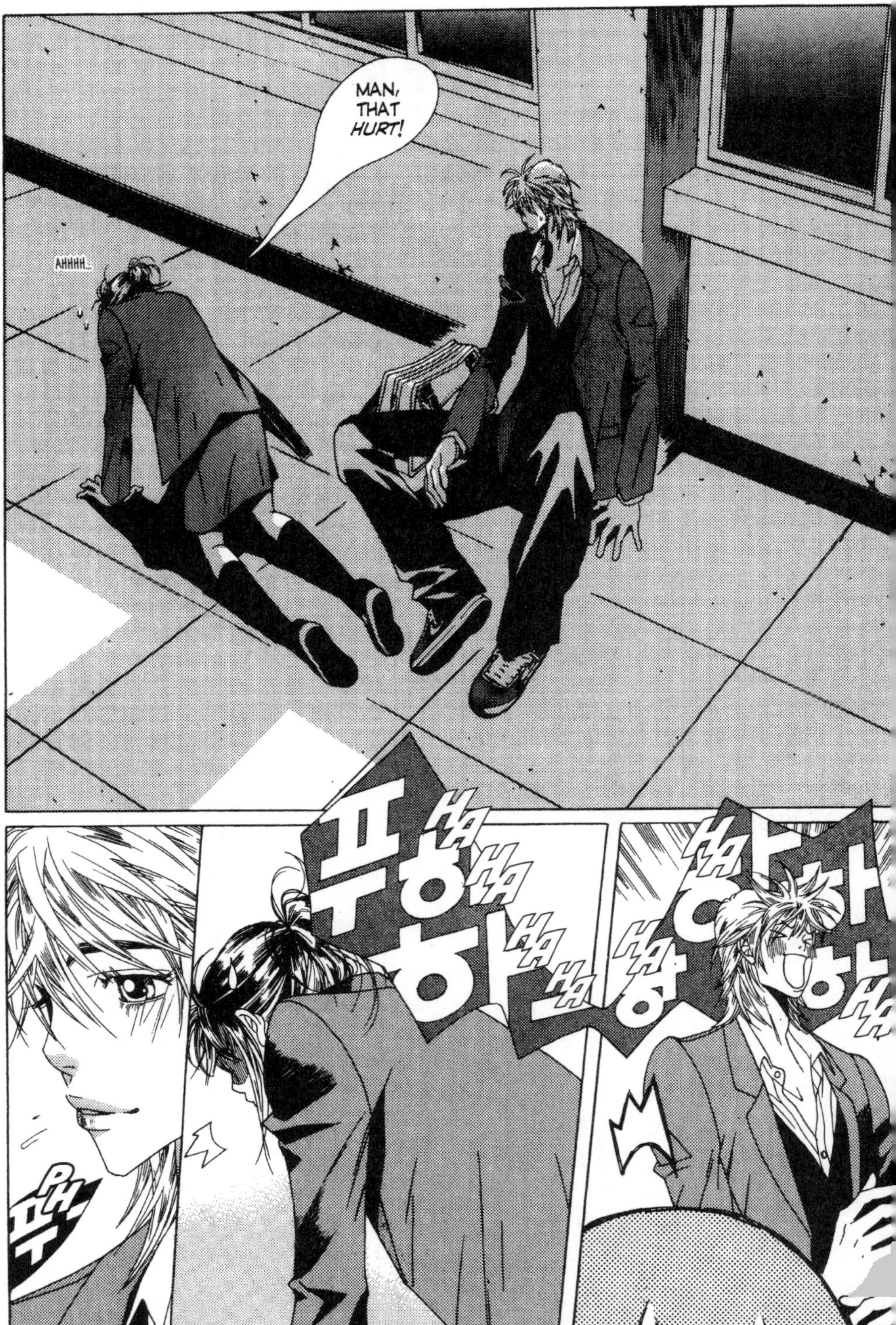
AHHHH...
MAN, THAT HURT!
PH
푸
푸하하
HA HA HA HA HA
HA HA
HA

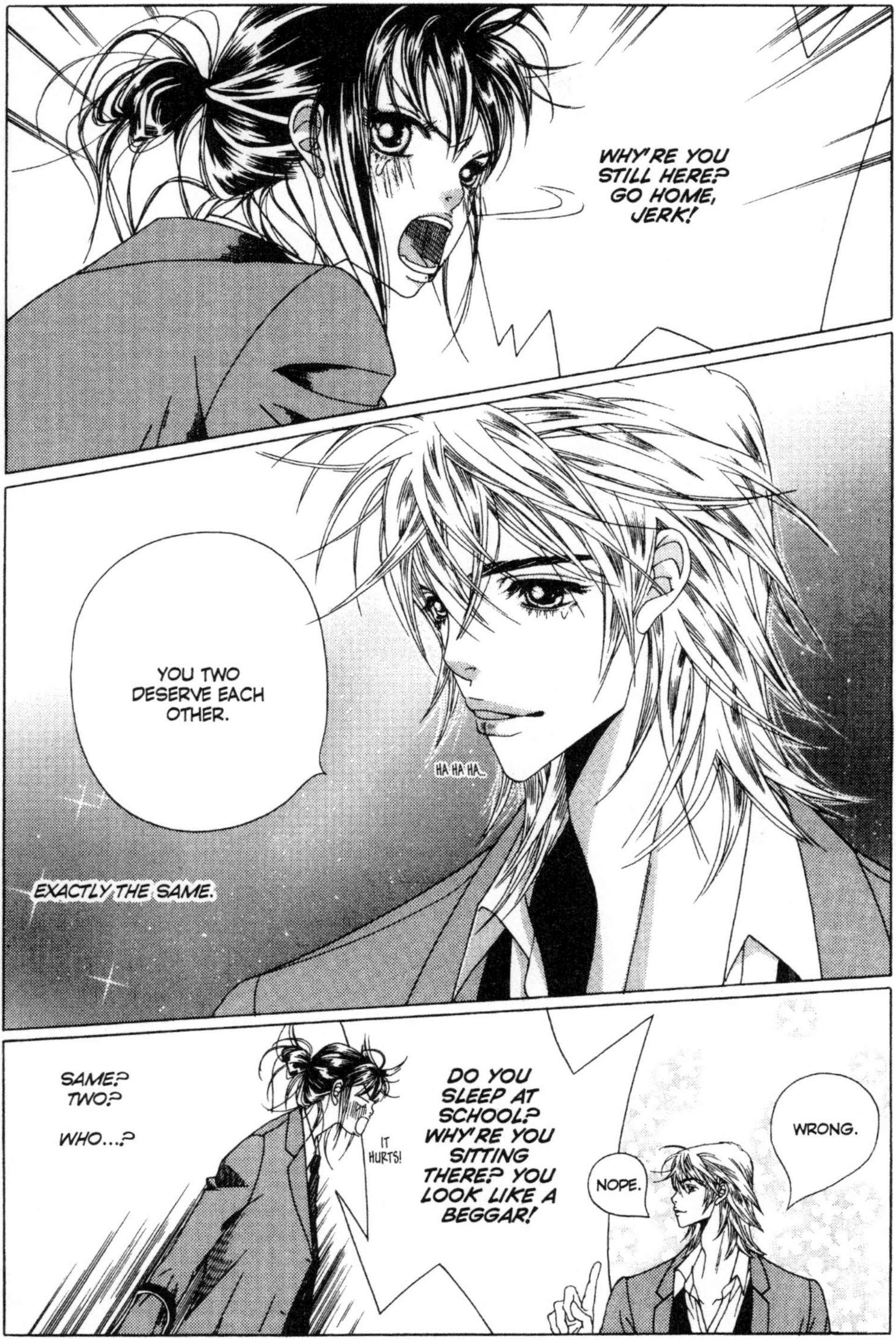
WHY'RE YOU STILL HERE? GO HOME, JERK!
YOU TWO DESERVE EACH OTHER.
HA HA HA...
EXACTLY THE SAME.
WRONG.
NOPE.
DO YOU SLEEP AT SCHOOL? WHY'RE YOU SITTING THERE? YOU LOOK LIKE A BEGGAR!
IT HURTS!
SAME? TWO?
WHO...?

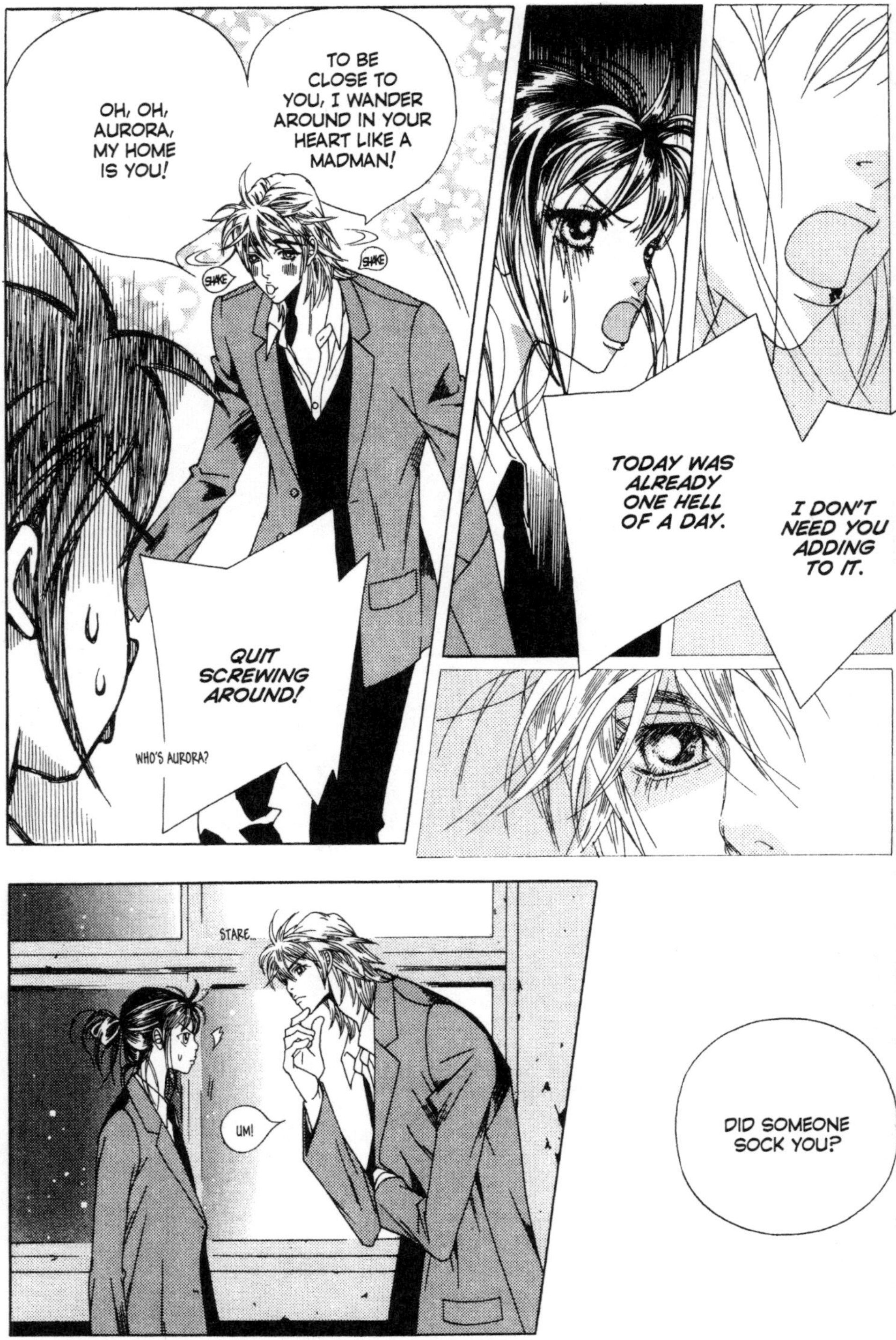
OH, OH, AURORA, MY HOME IS YOU!
TO BE CLOSE TO YOU, I WANDER AROUND IN YOUR HEART LIKE A MADMAN!
SHAKE
SHAKE
QUIT SCREWING AROUND!
WHO'S AURORA?
TODAY WAS ALREADY ONE HELL OF A DAY.
I DON'T NEED YOU ADDING TO IT.
STARE...
UM!
DID SOMEONE SOCK YOU?

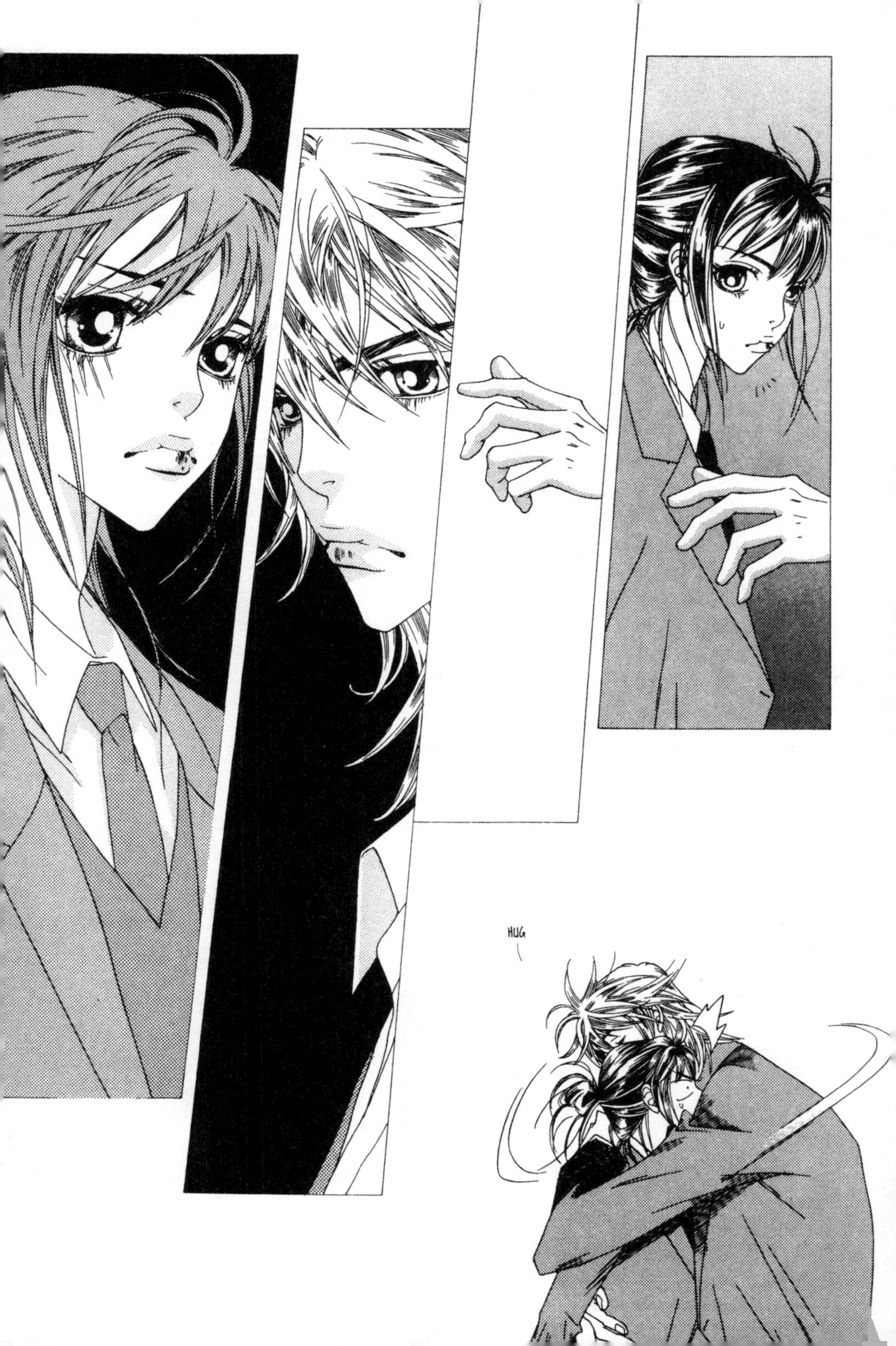
HUG

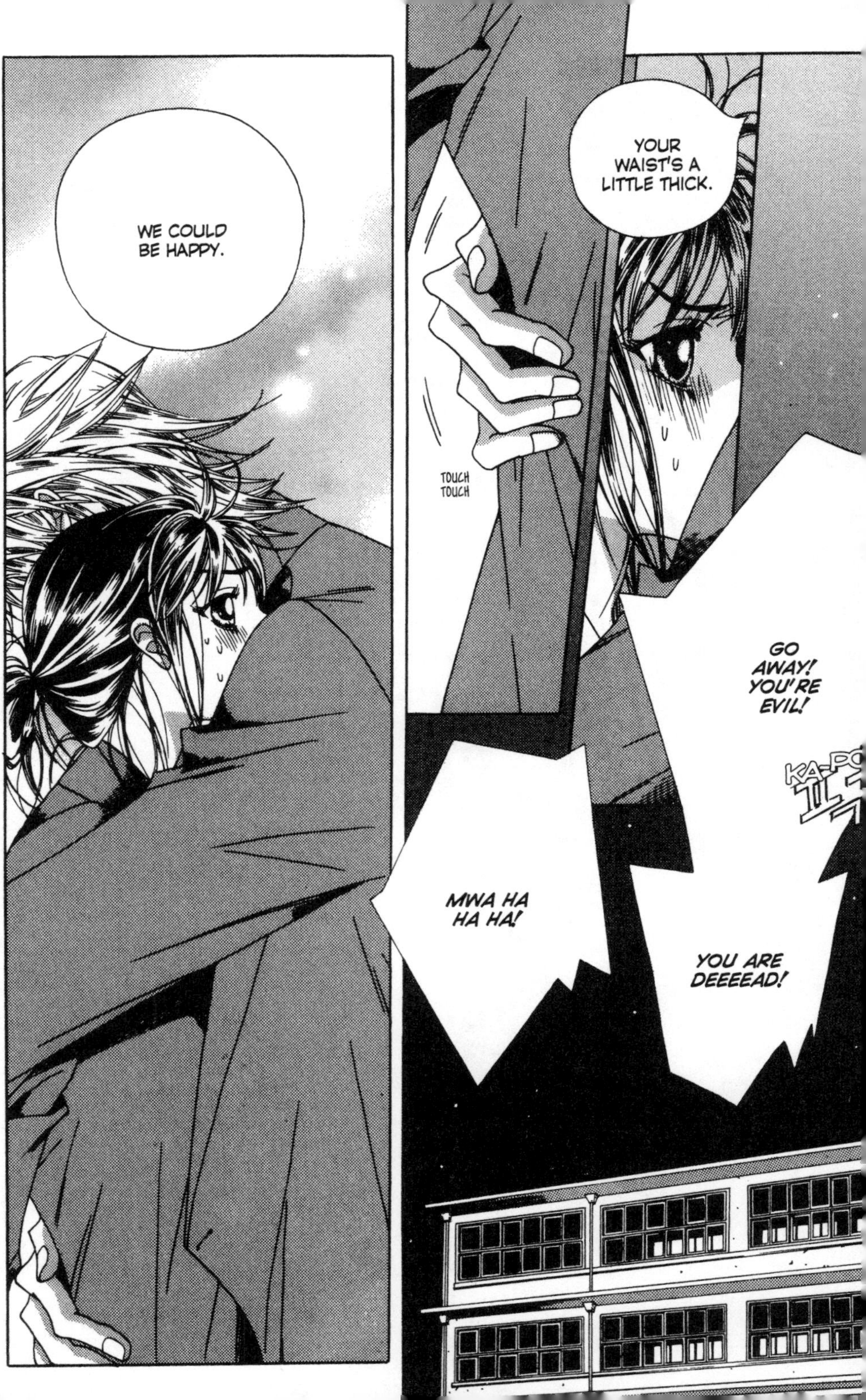
WE COULD BE HAPPY.
YOUR WAIST'S A LITTLE THICK.
TOUCH TOUCH
GO AWAY! YOU'RE EVIL!
MWA HA HA HA!
YOU ARE DEEEEAD!

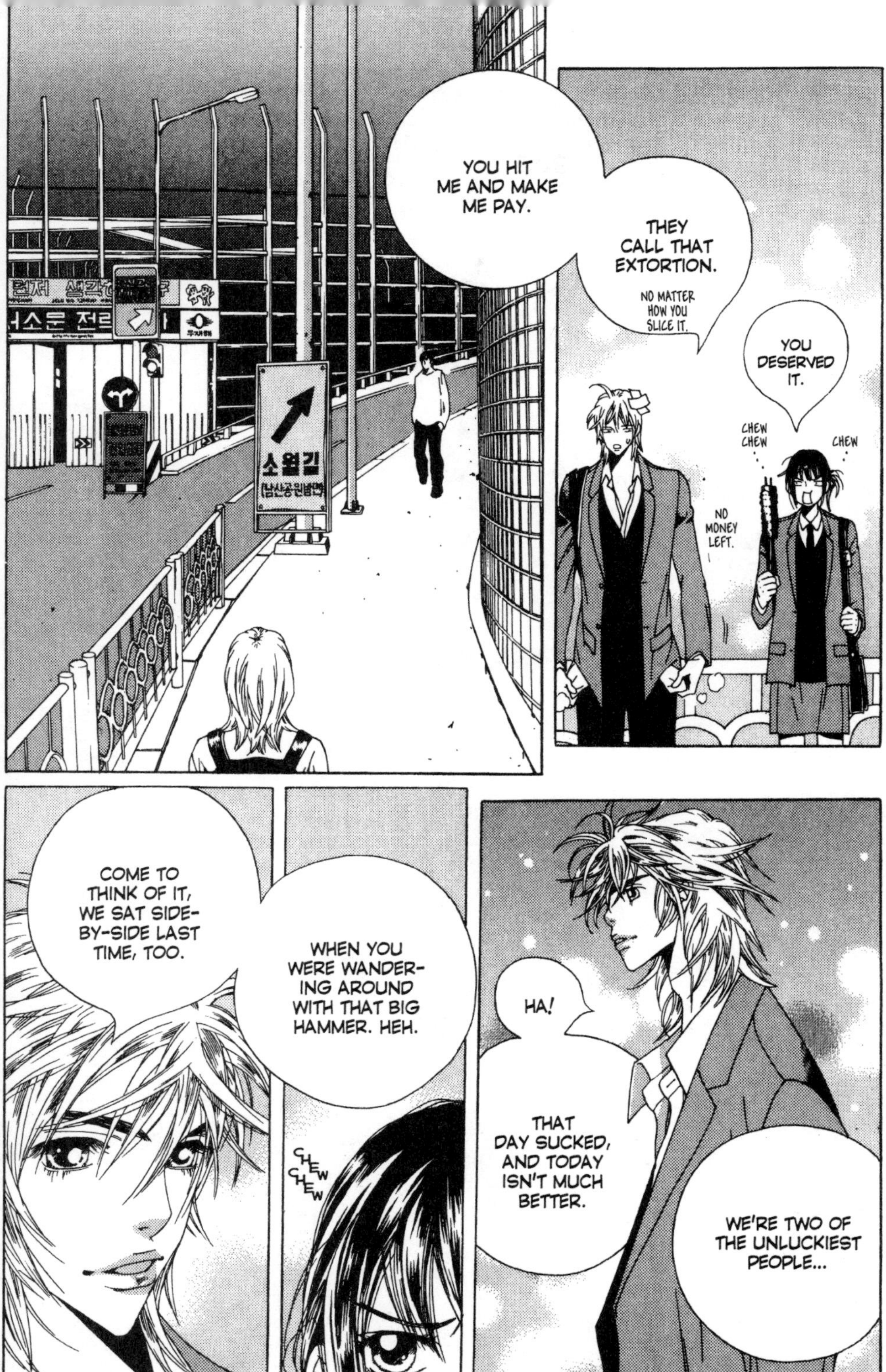
YOU HIT ME AND MAKE ME PAY.
THEY CALL THAT EXTORTION.
NO MATTER HOW YOU SLICE IT.
YOU DESERVED IT.
CHEW CHEW
CHEW
NO MONEY LEFT.
COME TO THINK OF IT, WE SAT SIDE-BY-SIDE LAST TIME, TOO.
WHEN YOU WERE WANDER-ING AROUND WITH THAT BIG HAMMER. HEH.
CHEW CHEW
HA!
THAT DAY SUCKED, AND TODAY ISN'T MUCH BETTER.
WE'RE TWO OF THE UNLUCKIEST PEOPLE...

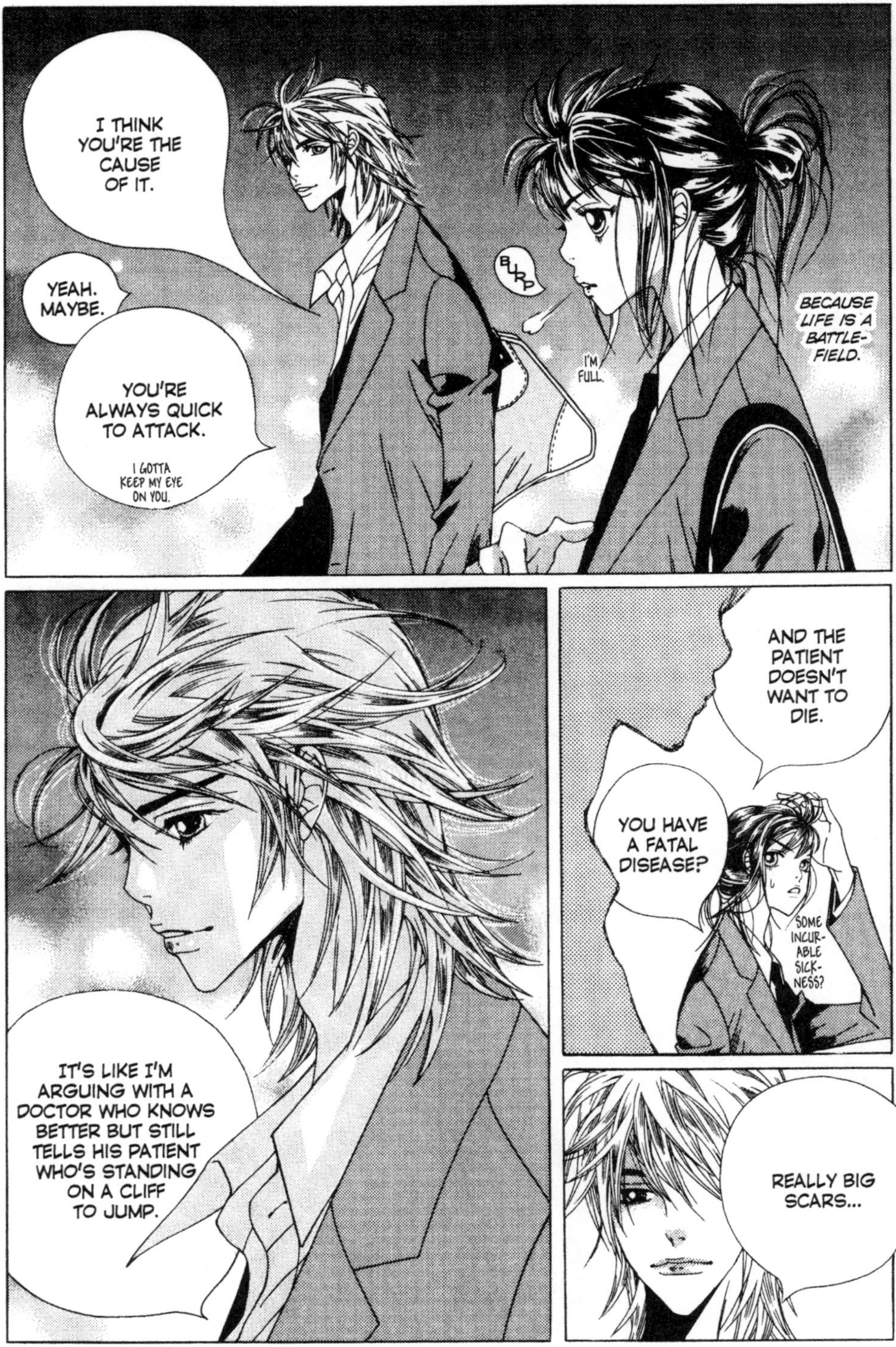
I THINK YOU'RE THE CAUSE OF IT.
YEAH. MAYBE.
YOU'RE ALWAYS QUICK TO ATTACK.
I GOTTA KEEP MY EYE ON YOU.
BURP
I'M FULL.
BECAUSE LIFE IS A BATTLE-FIELD.
IT'S LIKE I'M ARGUING WITH A DOCTOR WHO KNOWS BETTER BUT STILL TELLS HIS PATIENT WHO'S STANDING ON A CLIFF TO JUMP.
AND THE PATIENT DOESN'T WANT TO DIE.
YOU HAVE A FATAL DISEASE?
SOME INCUR-ABLE SICK-NESS?
REALLY BIG SCARS...

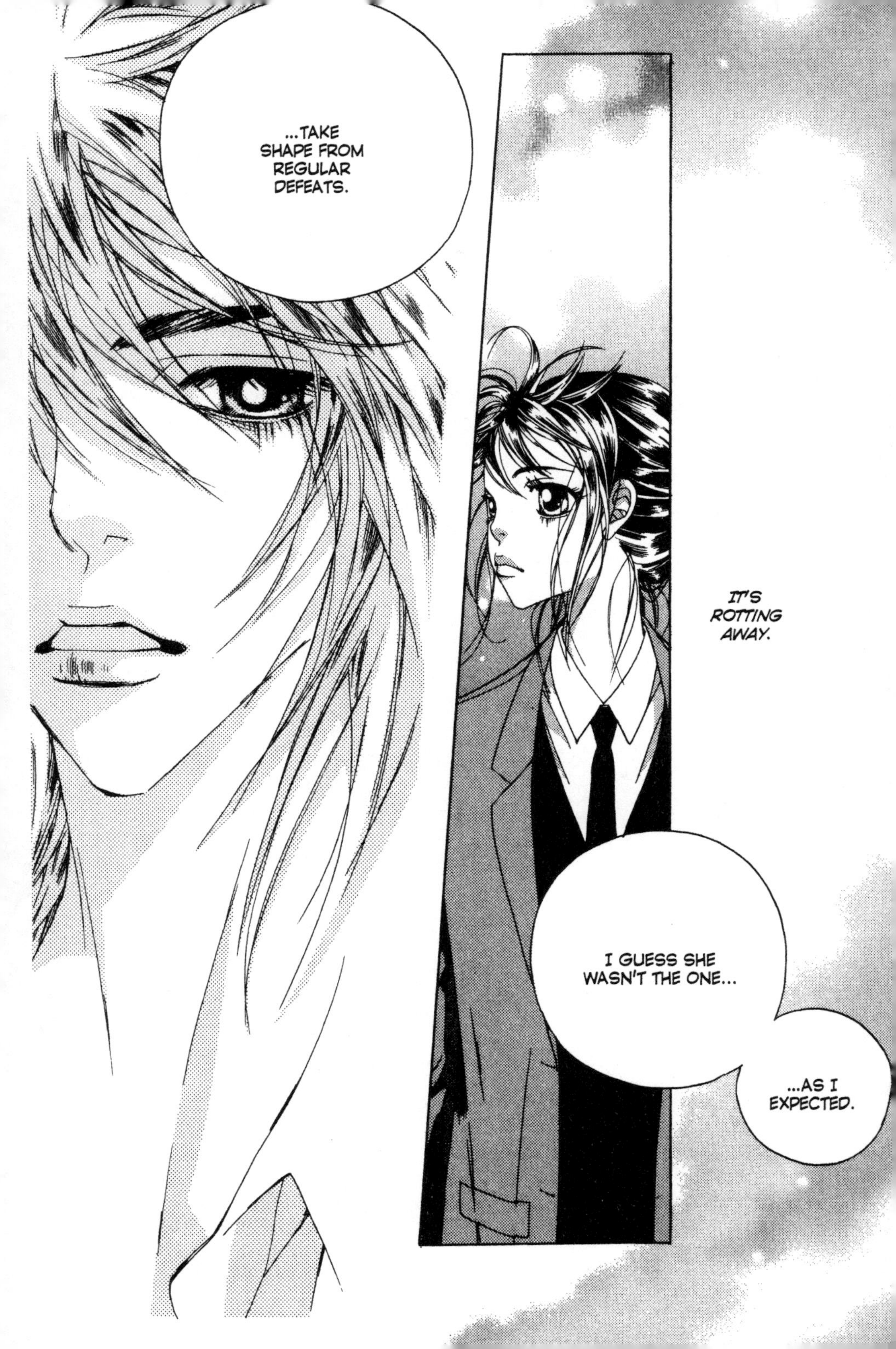
...TAKE SHAPE FROM REGULAR DEFEATS.
IT'S ROTTING AWAY.
I GUESS SHE WASN'T THE ONE...
...AS I EXPECTED.

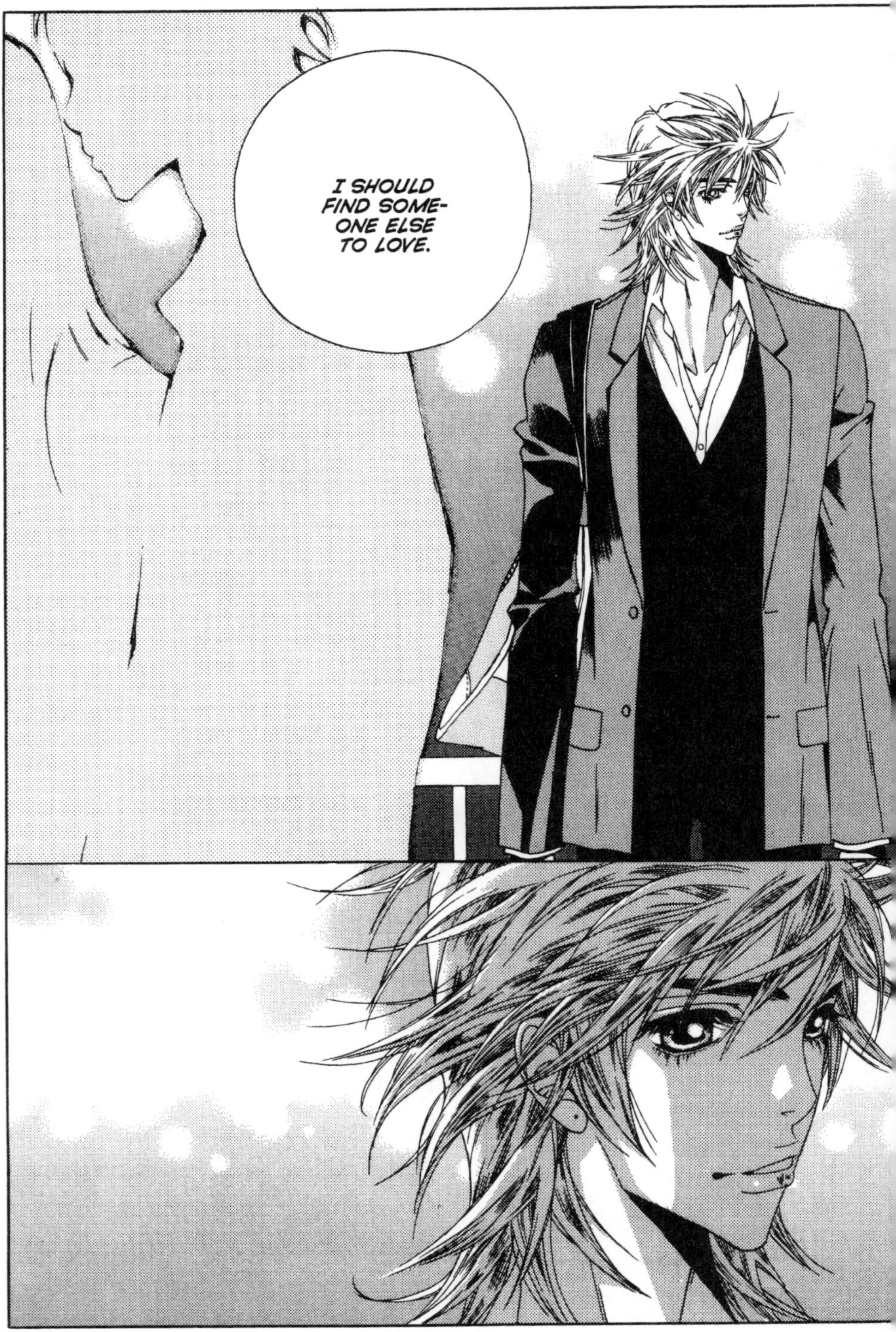
I SHOULD FIND SOME-ONE ELSE TO LOVE.

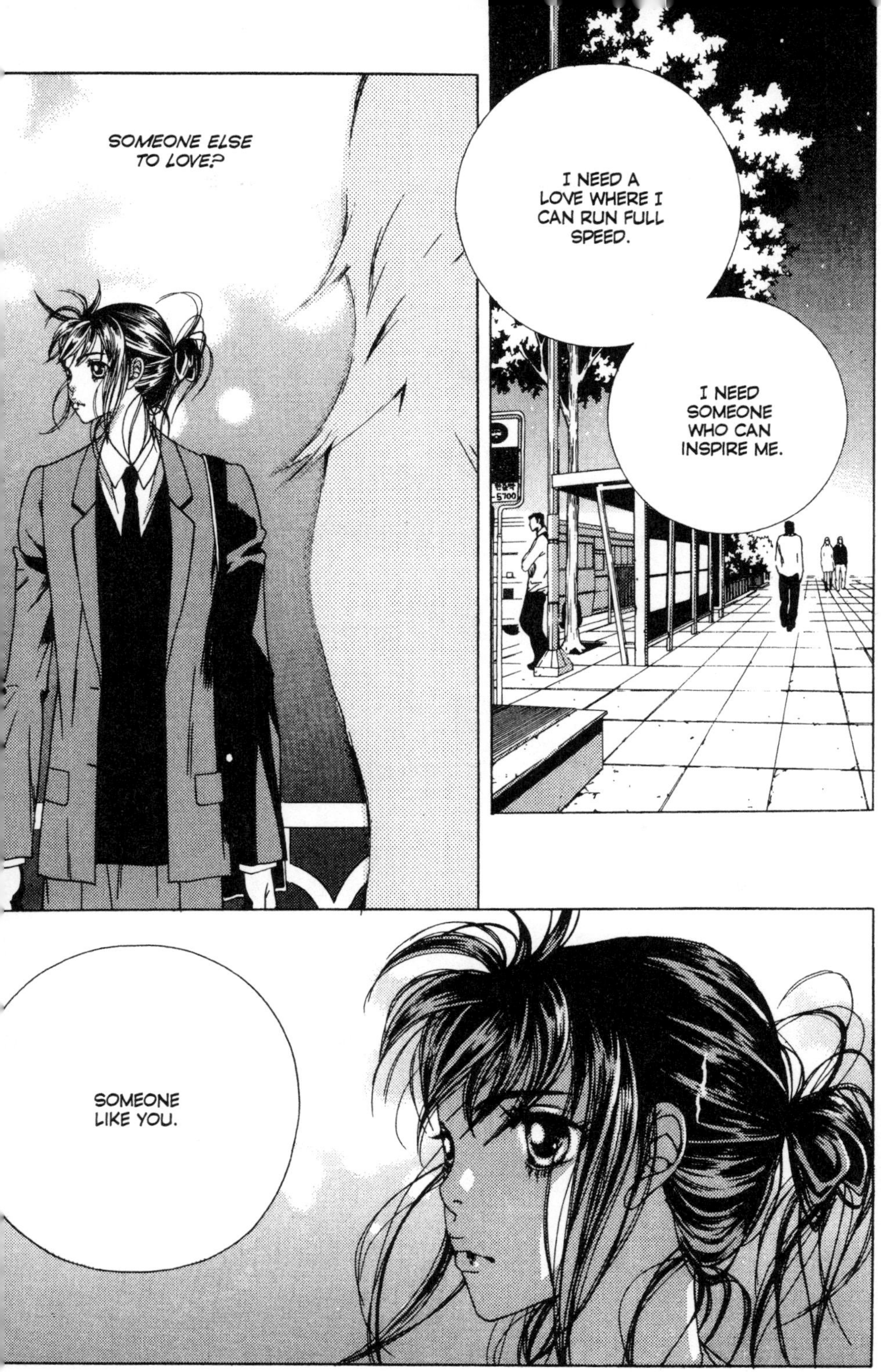
SOMEONE ELSE TO LOVE?
I NEED A LOVE WHERE I CAN RUN FULL SPEED.
I NEED SOMEONE WHO CAN INSPIRE ME.
SOMEONE LIKE YOU.

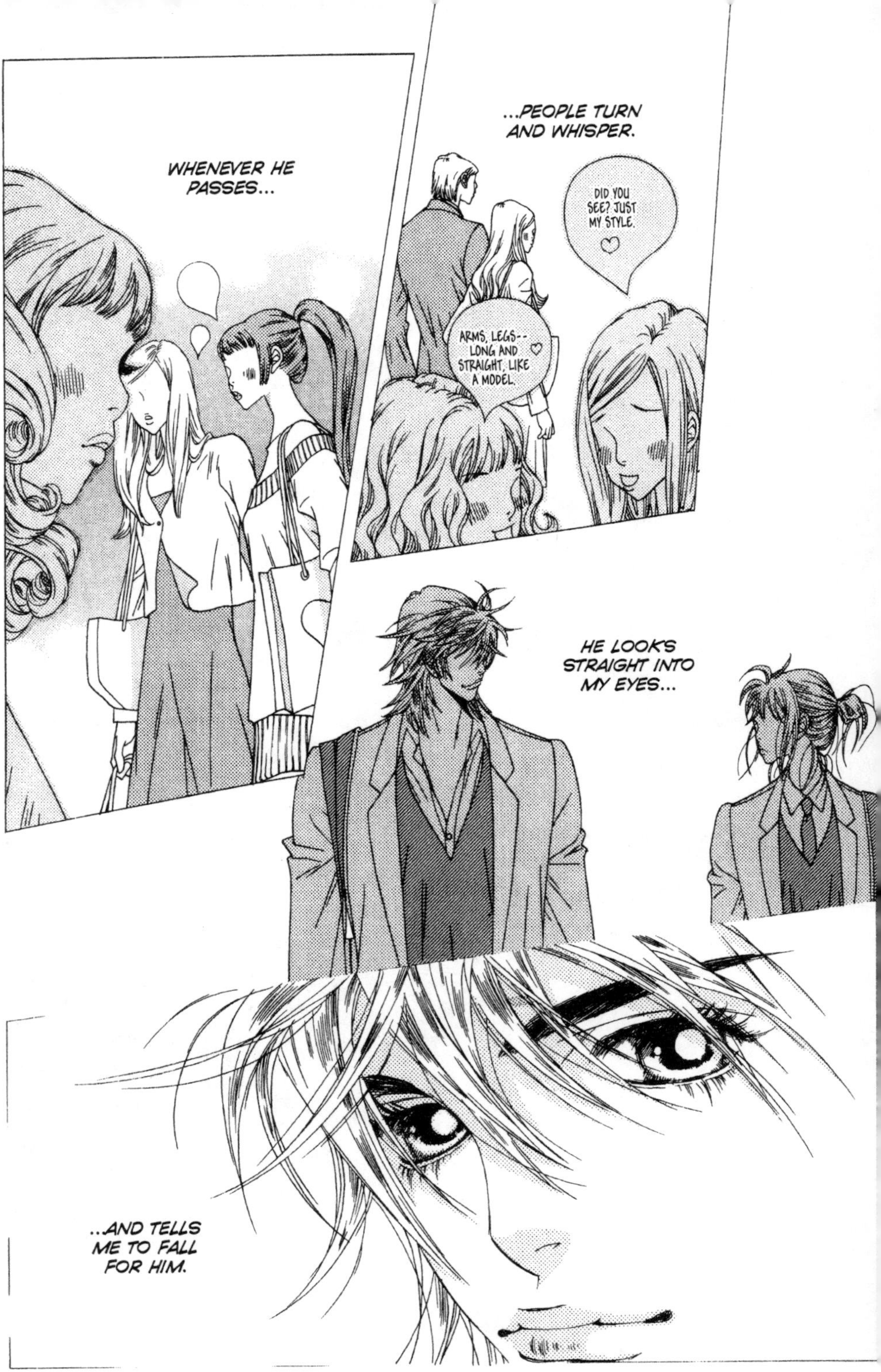
WHENEVER HE PASSES...
...PEOPLE TURN AND WHISPER.
DID YOU SEE? JUST MY STYLE.
ARMS, LEGS-- LONG AND STRAIGHT, LIKE A MODEL.
HE LOOKS STRAIGHT INTO MY EYES...
...AND TELLS ME TO FALL FOR HIM.

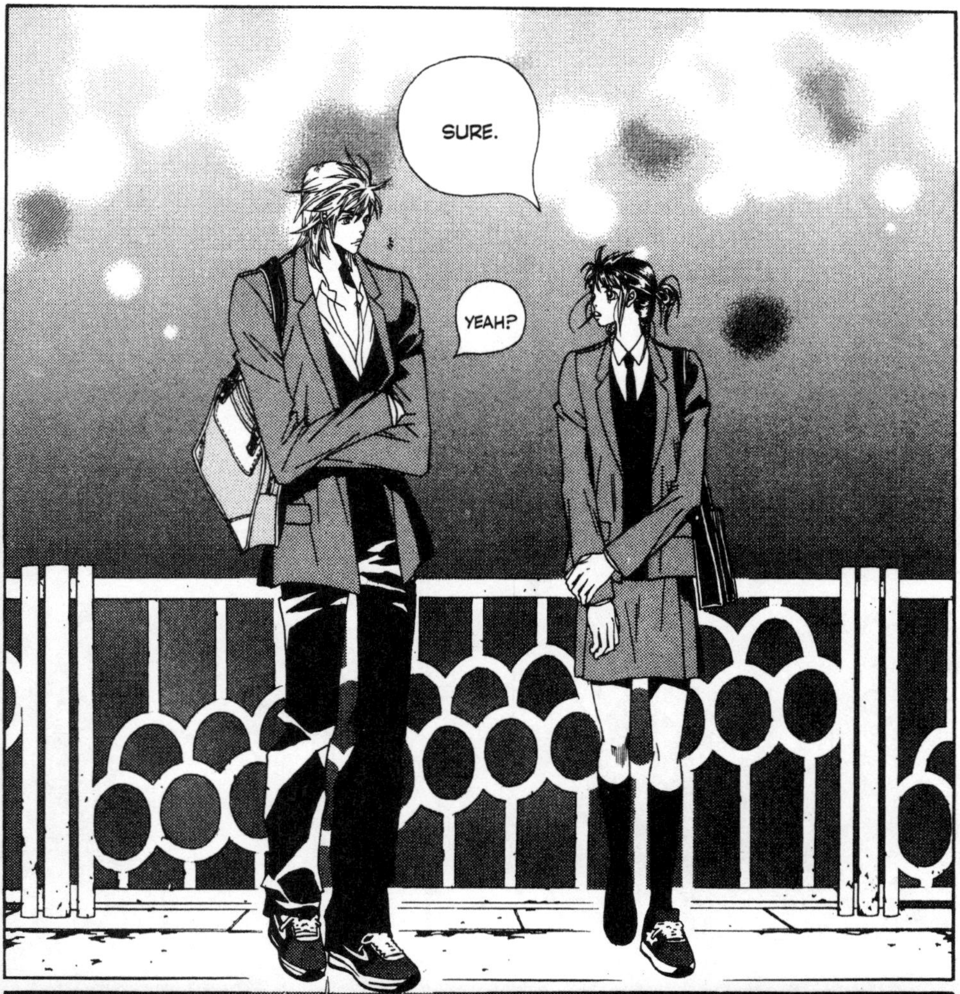
SURE.
YEAH?
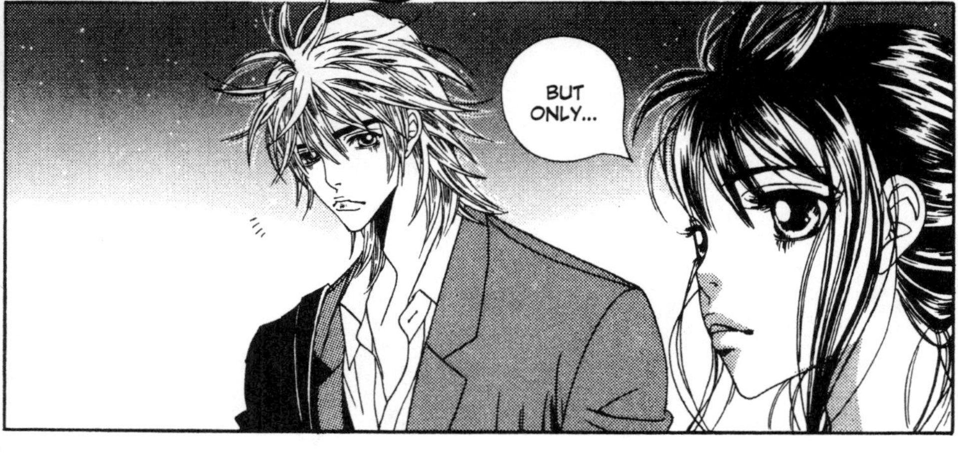
BUT ONLY...

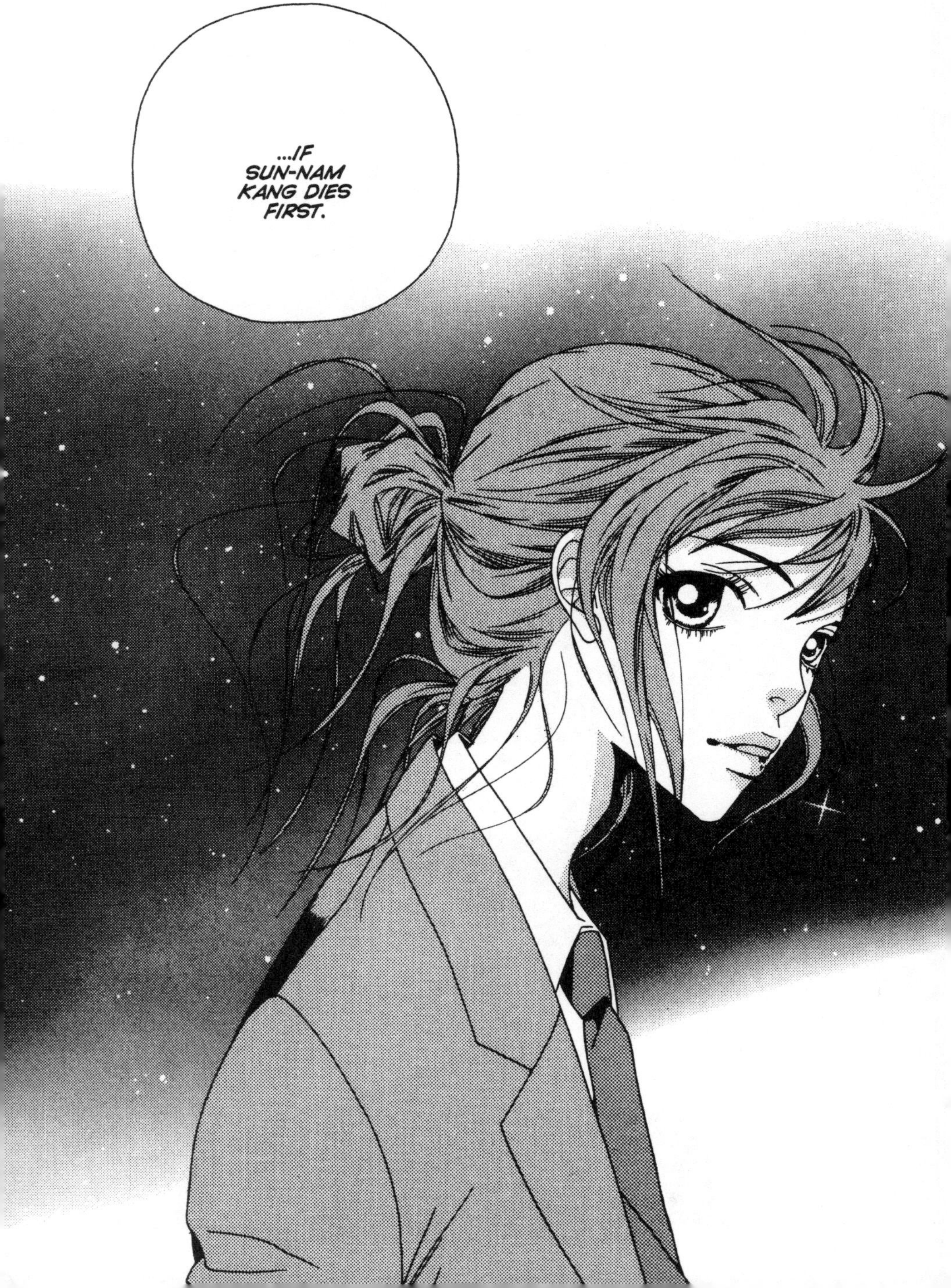
...IF SUN-NAM KANG DIES FIRST.

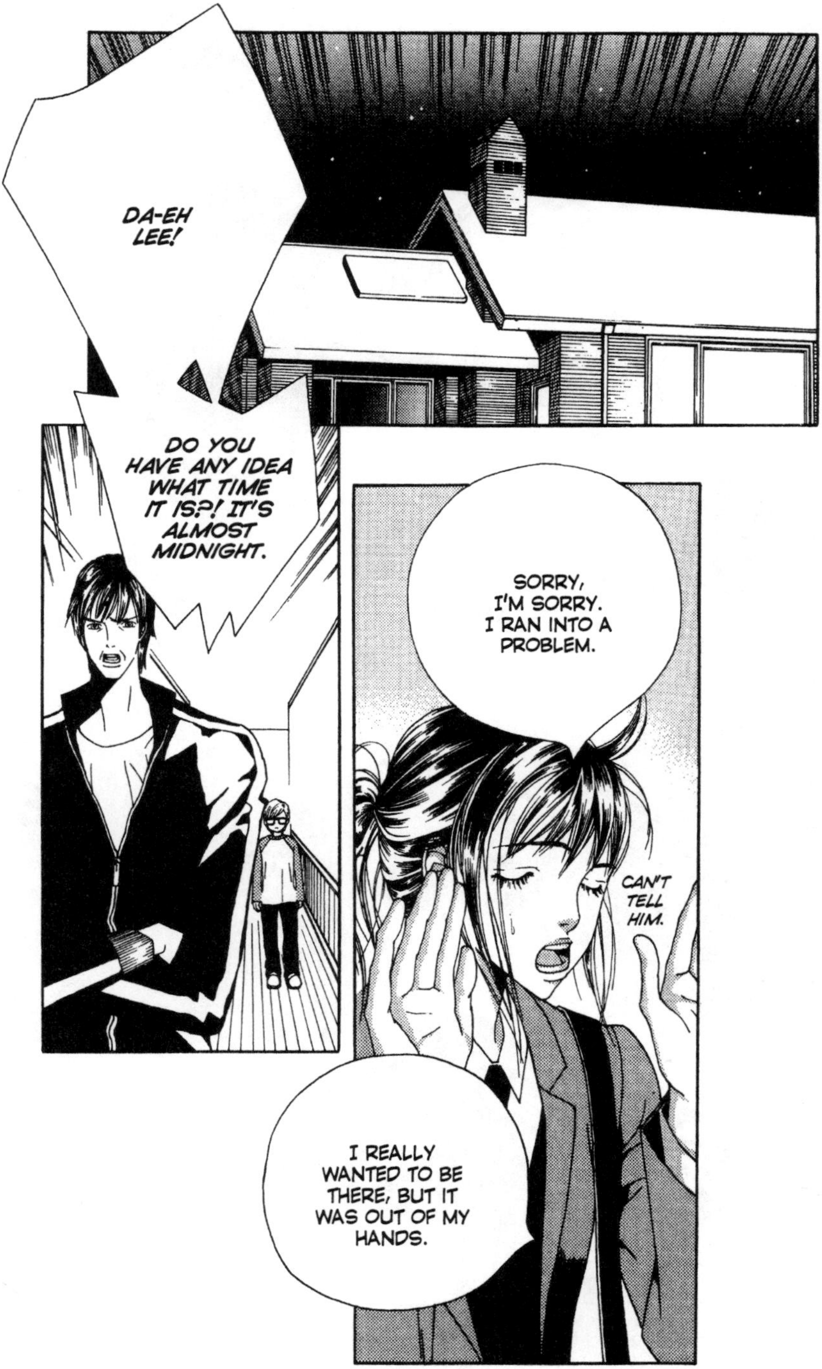
DA-EH LEE!
DO YOU HAVE ANY IDEA WHAT TIME IT IS?! IT'S ALMOST MIDNIGHT.
SORRY, I'M SORRY. I RAN INTO A PROBLEM.
CAN'T TELL HIM.
I REALLY WANTED TO BE THERE, BUT IT WAS OUT OF MY HANDS.

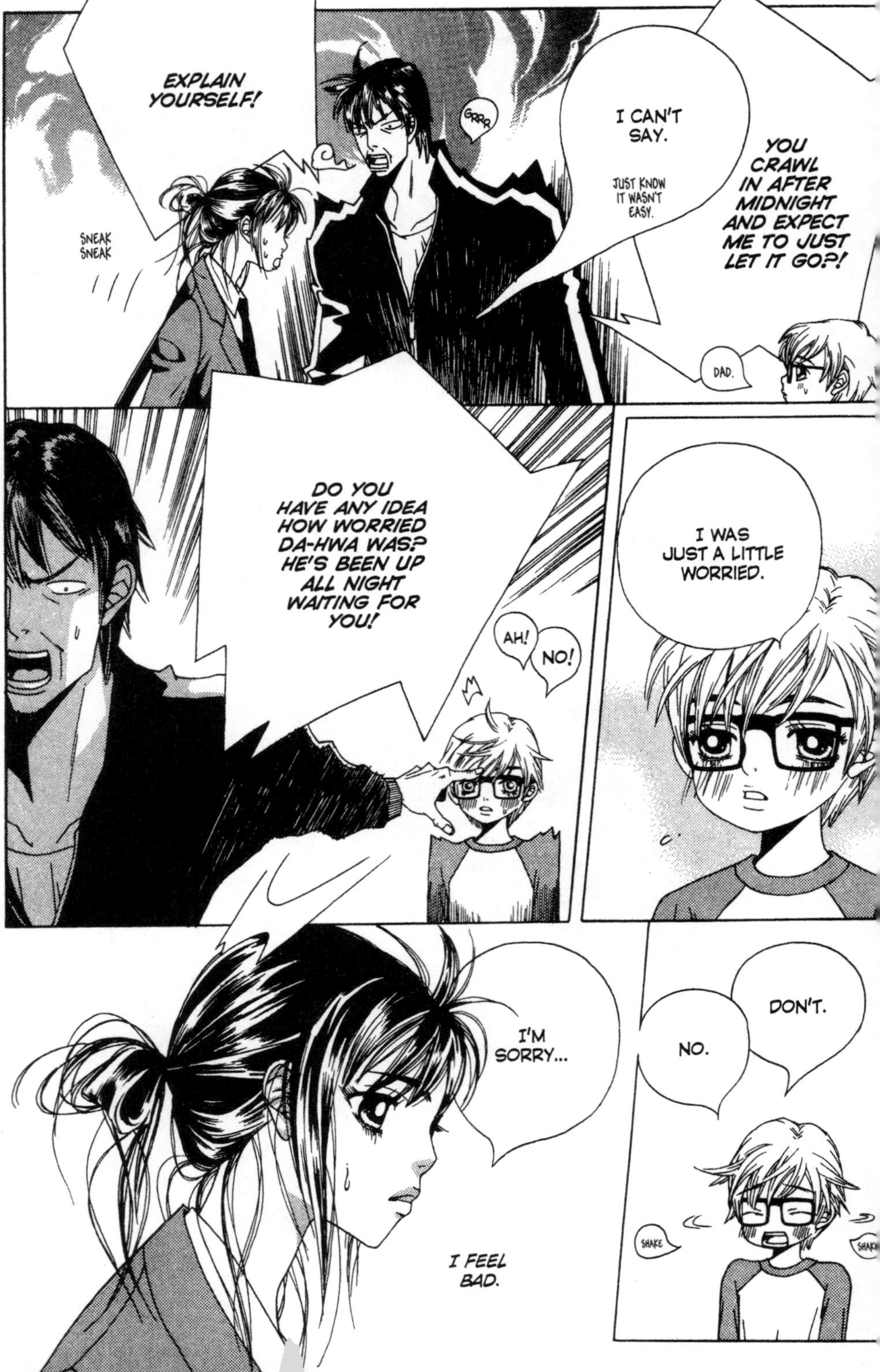

EXPLAIN YOURSELF!
GRRR
SNEAK SNEAK
I CAN'T SAY.
JUST KNOW IT WASN'T EASY.
YOU CRAWL IN AFTER MIDNIGHT AND EXPECT ME TO JUST LET IT GO?!
DAD.
DO YOU HAVE ANY IDEA HOW WORRIED DA-HWA WAS? HE'S BEEN UP ALL NIGHT WAITING FOR YOU!
AH!
NO!
I WAS JUST A LITTLE WORRIED.
I'M SORRY...
I FEEL BAD.
NO.
DON'T.
SHAKE

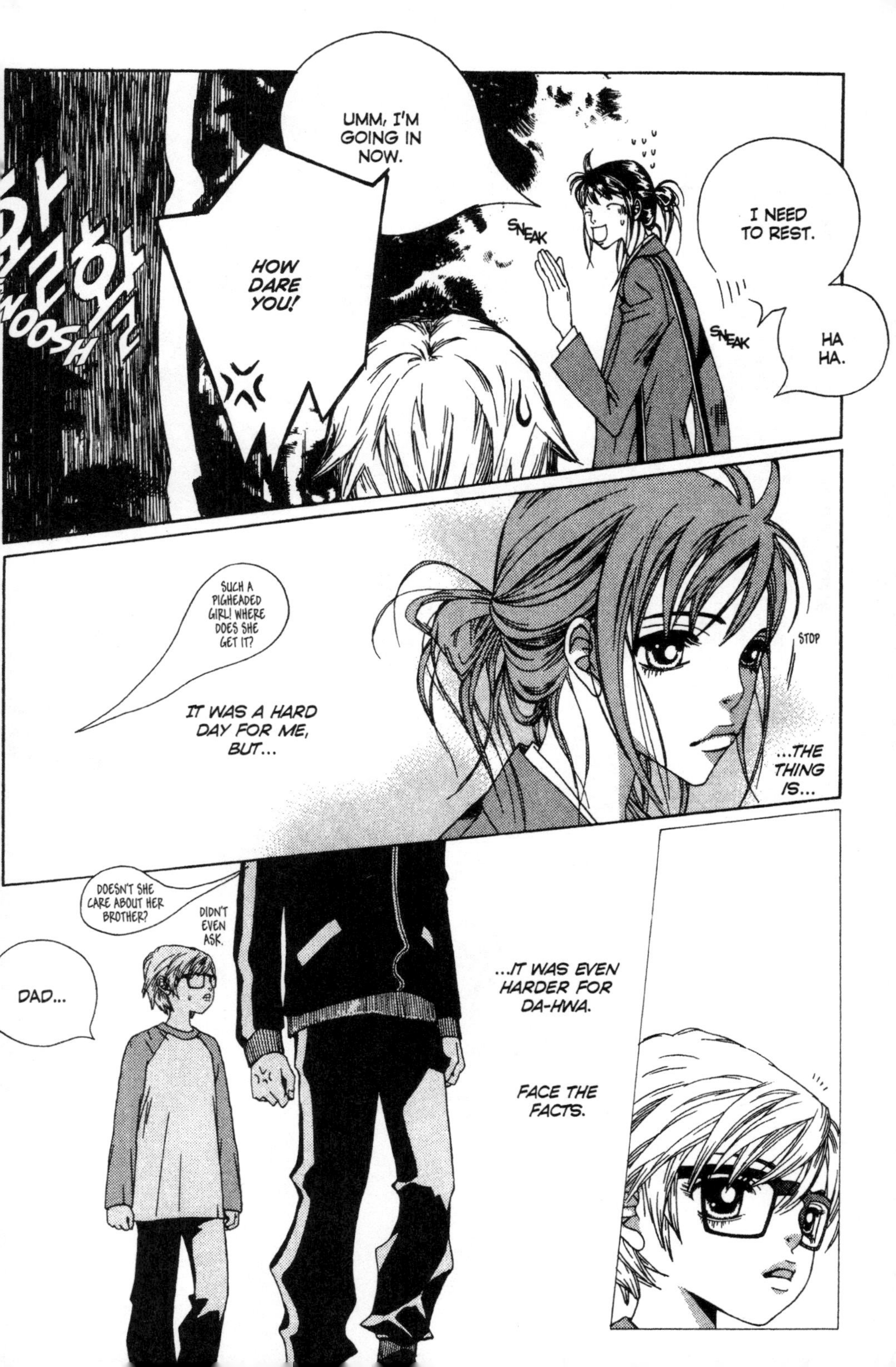
UMM, I'M GOING IN NOW.
HOW DARE YOU!
SNEAK
I NEED TO REST.
SNEAK
HA HA.
SUCH A PIGHEADED GIRL! WHERE DOES SHE GET IT?
IT WAS A HARD DAY FOR ME, BUT...
STOP
...THE THING IS...
DOESN'T SHE CARE ABOUT HER BROTHER?
DIDN'T EVEN ASK.
DAD...
...IT WAS EVEN HARDER FOR DA-HWA.
FACE THE FACTS.

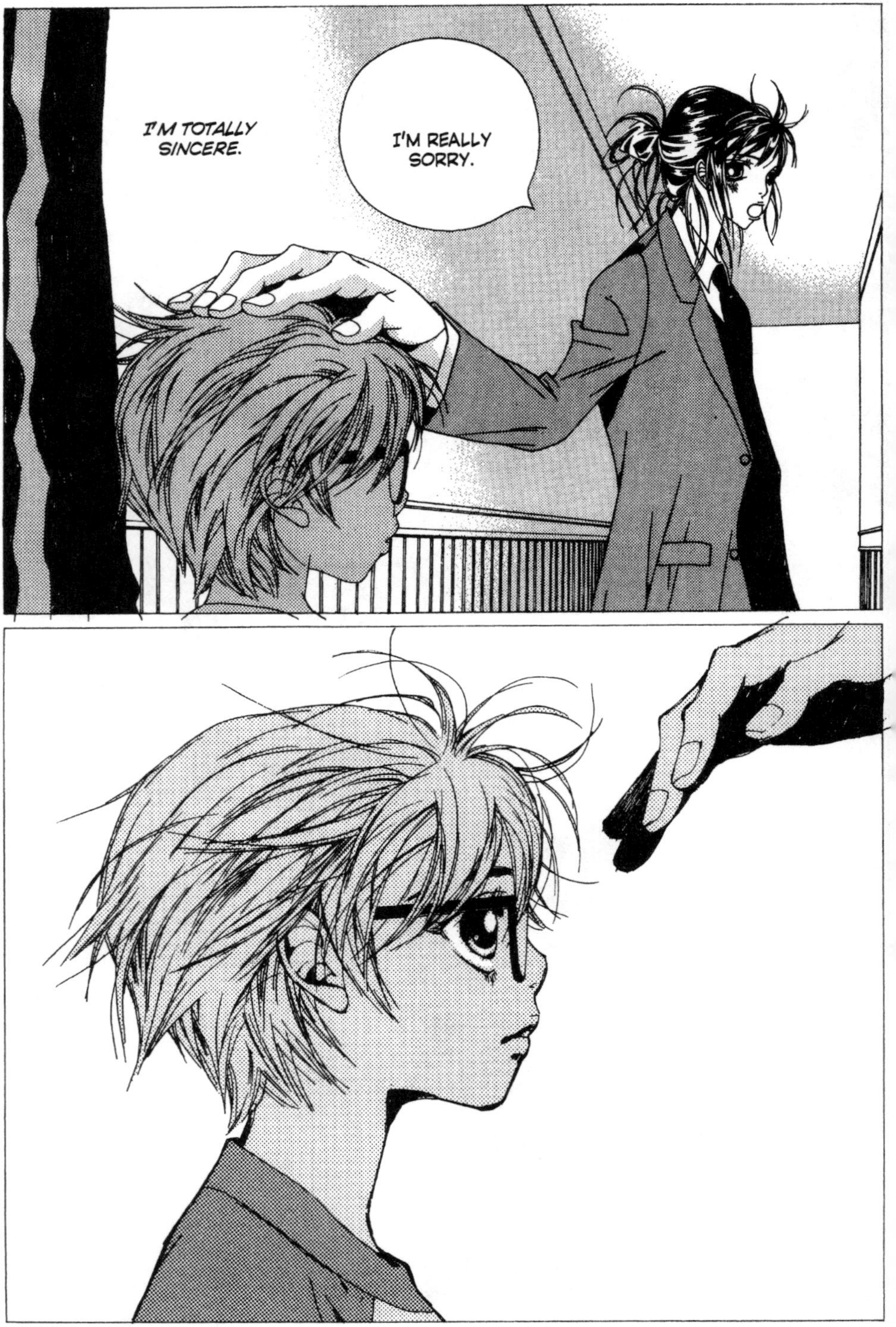
I'M TOTALLY SINCERE.
I'M REALLY SORRY.

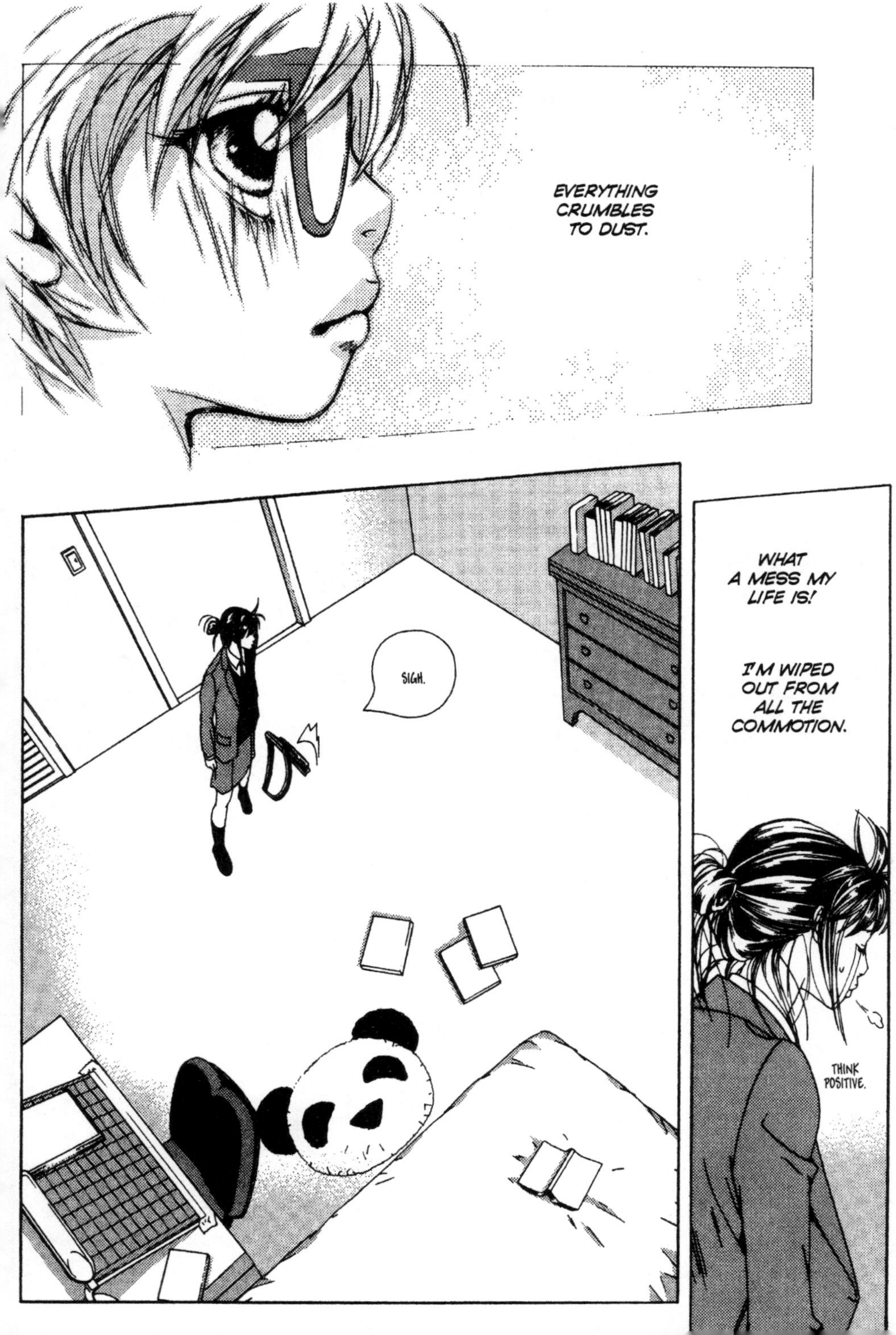
EVERYTHING CRUMBLES TO DUST.
SIGH.
WHAT A MESS MY LIFE IS!
I'M WIPED OUT FROM ALL THE COMMOTION.
THINK POSITIVE.

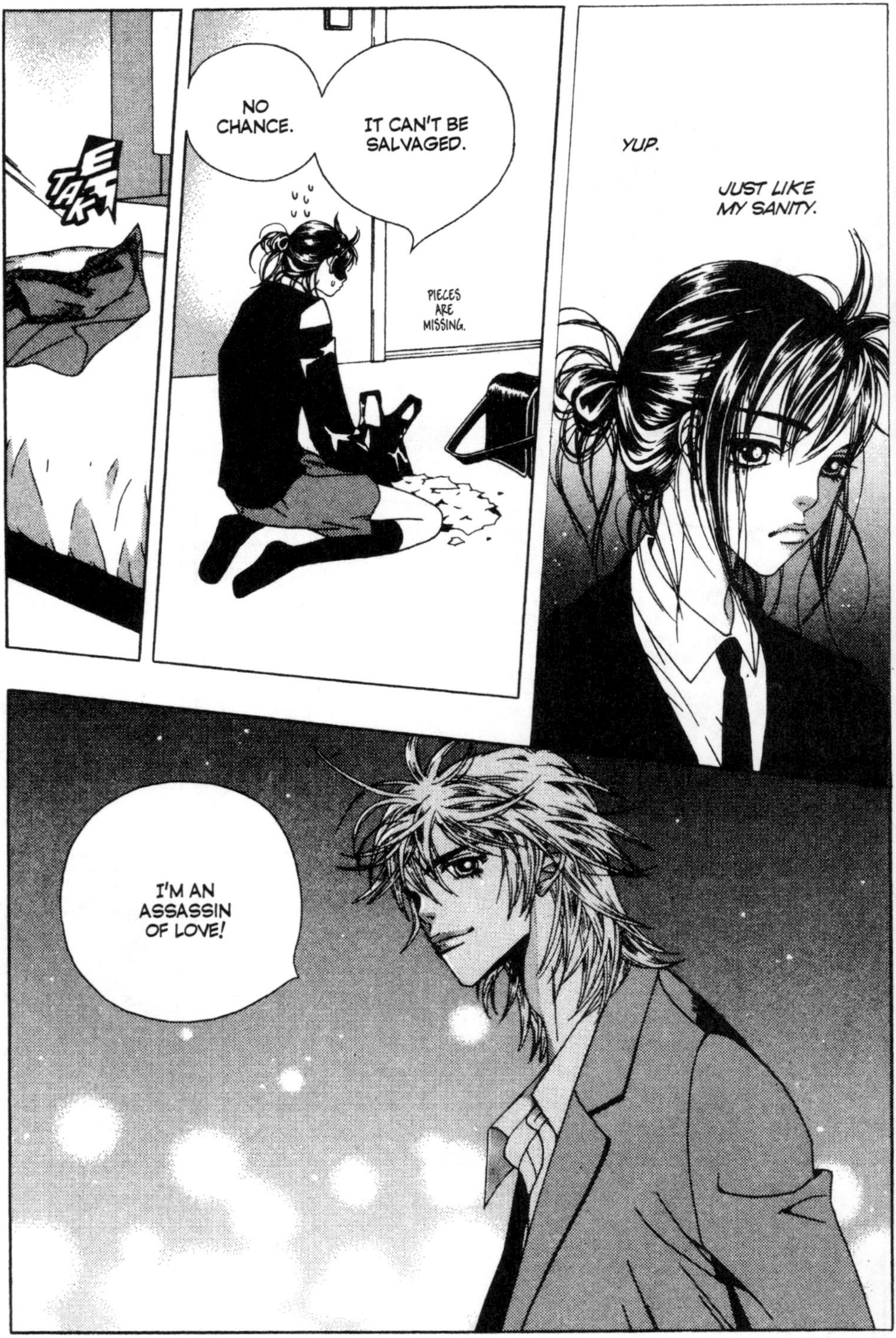
TAK
NO CHANCE.
IT CAN'T BE SALVAGED.
PIECES ARE MISSING.
YUP.
JUST LIKE MY SANITY.
I'M AN ASSASSIN OF LOVE!

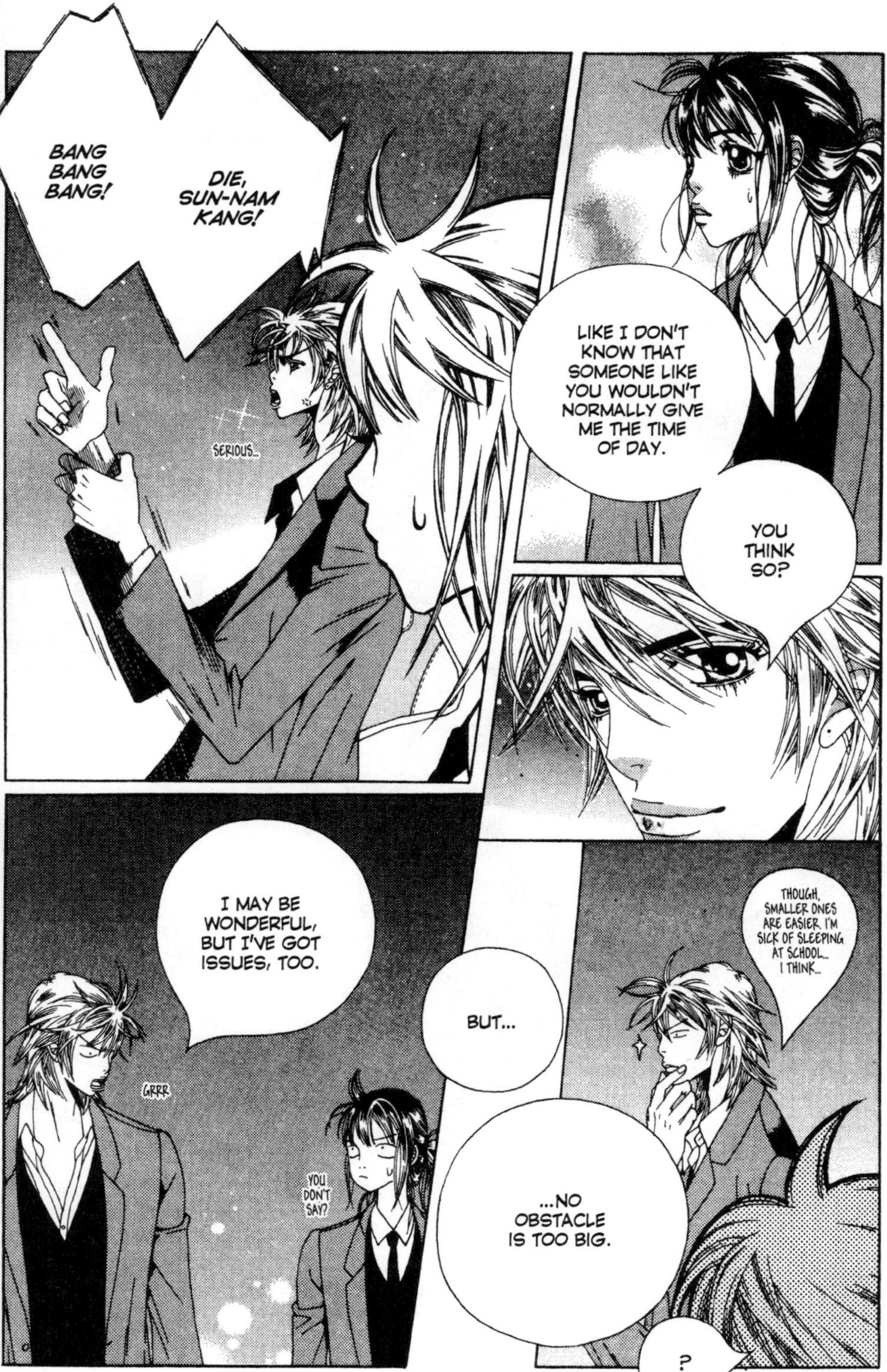
BANG BANG BANG!
DIE, SUN-NAM KANG!
SERIOUS...
LIKE I DON'T KNOW THAT SOMEONE LIKE YOU WOULDN'T NORMALLY GIVE ME THE TIME OF DAY.
YOU THINK SO?
I MAY BE WONDERFUL, BUT I'VE GOT ISSUES, TOO.
GRRR
YOU DON'T SAY?
BUT...
THOUGH, SMALLER ONES ARE EASIER. I'M SICK OF SLEEPING AT SCHOOL... I THINK...
...NO OBSTACLE IS TOO BIG.
?

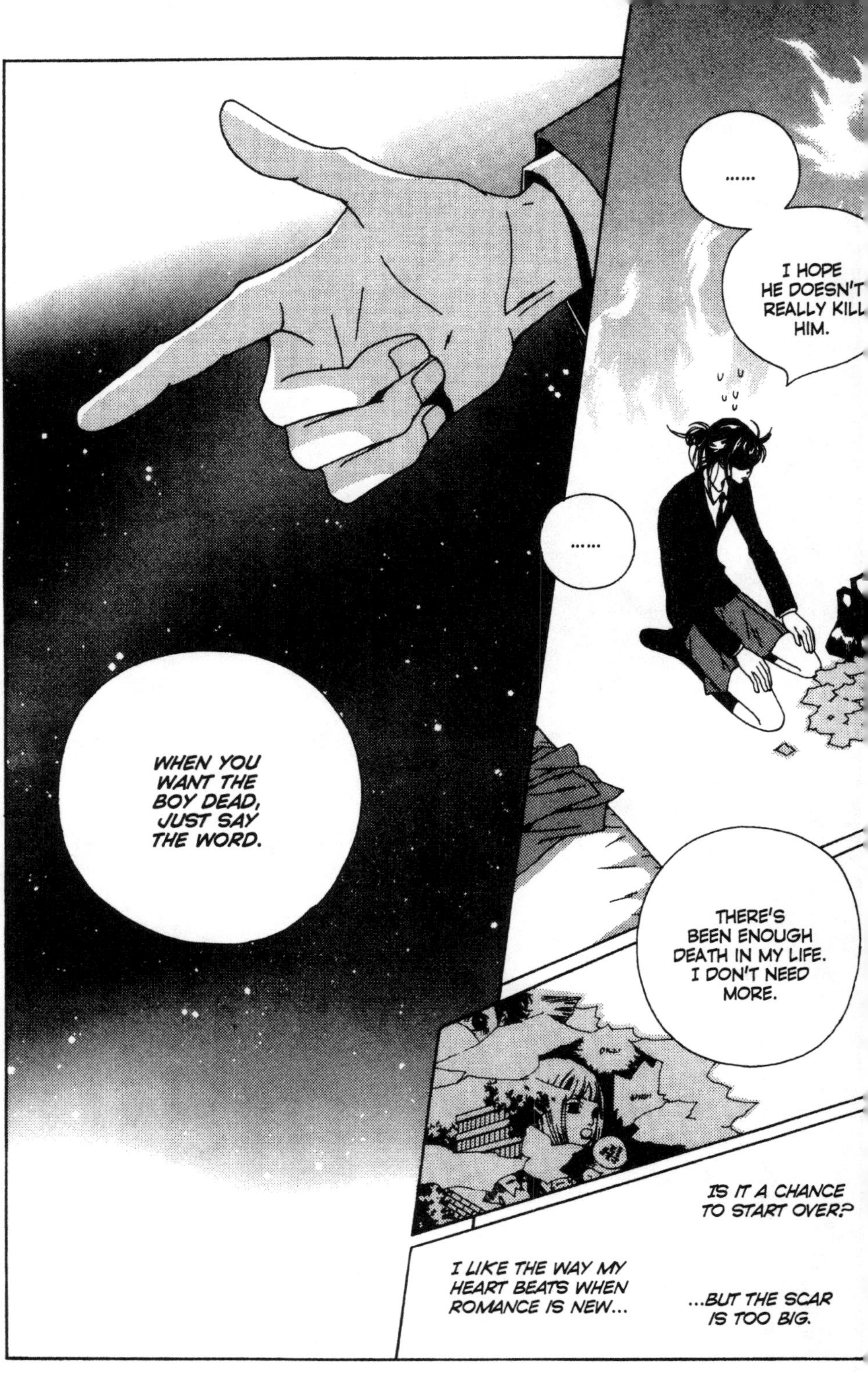
WHEN YOU WANT THE BOY DEAD, JUST SAY THE WORD.
......
I HOPE HE DOESN'T REALLY KILL HIM.
......
THERE'S BEEN ENOUGH DEATH IN MY LIFE. I DON'T NEED MORE.
IS IT A CHANCE TO START OVER?
I LIKE THE WAY MY HEART BEATS WHEN ROMANCE IS NEW...
...BUT THE SCAR IS TOO BIG.

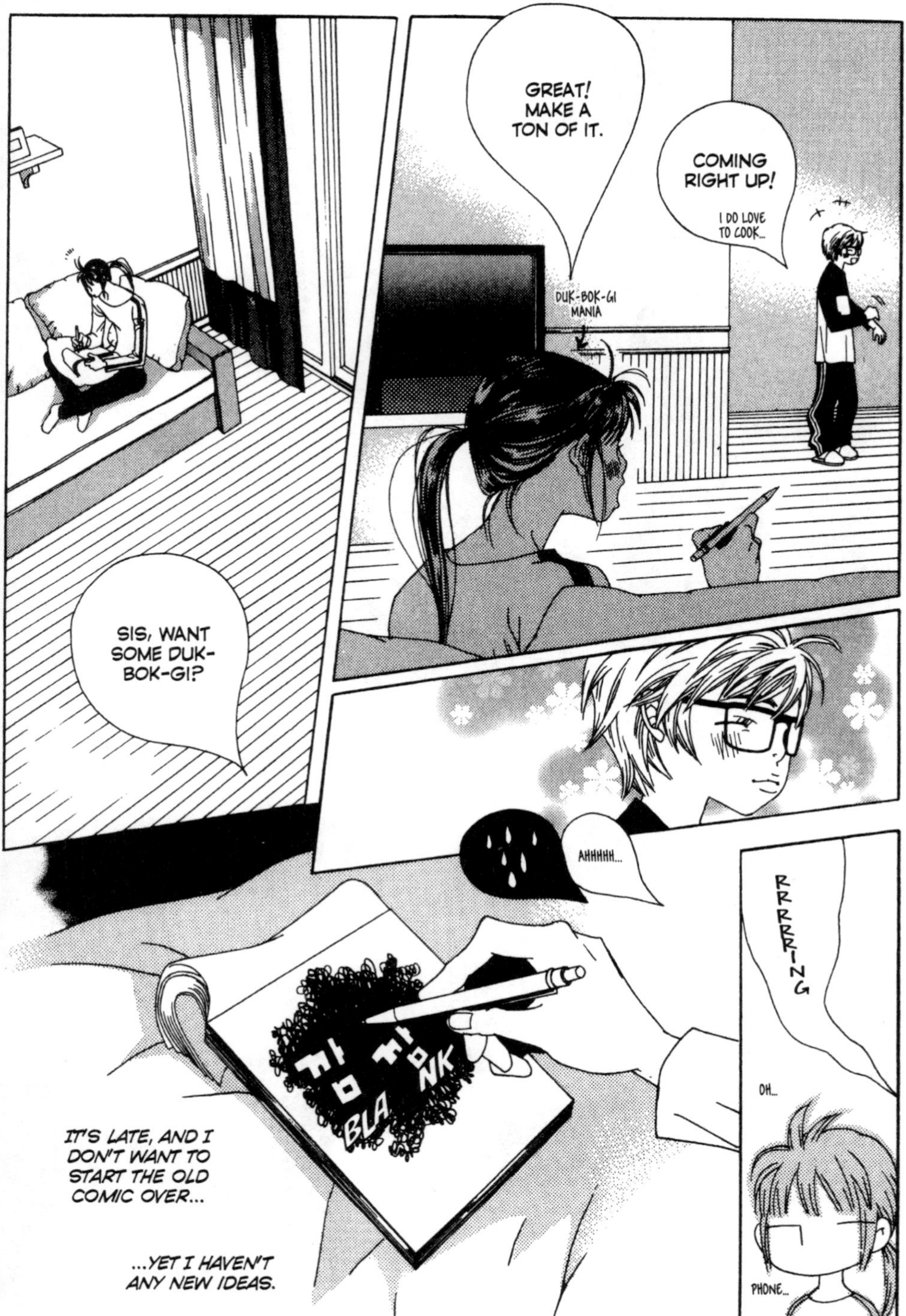

SIS, WANT SOME DUK-BOK-GI?
GREAT! MAKE A TON OF IT.
COMING RIGHT UP!
I DO LOVE TO COOK...
DUK-BOK-GI MANIA
AHHHHH...
BLANK
IT'S LATE, AND I DON'T WANT TO START THE OLD COMIC OVER...
...YET I HAVEN'T ANY NEW IDEAS.
RRRRRING
OH...
PHONE...

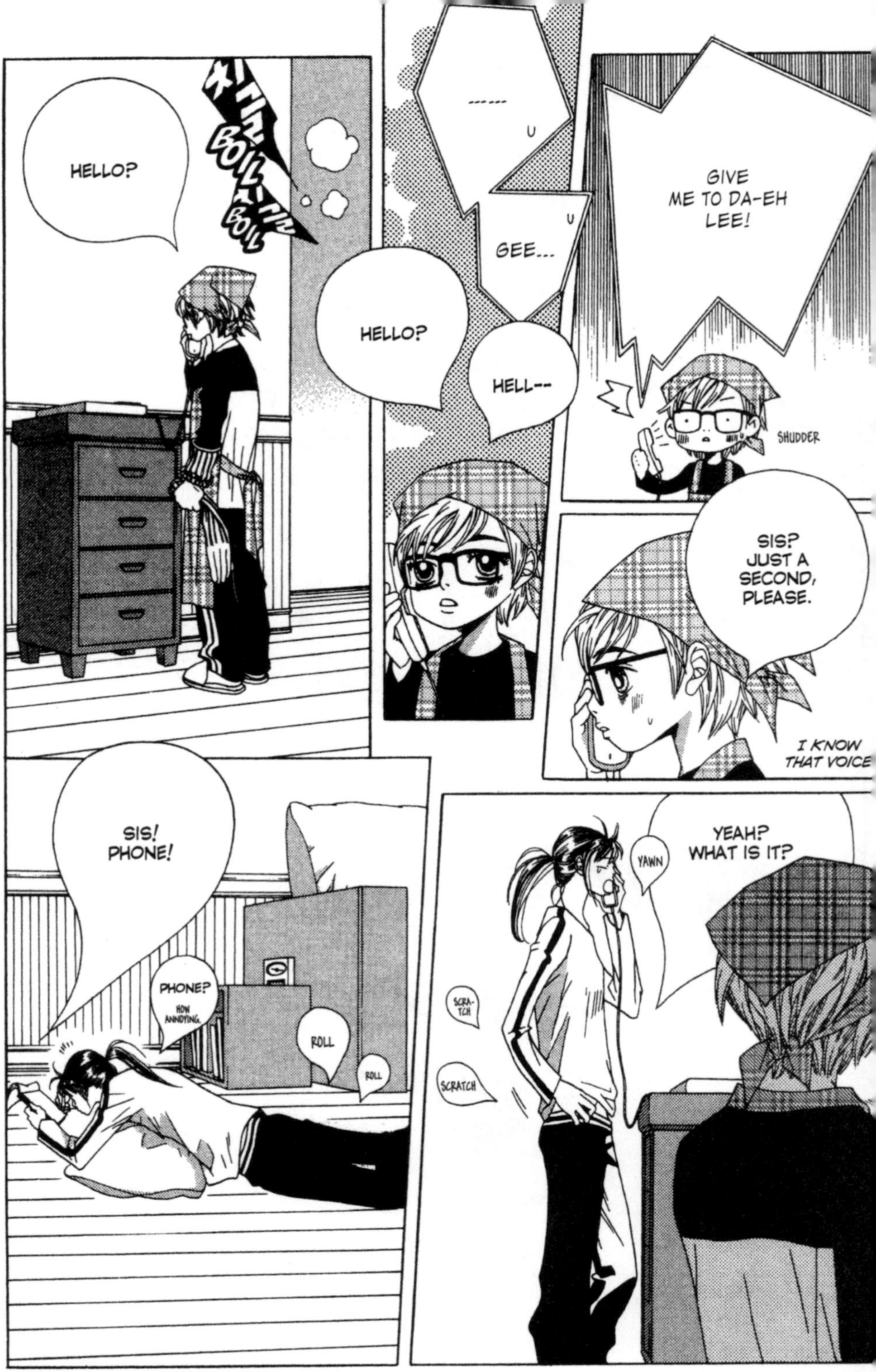
HELLO?
BOIL BOIL

GEE...
HELLO?
HELL--
GIVE ME TO DA-EH LEE!
SHUDDER
SIS? JUST A SECOND, PLEASE.
I KNOW THAT VOICE
SIS! PHONE!
PHONE? HOW ANNOYING.
ROLL
ROLL
YAWN
YEAH? WHAT IS IT?
SCRA-TCH
SCRATCH

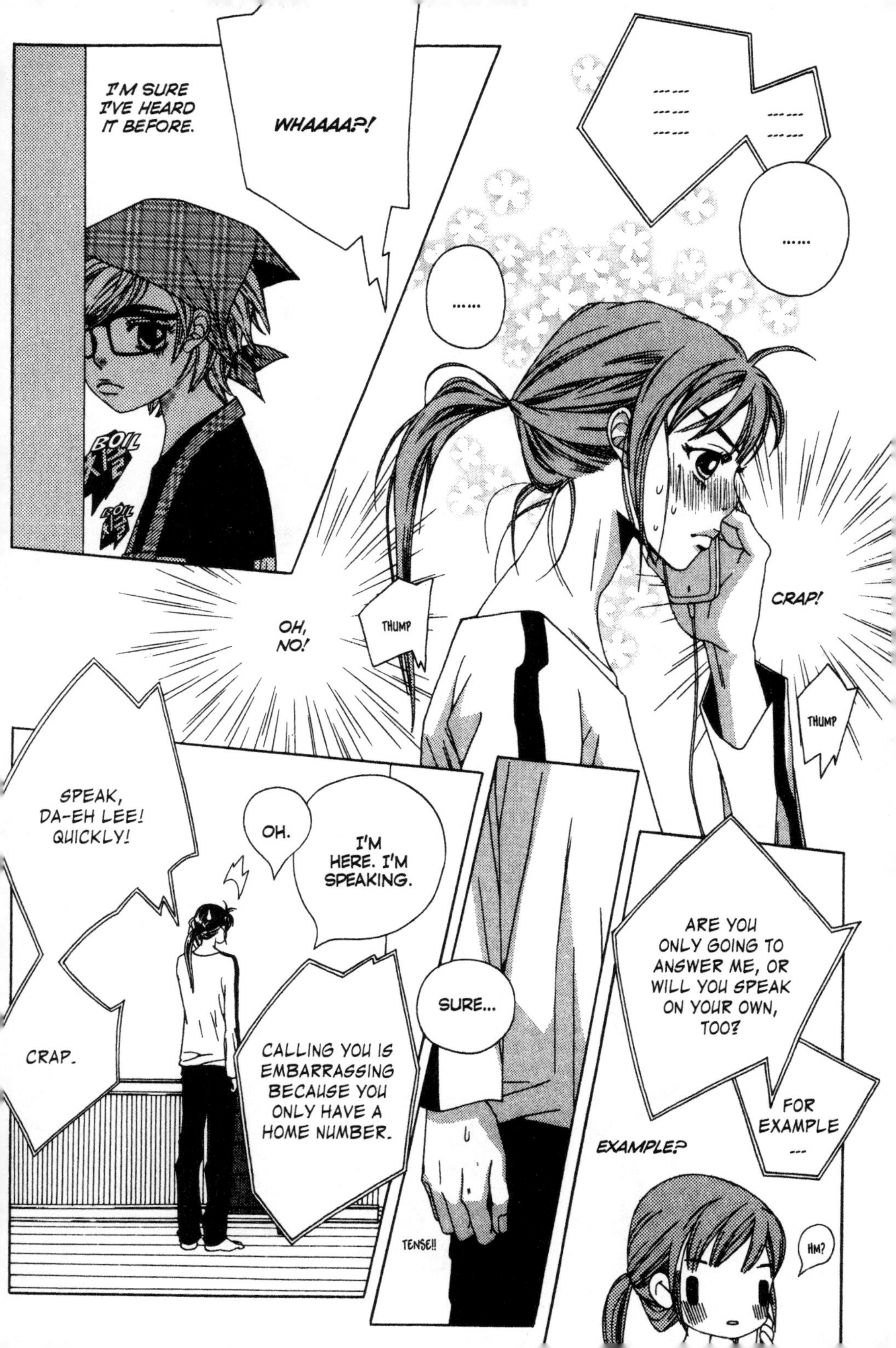

I'M SURE I'VE HEARD IT BEFORE.
WHAAAA?!
BOIL
BOIL
......
......
OH, NO!
THUMP
CRAP!
THUMP
SPEAK, DA-EH LEE! QUICKLY!
CRAP.
OH.
I'M HERE. I'M SPEAKING.
CALLING YOU IS EMBARRASSING BECAUSE YOU ONLY HAVE A HOME NUMBER.
SURE...
TENSE!!
ARE YOU ONLY GOING TO ANSWER ME, OR WILL YOU SPEAK ON YOUR OWN, TOO?
FOR EXAMPLE ---
EXAMPLE?
HM?

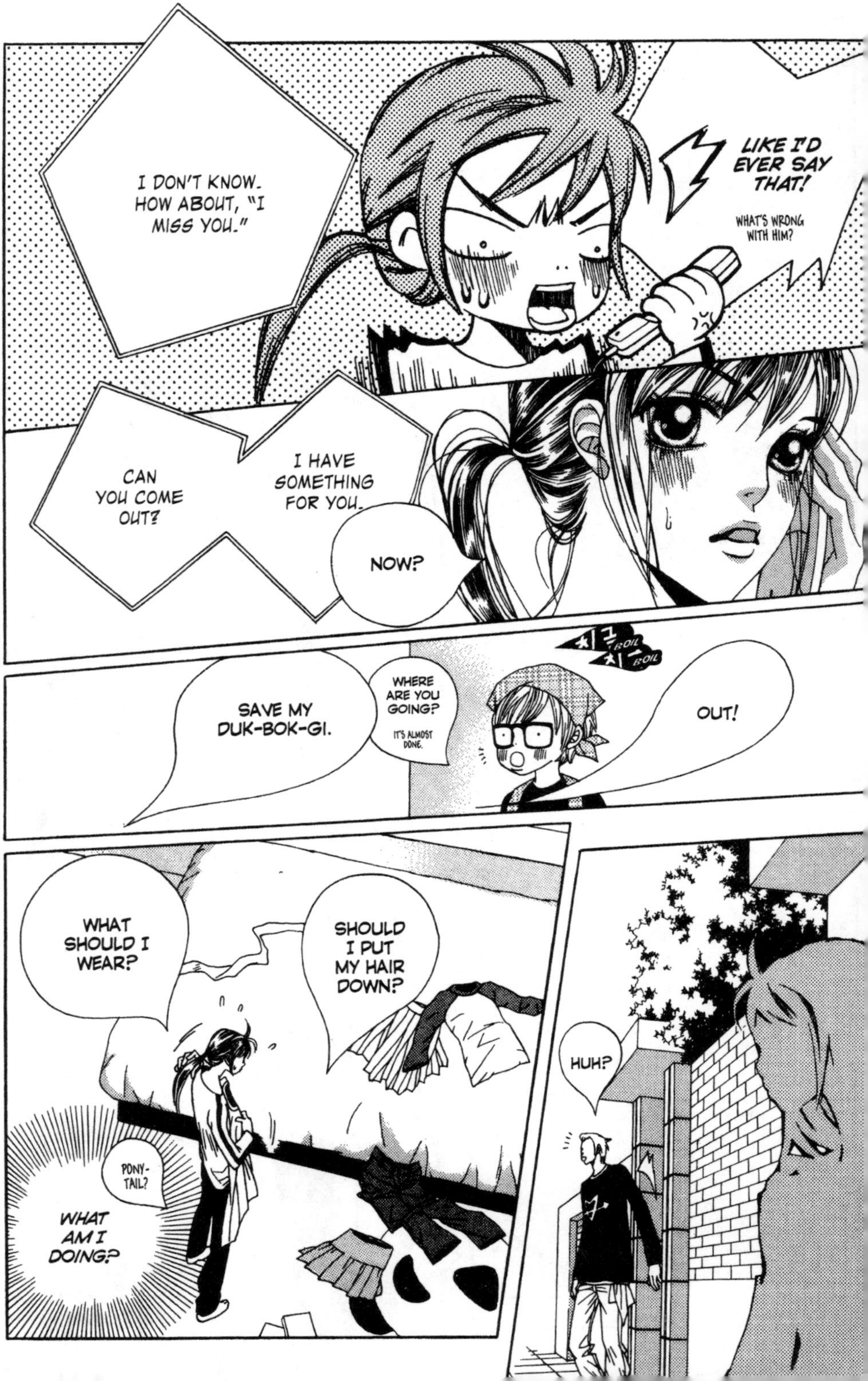
I DON'T KNOW. HOW ABOUT, "I MISS YOU."
LIKE I'D EVER SAY THAT!
WHAT'S WRONG WITH HIM?
CAN YOU COME OUT?
I HAVE SOMETHING FOR YOU.
NOW?
SAVE MY DUK-BOK-GI.
WHERE ARE YOU GOING?
IT'S ALMOST DONE.
BOIL BOIL
OUT!
WHAT SHOULD I WEAR?
SHOULD I PUT MY HAIR DOWN?
PONY-TAIL?
WHAT AM I DOING?
HUH?

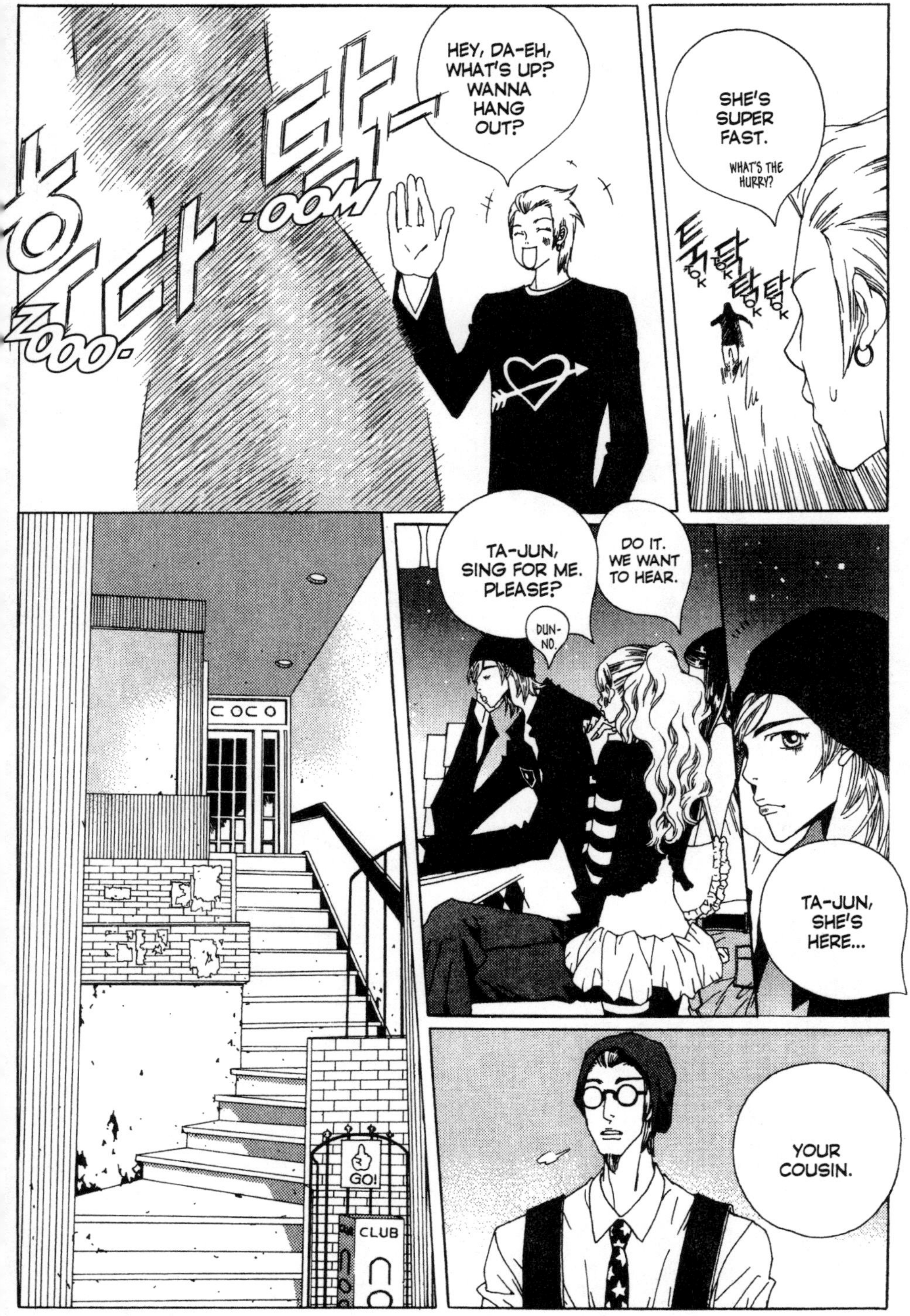
ZOOO-
-OOM
HEY, DA-EH, WHAT'S UP? WANNA HANG OUT?
SHE'S SUPER FAST.
WHAT'S THE HURRY?
TOK TOK TOK TOK
COCO
GO!
CLUB
TA-JUN, SING FOR ME. PLEASE?
DUN-NO.
DO IT. WE WANT TO HEAR.
TA-JUN, SHE'S HERE...
YOUR COUSIN.

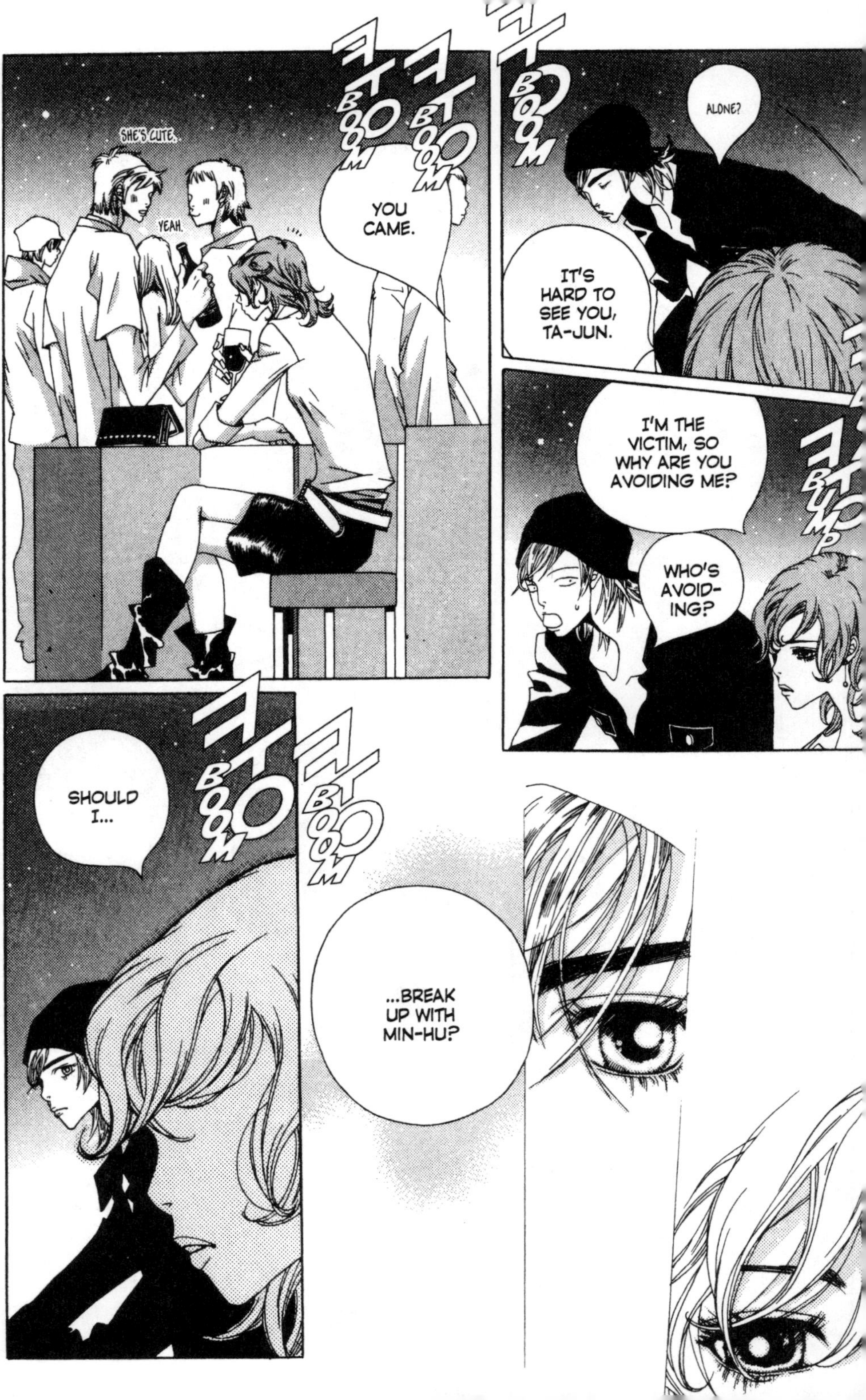
SHE'S CUTE.
YEAH.
BOOM
BOOM
YOU CAME.
BOOM
ALONE?
IT'S HARD TO SEE YOU, TA-JUN.
I'M THE VICTIM, SO WHY ARE YOU AVOIDING ME?
BUMP
WHO'S AVOID-ING?
SHOULD I...
BOOM
BOOM
...BREAK UP WITH MIN-HU?

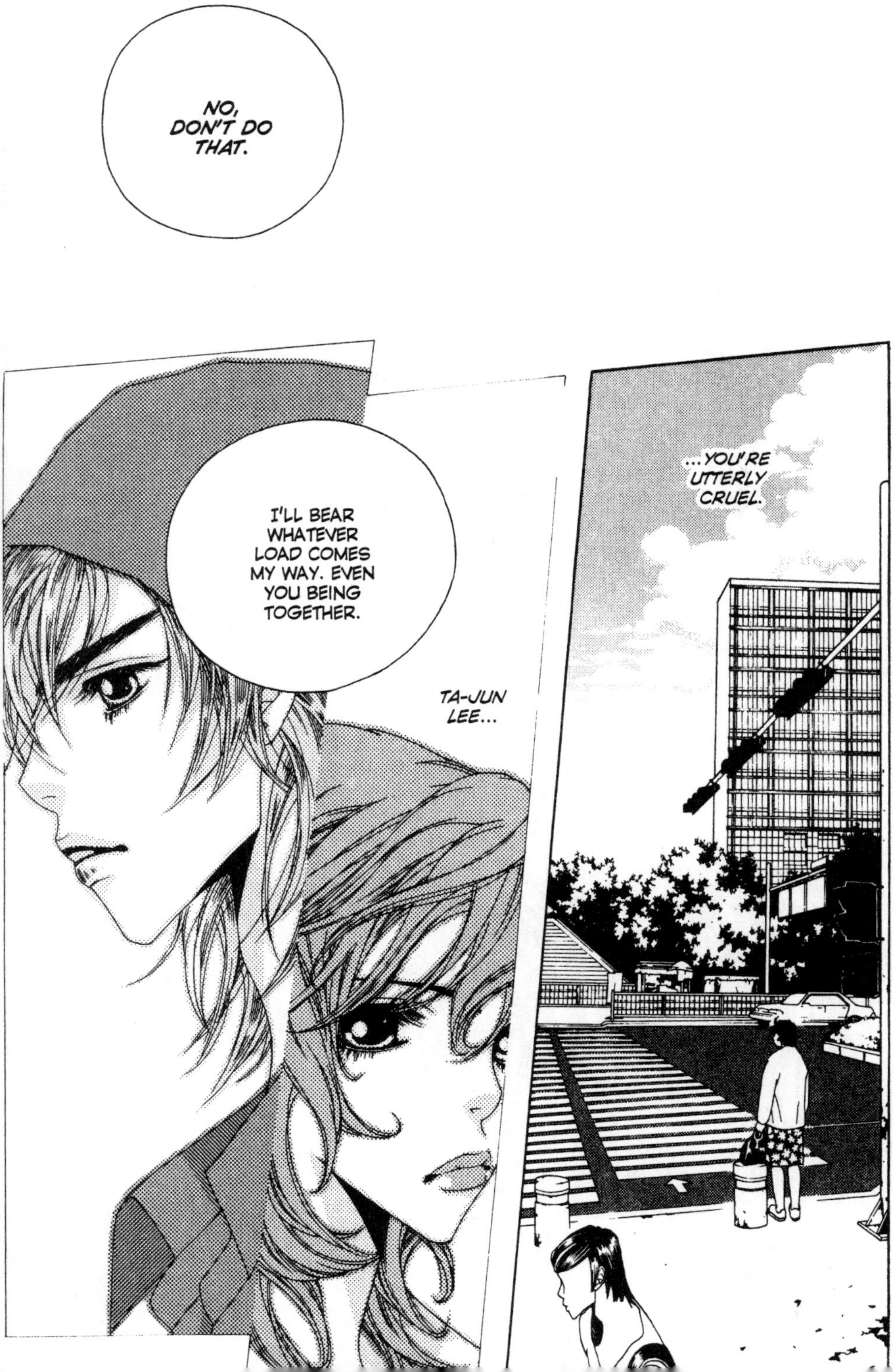
NO, DON'T DO THAT.
I'LL BEAR WHATEVER LOAD COMES MY WAY. EVEN YOU BEING TOGETHER.
TA-JUN LEE...
...YOU'RE UTTERLY CRUEL.

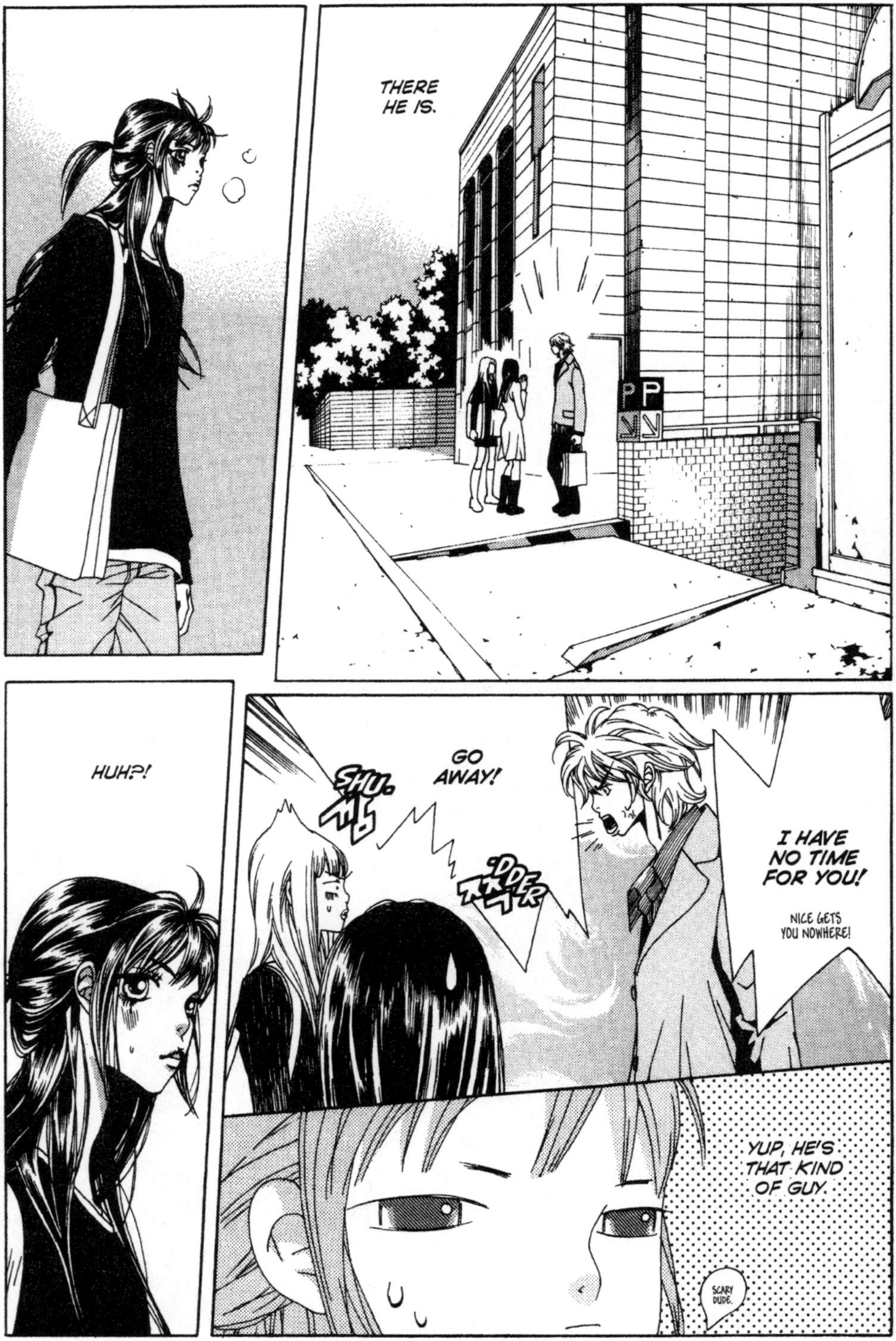
THERE HE IS.
HUH?!
SHU-
GO AWAY!
-DDER
I HAVE NO TIME FOR YOU!
NICE GETS YOU NOWHERE!
YUP, HE'S THAT KIND OF GUY.
SCARY DUDE.

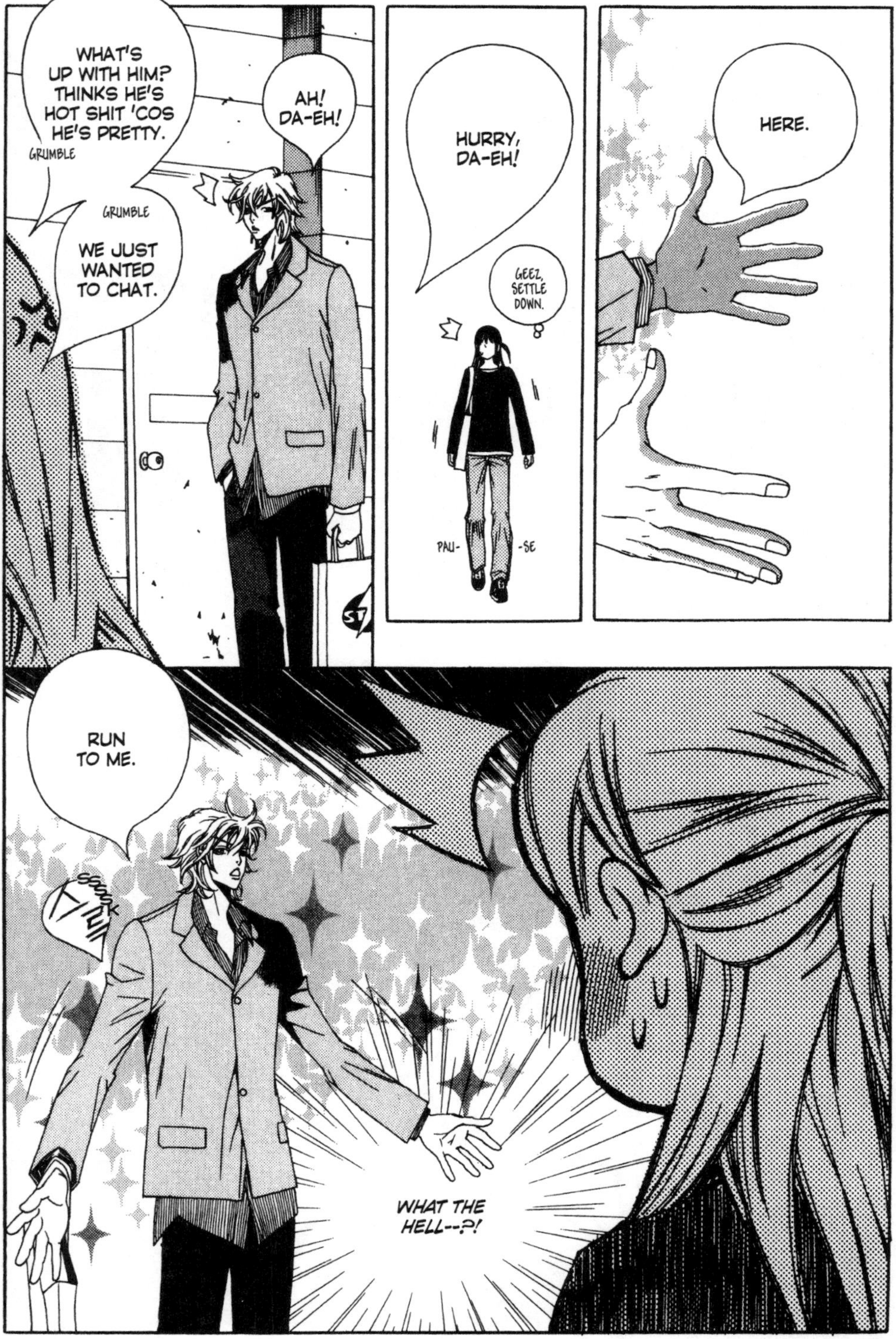
WHAT'S UP WITH HIM? THINKS HE'S HOT SHIT 'COS HE'S PRETTY.
GRUMBLE
GRUMBLE
WE JUST WANTED TO CHAT.
AH! DA-EH!
HURRY, DA-EH!
GEEZ, SETTLE DOWN.
PAU- -SE
HERE.
RUN TO ME.
SSSSK
WHAT THE HELL--?!

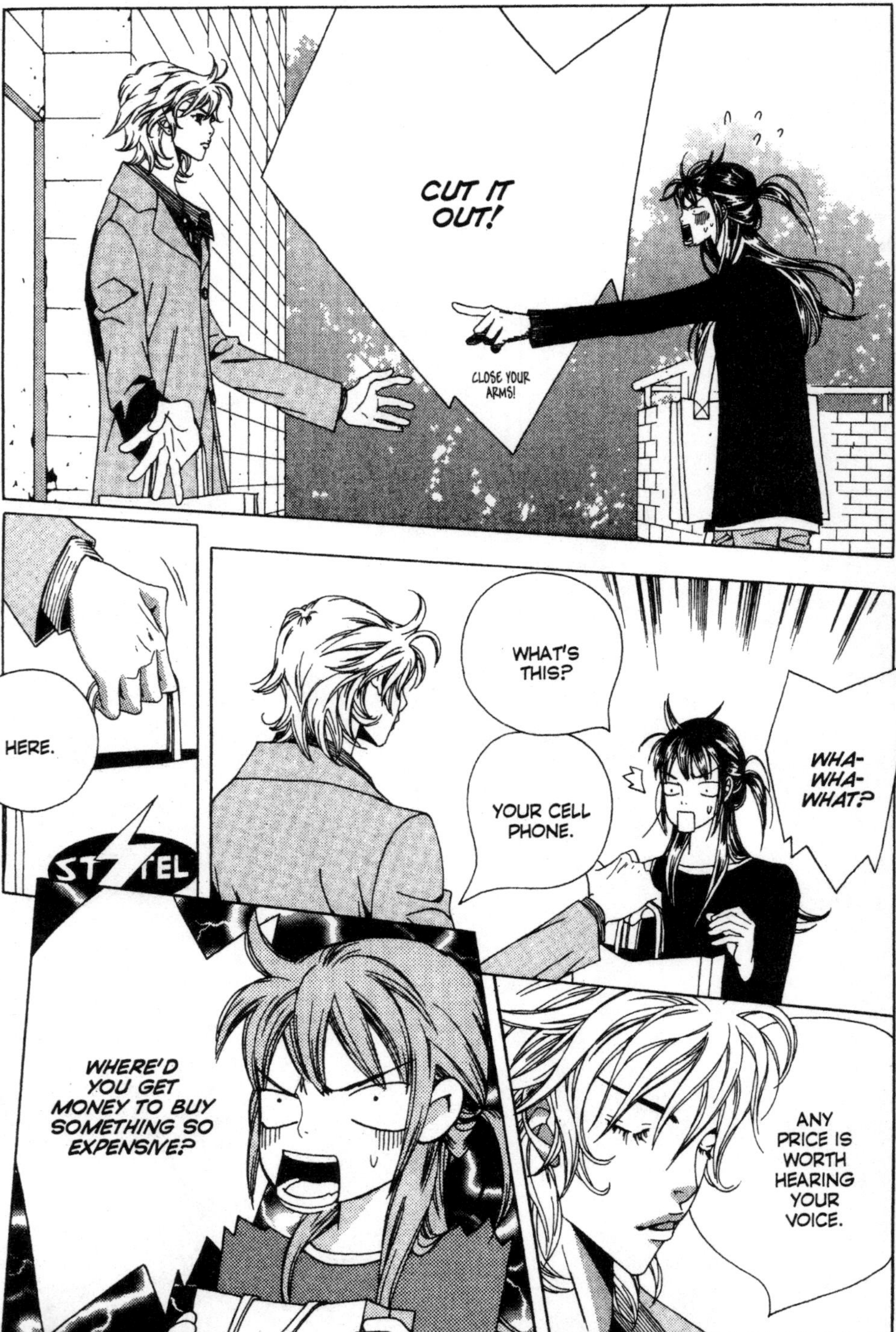
CUT IT OUT!
CLOSE YOUR ARMS!
HERE.
ST TEL
WHAT'S THIS?
YOUR CELL PHONE.
WHA-WHA-WHAT?
WHERE'D YOU GET MONEY TO BUY SOMETHING SO EXPENSIVE?
ANY PRICE IS WORTH HEARING YOUR VOICE.

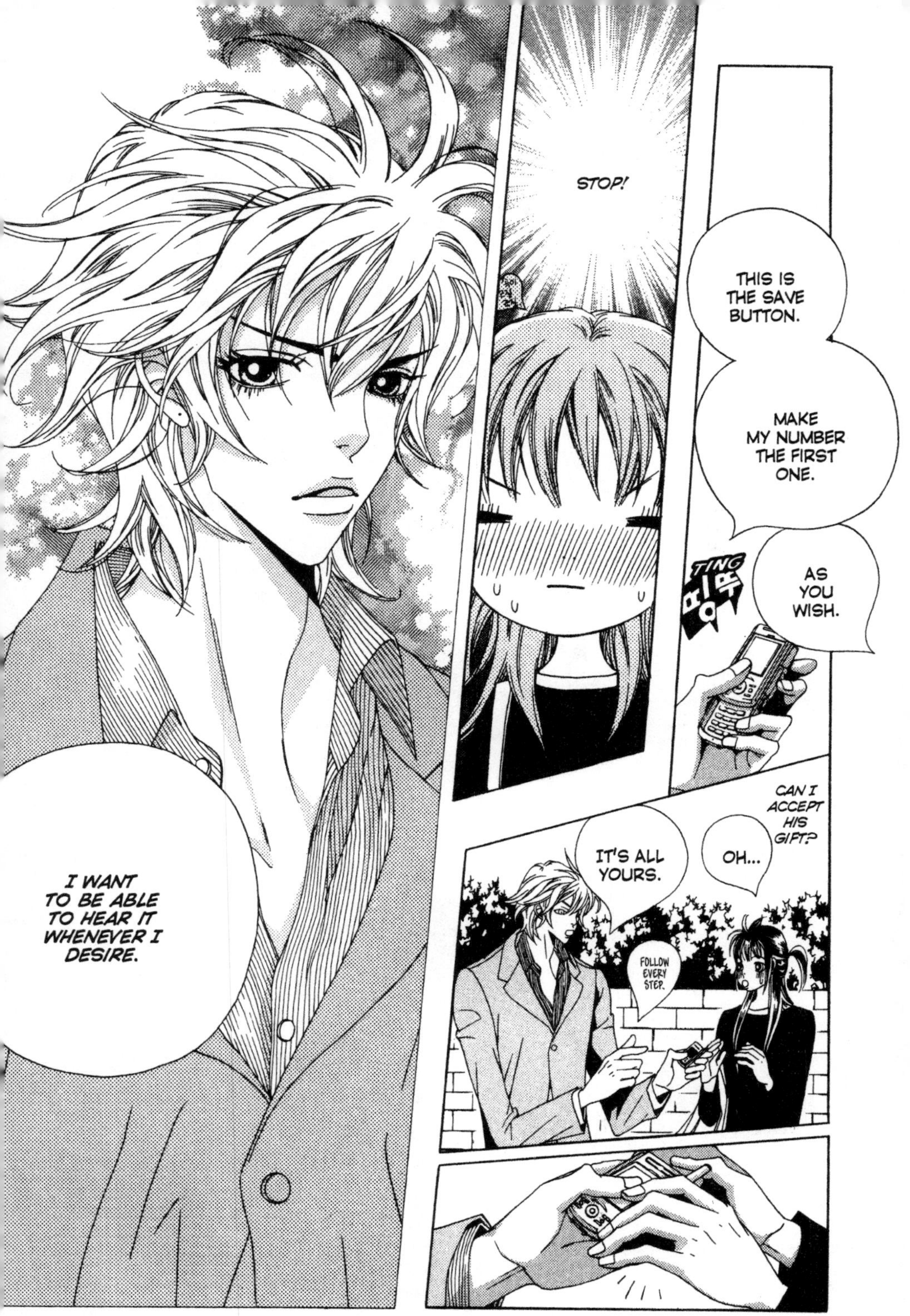
I WANT TO BE ABLE TO HEAR IT WHENEVER I DESIRE.
STOP!
THIS IS THE SAVE BUTTON.
MAKE MY NUMBER THE FIRST ONE.
TING
AS YOU WISH.
CAN I ACCEPT HIS GIFT?
IT'S ALL YOURS.
OH...
FOLLOW EVERY STEP.

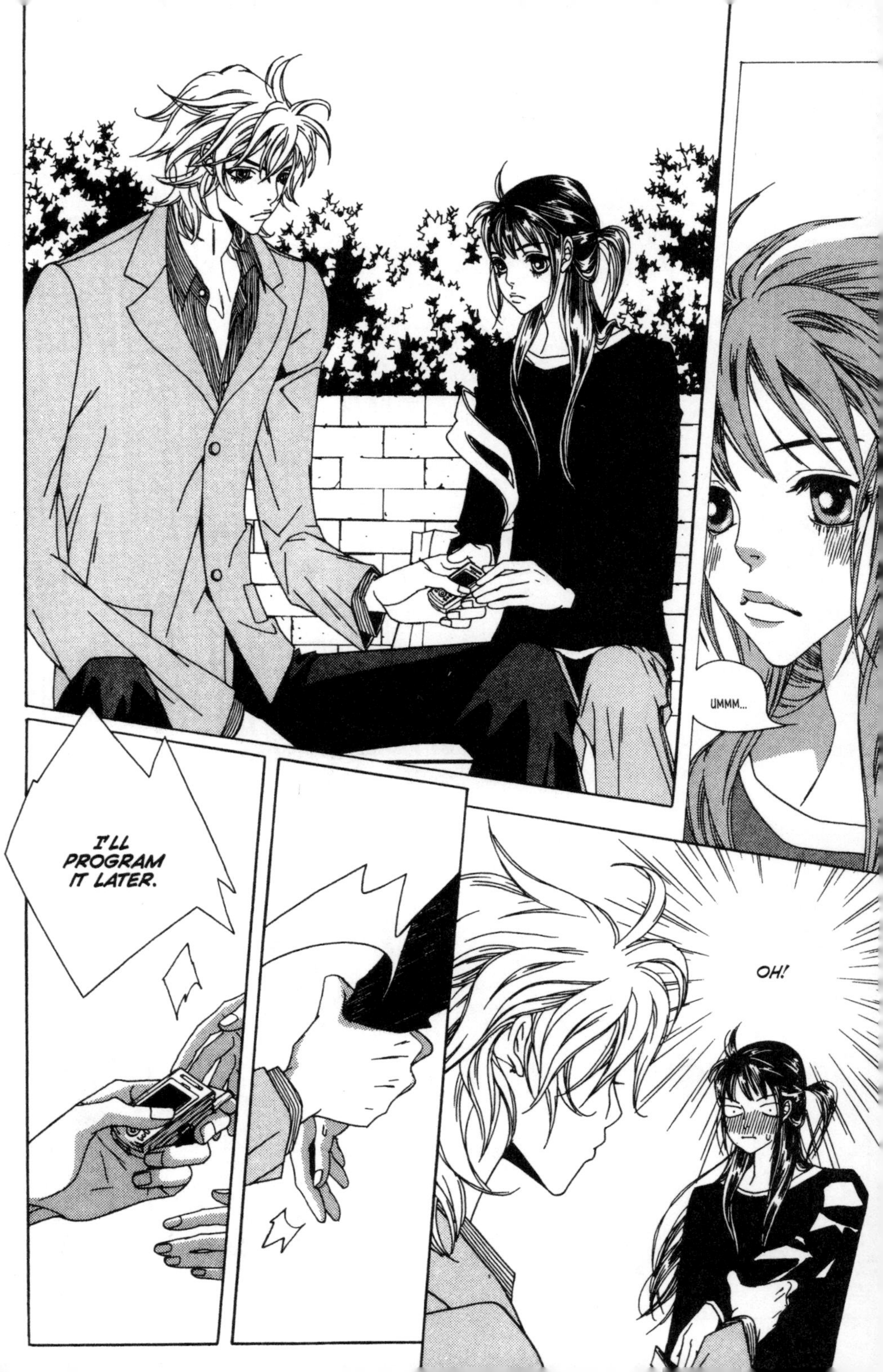
UMMM...
I'LL PROGRAM IT LATER.
OH!

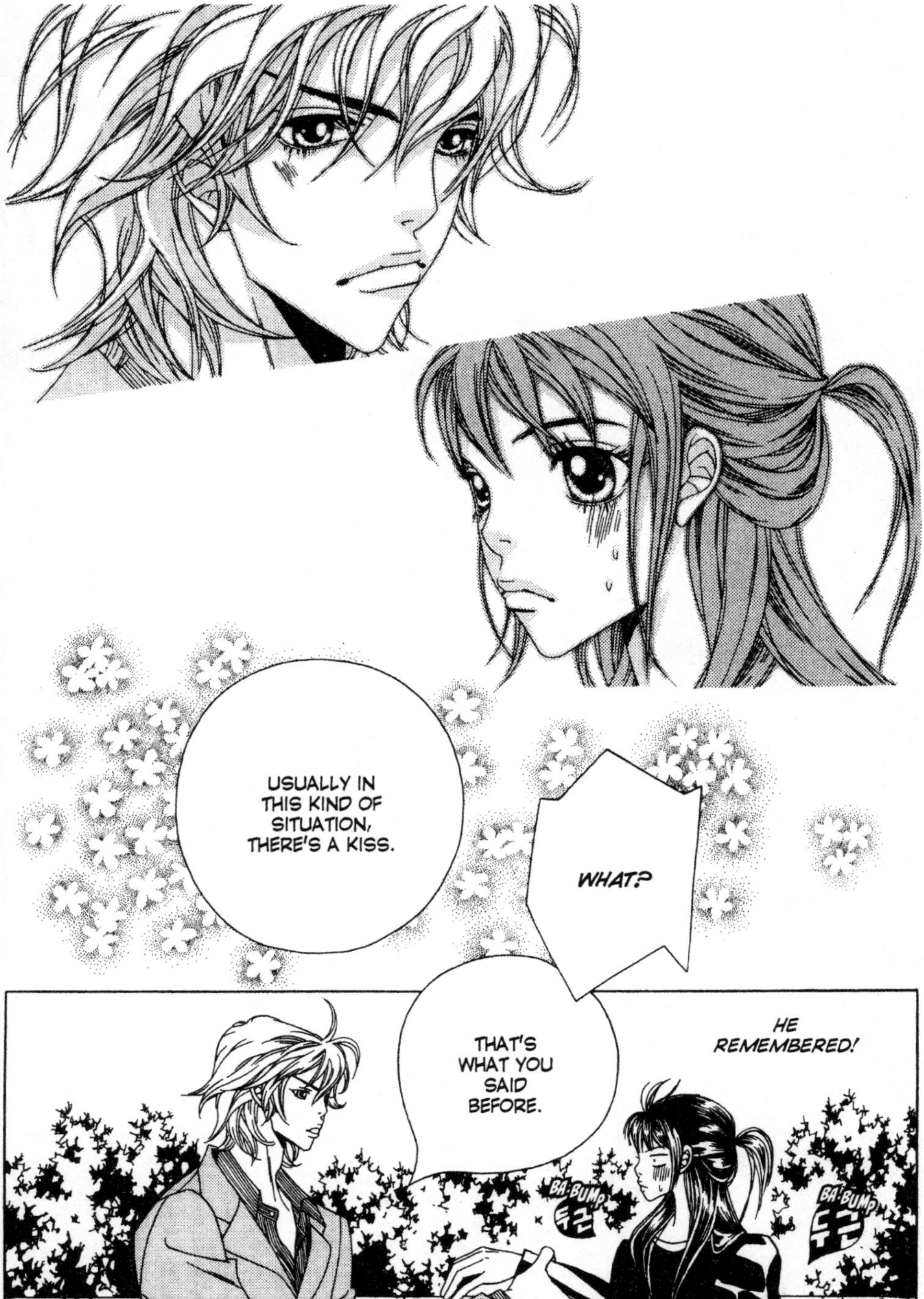
USUALLY IN THIS KIND OF SITUATION, THERE'S A KISS.
WHAT?
THAT'S WHAT YOU SAID BEFORE.
HE REMEMBERED!
BA-BUMP 두근
BA-BUMP 두근

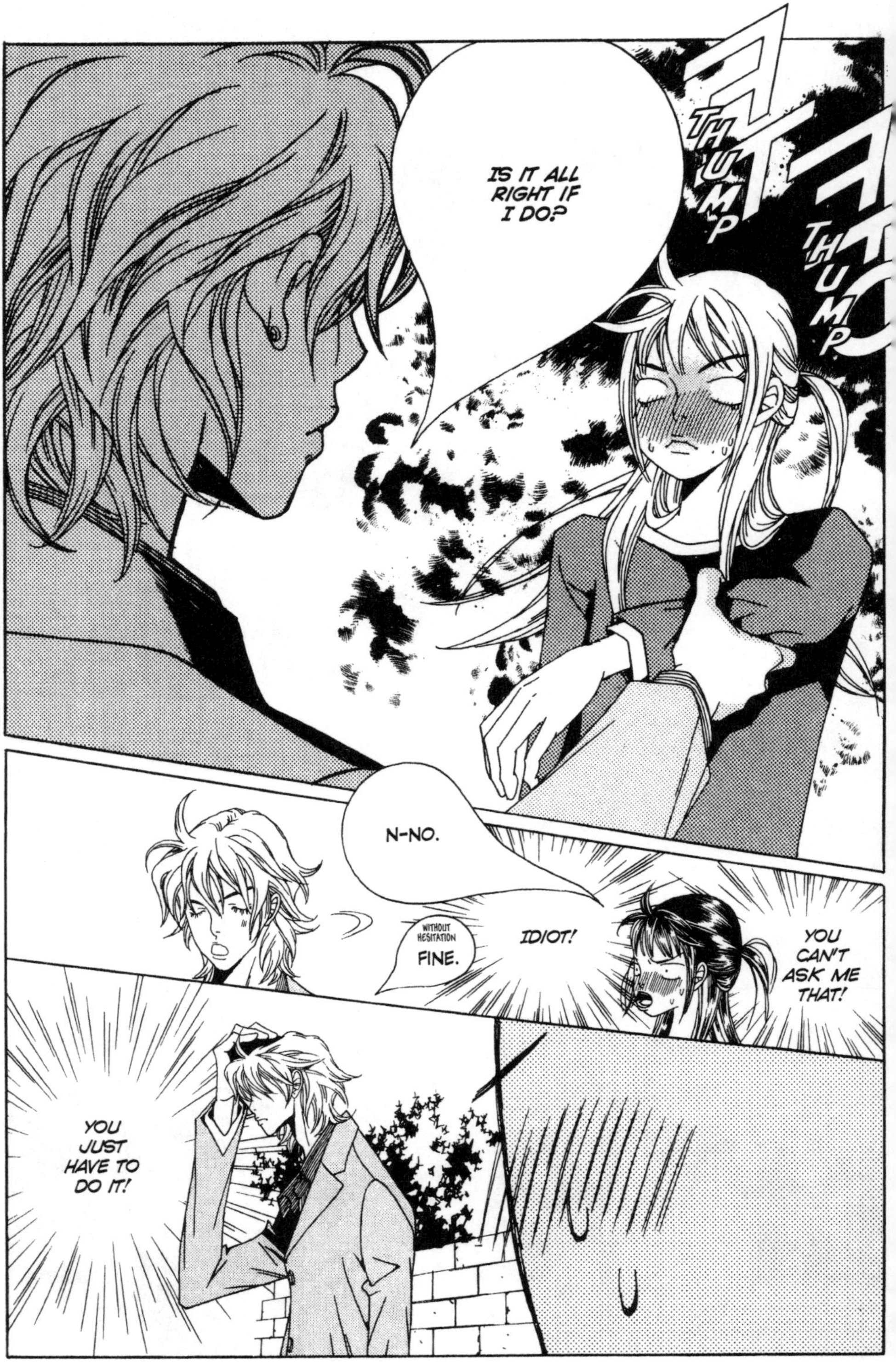
IS IT ALL RIGHT IF I DO?
THUMP
THUMP
N-NO.
WITHOUT HESITATION
FINE.
IDIOT!
YOU CAN'T ASK ME THAT!
YOU JUST HAVE TO DO IT!

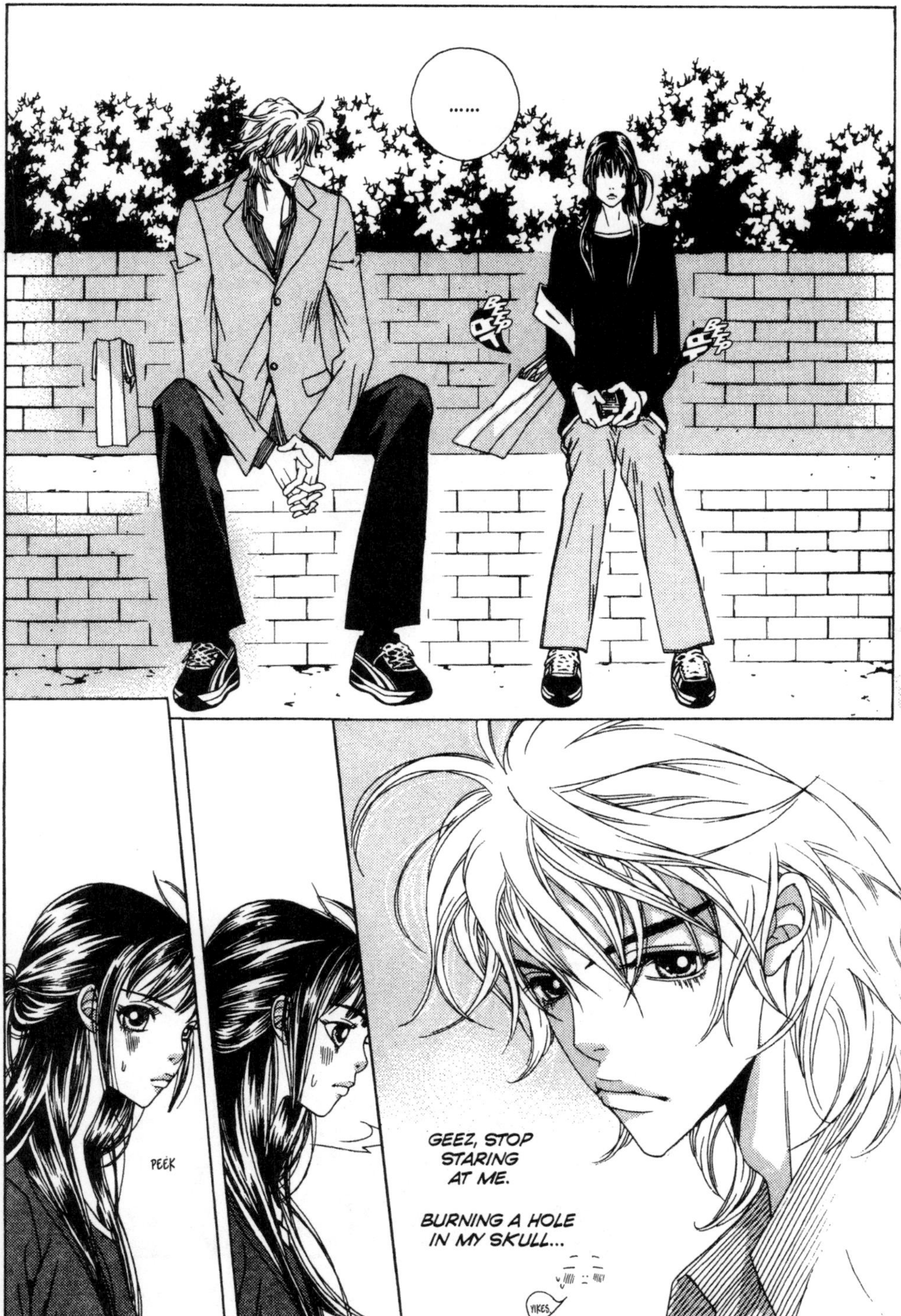
......
BEEP
BEEP
PEEK
GEEZ, STOP STARING AT ME.
BURNING A HOLE IN MY SKULL...
YIKES.

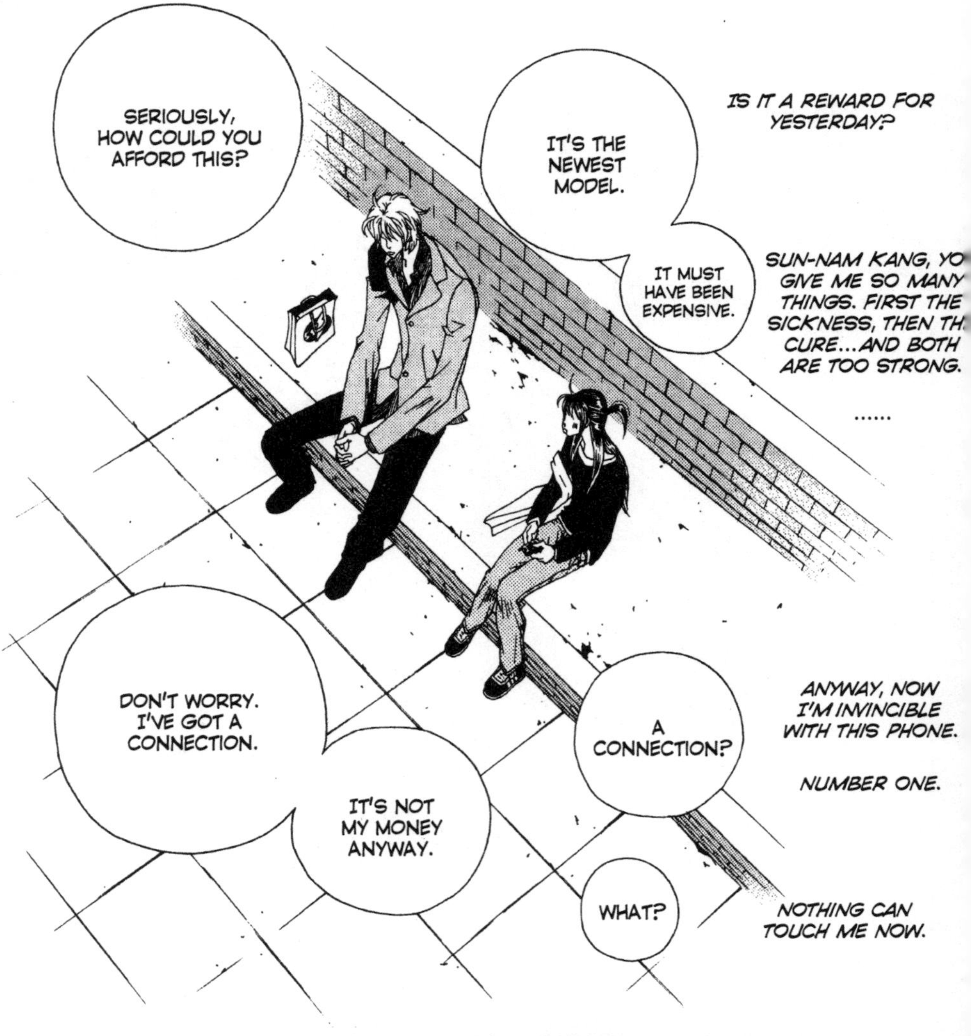
SERIOUSLY, HOW COULD YOU AFFORD THIS?
IT'S THE NEWEST MODEL.
IT MUST HAVE BEEN EXPENSIVE.
IS IT A REWARD FOR YESTERDAY?
SUN-NAM KANG, YO GIVE ME SO MANY THINGS. FIRST THE SICKNESS, THEN TH CURE...AND BOTH ARE TOO STRONG.
......
DON'T WORRY. I'VE GOT A CONNECTION.
IT'S NOT MY MONEY ANYWAY.
A CONNECTION?
WHAT?
ANYWAY, NOW I'M INVINCIBLE WITH THIS PHONE.
NUMBER ONE.
NOTHING CAN TOUCH ME NOW.

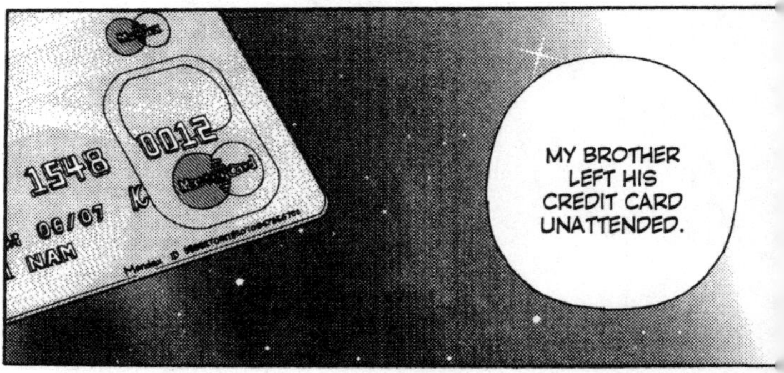
1548 0012
06/07
NAM
MY BROTHER LEFT HIS CREDIT CARD UNATTENDED.

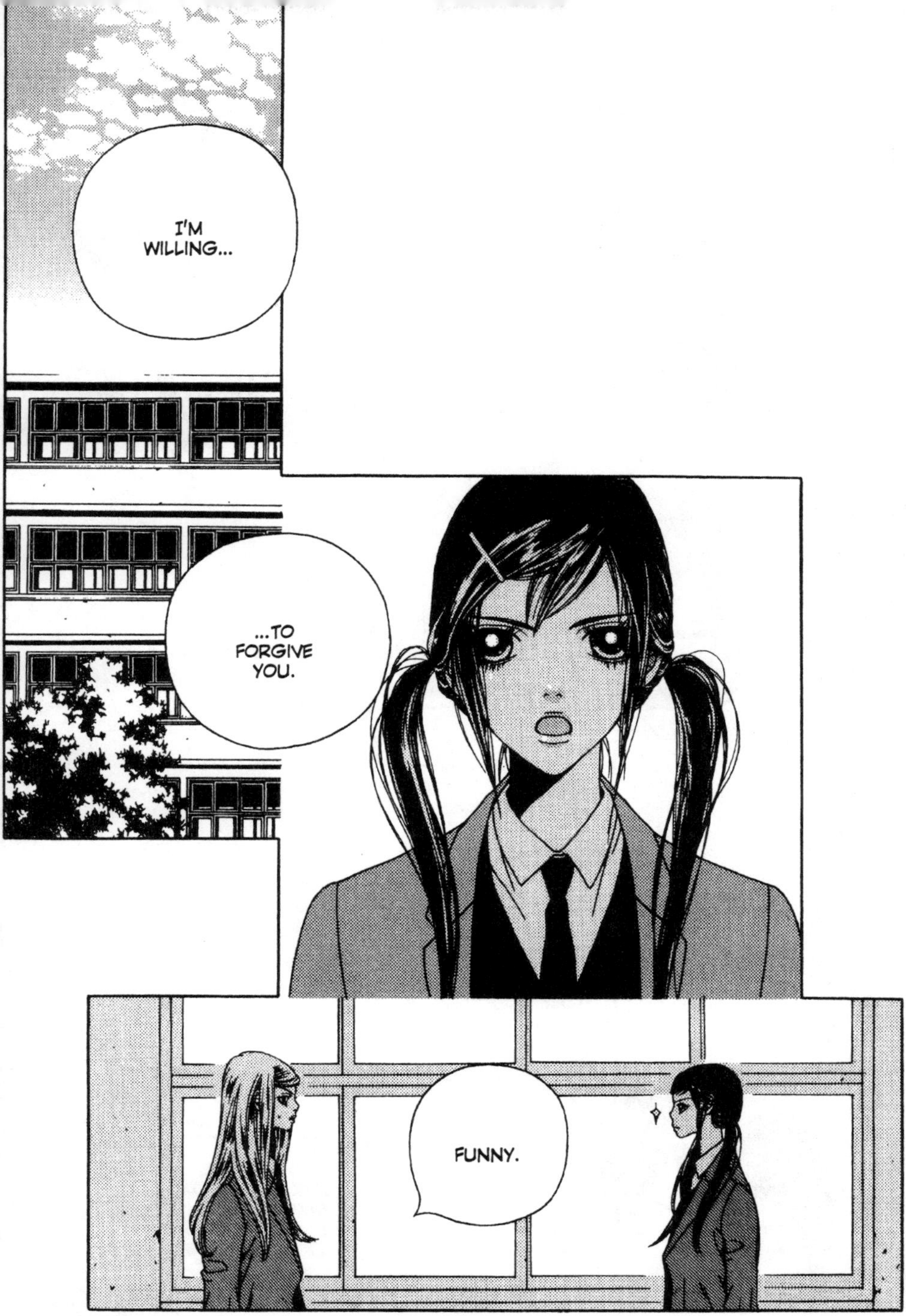
I'M WILLING...
...TO FORGIVE YOU.
FUNNY.

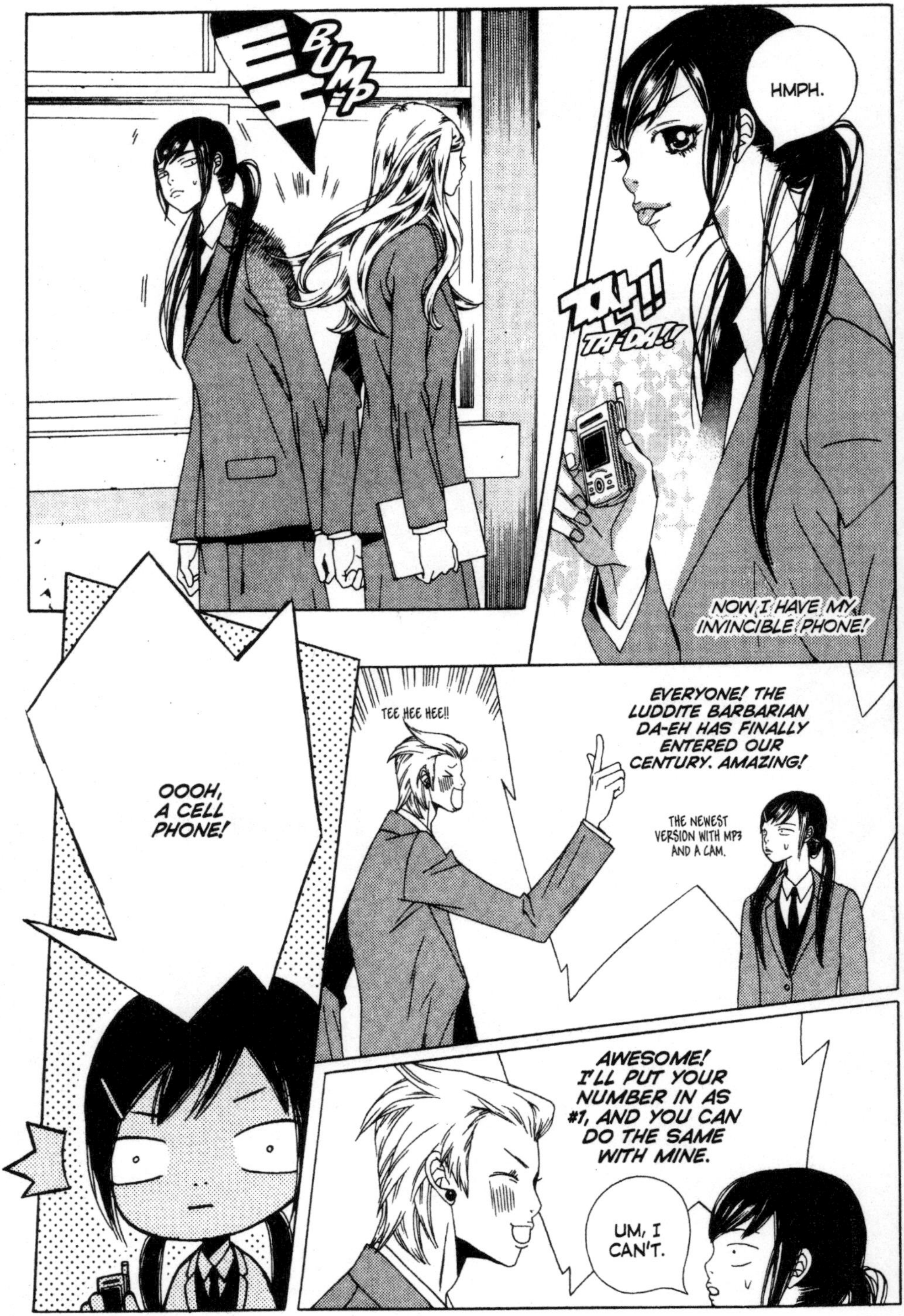
BUMP
HMPH.
TA-DA!!
NOW I HAVE MY INVINCIBLE PHONE!
OOOH, A CELL PHONE!
TEE HEE HEE!!
EVERYONE! THE LUDDITE BARBARIAN DA-EH HAS FINALLY ENTERED OUR CENTURY. AMAZING!
THE NEWEST VERSION WITH MP3 AND A CAM.
AWESOME! I'LL PUT YOUR NUMBER IN AS #1, AND YOU CAN DO THE SAME WITH MINE.
UM, I CAN'T.

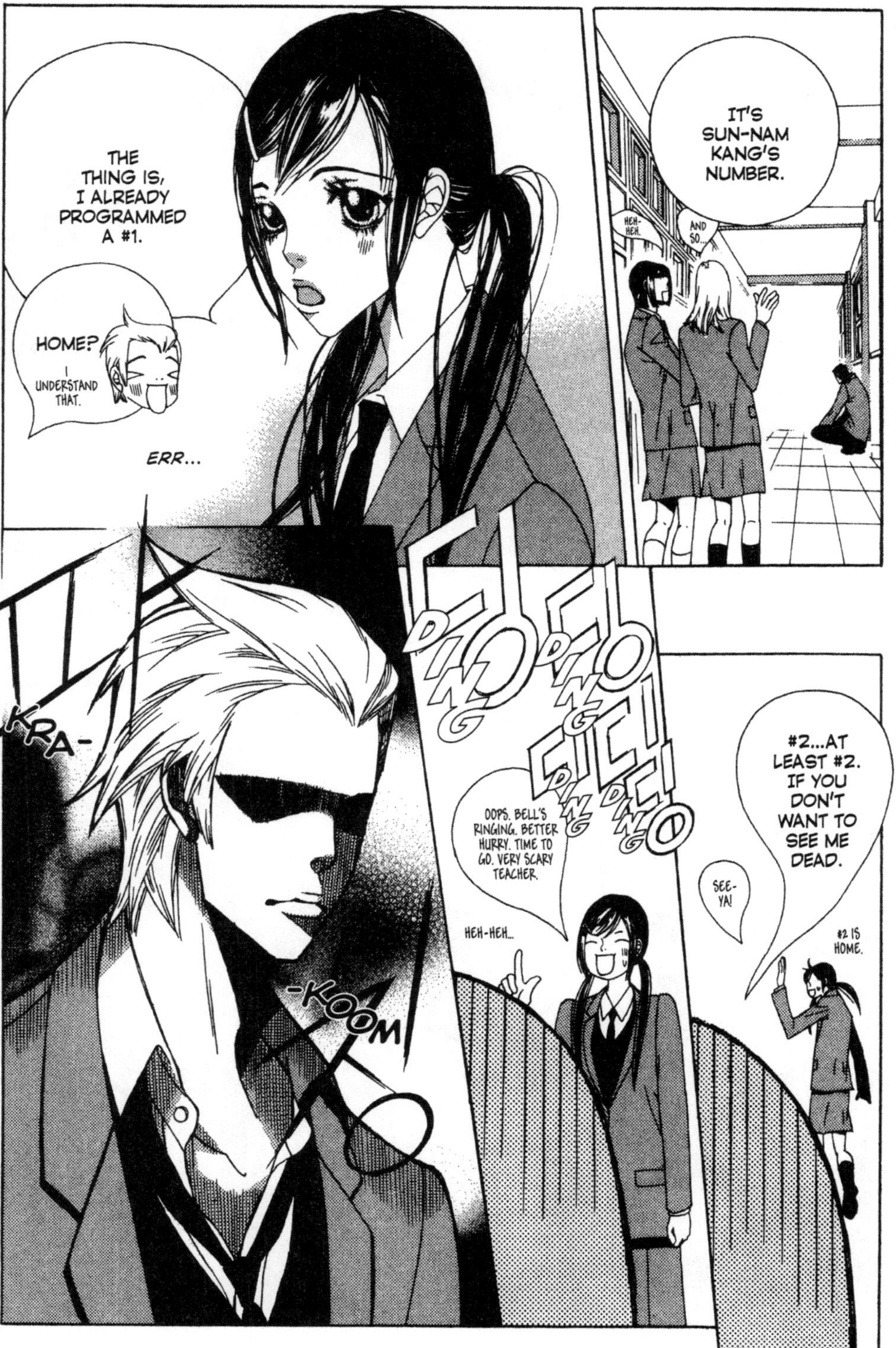
THE THING IS, I ALREADY PROGRAMMED A #1.
HOME?
I UNDERSTAND THAT.
ERR...
IT'S SUN-NAM KANG'S NUMBER.
HEH-HEH.
AND SO...
KRA-
-KOOM
DING DONG DING DONG
OOPS. BELL'S RINGING. BETTER HURRY. TIME TO GO. VERY SCARY TEACHER.
HEH-HEH...
#2...AT LEAST #2. IF YOU DON'T WANT TO SEE ME DEAD.
SEE-YA!
#2 IS HOME.

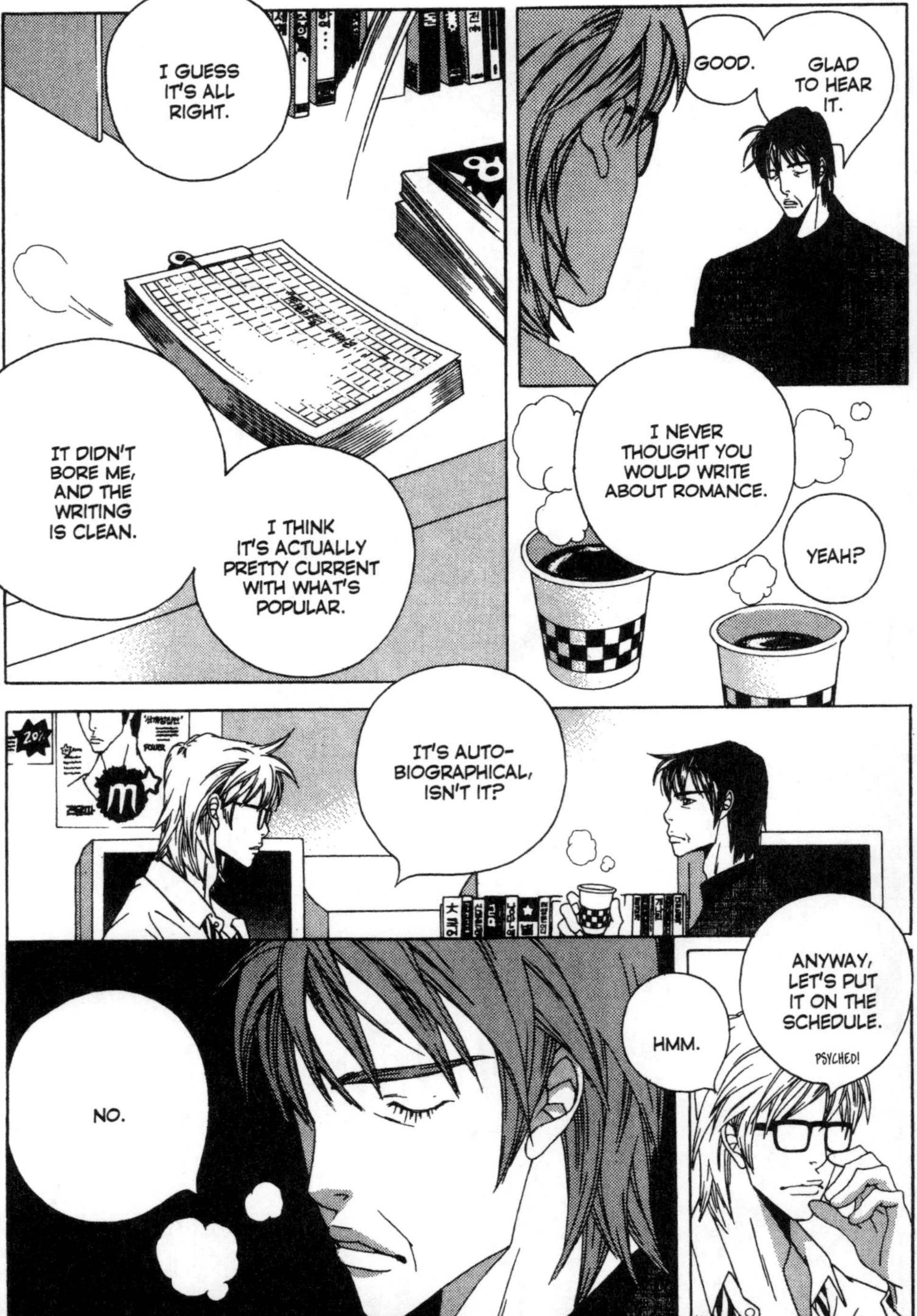
I GUESS IT'S ALL RIGHT.
IT DIDN'T BORE ME, AND THE WRITING IS CLEAN.
I THINK IT'S ACTUALLY PRETTY CURRENT WITH WHAT'S POPULAR.
GOOD.
GLAD TO HEAR IT.
I NEVER THOUGHT YOU WOULD WRITE ABOUT ROMANCE.
YEAH?
IT'S AUTO-BIOGRAPHICAL, ISN'T IT?
NO.
HMM.
ANYWAY, LET'S PUT IT ON THE SCHEDULE.
PSYCHED!

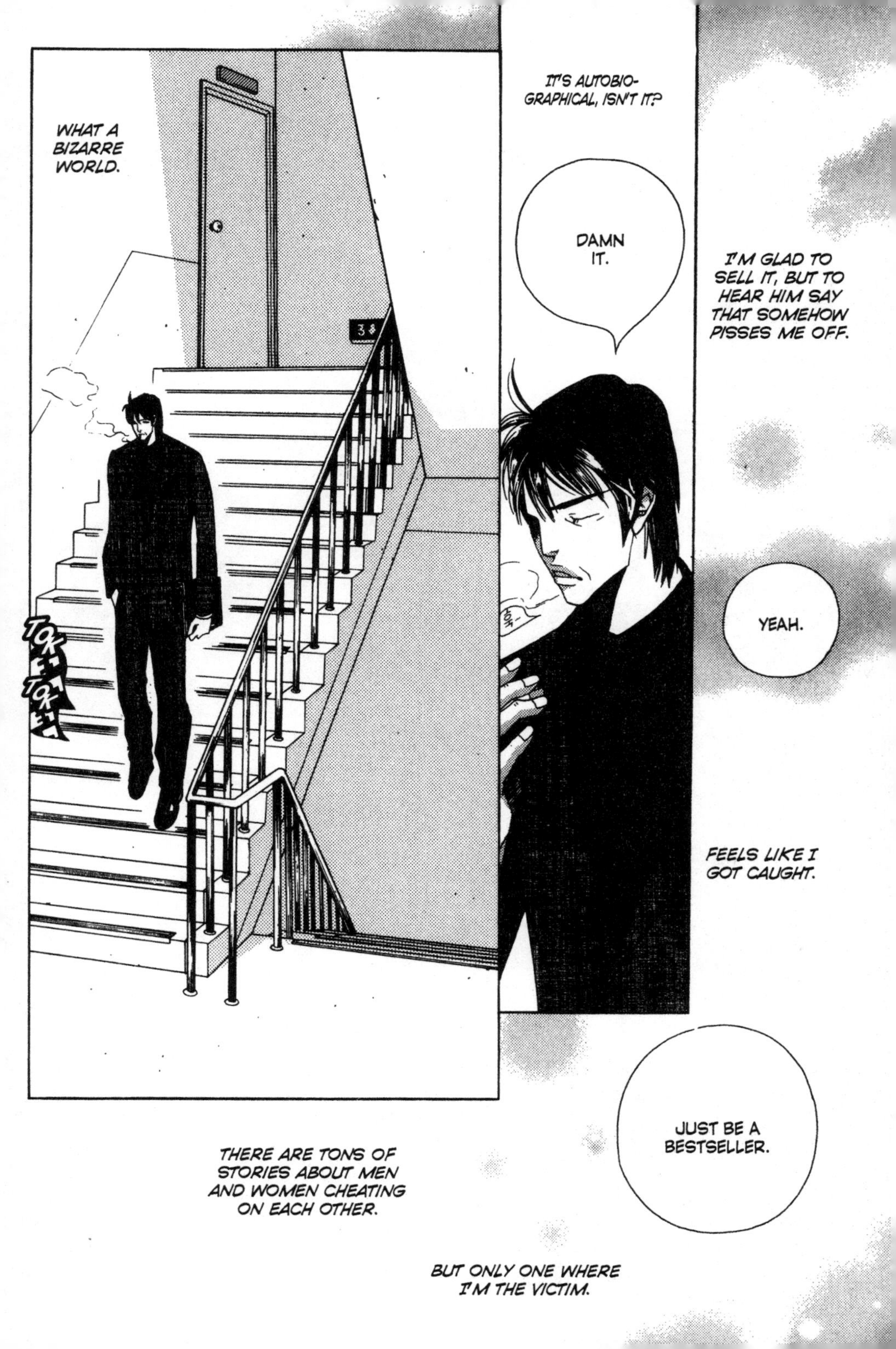

IT'S AUTOBIO-GRAPHICAL, ISN'T IT?
DAMN IT.
I'M GLAD TO SELL IT, BUT TO HEAR HIM SAY THAT SOMEHOW PISSES ME OFF.
YEAH.
FEELS LIKE I GOT CAUGHT.
WHAT A BIZARRE WORLD.
TOK TOK
JUST BE A BESTSELLER.
THERE ARE TONS OF STORIES ABOUT MEN AND WOMEN CHEATING ON EACH OTHER.
BUT ONLY ONE WHERE I'M THE VICTIM.

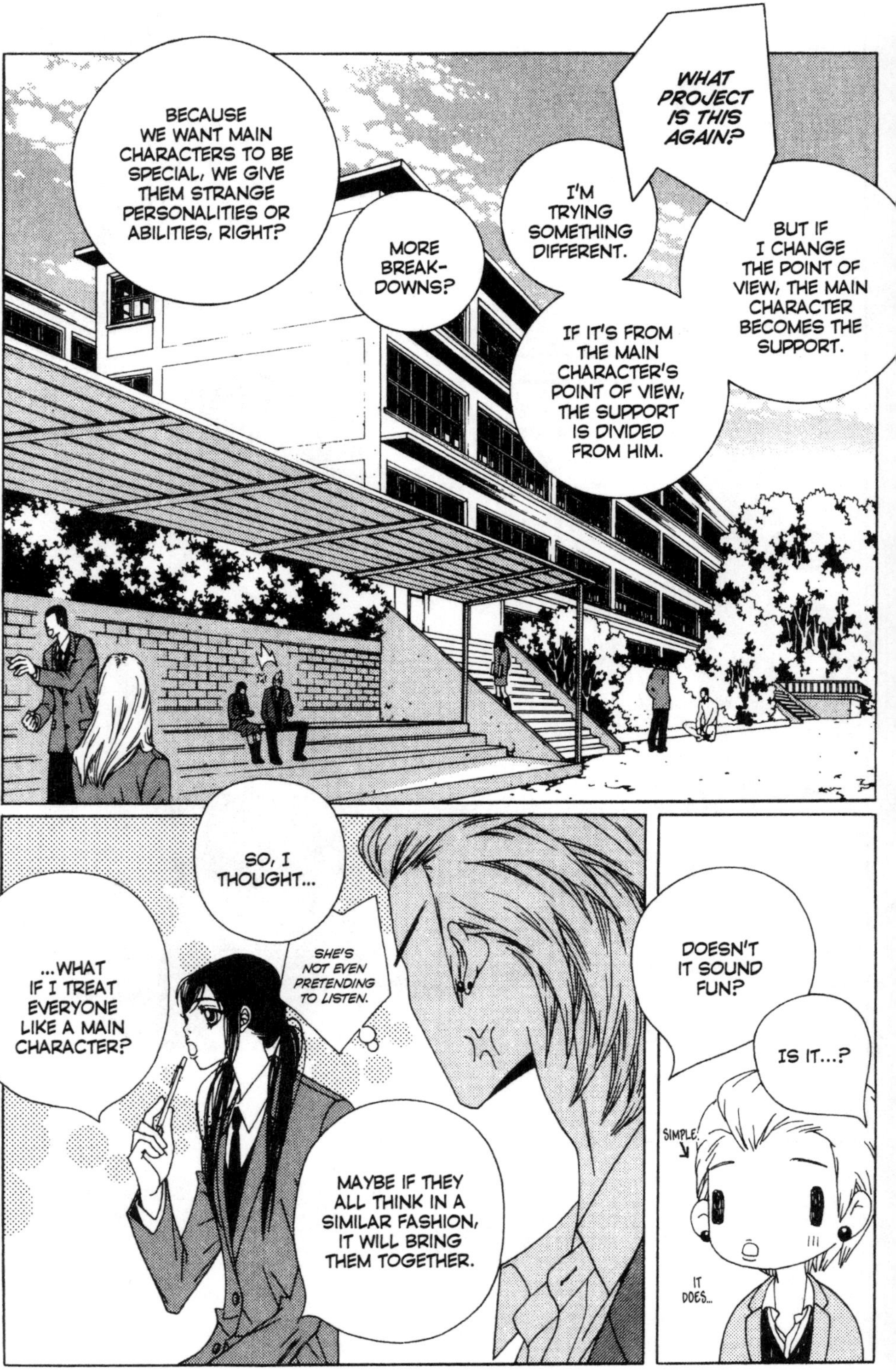
BECAUSE WE WANT MAIN CHARACTERS TO BE SPECIAL, WE GIVE THEM STRANGE PERSONALITIES OR ABILITIES, RIGHT?
MORE BREAK-DOWNS?
I'M TRYING SOMETHING DIFFERENT.
WHAT PROJECT IS THIS AGAIN?
BUT IF I CHANGE THE POINT OF VIEW, THE MAIN CHARACTER BECOMES THE SUPPORT.
IF IT'S FROM THE MAIN CHARACTER'S POINT OF VIEW, THE SUPPORT IS DIVIDED FROM HIM.
SO, I THOUGHT...
...WHAT IF I TREAT EVERYONE LIKE A MAIN CHARACTER?
SHE'S NOT EVEN PRETENDING TO LISTEN.
MAYBE IF THEY ALL THINK IN A SIMILAR FASHION, IT WILL BRING THEM TOGETHER.
DOESN'T IT SOUND FUN?
IS IT...?
SIMPLE.
IT DOES...

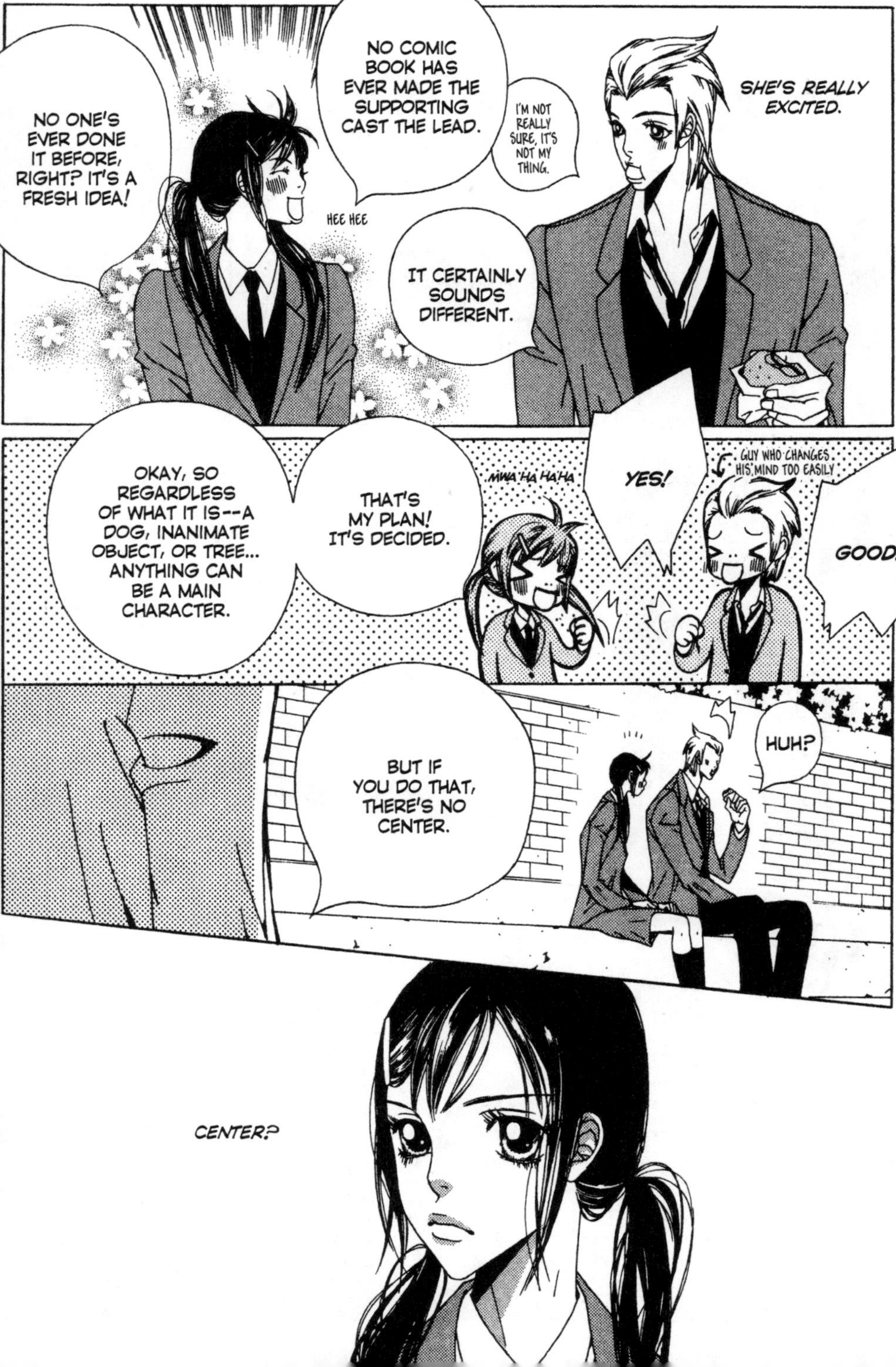
NO ONE'S EVER DONE IT BEFORE, RIGHT? IT'S A FRESH IDEA!
NO COMIC BOOK HAS EVER MADE THE SUPPORTING CAST THE LEAD.
HEE HEE
I'M NOT REALLY SURE, IT'S NOT MY THING.
IT CERTAINLY SOUNDS DIFFERENT.
SHE'S REALLY EXCITED.
OKAY, SO REGARDLESS OF WHAT IT IS--A DOG, INANIMATE OBJECT, OR TREE... ANYTHING CAN BE A MAIN CHARACTER.
THAT'S MY PLAN! IT'S DECIDED.
MWA HA HA HA
YES!
GUY WHO CHANGES HIS MIND TOO EASILY
GOOD!
BUT IF YOU DO THAT, THERE'S NO CENTER.
HUH?
CENTER?

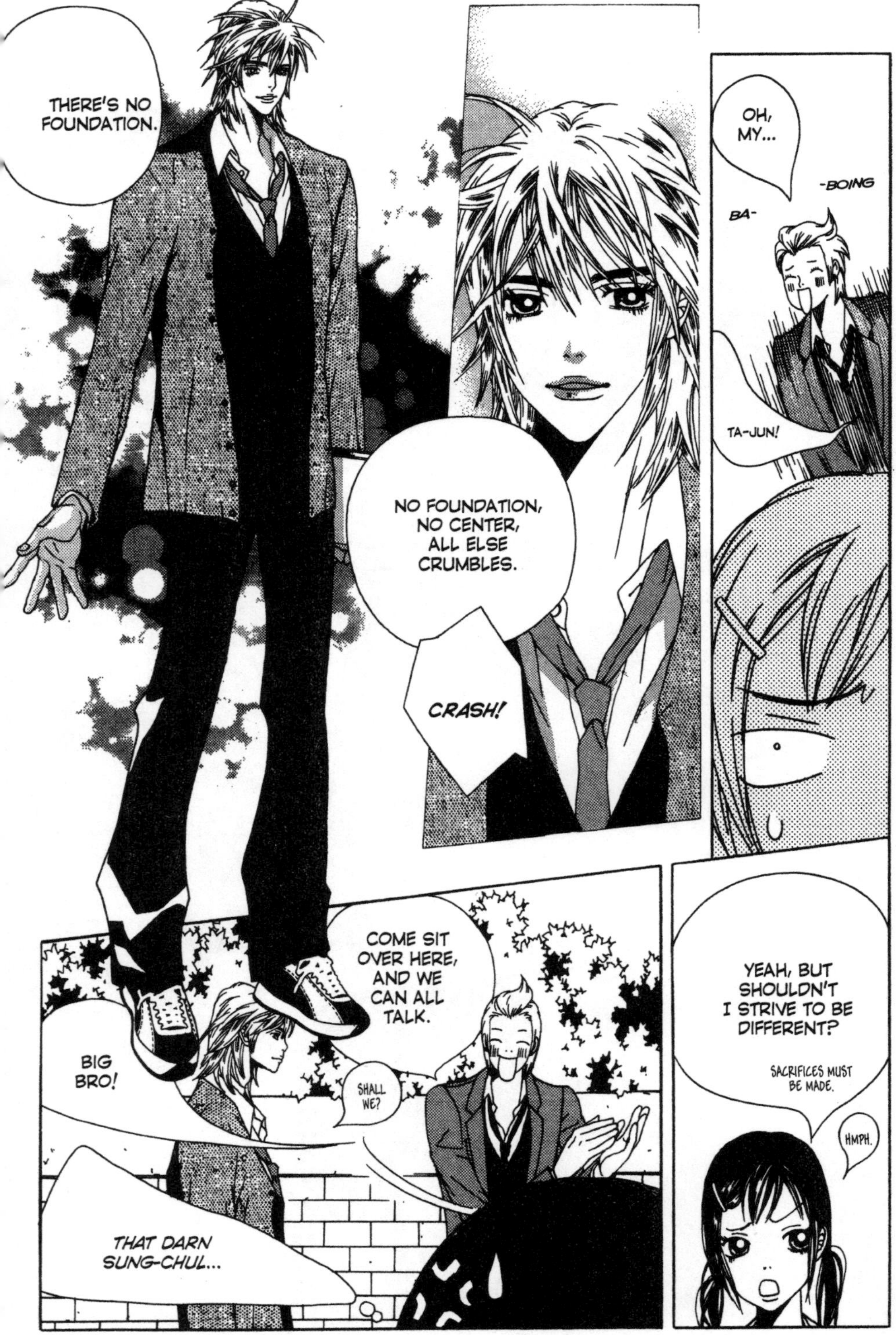
THERE'S NO FOUNDATION.
NO FOUNDATION, NO CENTER, ALL ELSE CRUMBLES.
CRASH!
OH, MY...
BA-
-BOING
TA-JUN!
COME SIT OVER HERE, AND WE CAN ALL TALK.
BIG BRO!
SHALL WE?
THAT DARN SUNG-CHUL...
YEAH, BUT SHOULDN'T I STRIVE TO BE DIFFERENT?
SACRIFICES MUST BE MADE.
HMPH.

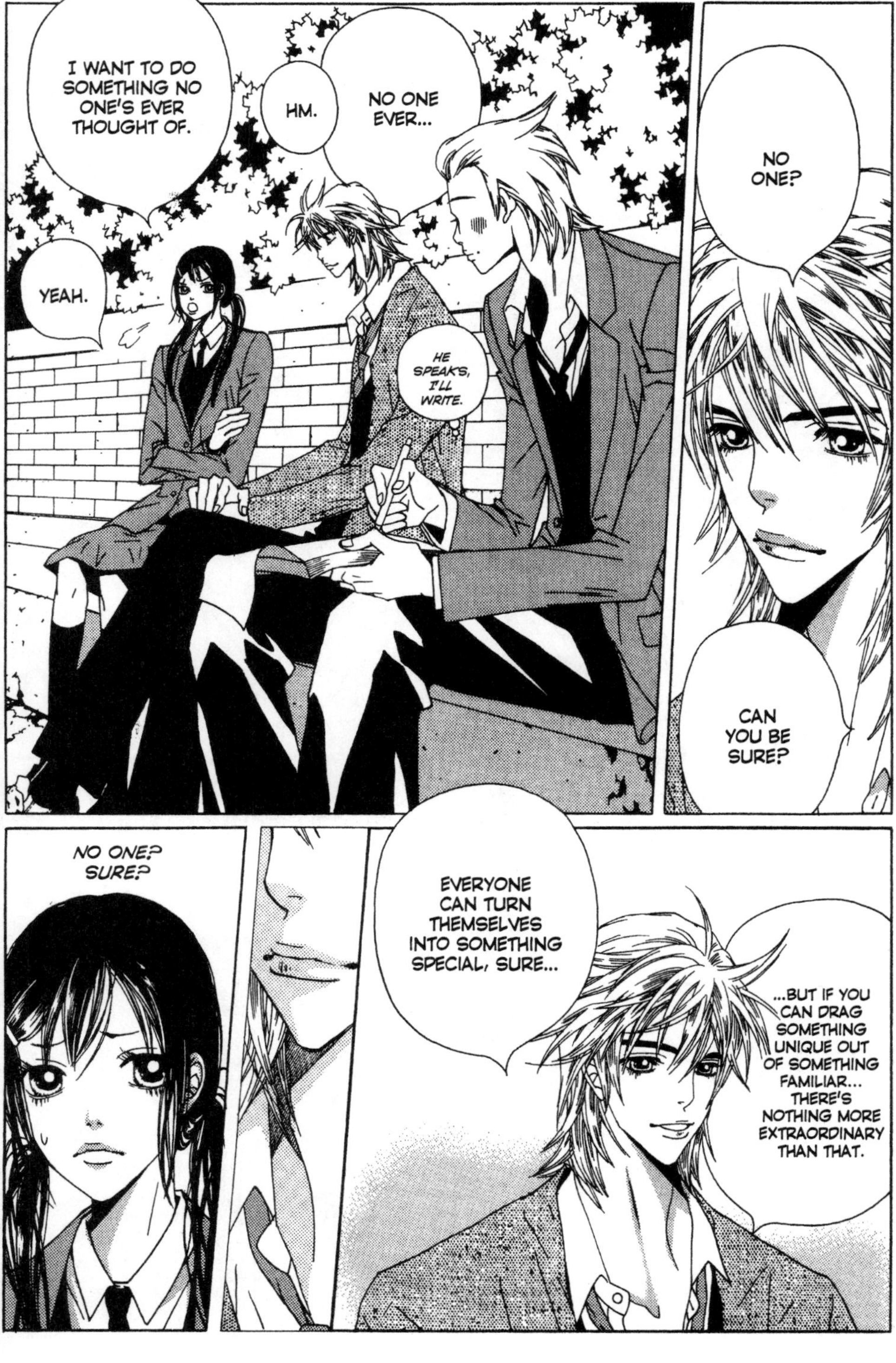
I WANT TO DO SOMETHING NO ONE'S EVER THOUGHT OF.
HM.
NO ONE EVER...
YEAH.
HE SPEAKS, I'LL WRITE.
NO ONE?
CAN YOU BE SURE?
NO ONE? SURE?
EVERYONE CAN TURN THEMSELVES INTO SOMETHING SPECIAL, SURE...
...BUT IF YOU CAN DRAG SOMETHING UNIQUE OUT OF SOMETHING FAMILIAR... THERE'S NOTHING MORE EXTRAORDINARY THAN THAT.

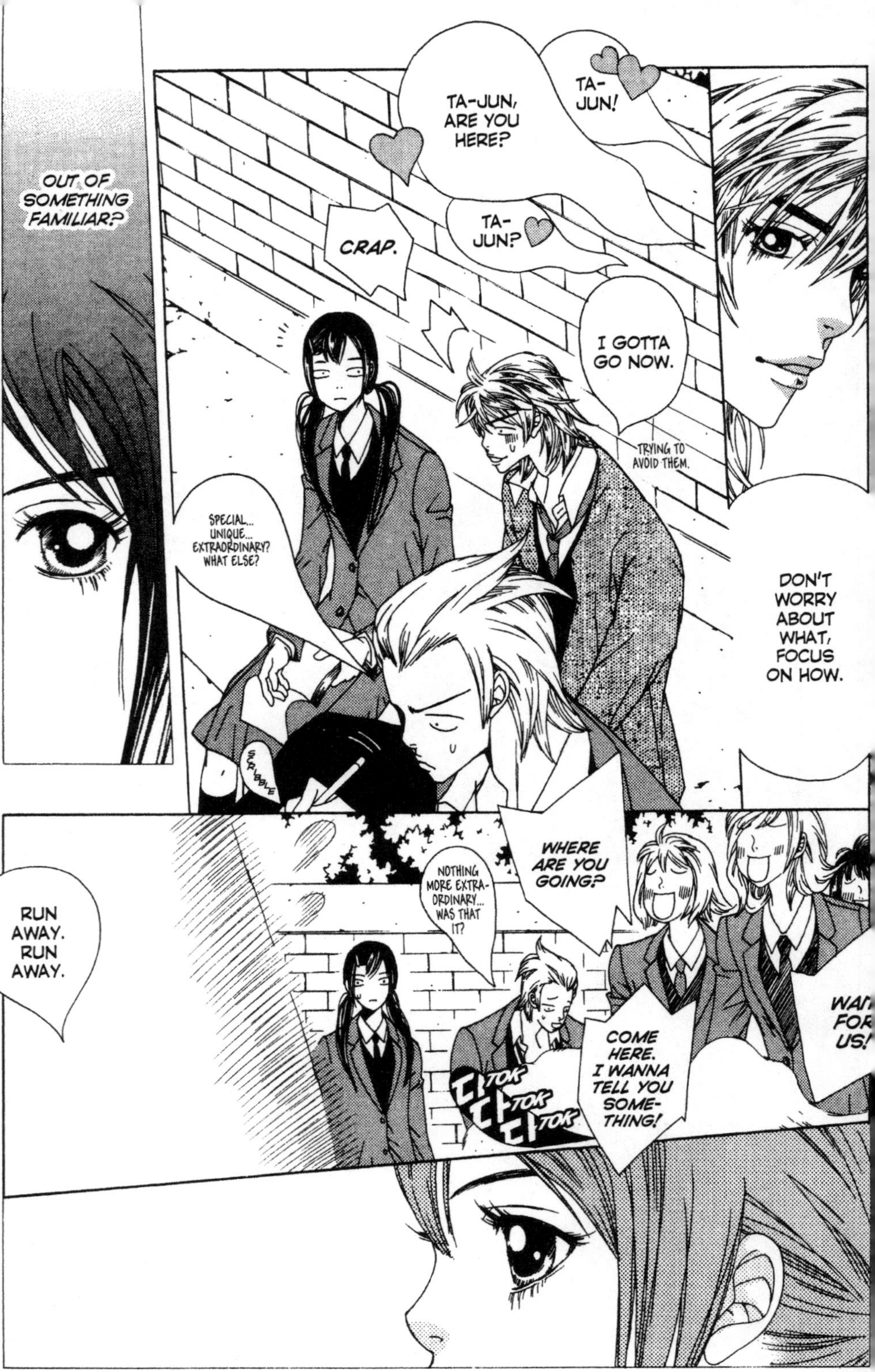

OUT OF SOMETHING FAMILIAR?
TA-JUN, ARE YOU HERE?
TA-JUN!
CRAP.
TA-JUN?
I GOTTA GO NOW.
TRYING TO AVOID THEM.
SPECIAL... UNIQUE... EXTRAORDINARY? WHAT ELSE?
SCRIBBLE
DON'T WORRY ABOUT WHAT, FOCUS ON HOW.
RUN AWAY. RUN AWAY.
NOTHING MORE EXTRA-ORDINARY... WAS THAT IT?
WHERE ARE YOU GOING?
TOK TOK TOK
COME HERE. I WANNA TELL YOU SOME-THING!

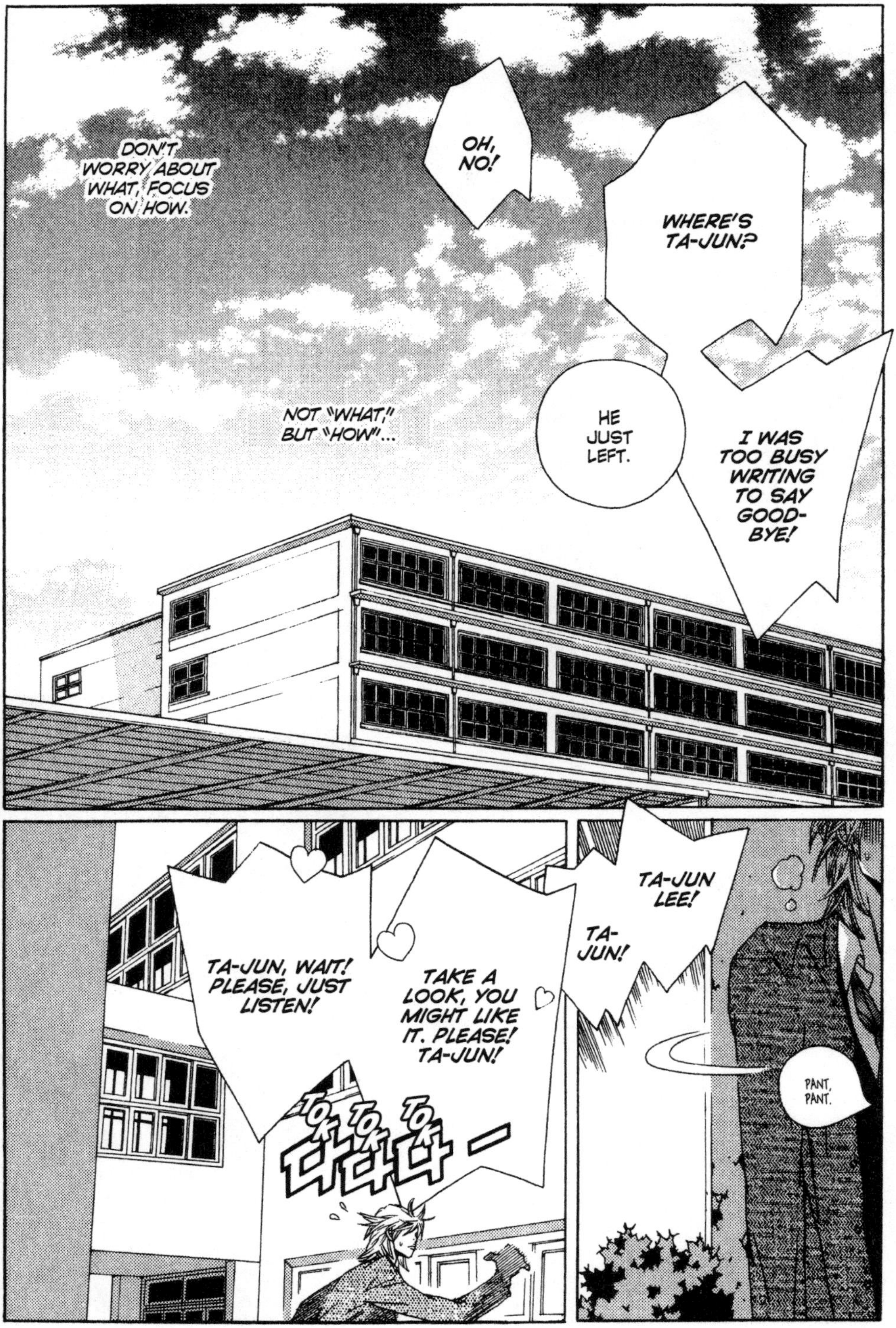
DON'T WORRY ABOUT WHAT, FOCUS ON HOW.
OH, NO!
WHERE'S TA-JUN?
NOT "WHAT," BUT "HOW"...
HE JUST LEFT.
I WAS TOO BUSY WRITING TO SAY GOOD-BYE!
TA-JUN, WAIT! PLEASE, JUST LISTEN!
TAKE A LOOK, YOU MIGHT LIKE IT. PLEASE! TA-JUN!
TOK TOK TOK
다다다 —
TA-JUN LEE!
TA-JUN!
PANT, PANT.

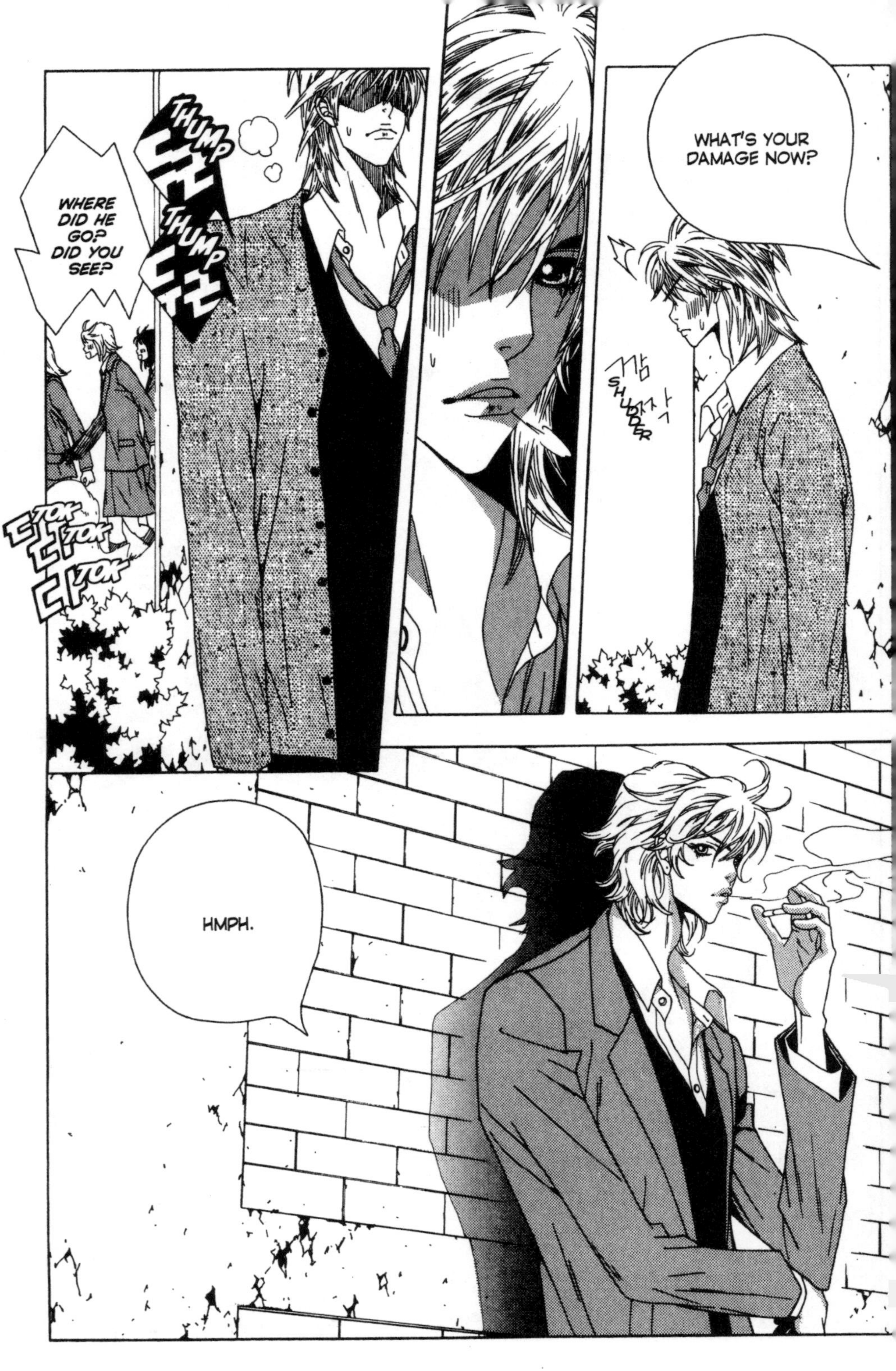
WHERE DID HE GO? DID YOU SEE?
THUMP THUMP
TOK TOK TOK
WHAT'S YOUR DAMAGE NOW?
SHUDDER
HMPH.

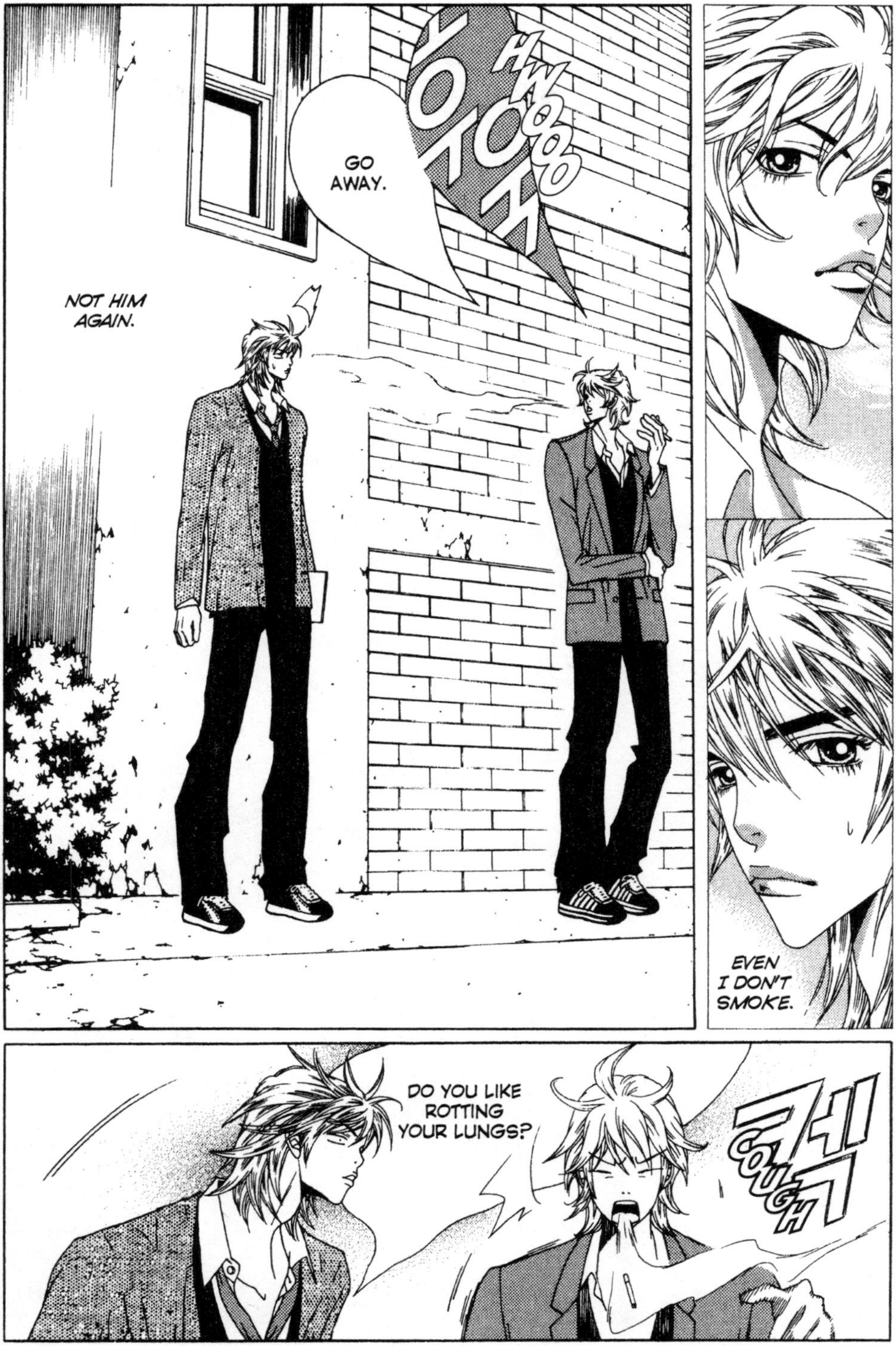
HWOOOO
GO AWAY.
NOT HIM AGAIN.
EVEN I DON'T SMOKE.
DO YOU LIKE ROTTING YOUR LUNGS?
COUGH

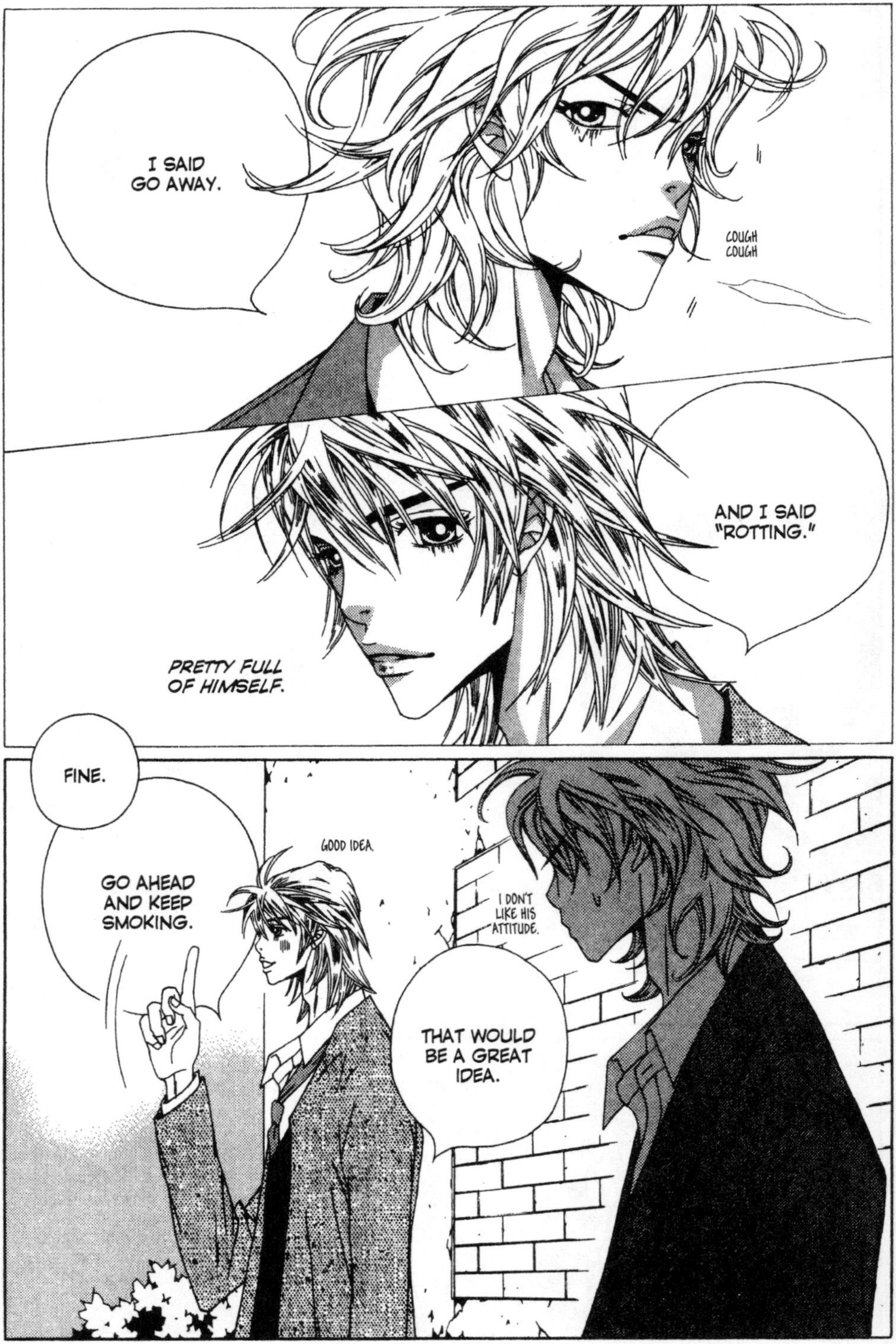
I SAID GO AWAY.
COUGH COUGH
AND I SAID "ROTTING."
PRETTY FULL OF HIMSELF.
FINE.
GO AHEAD AND KEEP SMOKING.
GOOD IDEA.
I DON'T LIKE HIS ATTITUDE.
THAT WOULD BE A GREAT IDEA.

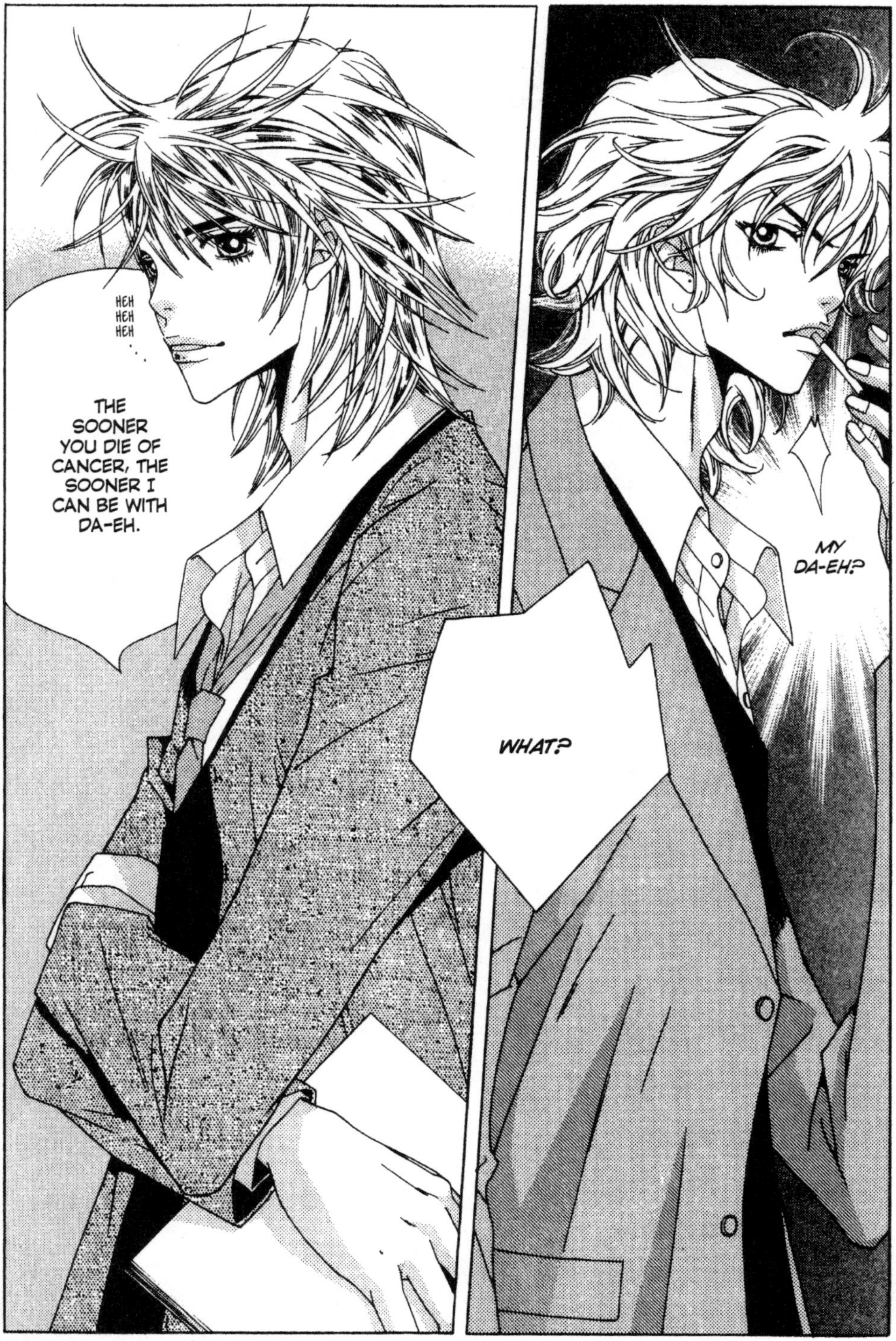
HEH HEH HEH . . .
THE SOONER YOU DIE OF CANCER, THE SOONER I CAN BE WITH DA-EH.
MY DA-EH?
WHAT?

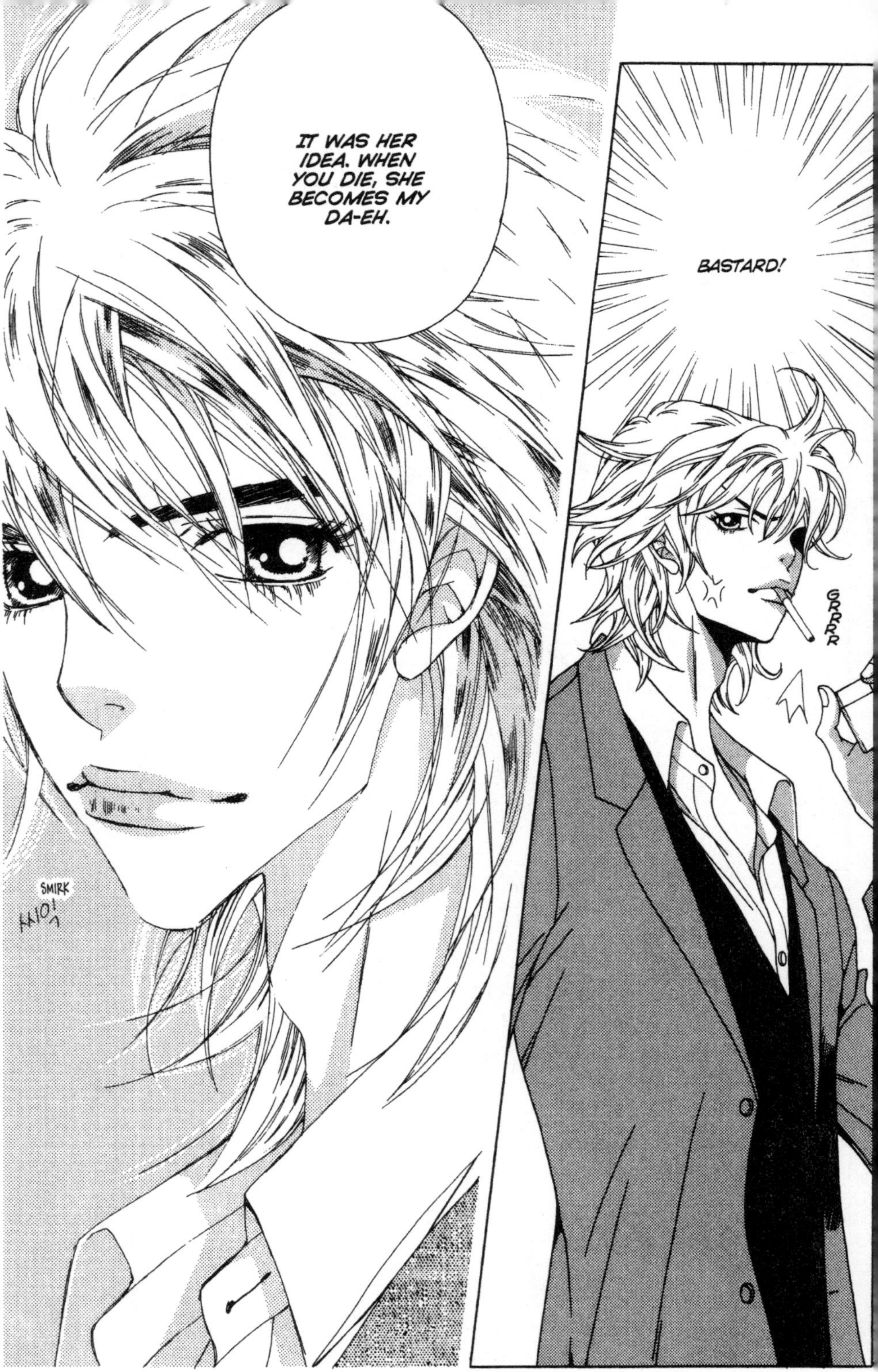
IT WAS HER IDEA. WHEN YOU DIE, SHE BECOMES MY DA-EH.
SMIRK
BASTARD!
GRRRR

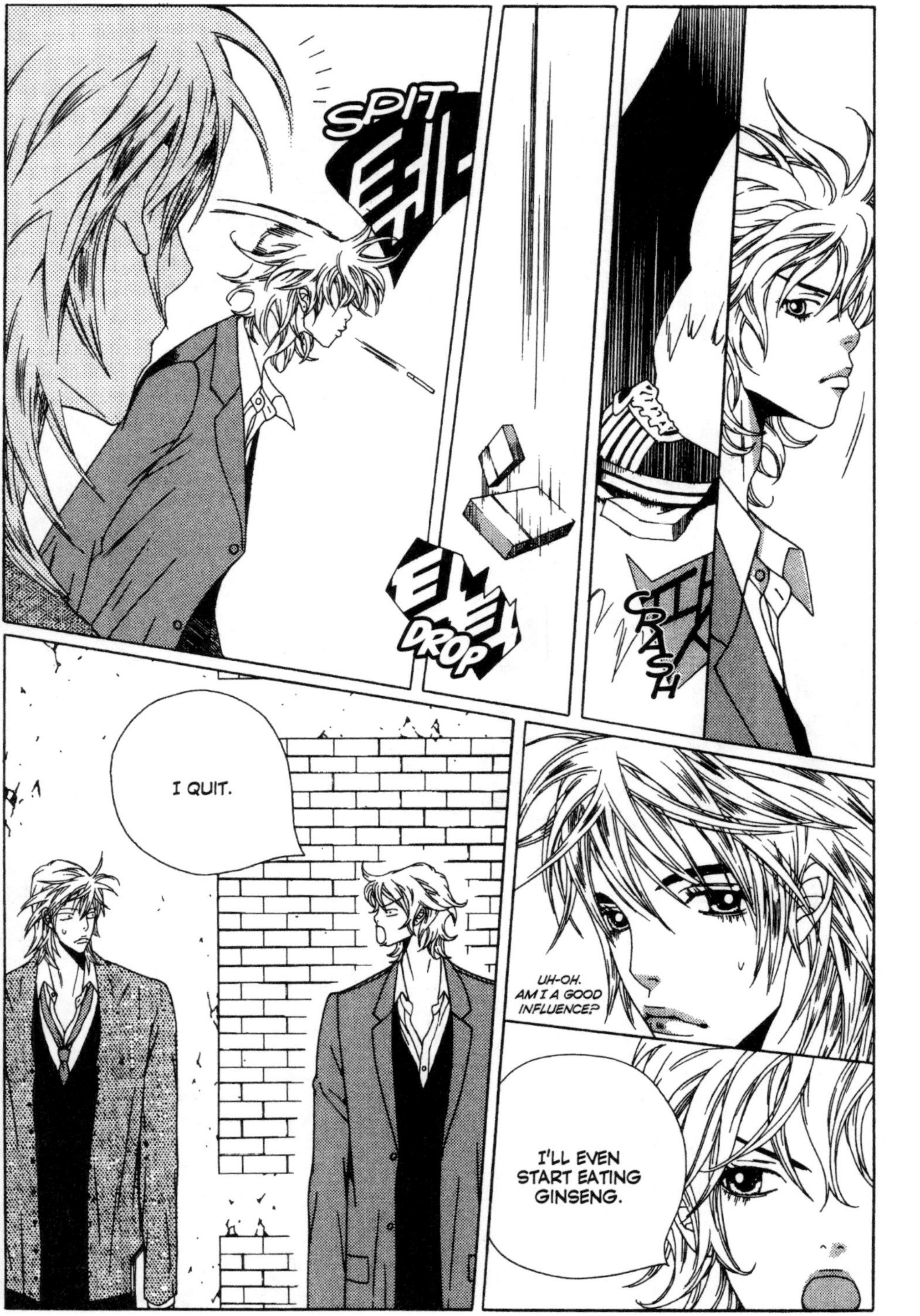
SPIT
DROP
CRASH
I QUIT.
UH-OH. AM I A GOOD INFLUENCE?
I'LL EVEN START EATING GINSENG.

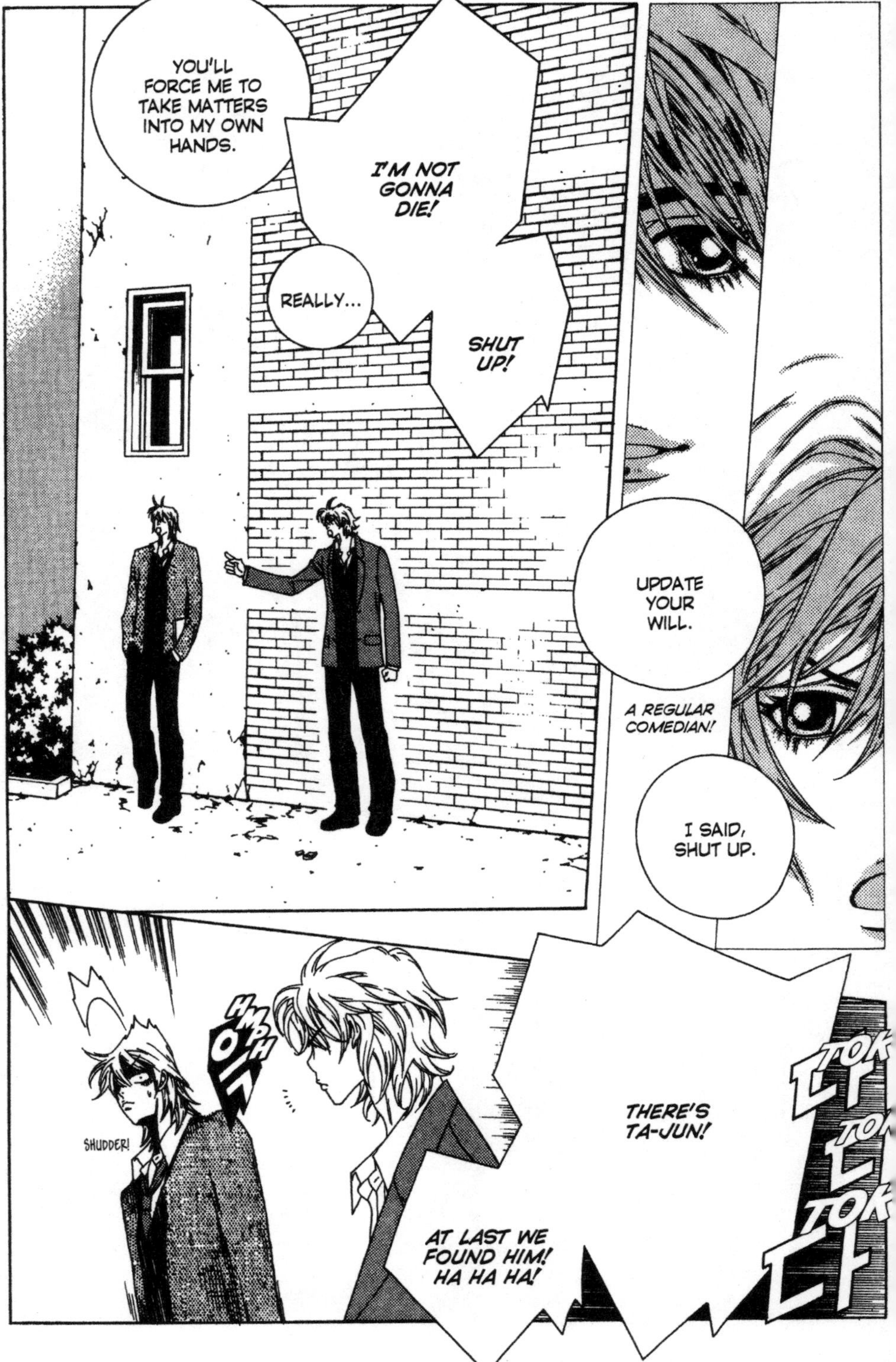
YOU'LL FORCE ME TO TAKE MATTERS INTO MY OWN HANDS.
I'M NOT GONNA DIE!
REALLY...
SHUT UP!
UPDATE YOUR WILL.
A REGULAR COMEDIAN!
I SAID, SHUT UP.
SHUDDER!
HMPH
...
THERE'S TA-JUN!
AT LAST WE FOUND HIM! HA HA HA!
TOK TOK TOK

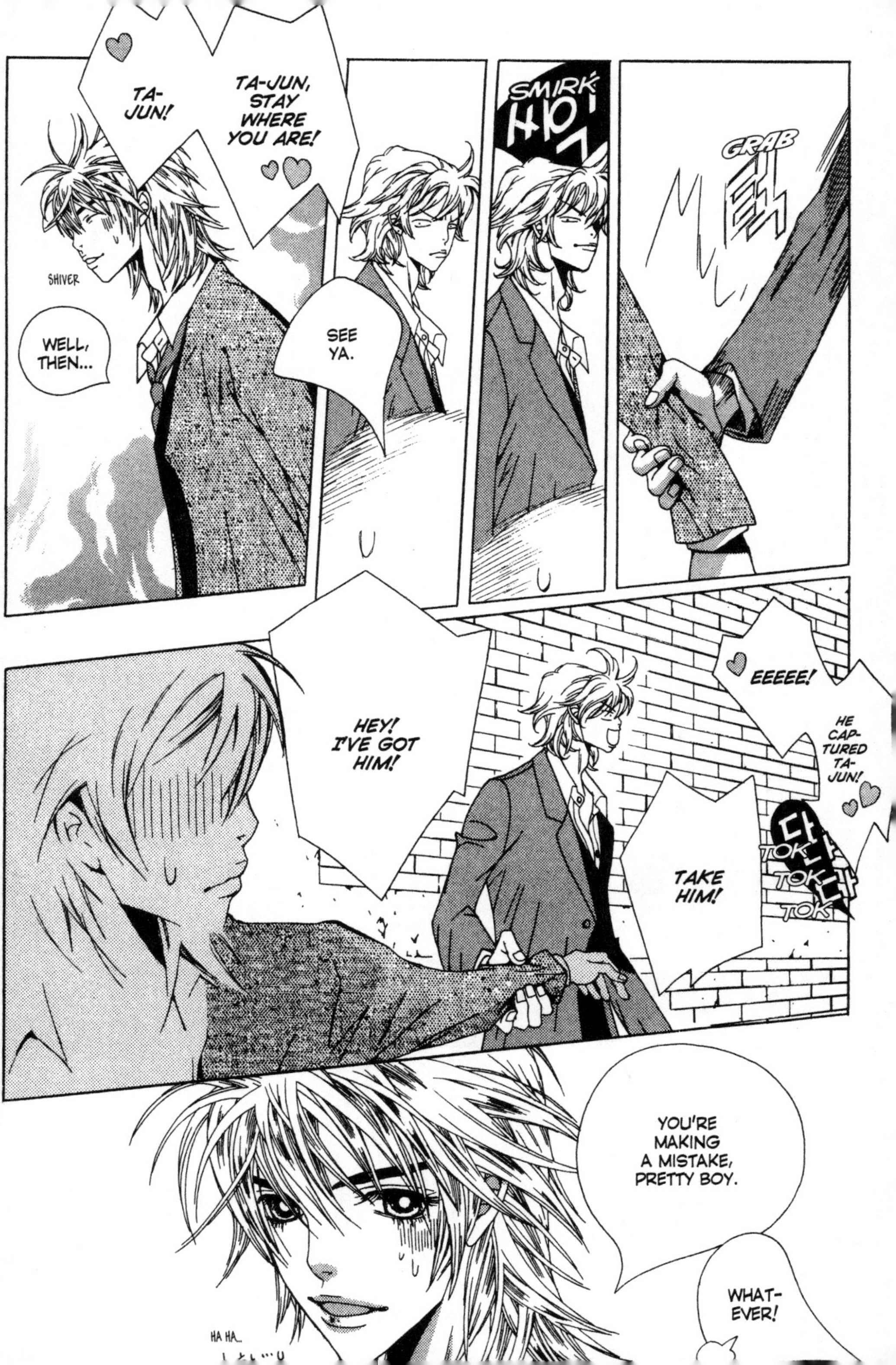
TA-JUN!
TA-JUN, STAY WHERE YOU ARE!
SHIVER
WELL, THEN...
SEE YA.
SMIRK
GRAB
HEY! I'VE GOT HIM!
EEEEE!
HE CAPTURED TA-JUN!
TAKE HIM!
TOK TOK TOK
YOU'RE MAKING A MISTAKE, PRETTY BOY.
WHAT-EVER!
HA HA..

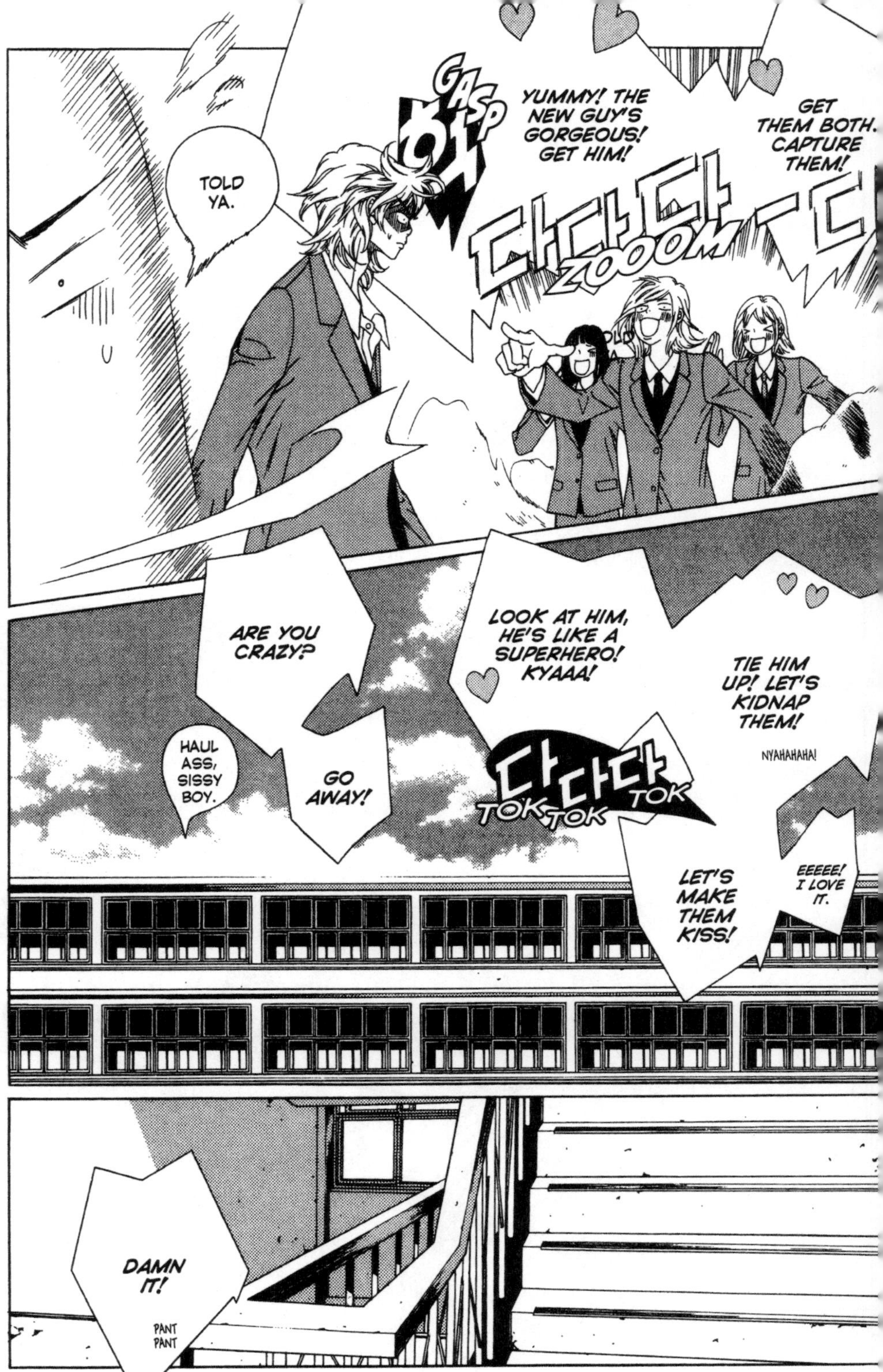
TOLD YA.
GASP
YUMMY! THE NEW GUY'S GORGEOUS! GET HIM!
GET THEM BOTH. CAPTURE THEM!
ZOOOM
ARE YOU CRAZY?
HAUL ASS, SISSY BOY.
GO AWAY!
LOOK AT HIM, HE'S LIKE A SUPERHERO! KYAAA!
TIE HIM UP! LET'S KIDNAP THEM!
NYAHAHAHA!
TOK TOK TOK
LET'S MAKE THEM KISS!
EEEEE! I LOVE IT.
DAMN IT!
PANT PANT

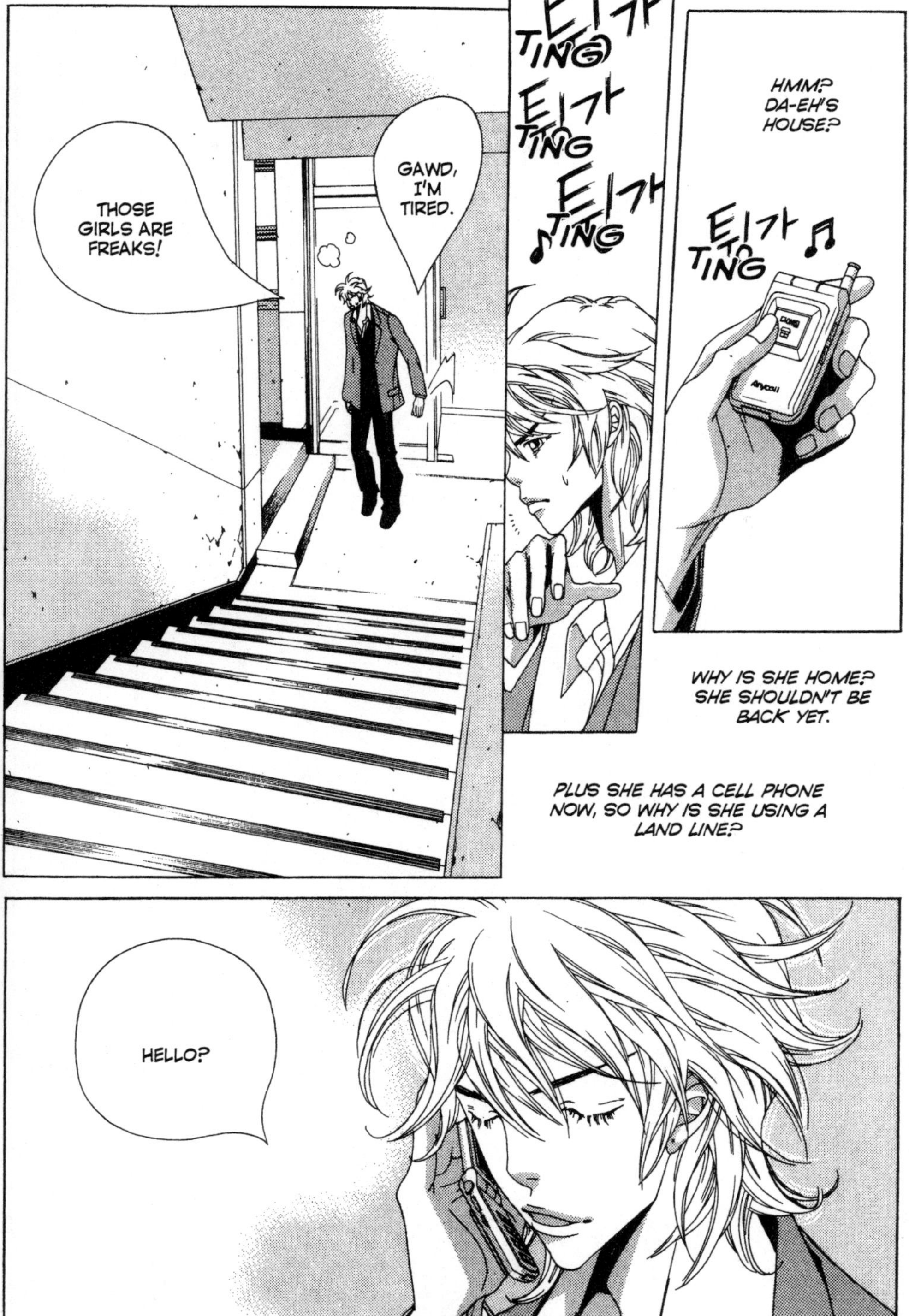
THOSE GIRLS ARE FREAKS!
GAWD, I'M TIRED.
티가 TING
티가 TING
티가 TING
티가 TING
HMM? DA-EH'S HOUSE?
WHY IS SHE HOME? SHE SHOULDN'T BE BACK YET.
PLUS SHE HAS A CELL PHONE NOW, SO WHY IS SHE USING A LAND LINE?
HELLO?

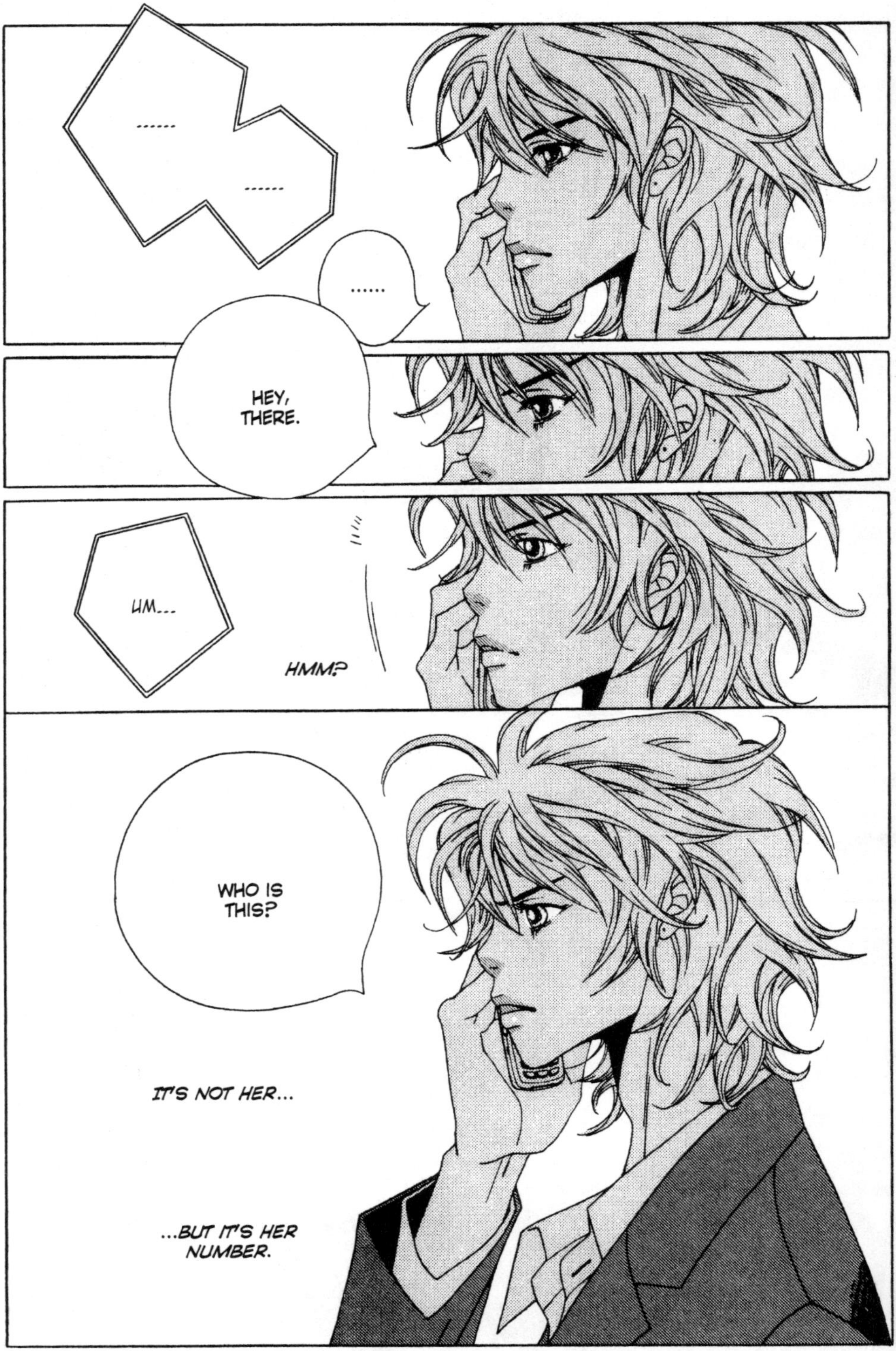
......
......
......
HEY, THERE.
UM...
HMM?
WHO IS THIS?
IT'S NOT HER...
...BUT IT'S HER NUMBER.

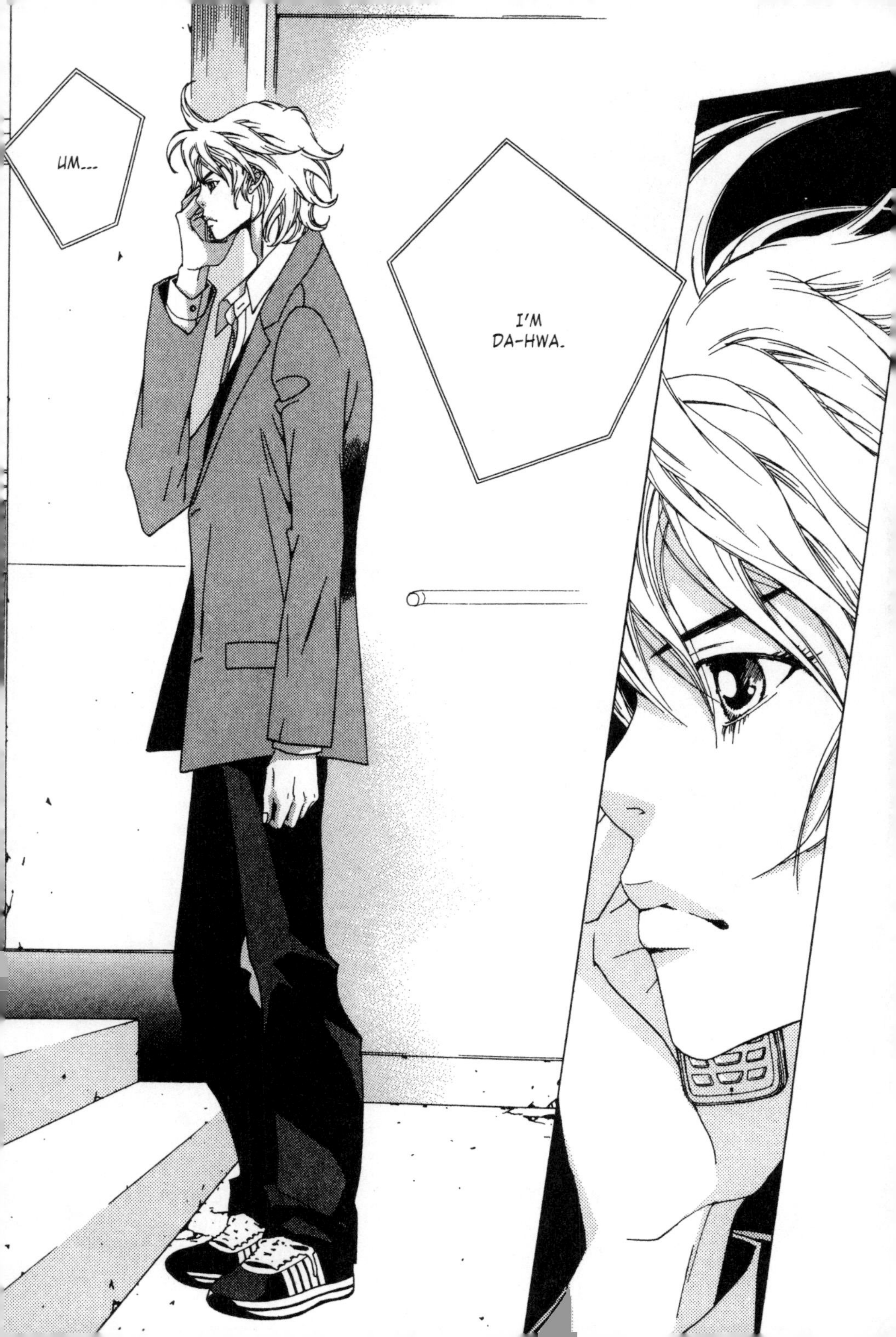
UM...
I'M DA-HWA.

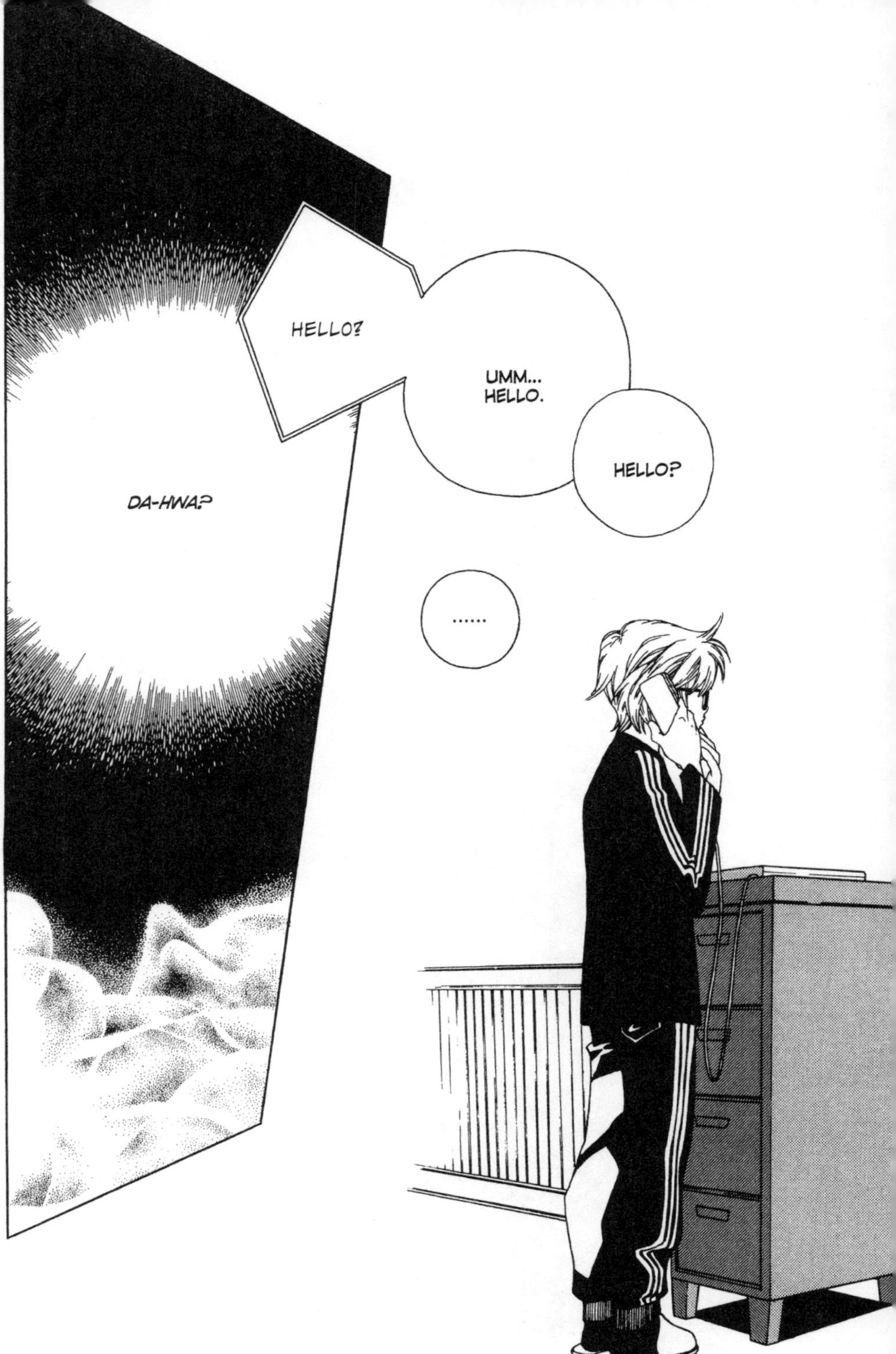
DA-HWA?
HELLO?
UMM... HELLO.
HELLO?
......

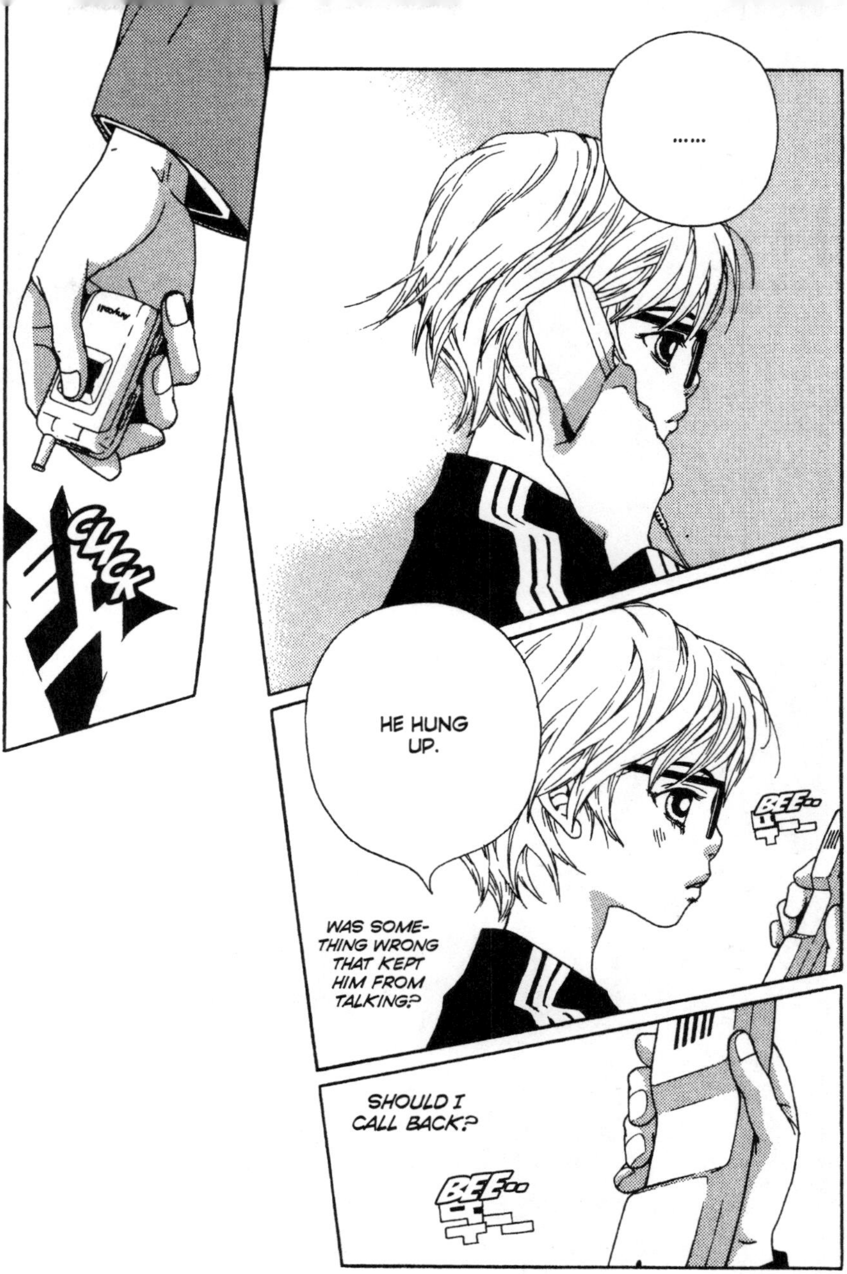
CLICK
......
HE HUNG UP.
WAS SOME-THING WRONG THAT KEPT HIM FROM TALKING?
BEE..
SHOULD I CALL BACK?
BEE..

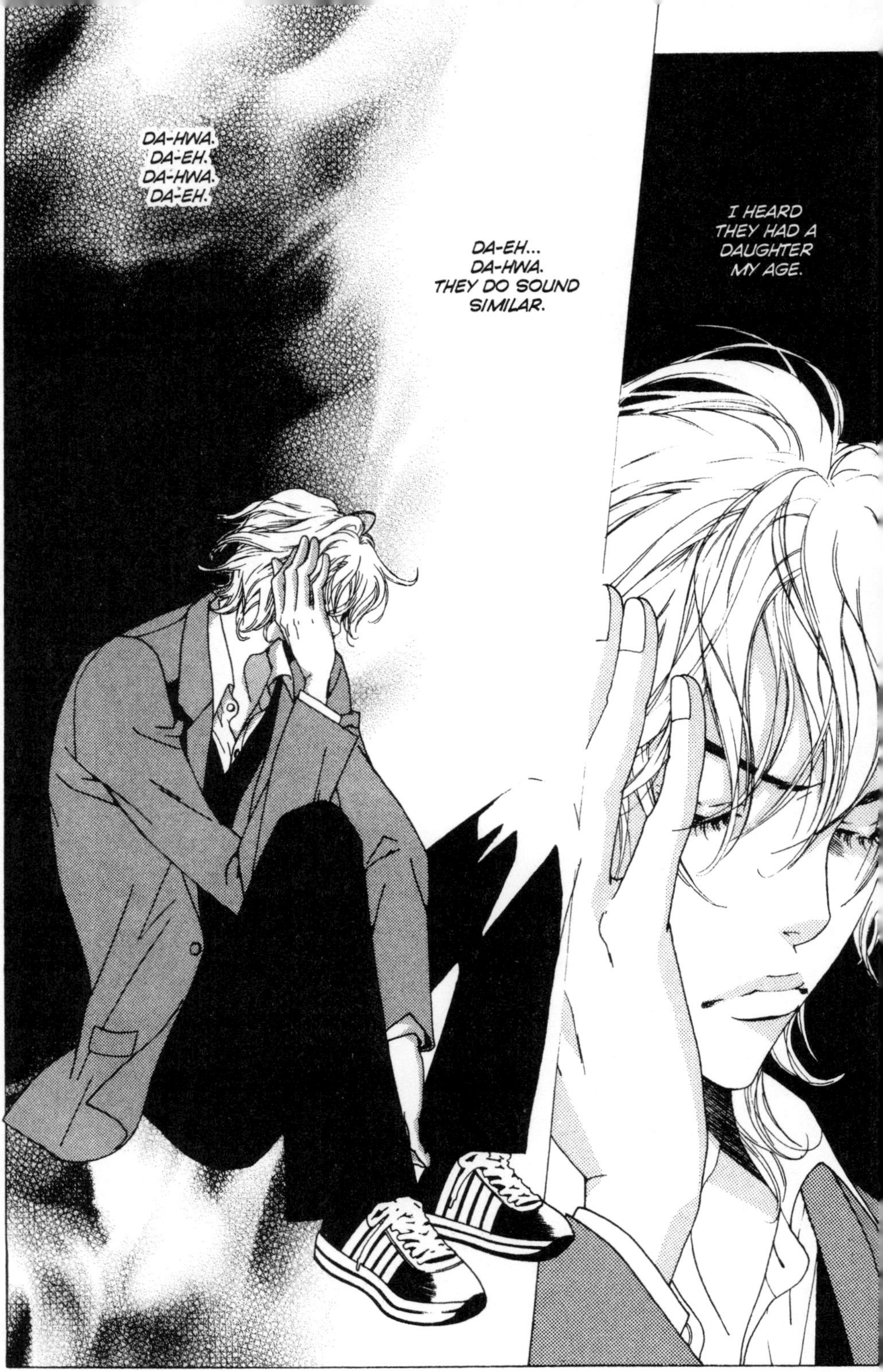
DA-HWA.
DA-EH.
DA-HWA.
DA-EH.
DA-EH... DA-HWA. THEY DO SOUND SIMILAR.
I HEARD THEY HAD A DAUGHTER MY AGE.

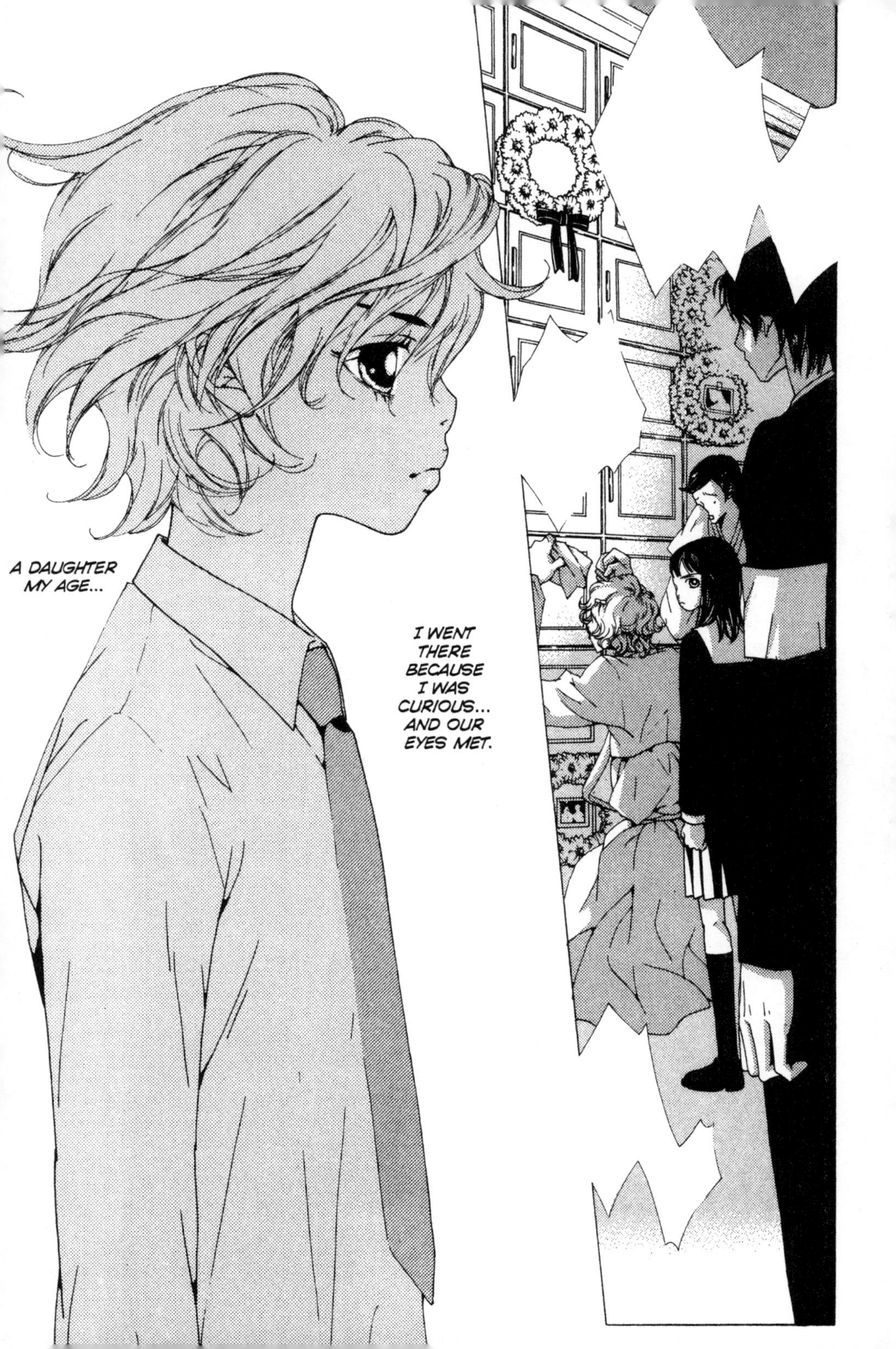
A DAUGHTER MY AGE...
I WENT THERE BECAUSE I WAS CURIOUS... AND OUR EYES MET.

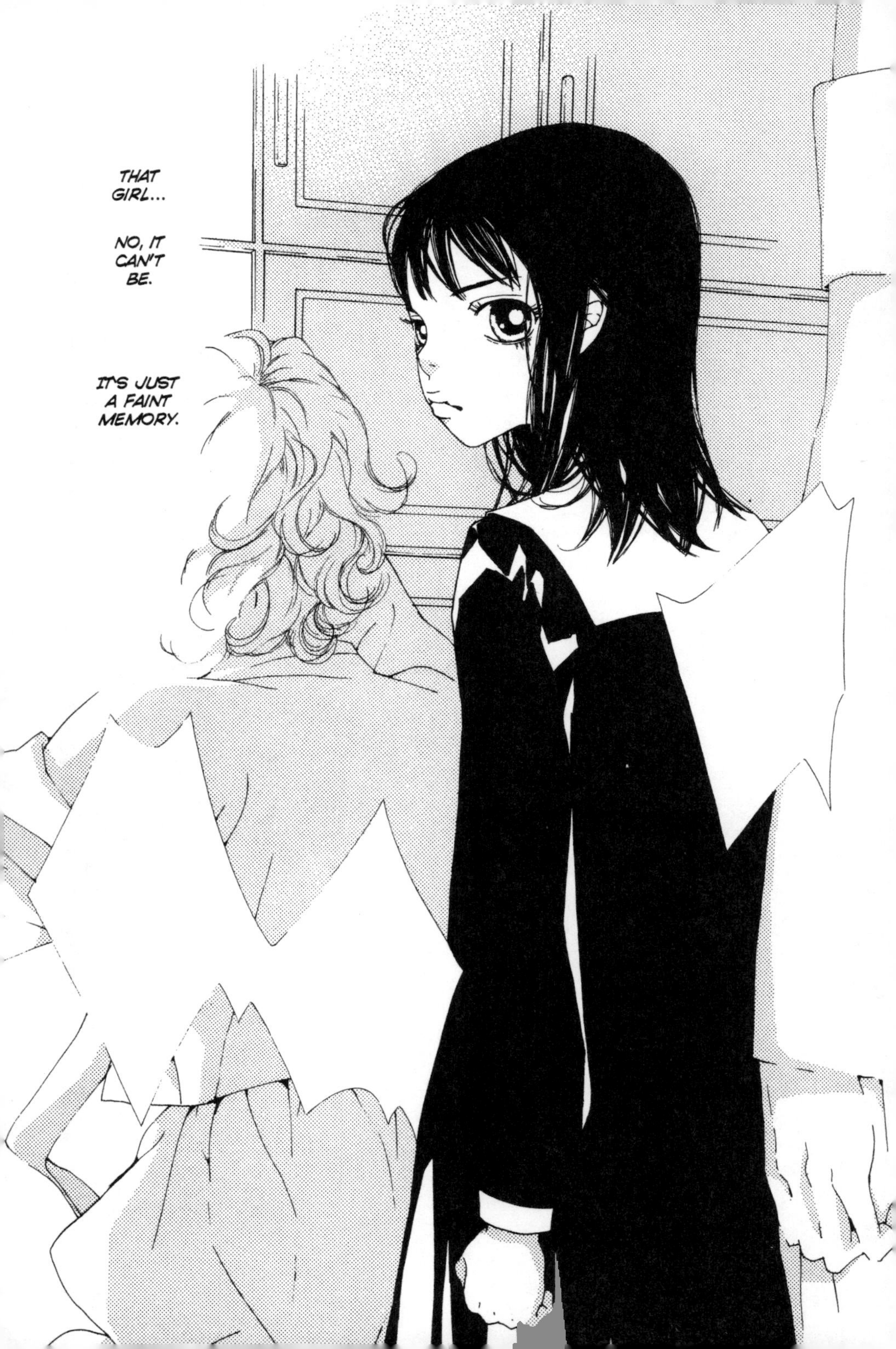
THAT GIRL...
NO, IT CAN'T BE.
IT'S JUST A FAINT MEMORY.

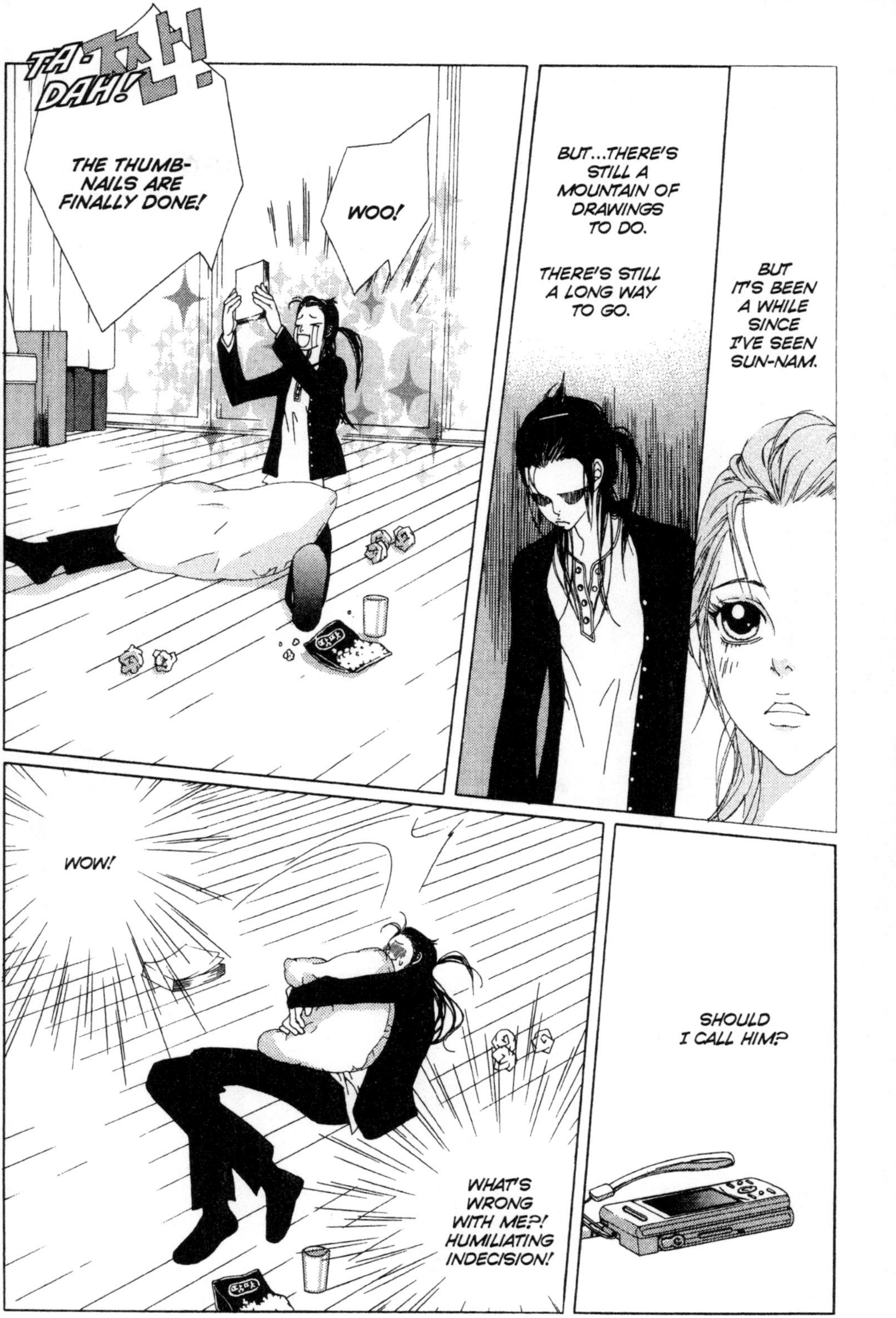
TA-DAH!
THE THUMB-NAILS ARE FINALLY DONE!
WOO!
BUT...THERE'S STILL A MOUNTAIN OF DRAWINGS TO DO.
THERE'S STILL A LONG WAY TO GO.
BUT IT'S BEEN A WHILE SINCE I'VE SEEN SUN-NAM.
WOW!
WHAT'S WRONG WITH ME?! HUMILIATING INDECISION!
SHOULD I CALL HIM?

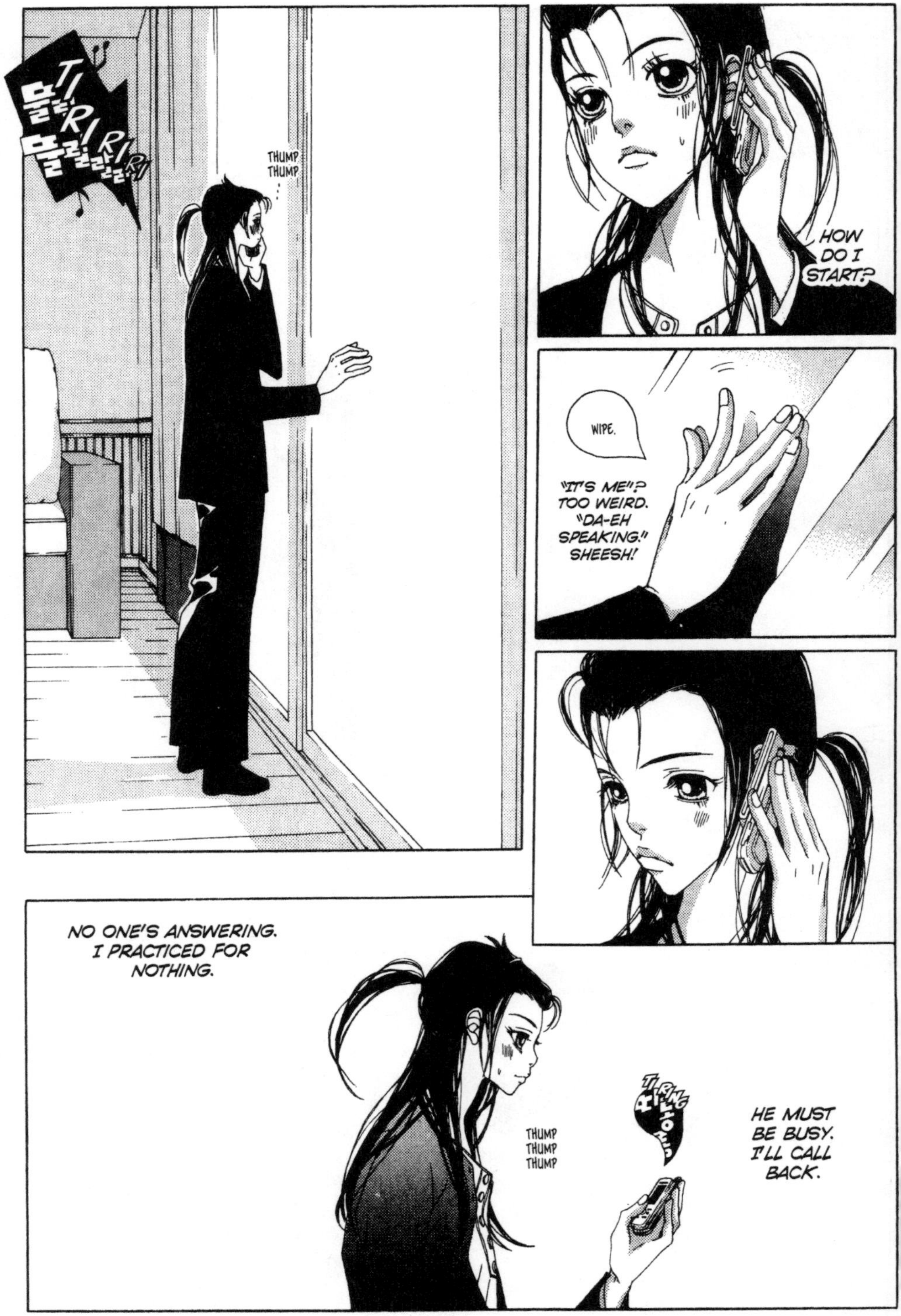
TIRIRIRI
THUMP THUMP
HOW DO I START?
WIPE.
"IT'S ME"? TOO WEIRD. "DA-EH SPEAKING." SHEESH!
NO ONE'S ANSWERING. I PRACTICED FOR NOTHING.
THUMP THUMP THUMP
TIRING
HE MUST BE BUSY. I'LL CALL BACK.

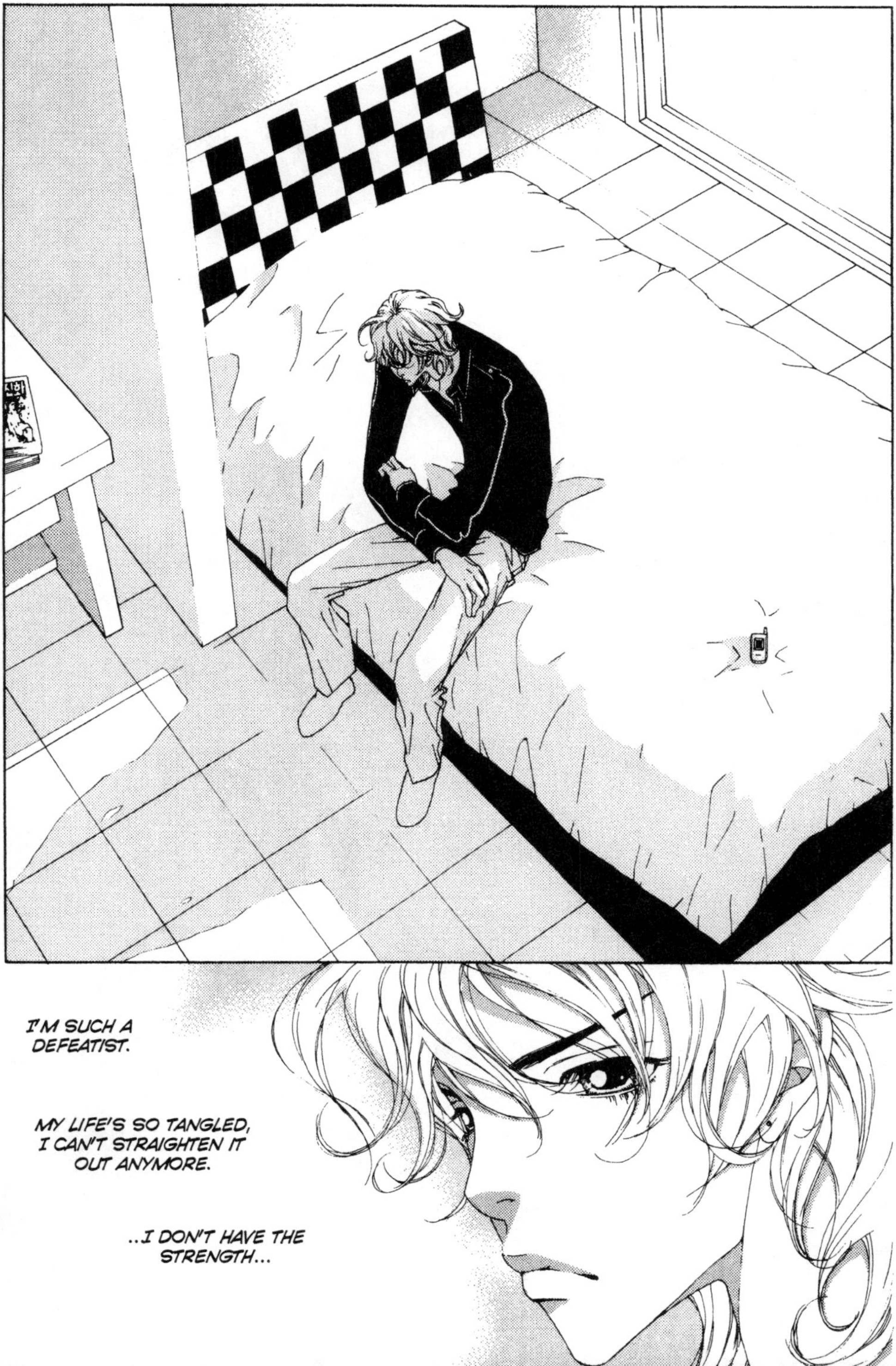
I'M SUCH A DEFEATIST.
MY LIFE'S SO TANGLED, I CAN'T STRAIGHTEN IT OUT ANYMORE.
...I DON'T HAVE THE STRENGTH...

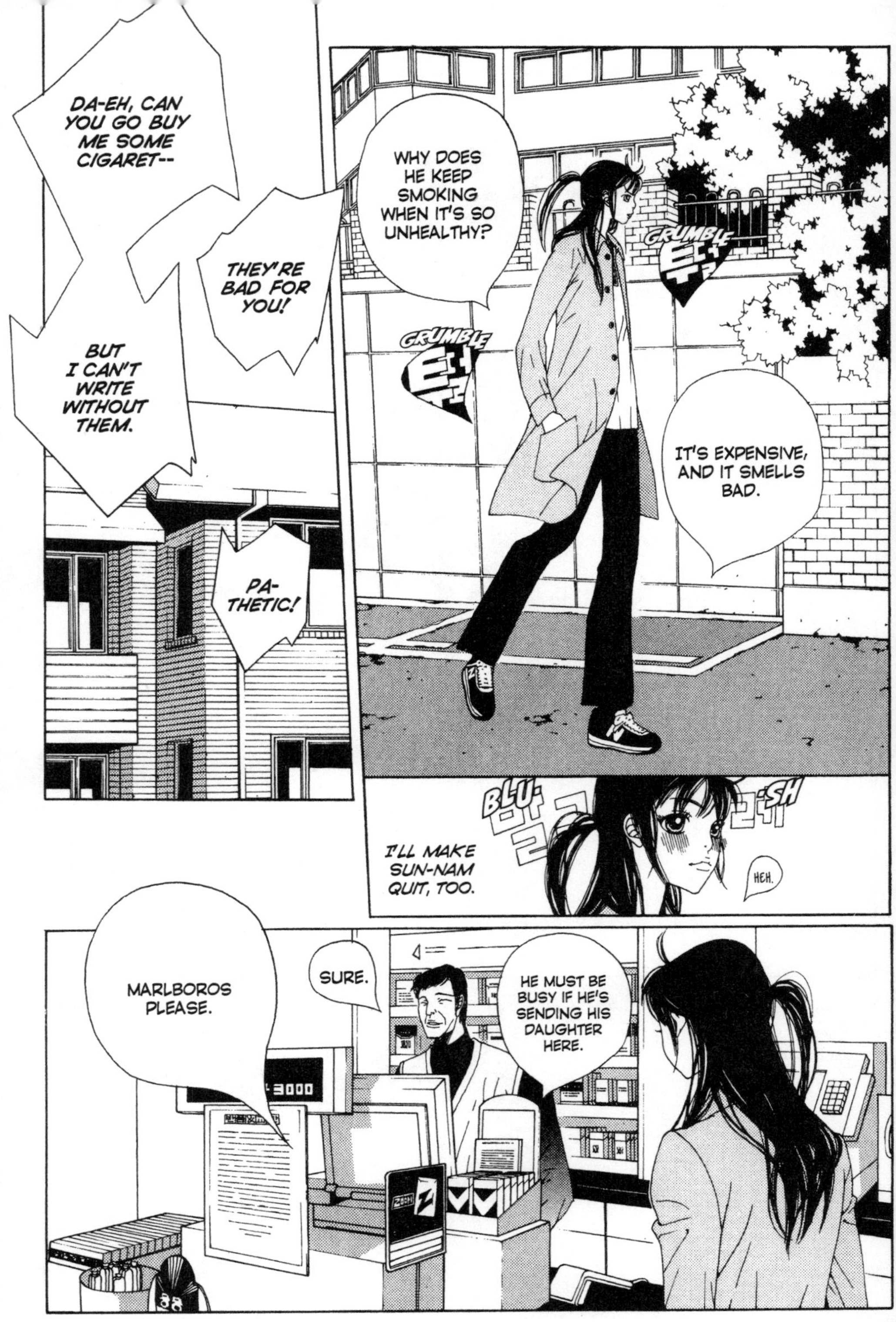
DA-EH, CAN YOU GO BUY ME SOME CIGARET--
THEY'RE BAD FOR YOU!
BUT I CAN'T WRITE WITHOUT THEM.
PA-THETIC!
WHY DOES HE KEEP SMOKING WHEN IT'S SO UNHEALTHY?
GRUMBLE
GRUMBLE
IT'S EXPENSIVE, AND IT SMELLS BAD.
BLU-SH
I'LL MAKE SUN-NAM QUIT, TOO.
HEH.
MARLBOROS PLEASE.
SURE.
HE MUST BE BUSY IF HE'S SENDING HIS DAUGHTER HERE.

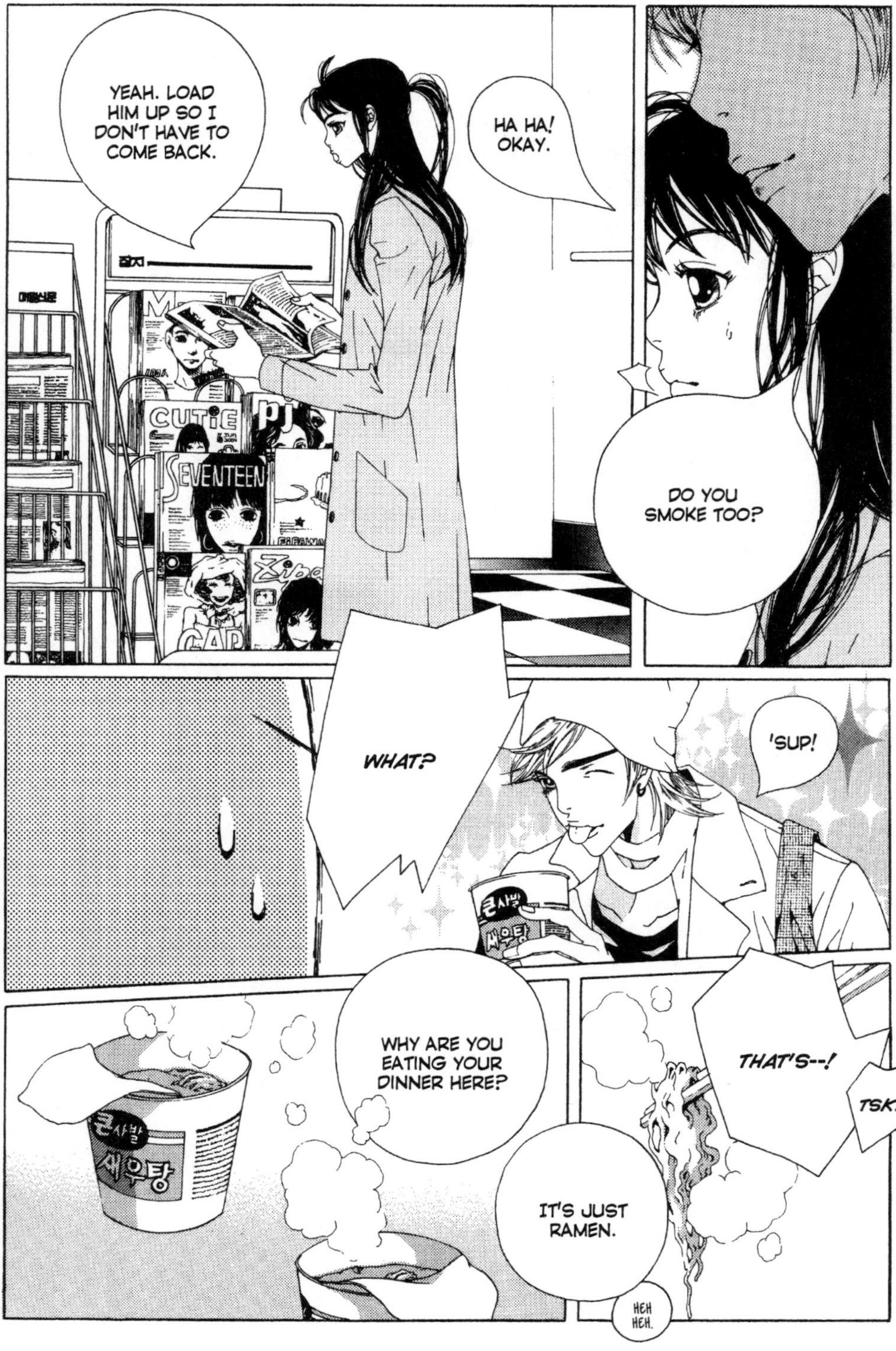
YEAH. LOAD HIM UP SO I DON'T HAVE TO COME BACK.
HA HA! OKAY.
DO YOU SMOKE TOO?
WHAT?
'SUP!
WHY ARE YOU EATING YOUR DINNER HERE?
THAT'S--!
TSK.
IT'S JUST RAMEN.
HEH HEH.

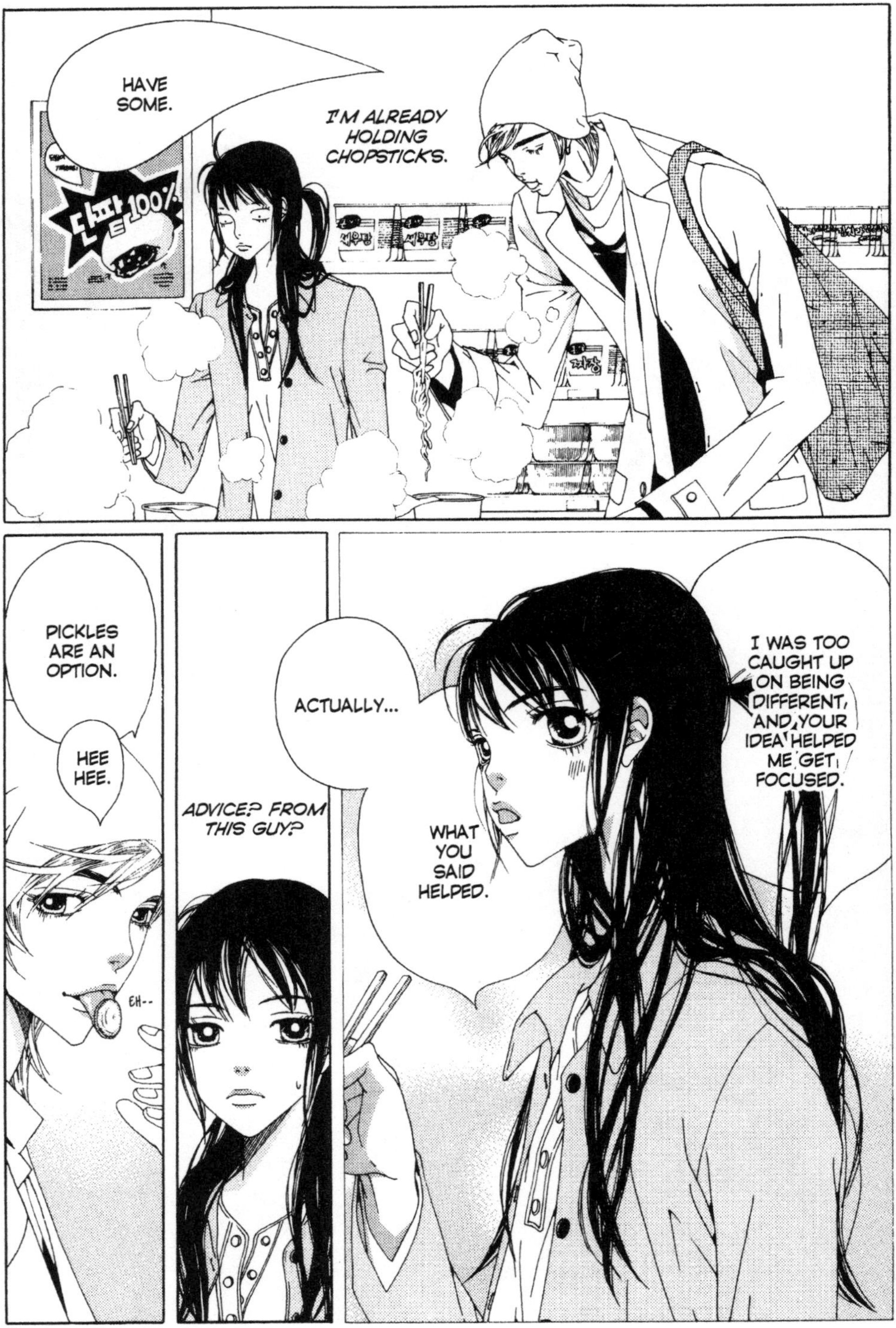
HAVE SOME.
I'M ALREADY HOLDING CHOPSTICKS.
PICKLES ARE AN OPTION.
HEE HEE.
EH--
ADVICE? FROM THIS GUY?
ACTUALLY...
WHAT YOU SAID HELPED.
I WAS TOO CAUGHT UP ON BEING DIFFERENT, AND YOUR IDEA HELPED ME GET FOCUSED.

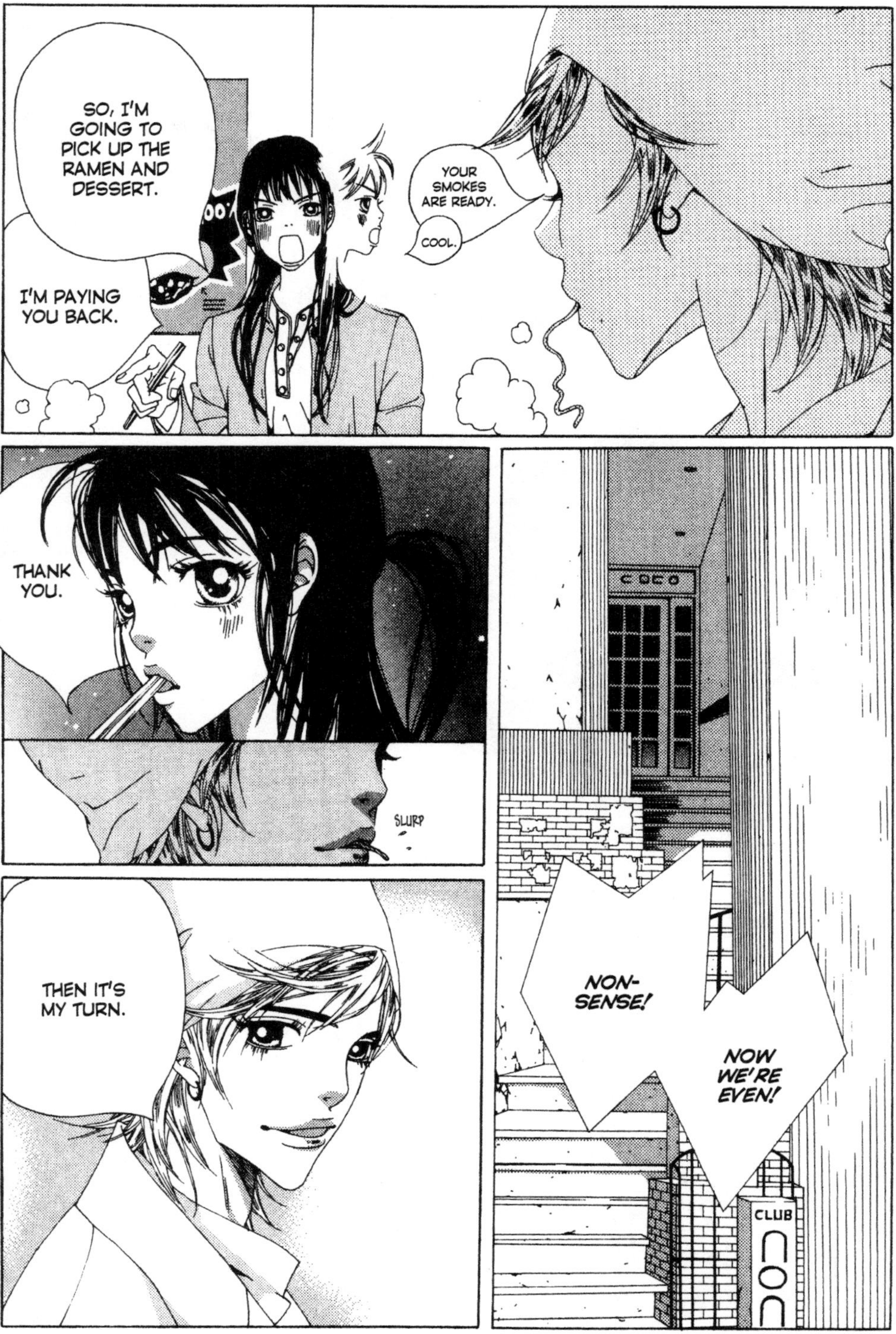
SO, I'M GOING TO PICK UP THE RAMEN AND DESSERT.
I'M PAYING YOU BACK.
YOUR SMOKES ARE READY.
COOL.
THANK YOU.
SLURP
THEN IT'S MY TURN.
COCO
NON-SENSE!
NOW WE'RE EVEN!
CLUB

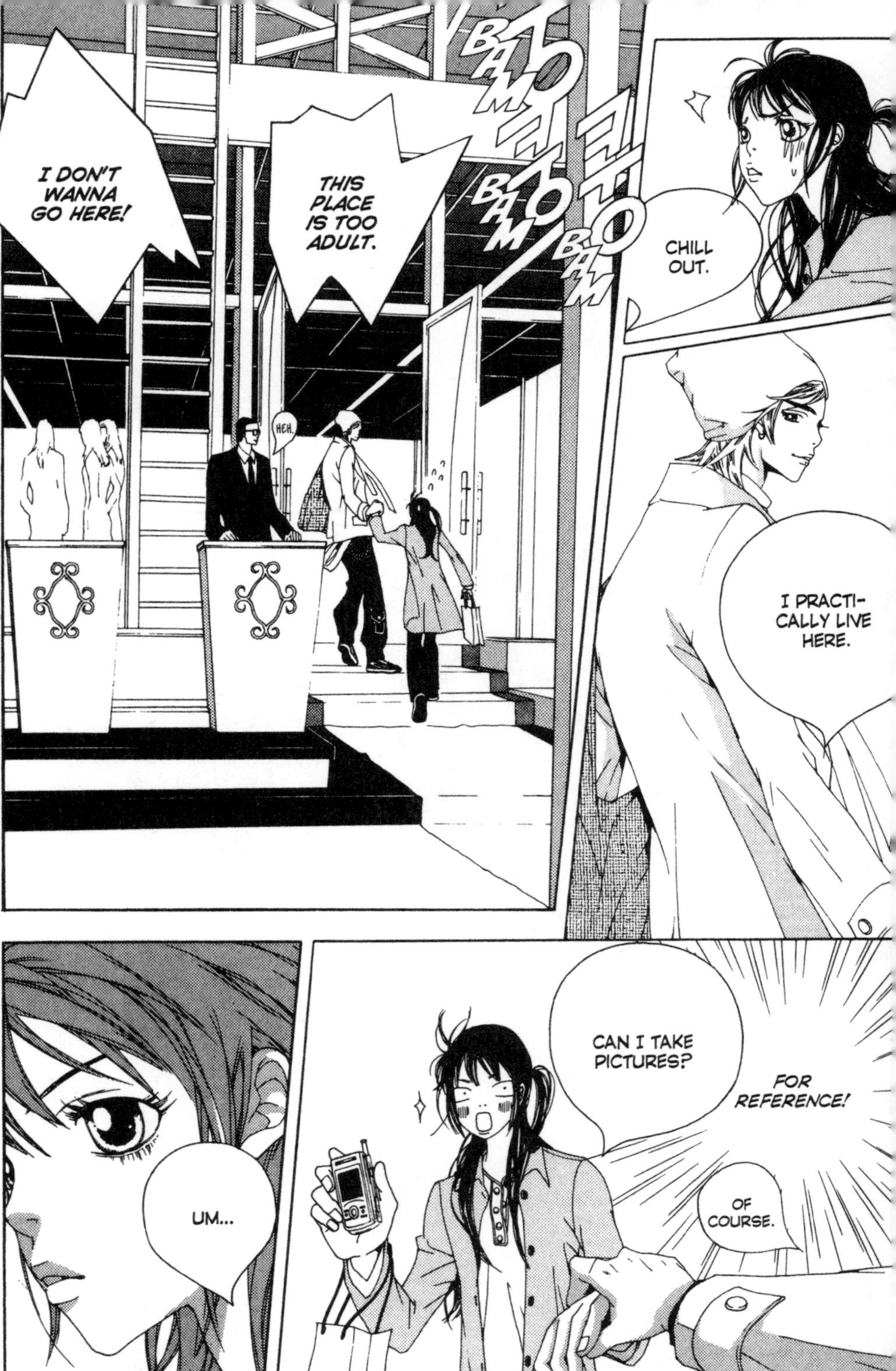
I DON'T WANNA GO HERE!
THIS PLACE IS TOO ADULT.
HEH.
BAM BAM BAM
CHILL OUT.
I PRACTI-CALLY LIVE HERE.
UM...
CAN I TAKE PICTURES?
FOR REFERENCE!
OF COURSE.

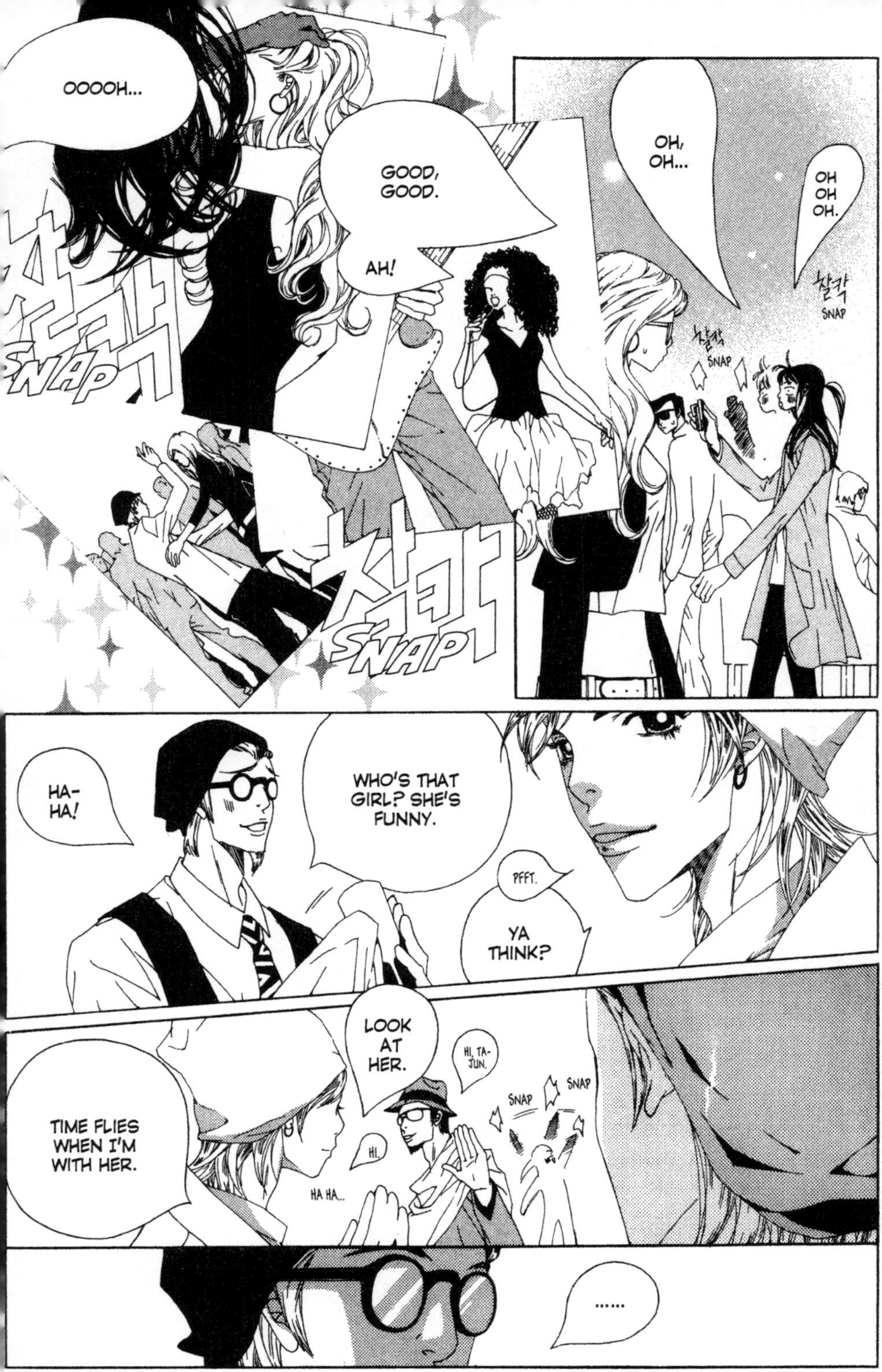
OOOOH...
찰칵
SNAP
GOOD, GOOD.
AH!
찰칵
SNAP
OH, OH...
OH OH OH.
찰칵
SNAP
찰칵
SNAP
HA-HA!
WHO'S THAT GIRL? SHE'S FUNNY.
PFFT.
YA THINK?
TIME FLIES WHEN I'M WITH HER.
LOOK AT HER.
HI, TA-JUN.
HI.
HA HA...
SNAP
SNAP
......

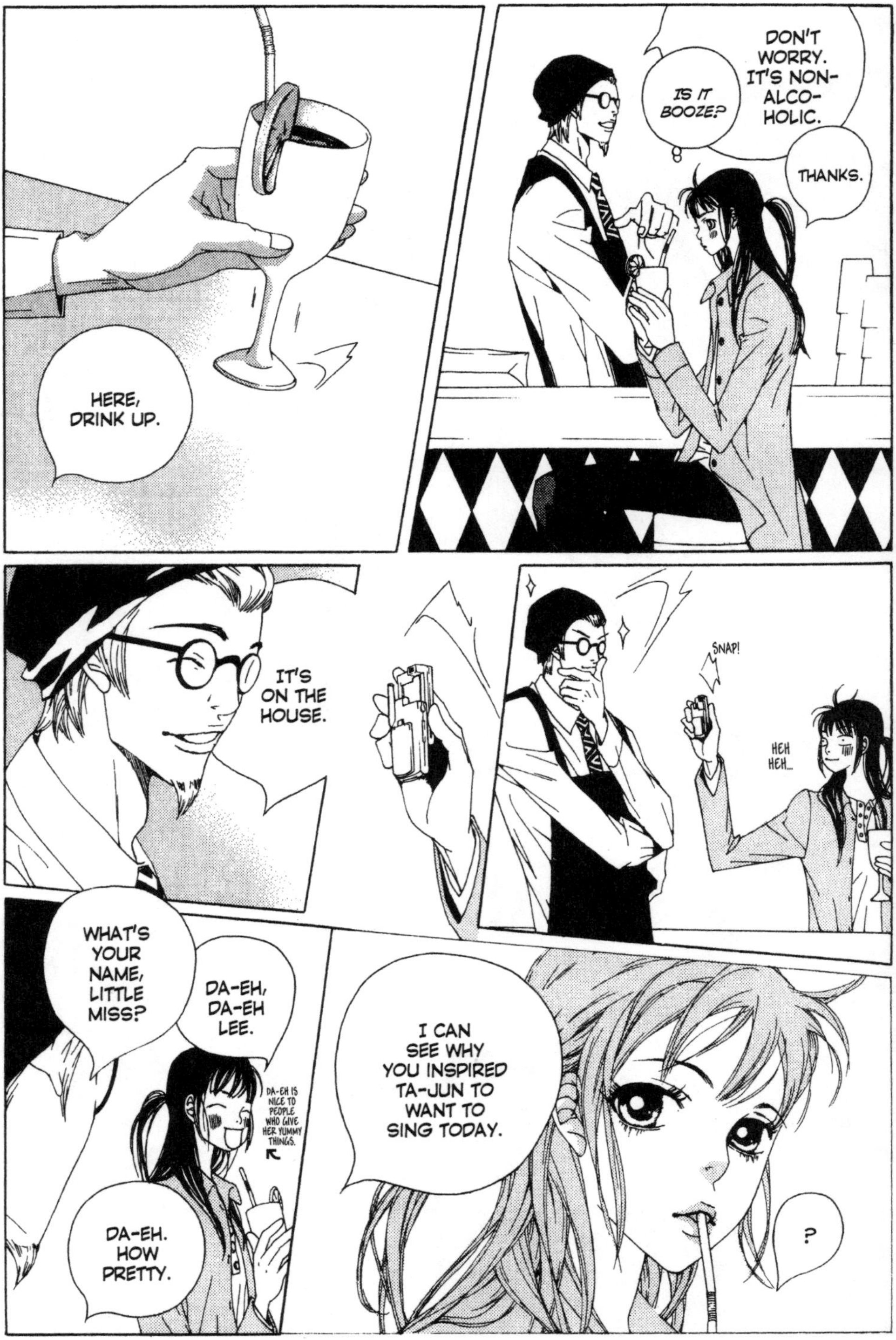
HERE, DRINK UP.
DON'T WORRY. IT'S NON-ALCO-HOLIC.
IS IT BOOZE?
THANKS.
IT'S ON THE HOUSE.
SNAP!
HEH HEH...
WHAT'S YOUR NAME, LITTLE MISS?
DA-EH, DA-EH LEE.
DA-EH IS NICE TO PEOPLE WHO GIVE HER YUMMY THINGS.
DA-EH. HOW PRETTY.
I CAN SEE WHY YOU INSPIRED TA-JUN TO WANT TO SING TODAY.
?

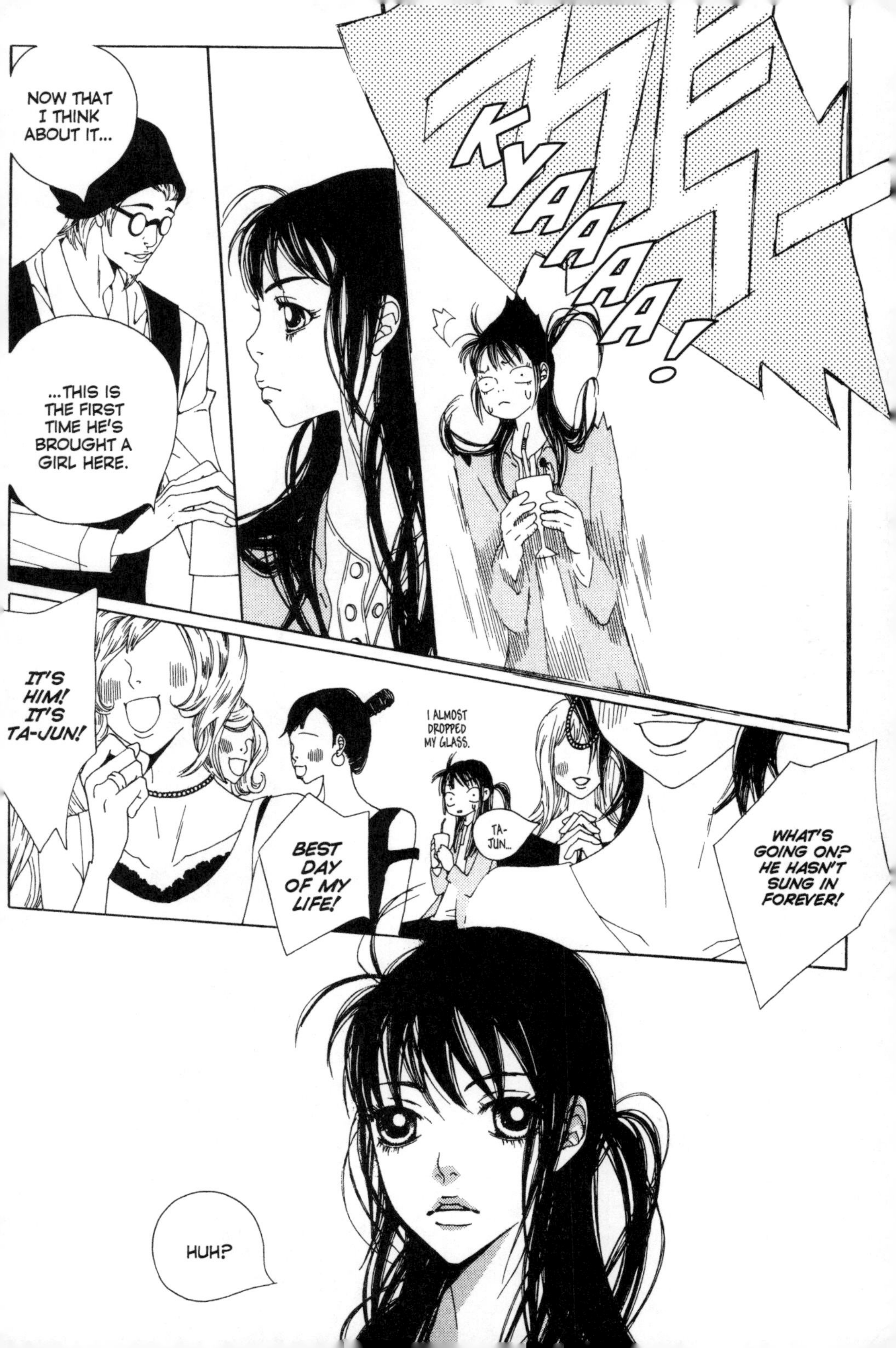
NOW THAT I THINK ABOUT IT...
...THIS IS THE FIRST TIME HE'S BROUGHT A GIRL HERE.
KYAAAAA!
IT'S HIM! IT'S TA-JUN!
BEST DAY OF MY LIFE!
I ALMOST DROPPED MY GLASS.
TA-JUN...
WHAT'S GOING ON? HE HASN'T SUNG IN FOREVER!
HUH?

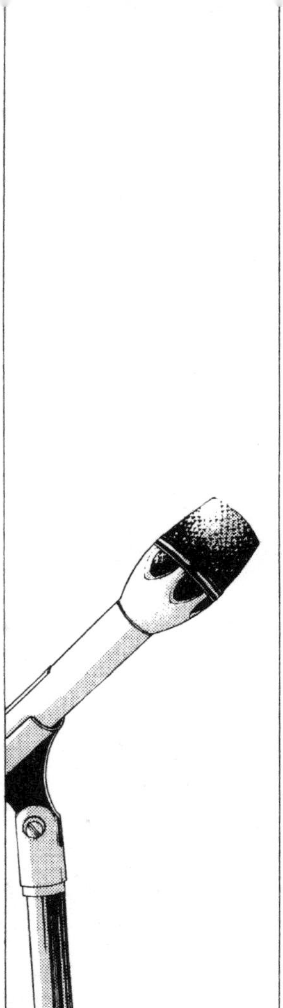

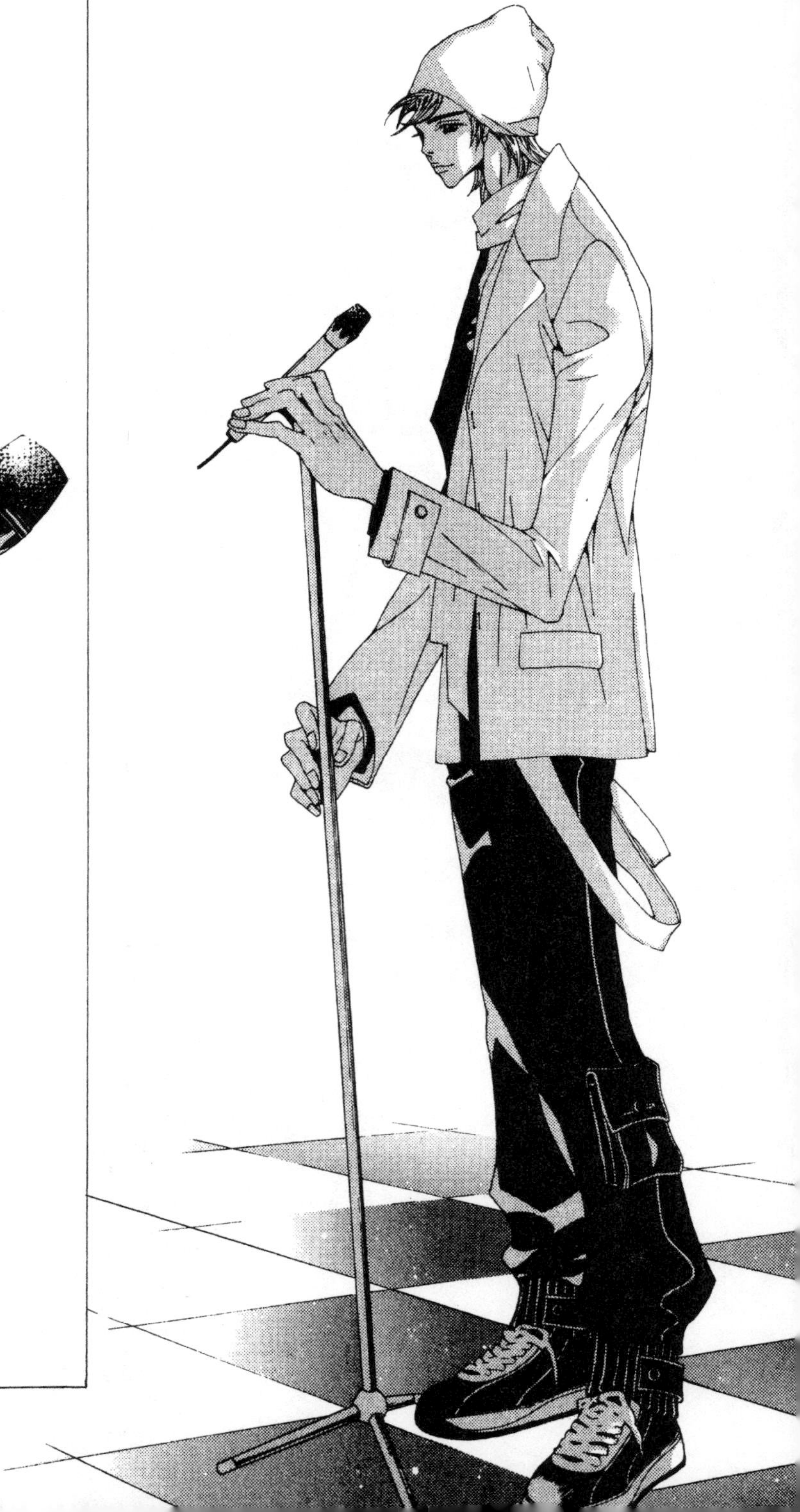

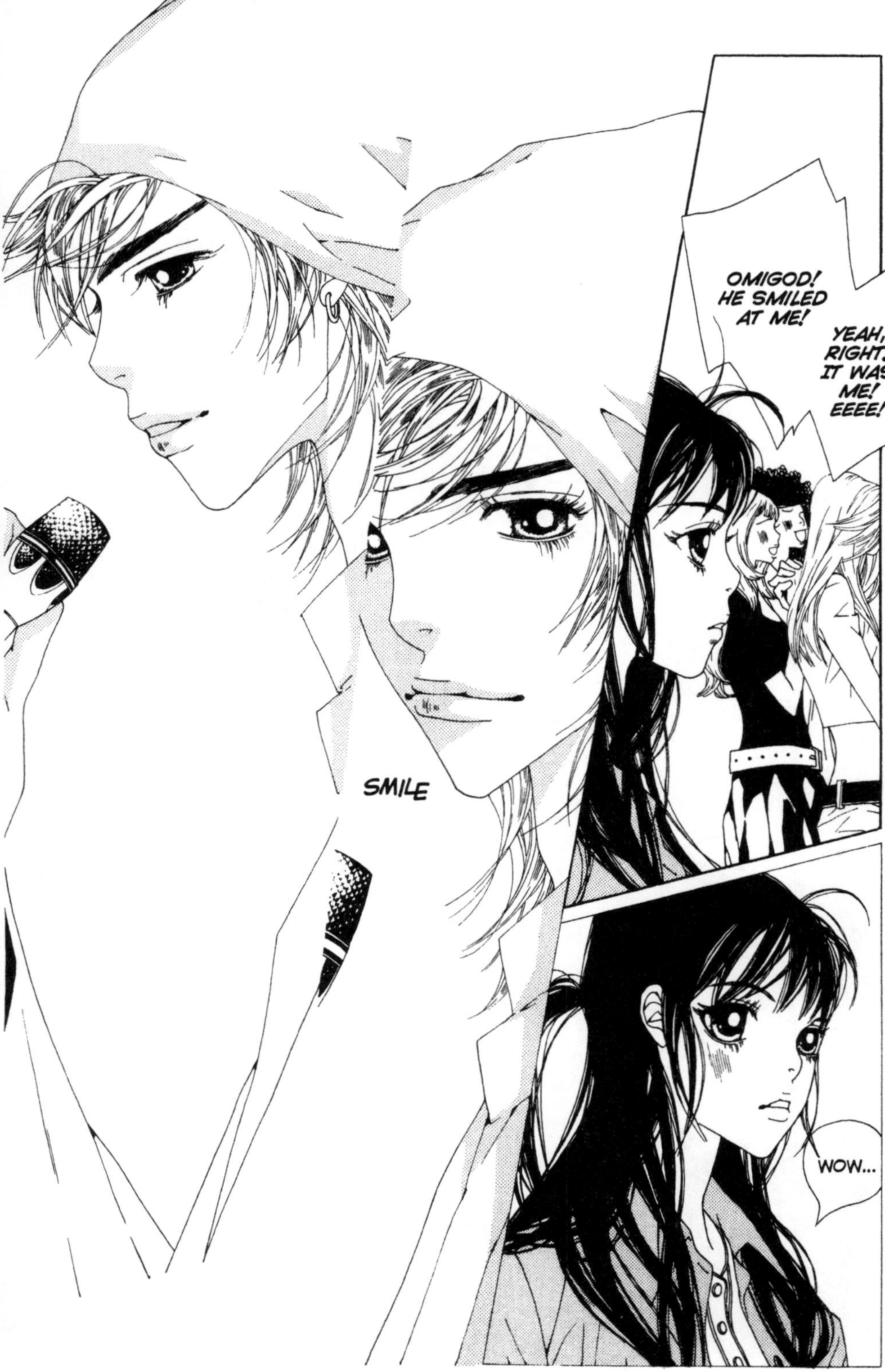
SMILE
OMIGOD! HE SMILED AT ME!
YEAH, RIGHT! IT WAS ME! EEEE!
WOW...

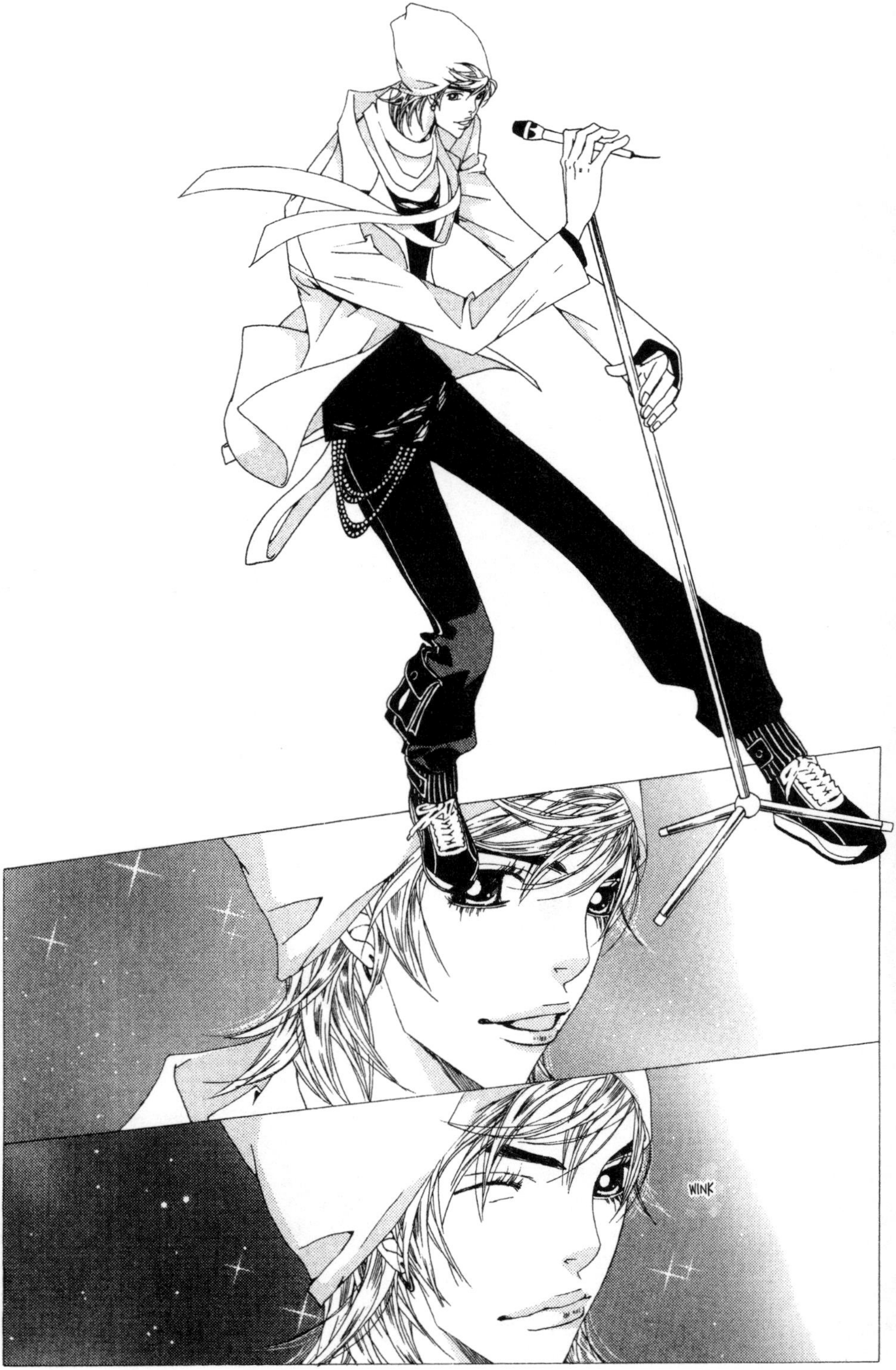
WINK

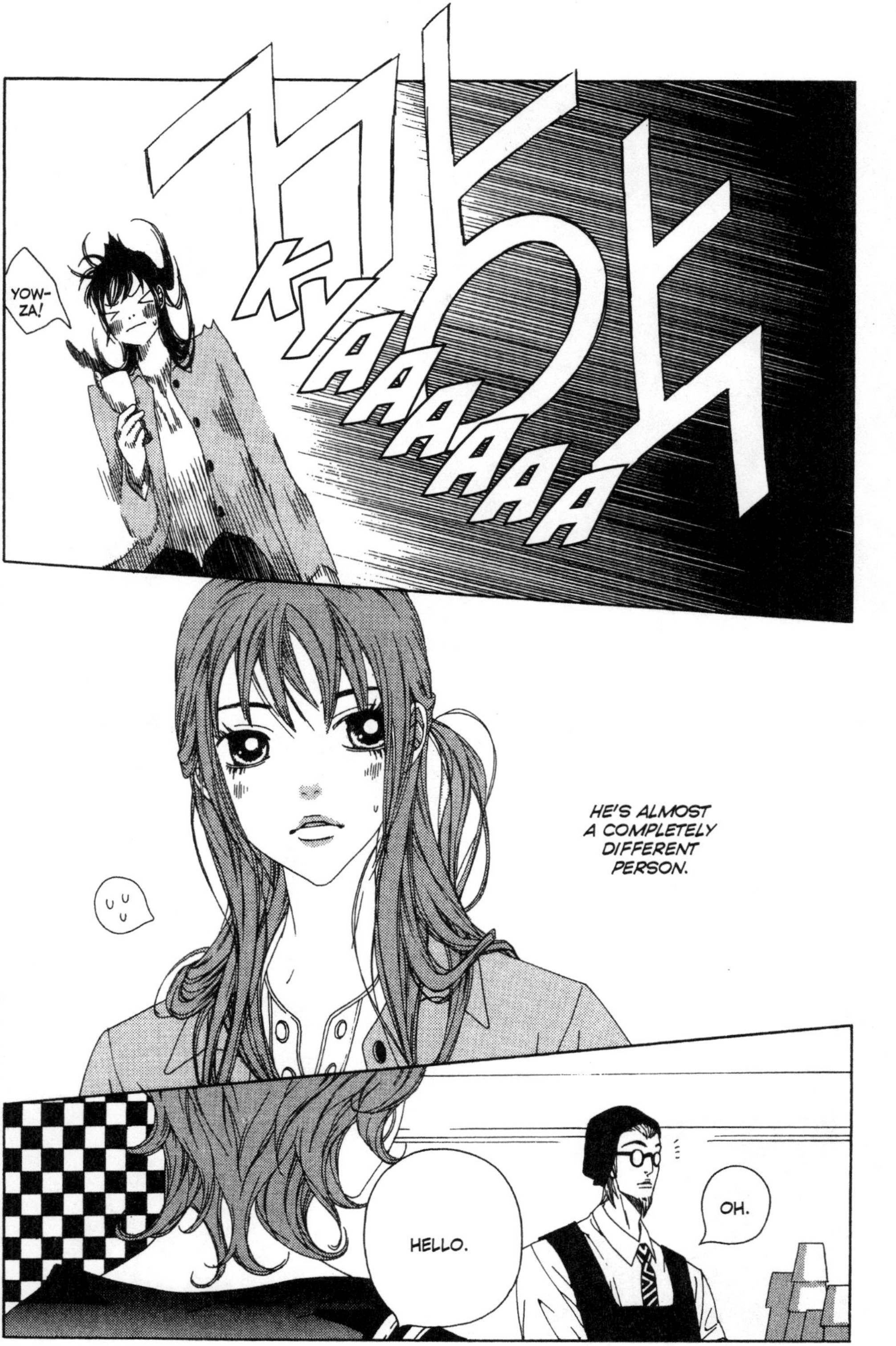
YOW-ZA!
KYAAAAAAAA
HE'S ALMOST A COMPLETELY DIFFERENT PERSON.
HELLO.
OH.

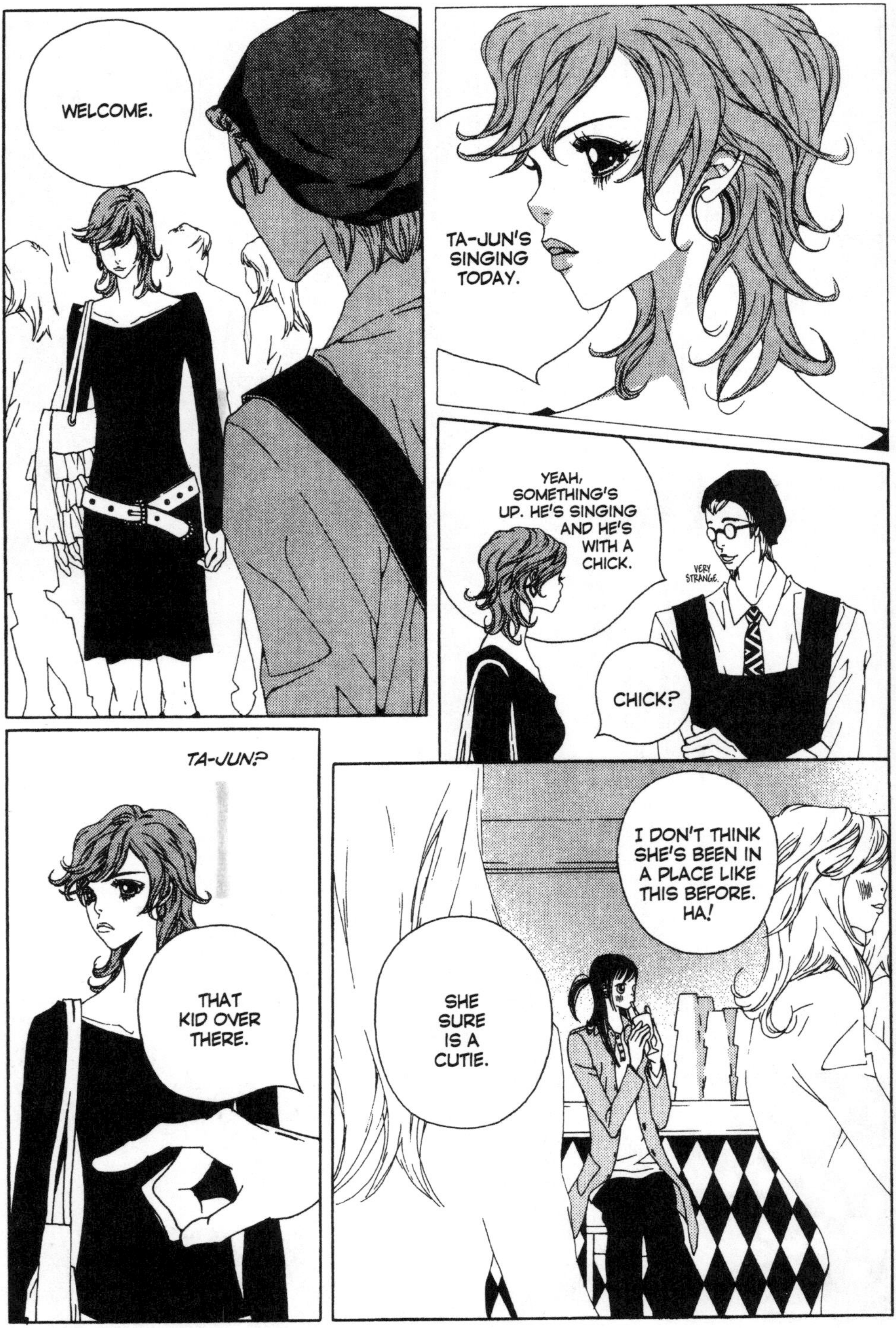
WELCOME.
TA-JUN'S SINGING TODAY.
YEAH, SOMETHING'S UP. HE'S SINGING AND HE'S WITH A CHICK.
VERY STRANGE.
CHICK?
TA-JUN?
THAT KID OVER THERE.
I DON'T THINK SHE'S BEEN IN A PLACE LIKE THIS BEFORE. HA!
SHE SURE IS A CUTIE.

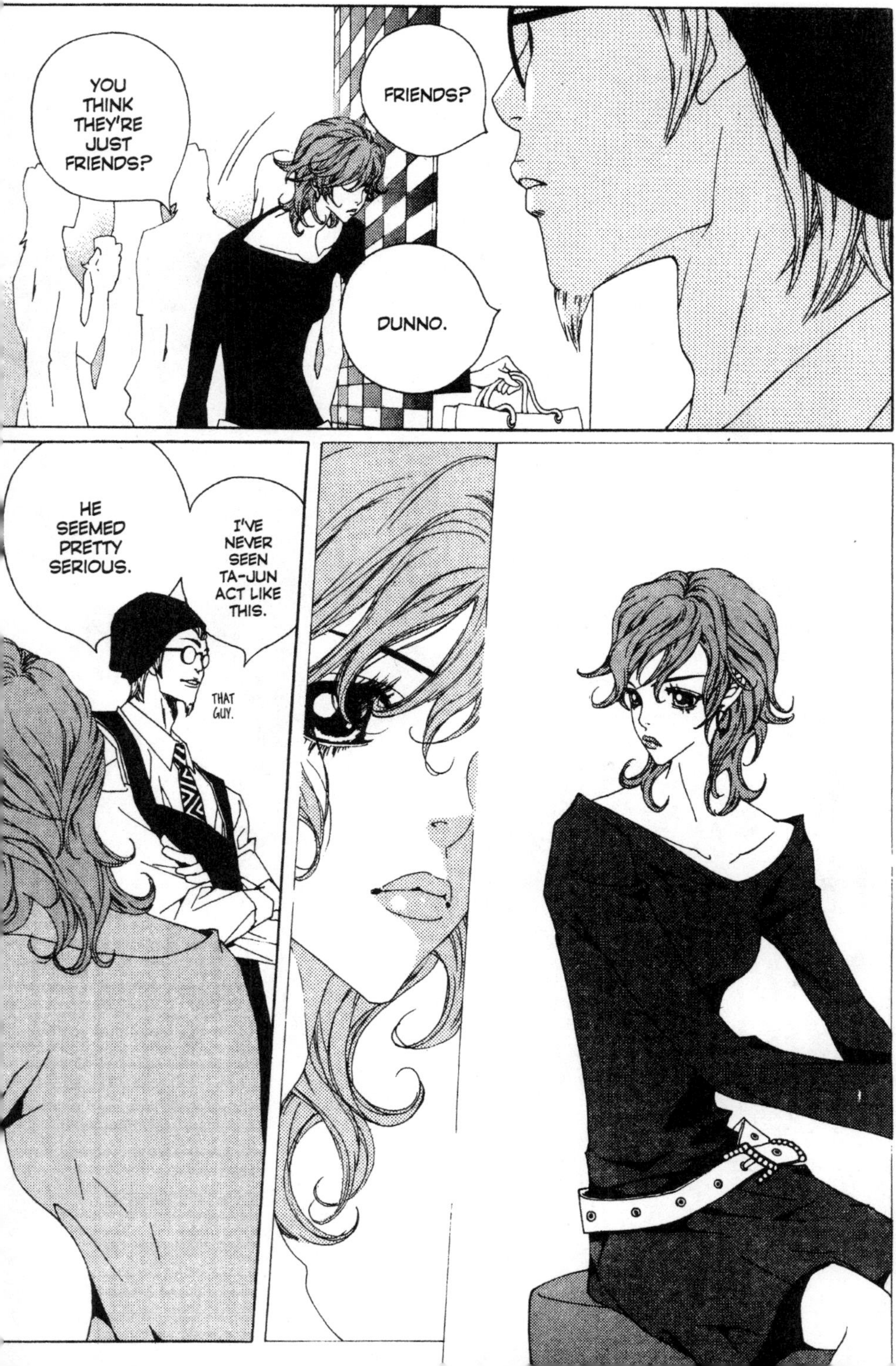
YOU THINK THEY'RE JUST FRIENDS?
FRIENDS?
DUNNO.
HE SEEMED PRETTY SERIOUS.
I'VE NEVER SEEN TA-JUN ACT LIKE THIS.
THAT GUY.

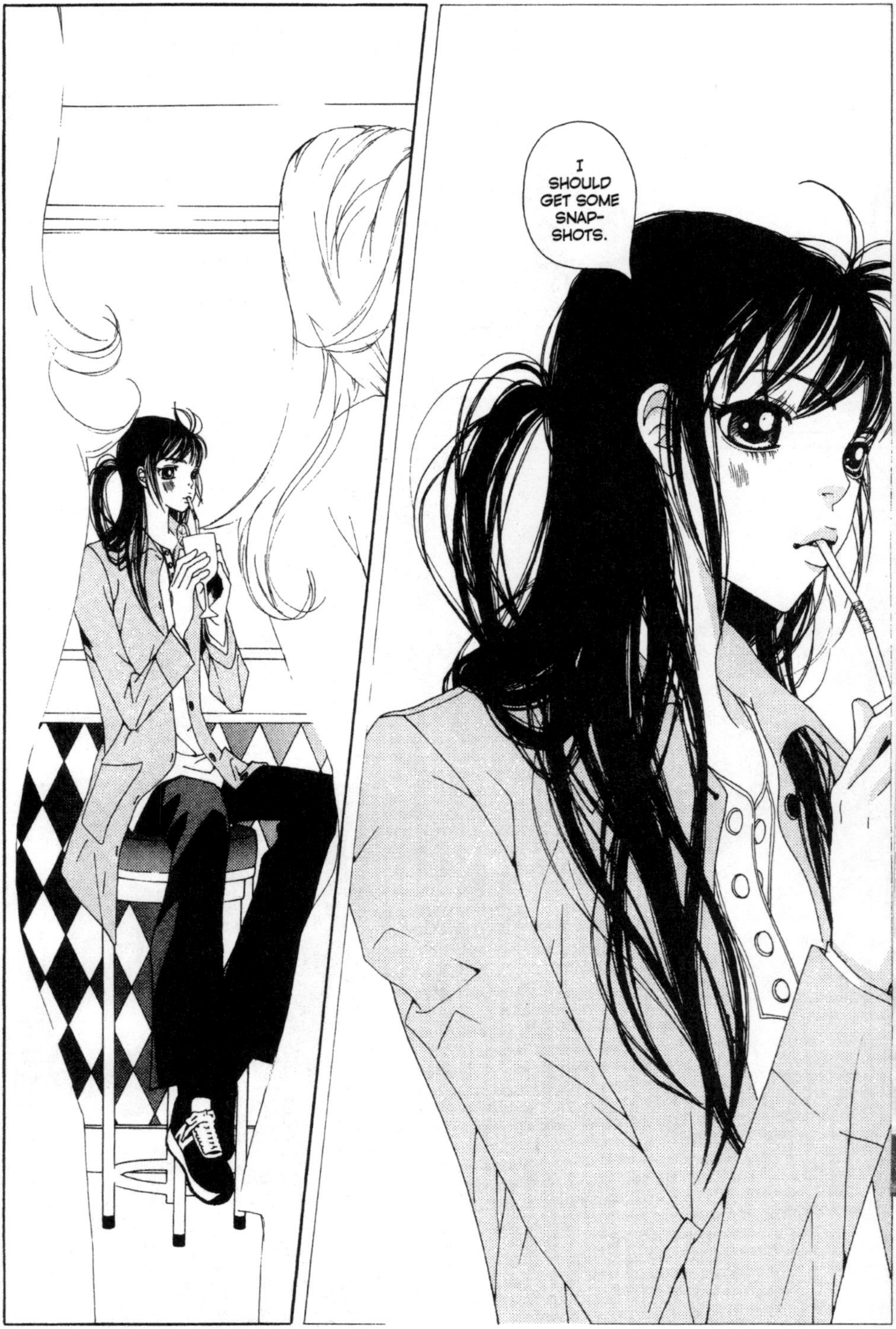
I SHOULD GET SOME SNAP-SHOTS.

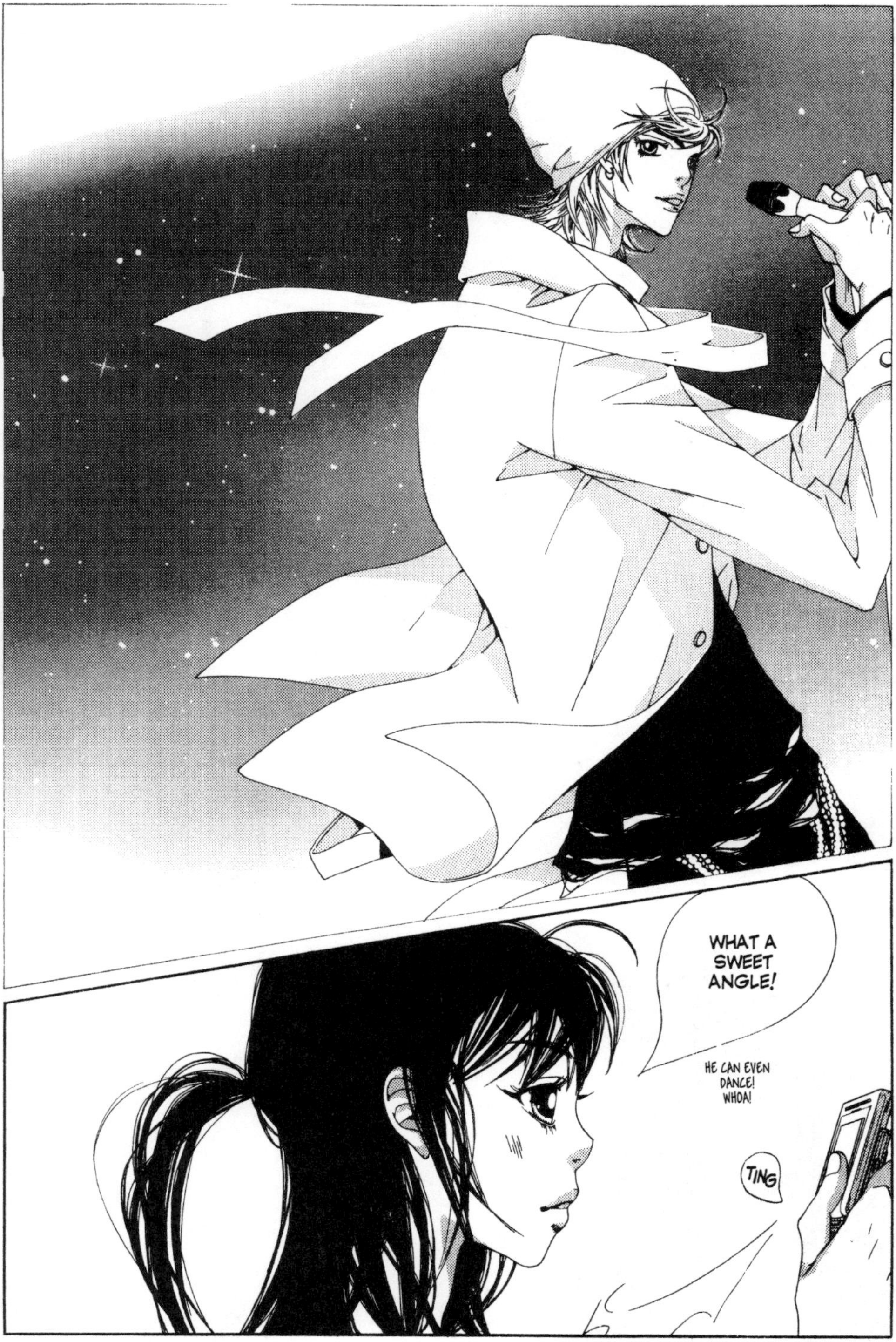
WHAT A SWEET ANGLE!
HE CAN EVEN DANCE! WHOA!
TING

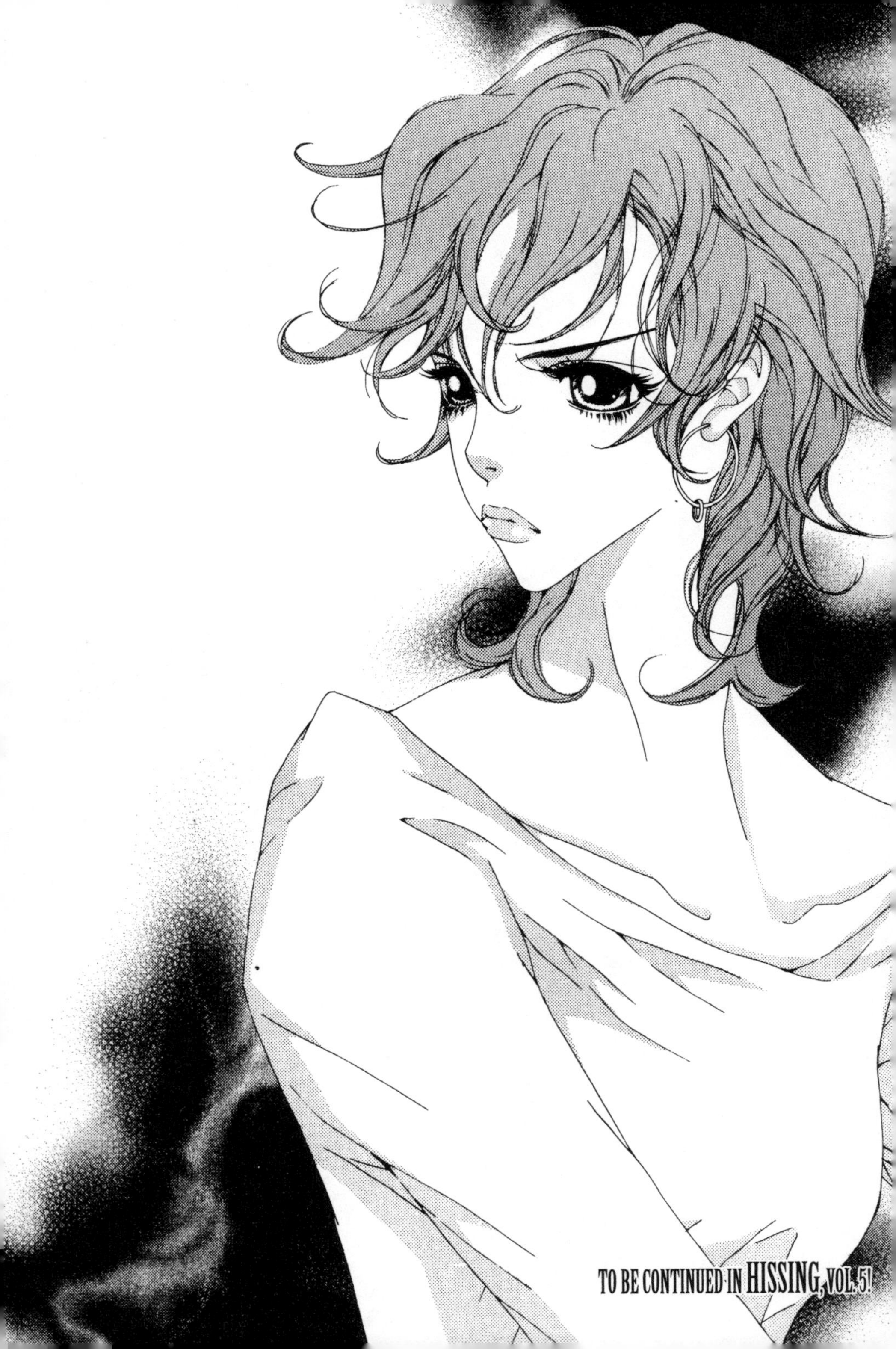
TO BE CONTINUED IN HISSING, VOL. 5!

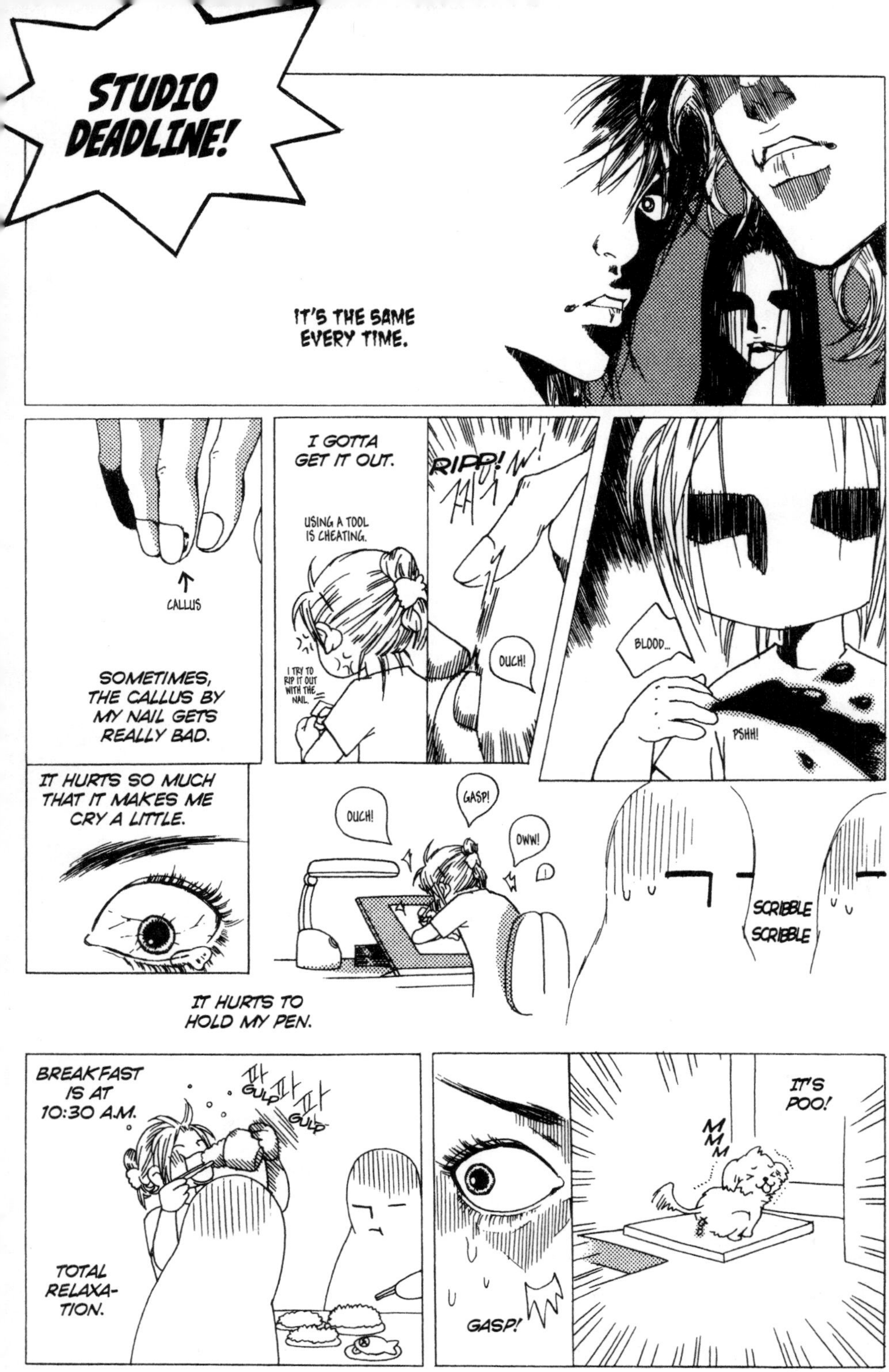
STUDIO DEADLINE!
IT'S THE SAME EVERY TIME.
CALLUS
SOMETIMES, THE CALLUS BY MY NAIL GETS REALLY BAD.
I GOTTA GET IT OUT.
USING A TOOL IS CHEATING.
I TRY TO RIP IT OUT WITH THE NAIL.
RIPP!
OUCH!
BLOOD...
PSHH!
IT HURTS SO MUCH THAT IT MAKES ME CRY A LITTLE.
OUCH!
GASP!
OWW!
SCRIBBLE
SCRIBBLE
IT HURTS TO HOLD MY PEN.
BREAKFAST IS AT 10:30 A.M.
GULP
GULP
TOTAL RELAXA-TION.
GASP!
IT'S POO!
MMM

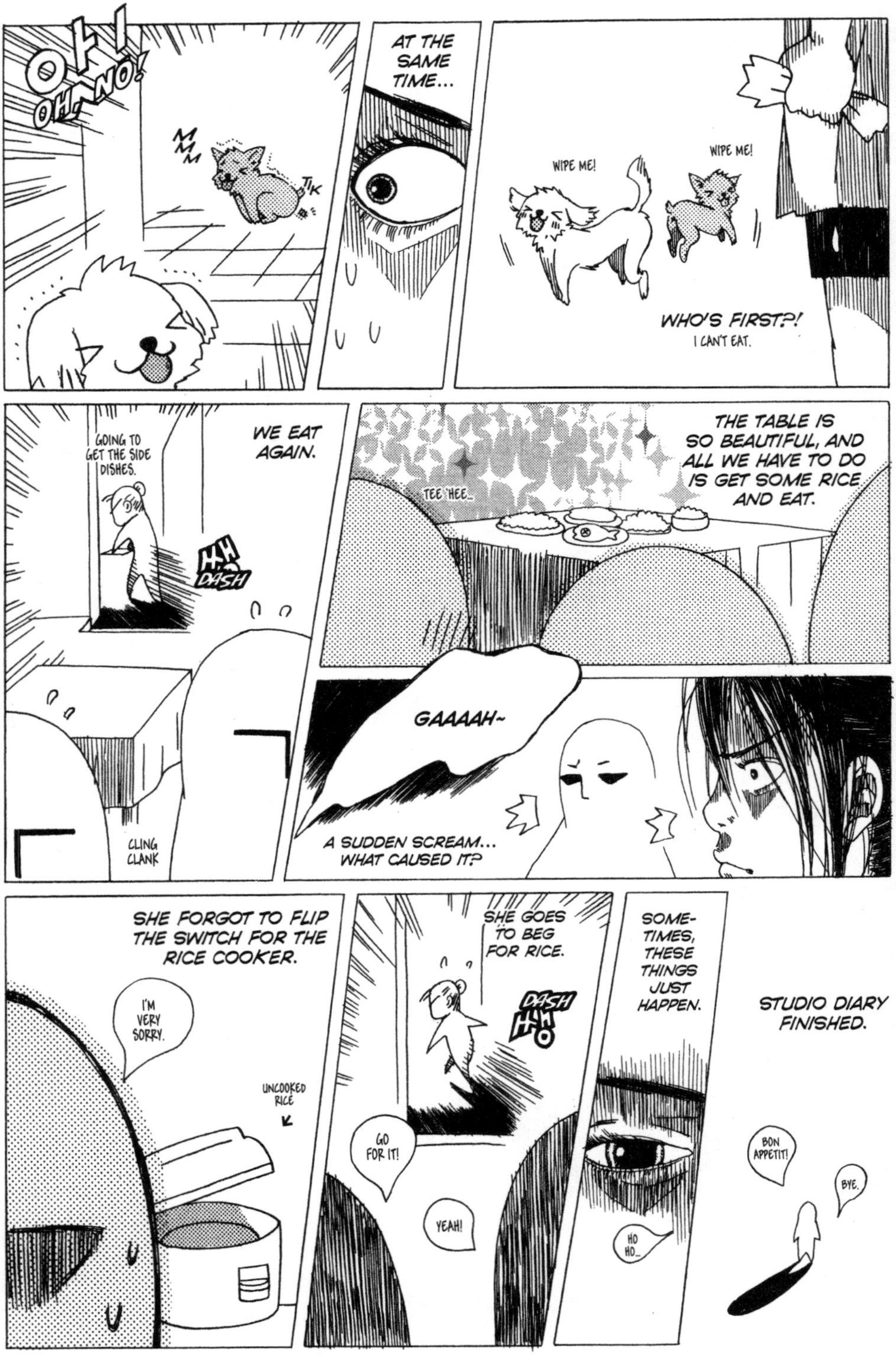
아니!
OH~NO!
MMM
TIK
AT THE SAME TIME...
WIPE ME!
WIPE ME!
WHO'S FIRST?!
I CAN'T EAT.
GOING TO GET THE SIDE DISHES.
WE EAT AGAIN.
DASH
CLING CLANK
TEE HEE...
THE TABLE IS SO BEAUTIFUL, AND ALL WE HAVE TO DO IS GET SOME RICE AND EAT.
GAAAAH~
A SUDDEN SCREAM... WHAT CAUSED IT?
SHE FORGOT TO FLIP THE SWITCH FOR THE RICE COOKER.
I'M VERY SORRY.
UNCOOKED RICE
SHE GOES TO BEG FOR RICE.
DASH
GO FOR IT!
YEAH!
SOME-TIMES, THESE THINGS JUST HAPPEN.
HO HO...
STUDIO DIARY FINISHED.
BON APPETIT!
BYE.

The Antique Gift Shop 1~4

Lee Eun

Available at bookstores near you!

Yen Press

www.yenpress.com

CAN YOU FEEL THE SOULS OF THE ANTIQUES? DO YOU BELIEVE?

Did you know that an antique possesses a soul of its own?
The Antique Gift Shop specializes in such items that charm and captivate the buyers they are destined to belong to. Guided by a mysterious and charismatic shopkeeper, the enchanted relics lead their new owners on a journey into an alternate cosmic universe to their true destinies.
Eerily bittersweet and dolefully melancholy, The Antique Gift Shop opens up a portal to a world where torn lovers unite, broken friendships are mended, and regrets are resolved. Can you feel the power of the antiques?

Totally new Arabian nights, where Shahrazad is a guy!

Everyone knows the story of Shahrazad and her wonderful tales from the Arabian Nights. For one thousand and one nights, the stories that she created entertained the mad Sultan and eventually saved her life. In this version, Shahrazad is a guy who wanted to save his sister from the mad Sultan by disguising himself as a woman. When he puts his life on the line, what kind of strange and unique stories would he tell? This new twist on one of the greatest classical tales might just keep you awake for another ONE THOUSAND AND ONE NIGHTS.

Available at bookstores near you!

One thousand and one nights 1~4

Han SeungHee · Jeon JinSeok

Hissing vol. 4

Story and art by EunYoung Kang

Translation: June Um
English Adaptation: Jamie S. Rich
Lettering: Marshall Dillon · Terri Delgado

Yen Press
Hachette Book Group USA
237 Park Avenue, New York, NY 10017

Visit our Web sites at www.HachetteBookGroupUSA.com and www.YenPress.com.

Yen Press is an imprint of Hachette Book Group USA, Inc. The Yen Press name and logo are trademarks of Hachette Book Group USA, Inc.

First Yen Press Edition: July 2008

ISBN-10: 0-7595-2883-7
ISBN-13: 978-0-7595-2883-3

10 9 8 7 6 5 4 3 2 1

BVG

Printed in the United States of America